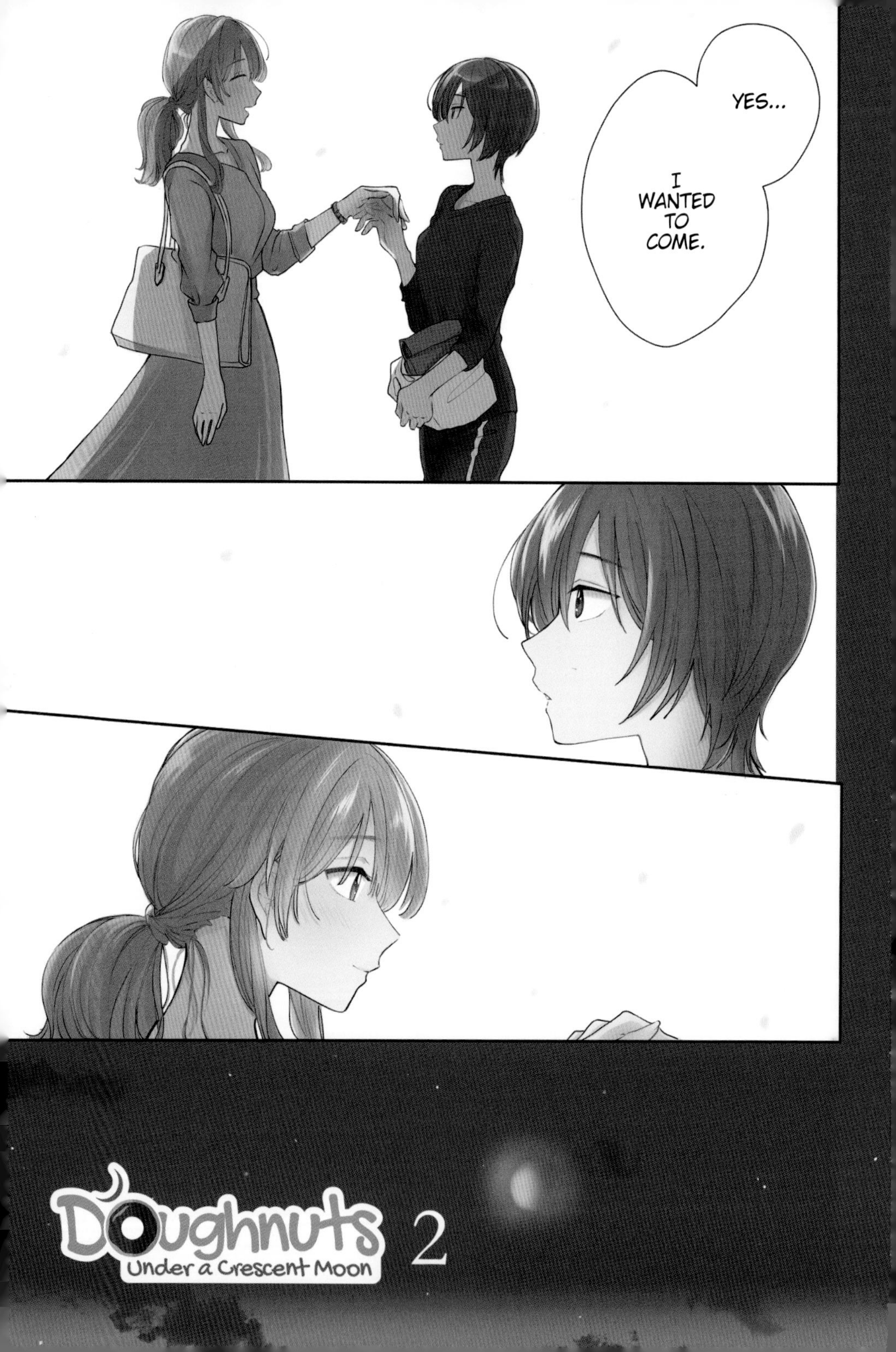
YES...
I WANTED TO COME.
Doughnuts Under a Crescent Moon 2

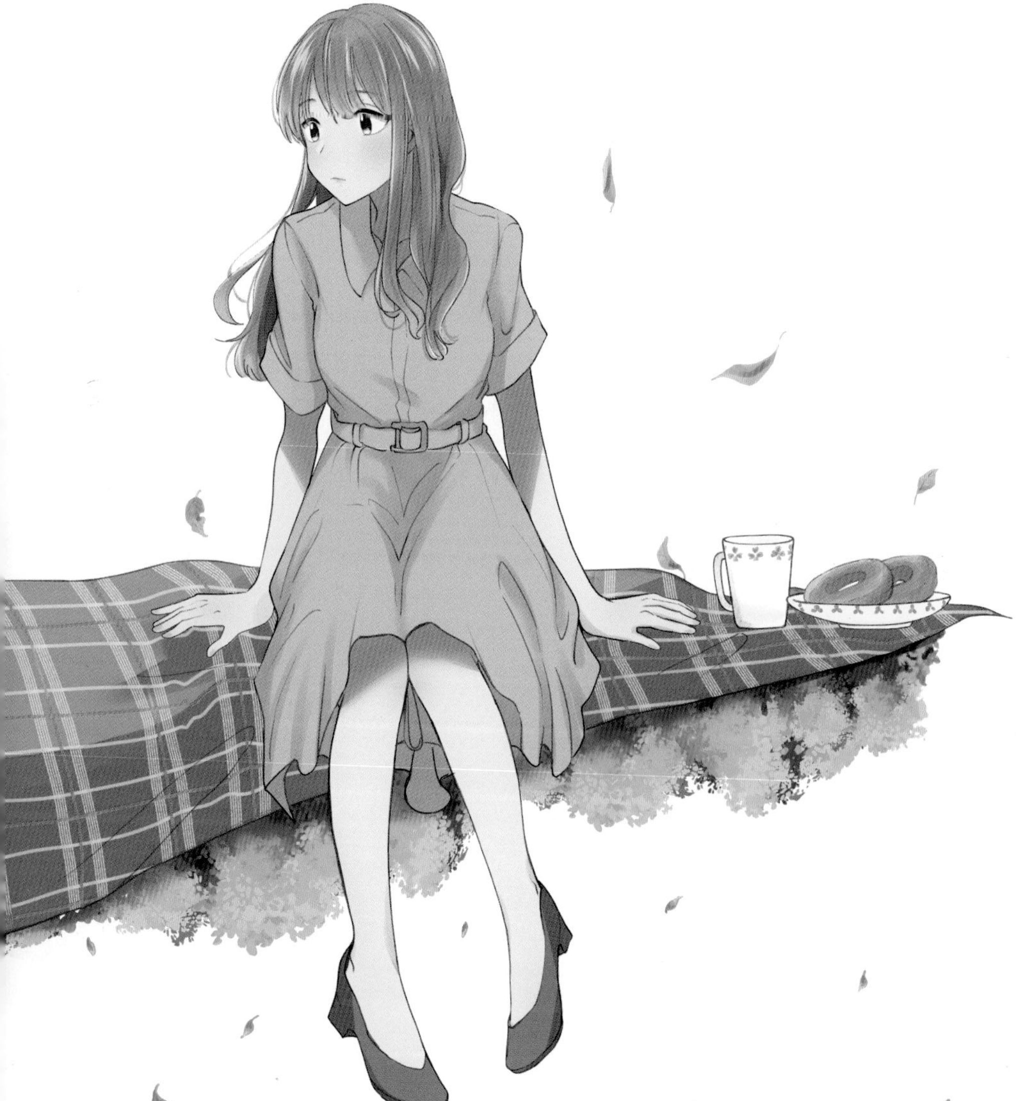

Chapter 6: The Dark Side of the Moon

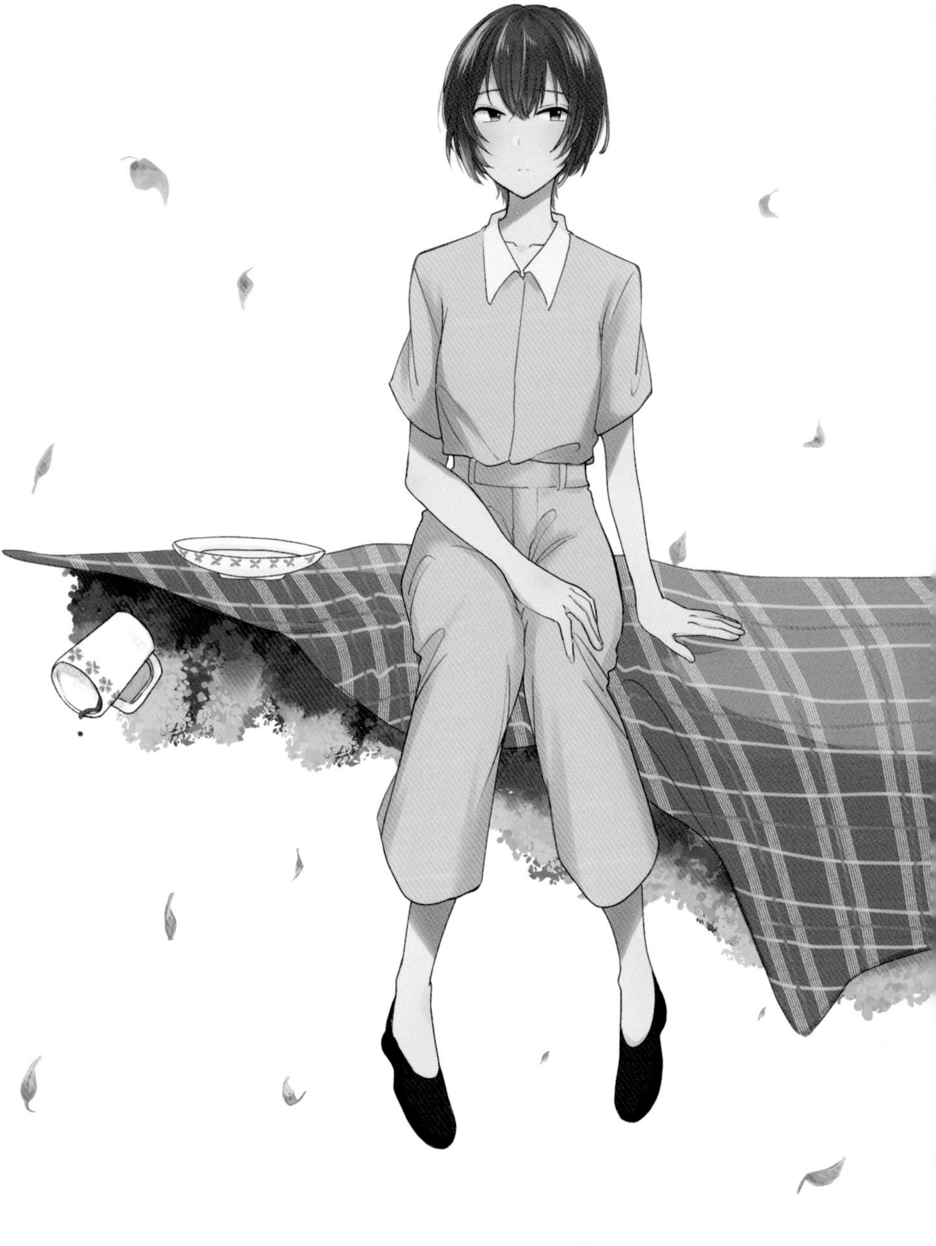

Doughnuts Under a Crescent Moon

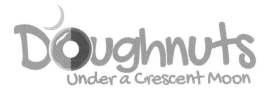

2

CONTENTS

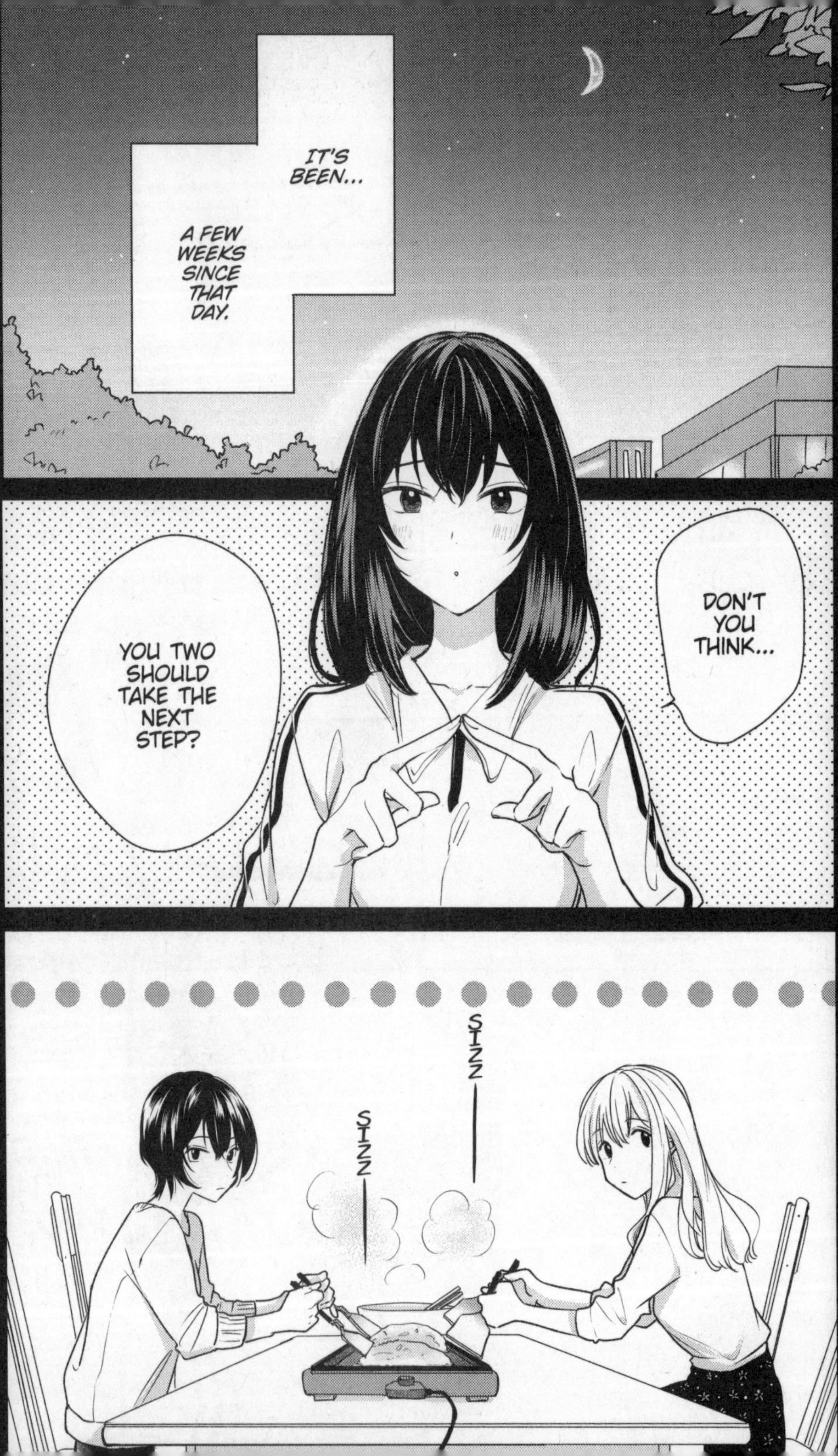
IT'S BEEN...
A FEW WEEKS SINCE THAT DAY.
DON'T YOU THINK...
YOU TWO SHOULD TAKE THE NEXT STEP?
SIZZ
SIZZ

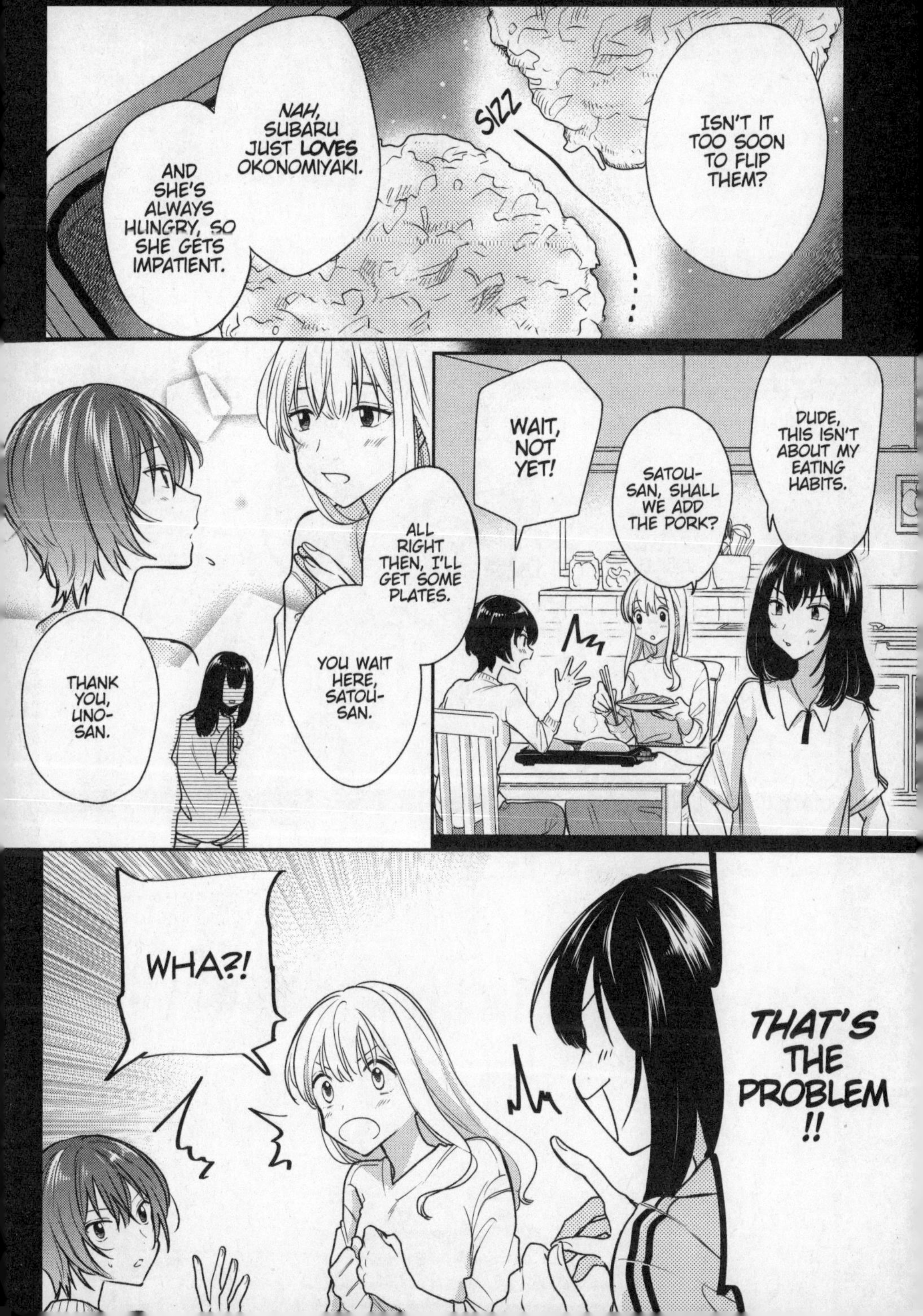
ISN'T IT TOO SOON TO FLIP THEM?
SIZZ
...
NAH, SUBARU JUST **LOVES** OKONOMIYAKI.
AND SHE'S ALWAYS HUNGRY, SO SHE GETS IMPATIENT.
DUDE, THIS ISN'T ABOUT MY EATING HABITS.
SATOU-SAN, SHALL WE ADD THE PORK?
WAIT, NOT YET!
ALL RIGHT THEN, I'LL GET SOME PLATES.
YOU WAIT HERE, SATOU-SAN.
THANK YOU, UNO-SAN.
THAT'S THE PROBLEM!!
WHA?!

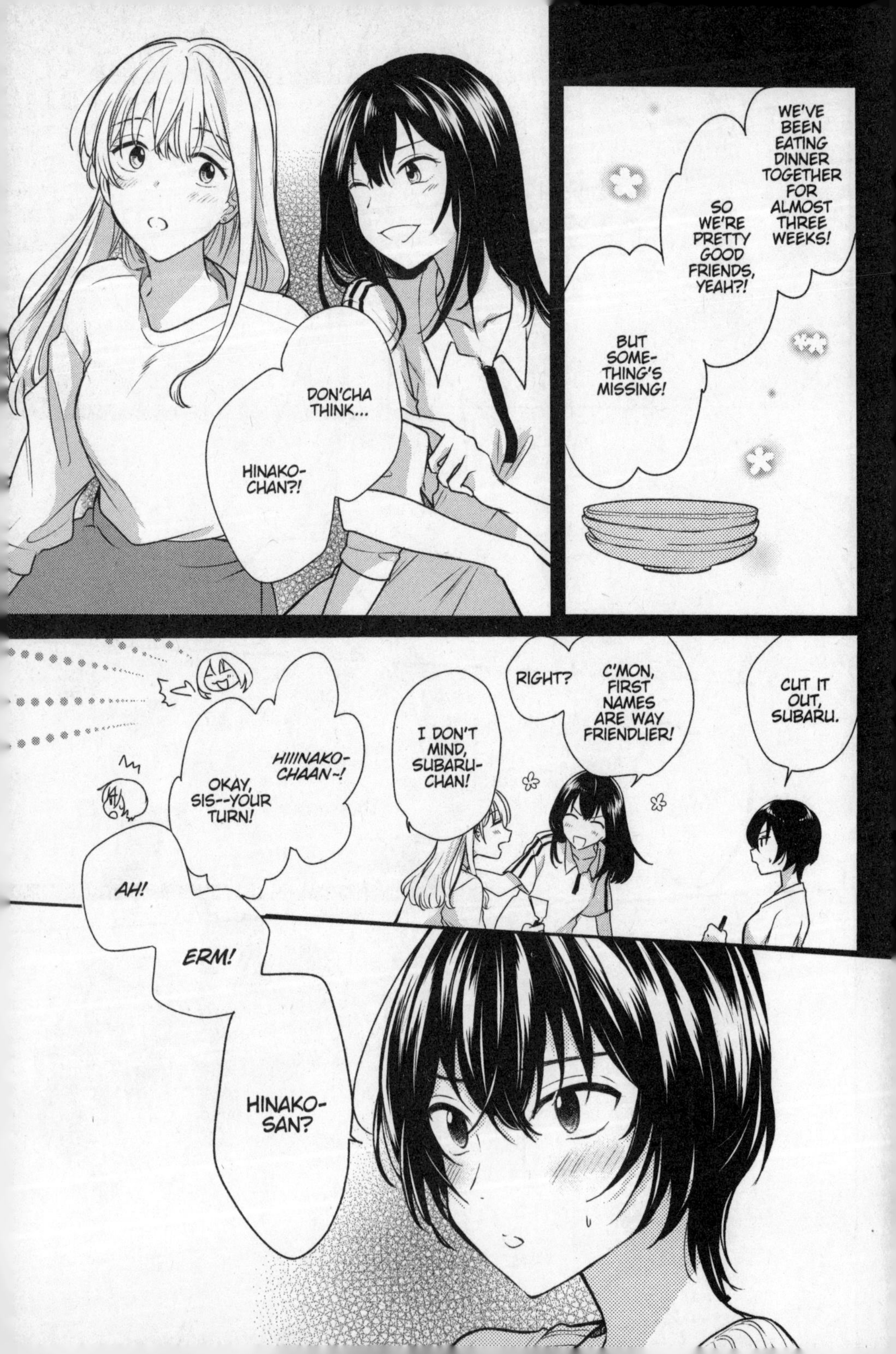
WE'VE BEEN EATING DINNER TOGETHER FOR ALMOST THREE WEEKS!
SO WE'RE PRETTY GOOD FRIENDS, YEAH?!
BUT SOME-THING'S MISSING!
DON'CHA THINK...
HINAKO-CHAN?!
CUT IT OUT, SUBARU.
C'MON, FIRST NAMES ARE WAY FRIENDLIER!
RIGHT?
I DON'T MIND, SUBARU-CHAN!
HIIINAKO-CHAAN~!
OKAY, SIS--YOUR TURN!
AH!
ERM!
HINAKO-SAN?

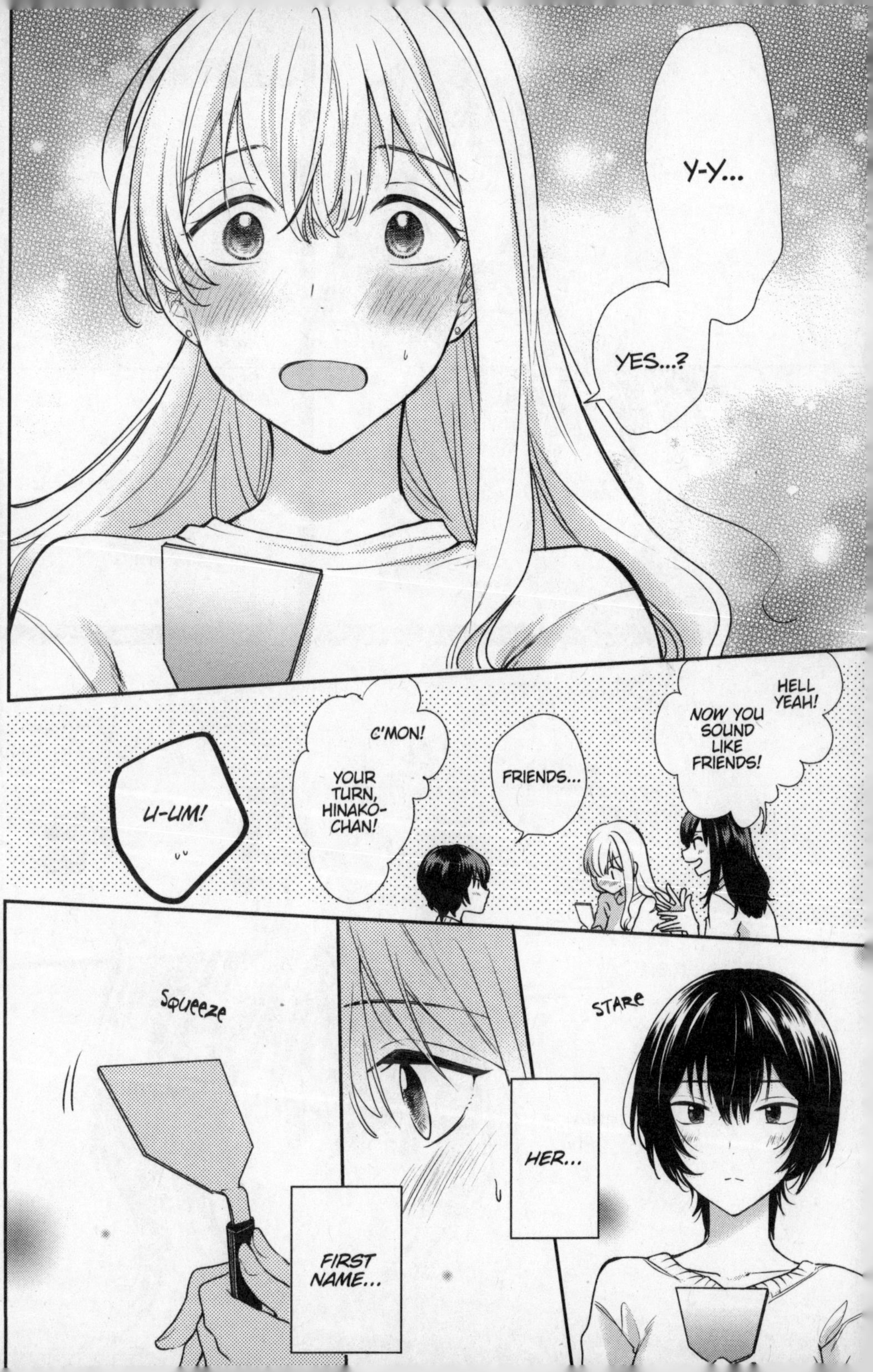
Y-Y...
YES...?
HELL YEAH!
NOW YOU SOUND LIKE FRIENDS!
FRIENDS...
C'MON!
YOUR TURN, HINAKO-CHAN!
U-UM!
STARE
HER...
Squeeze
FIRST NAME...

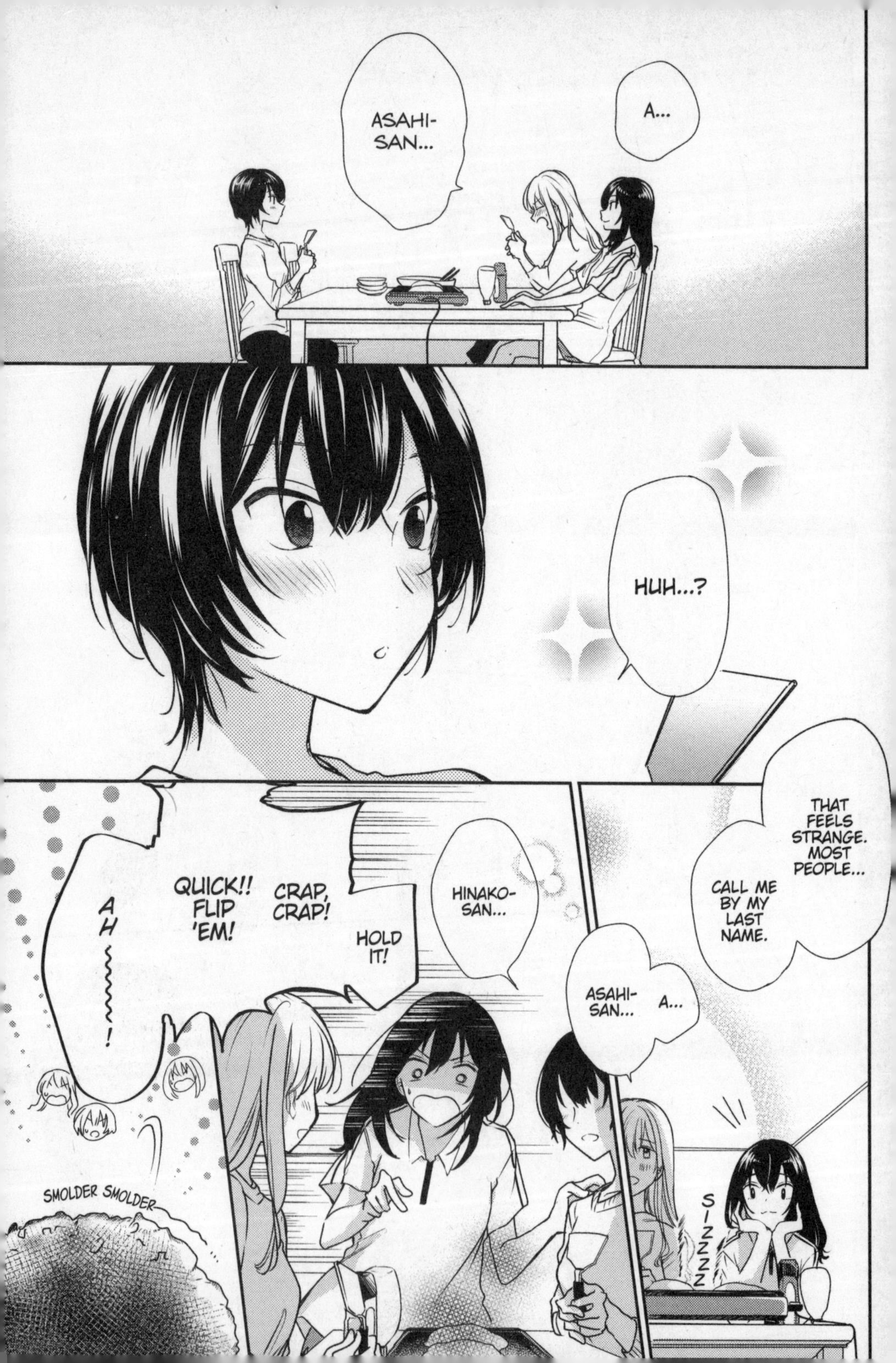
ASAHI-SAN...
A...
HUH...?
THAT FEELS STRANGE. MOST PEOPLE...
CALL ME BY MY LAST NAME.
ASAHI-SAN... A...
SIZZZZ
HINAKO-SAN...
HOLD IT!
CRAP, CRAP!
QUICK!! FLIP 'EM!
AH~~~!
SMOLDER SMOLDER

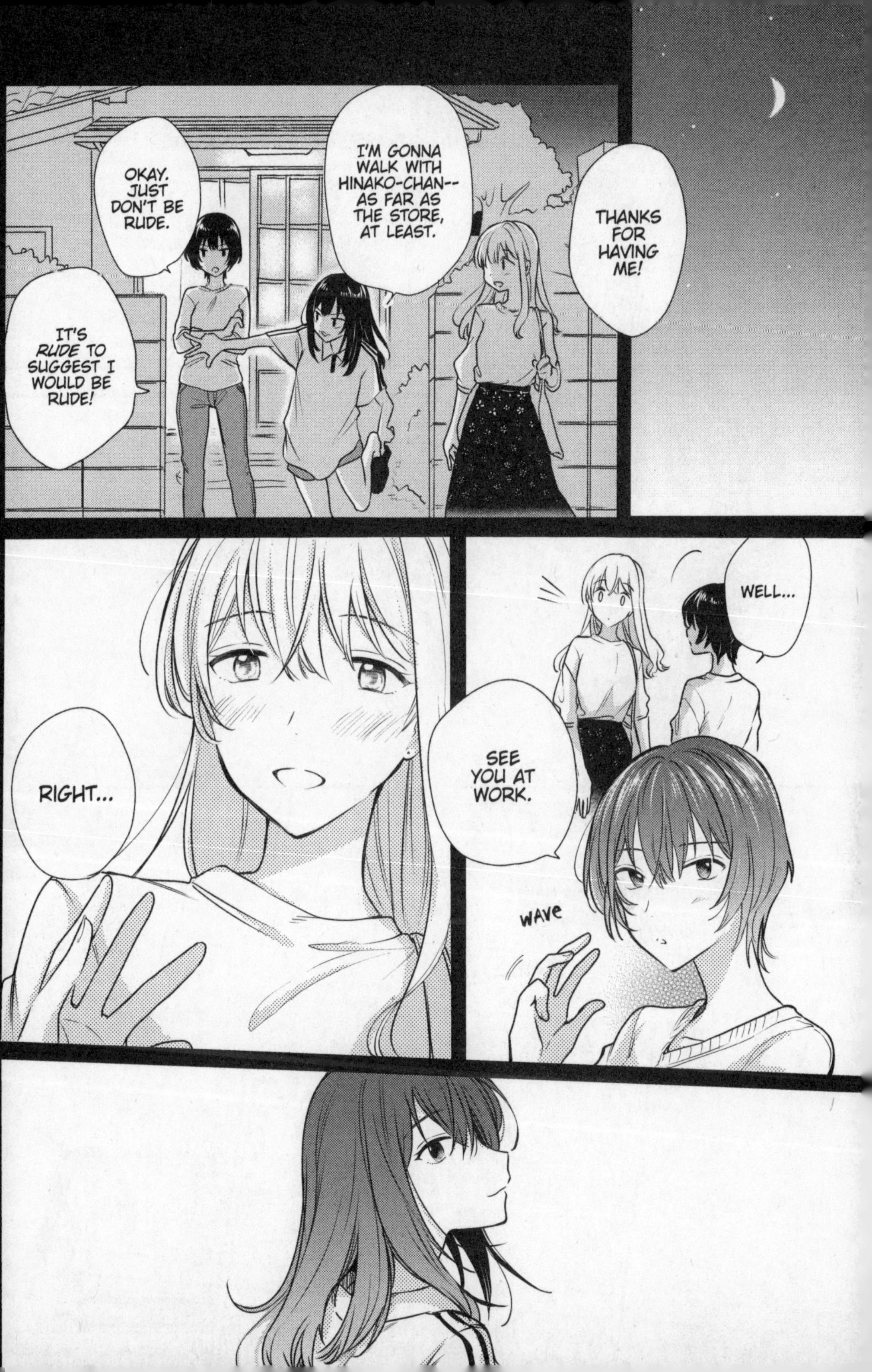
THANKS FOR HAVING ME!
I'M GONNA WALK WITH HINAKO-CHAN-- AS FAR AS THE STORE, AT LEAST.
OKAY. JUST DON'T BE RUDE.
IT'S *RUDE* TO SUGGEST I WOULD BE RUDE!
WELL...
SEE YOU AT WORK.
WAVE
RIGHT...

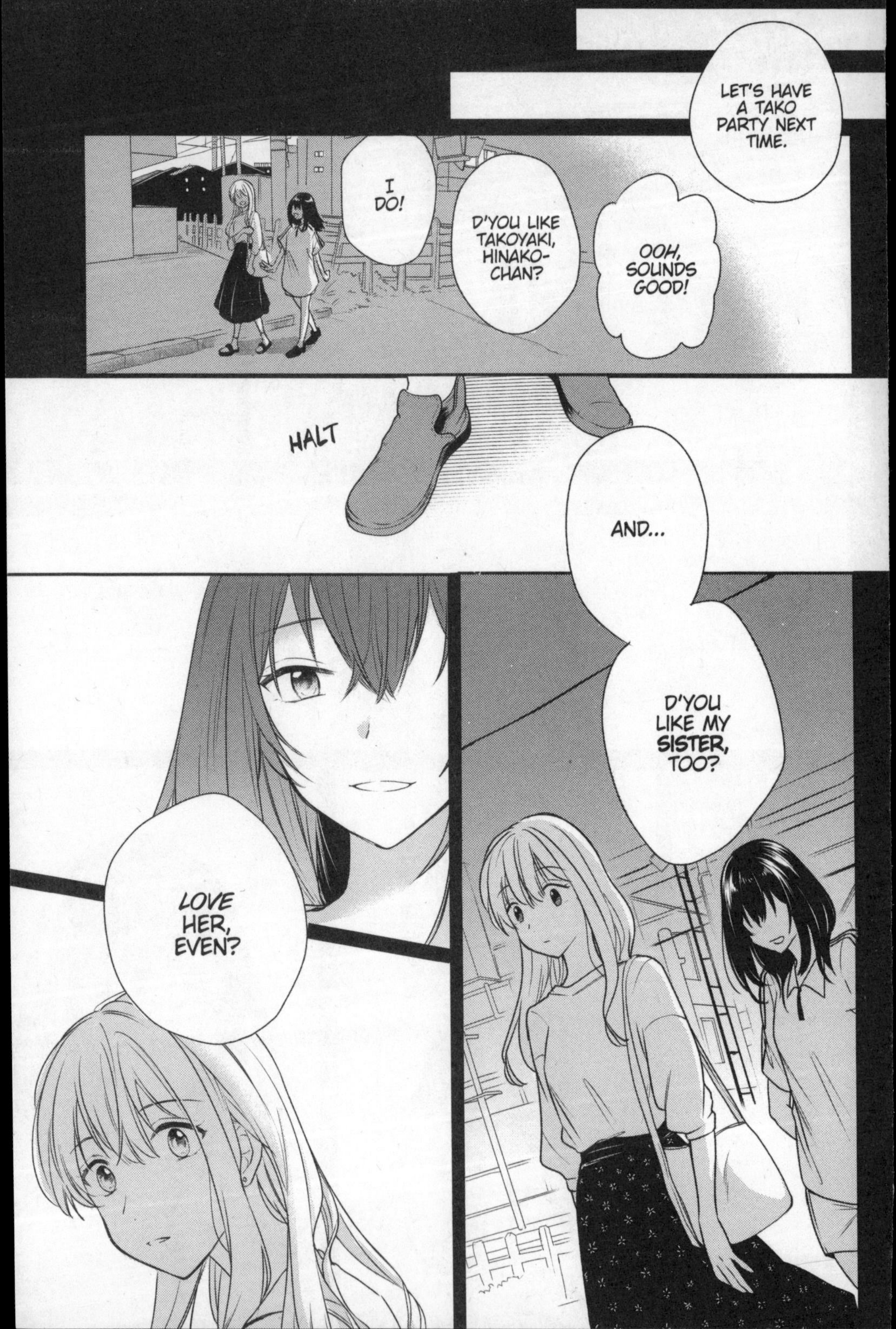
LET'S HAVE A TAKO PARTY NEXT TIME.
OOH, SOUNDS GOOD!
D'YOU LIKE TAKOYAKI, HINAKO-CHAN?
I DO!
AND...
HALT
D'YOU LIKE MY SISTER, TOO?
LOVE HER, EVEN?

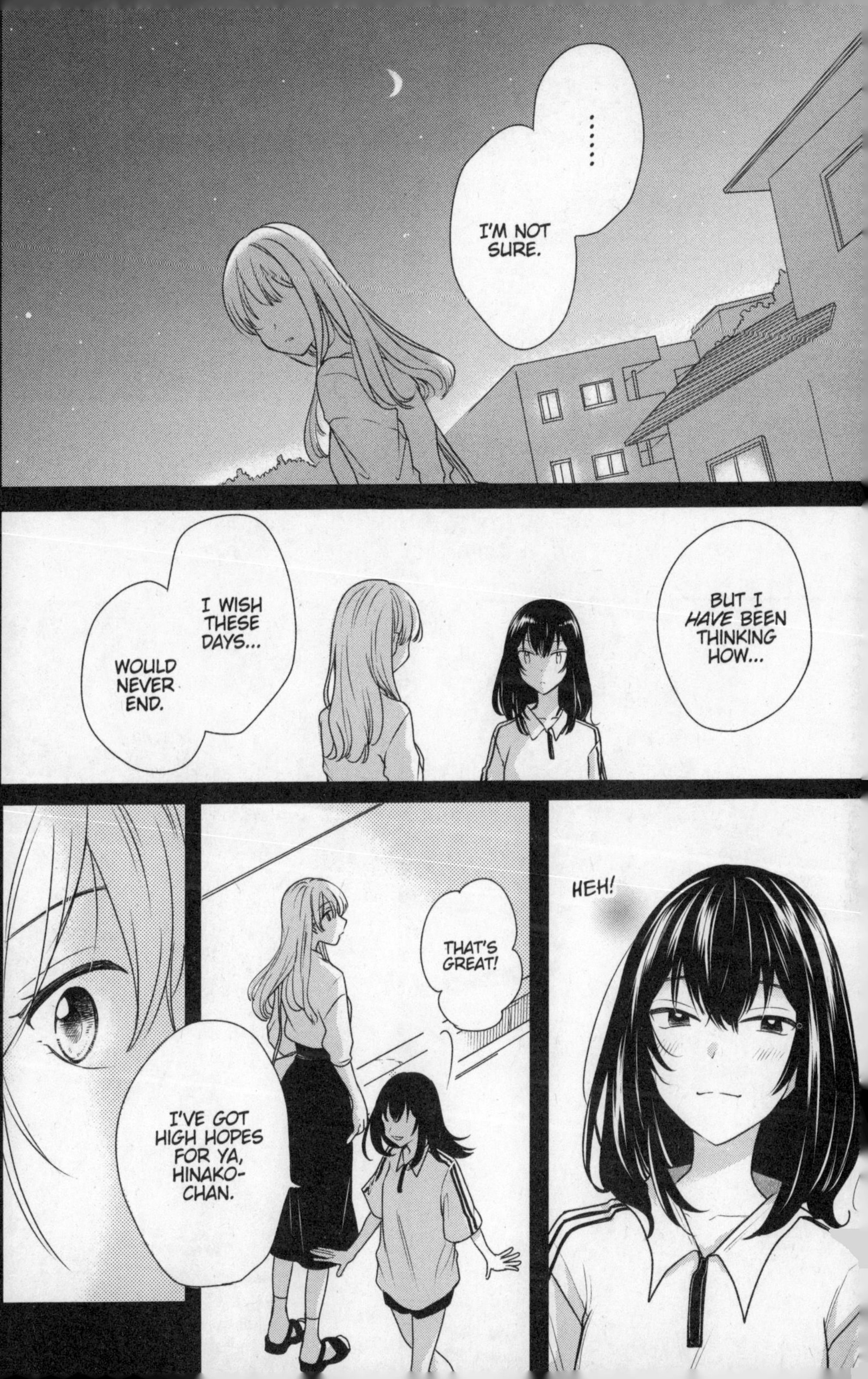
......
I'M NOT SURE.
BUT I *HAVE* BEEN THINKING HOW...
I WISH THESE DAYS... WOULD NEVER END.
HEH!
THAT'S GREAT!
I'VE GOT HIGH HOPES FOR YA, HINAKO-CHAN.

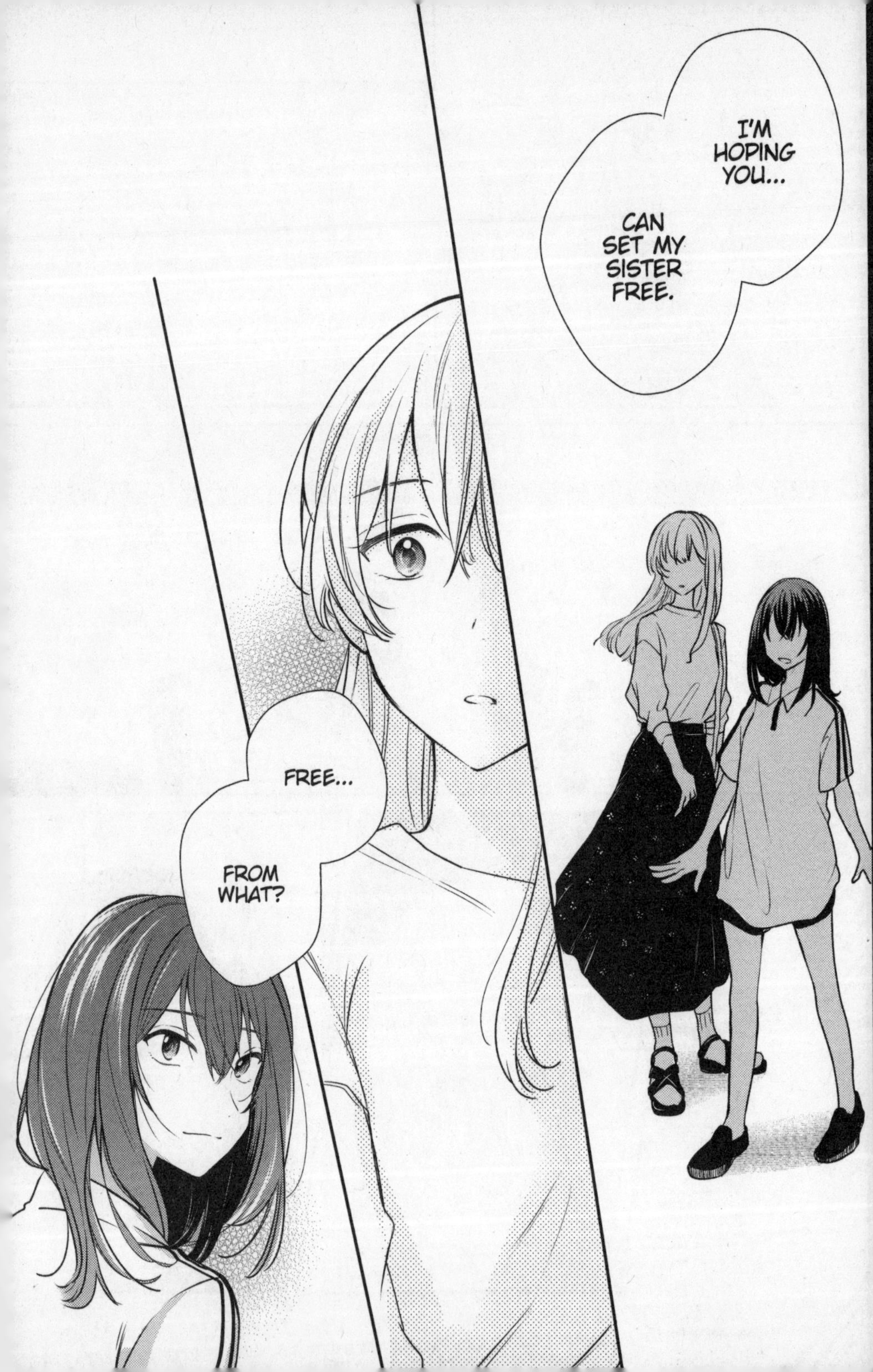
I'M HOPING YOU...
CAN SET MY SISTER FREE.
FREE...
FROM WHAT?

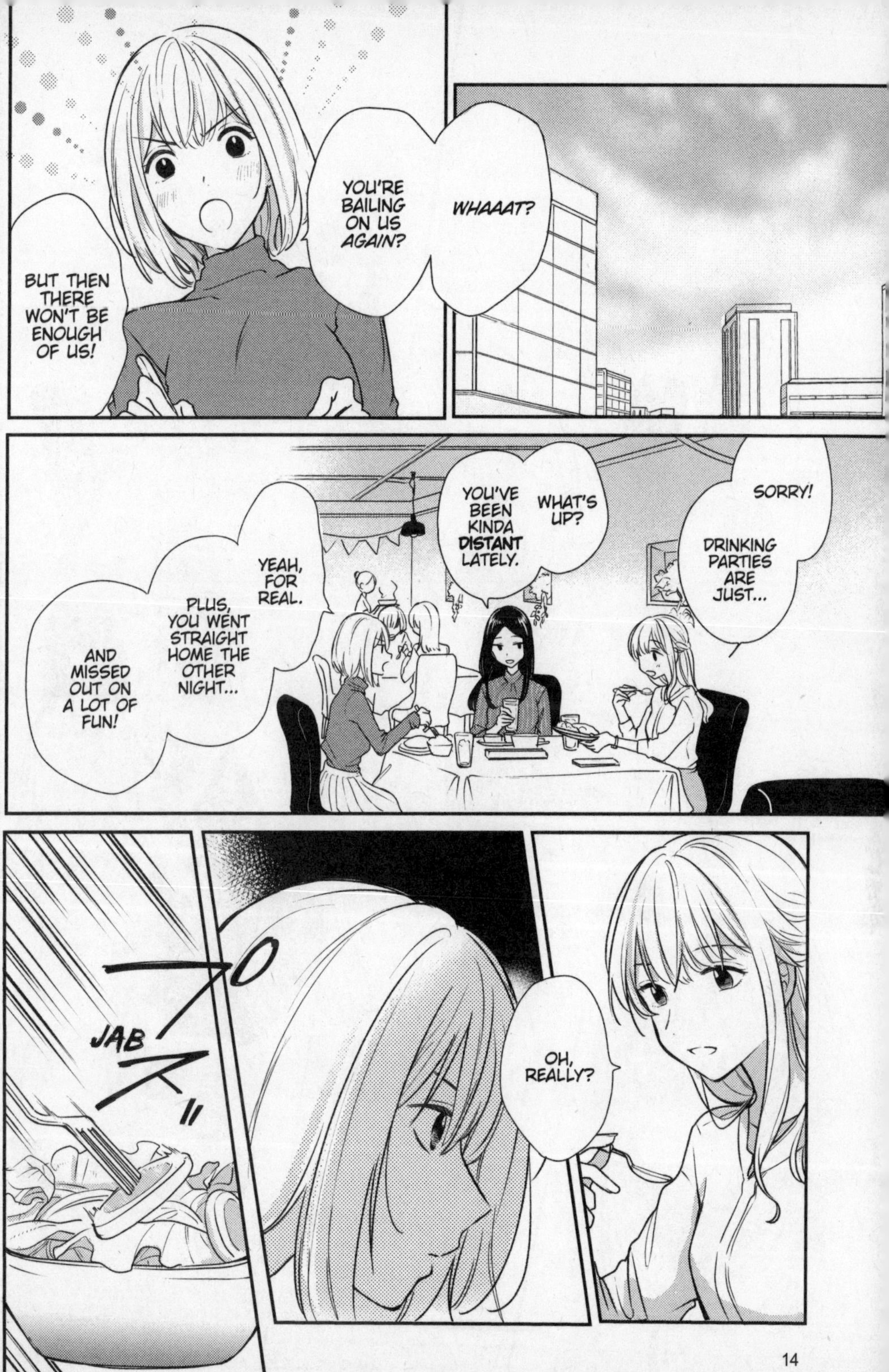
WHAAAT?
YOU'RE BAILING ON US AGAIN?
BUT THEN THERE WON'T BE ENOUGH OF US!
SORRY!
DRINKING PARTIES ARE JUST...
WHAT'S UP?
YOU'VE BEEN KINDA DISTANT LATELY.
YEAH, FOR REAL.
PLUS, YOU WENT STRAIGHT HOME THE OTHER NIGHT...
AND MISSED OUT ON A LOT OF FUN!
OH, REALLY?
JAB

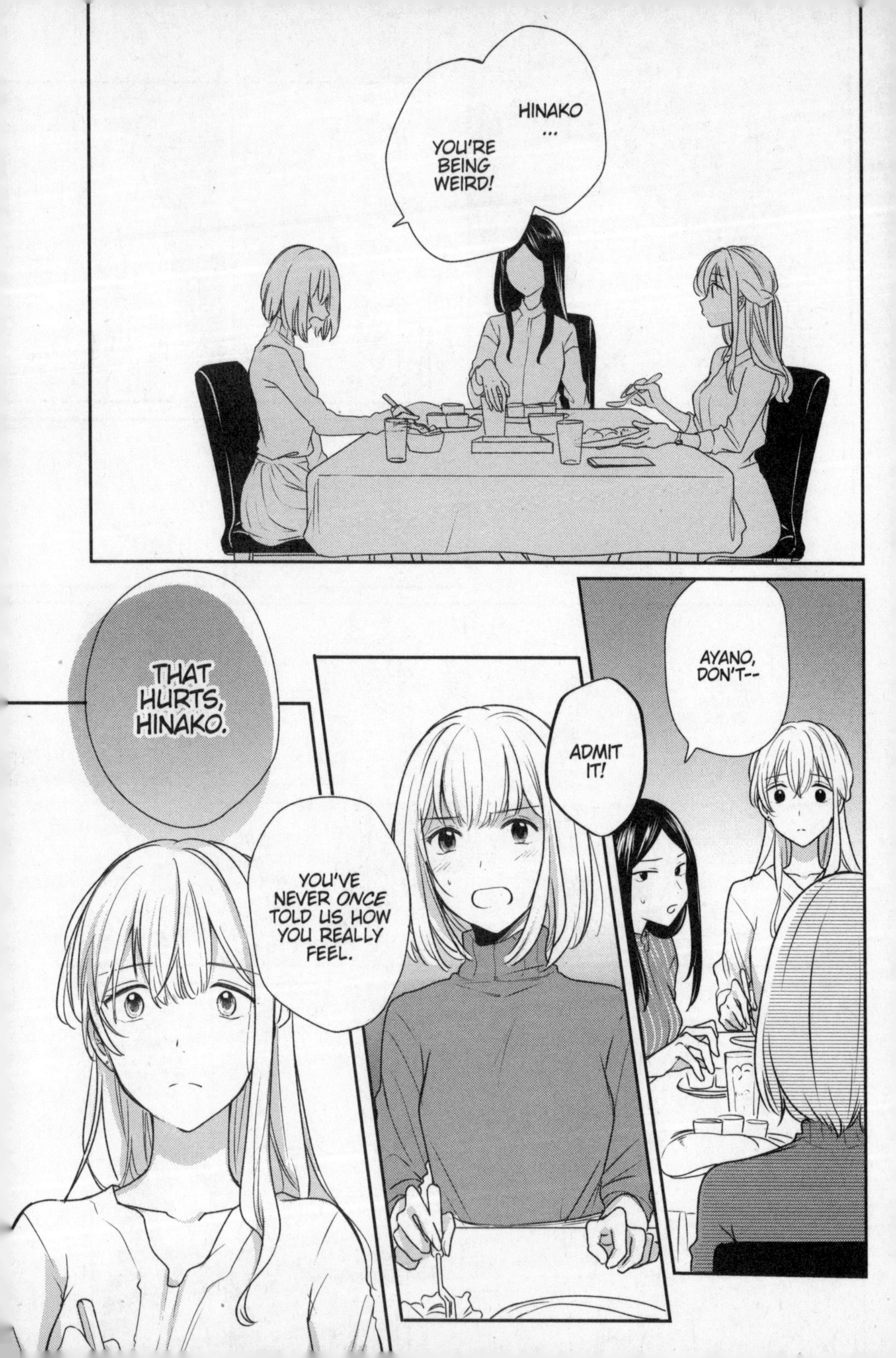
HINAKO ...
YOU'RE BEING WEIRD!
AYANO, DON'T--
ADMIT IT!
YOU'VE NEVER ONCE TOLD US HOW YOU REALLY FEEL.
THAT HURTS, HINAKO.

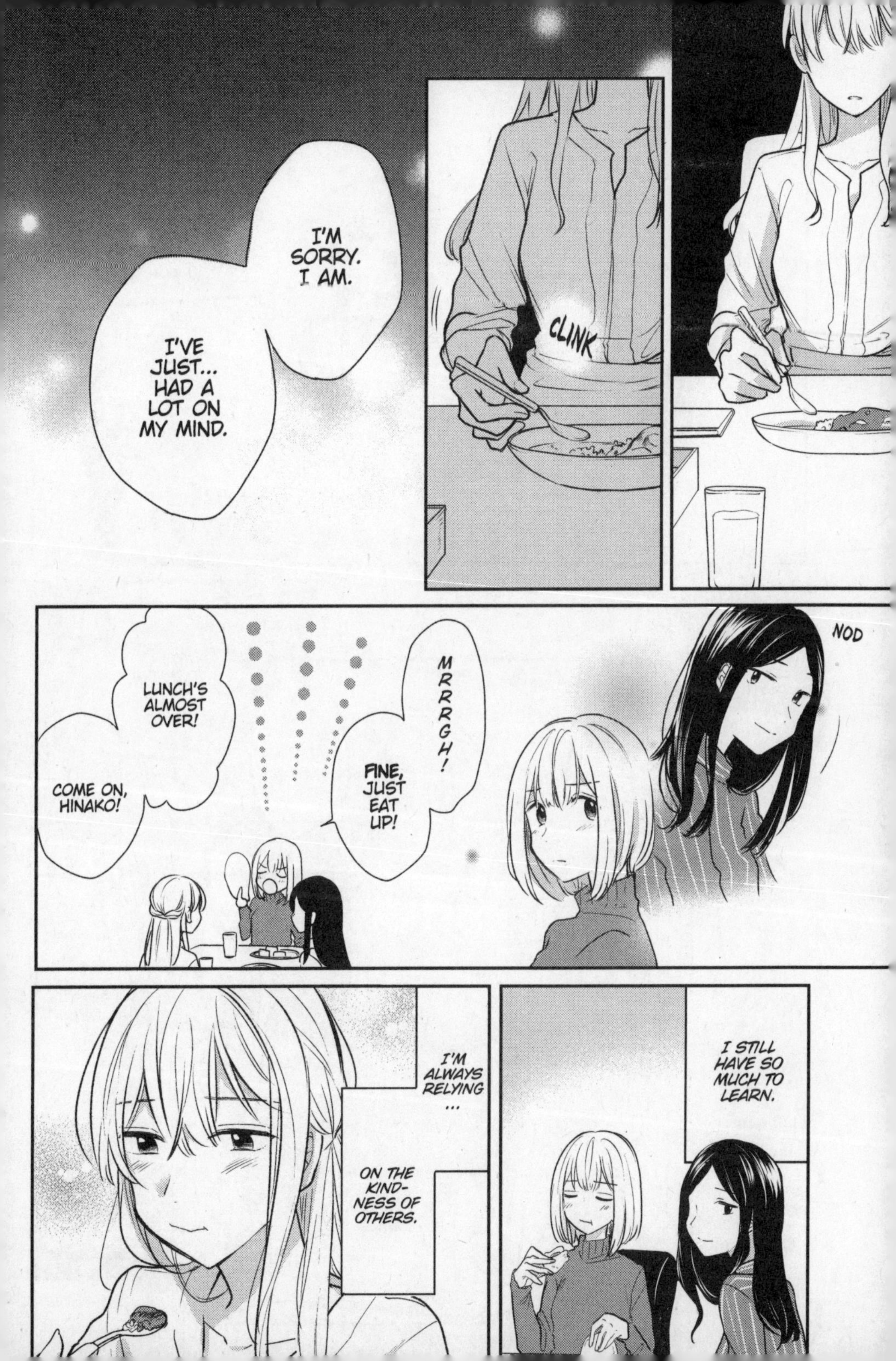
CLINK
I'M SORRY. I AM.
I'VE JUST... HAD A LOT ON MY MIND.
NOD
MRRRGH!
FINE, JUST EAT UP!
LUNCH'S ALMOST OVER!
COME ON, HINAKO!
I STILL HAVE SO MUCH TO LEARN.
I'M ALWAYS RELYING...
ON THE KINDNESS OF OTHERS.

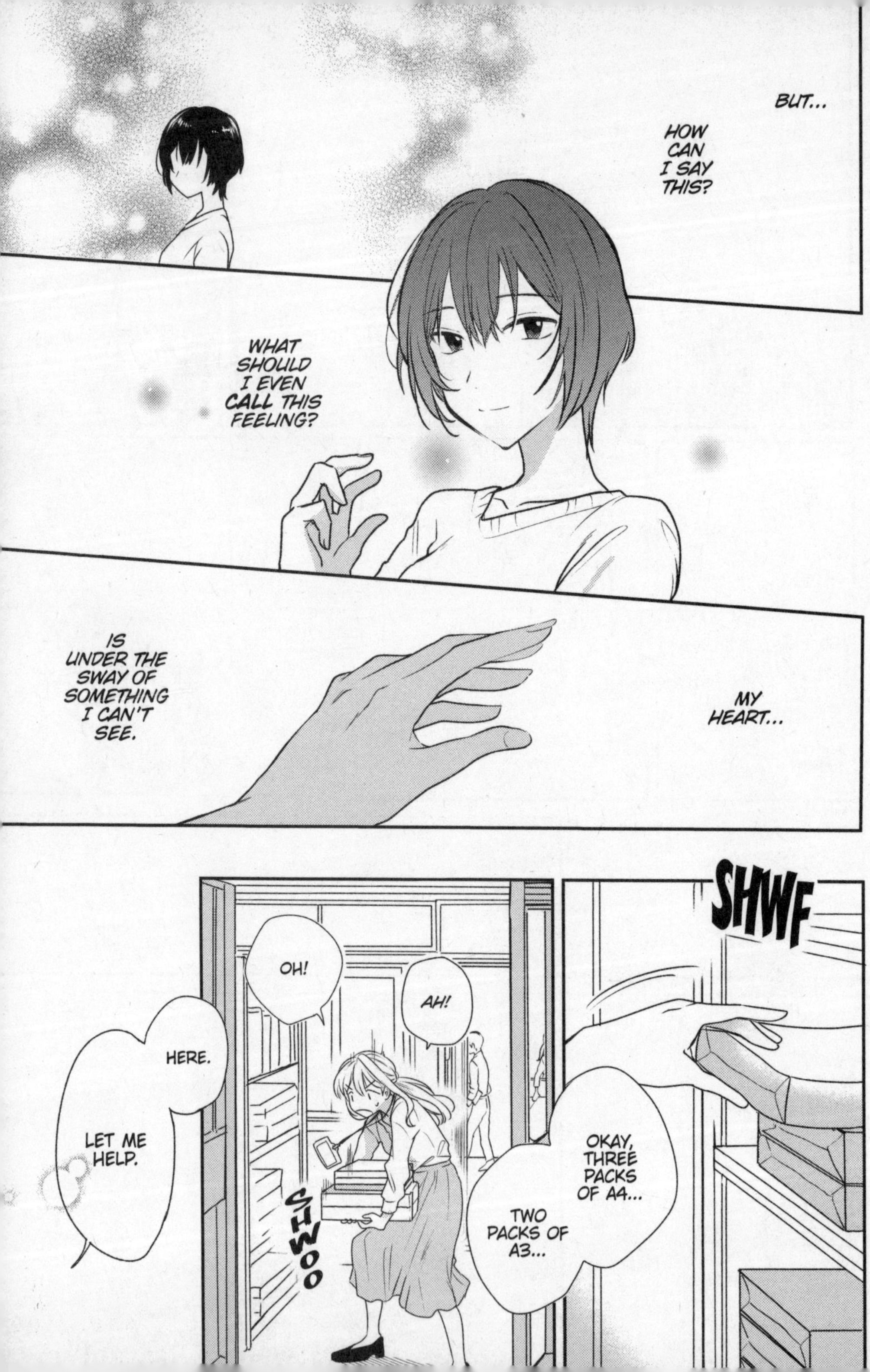

BUT...
HOW CAN I SAY THIS?
WHAT SHOULD I EVEN CALL THIS FEELING?
MY HEART...
IS UNDER THE SWAY OF SOMETHING I CAN'T SEE.
SHWF
OKAY, THREE PACKS OF A4...
TWO PACKS OF A3...
AH!
OH!
SHWOO
HERE.
LET ME HELP.

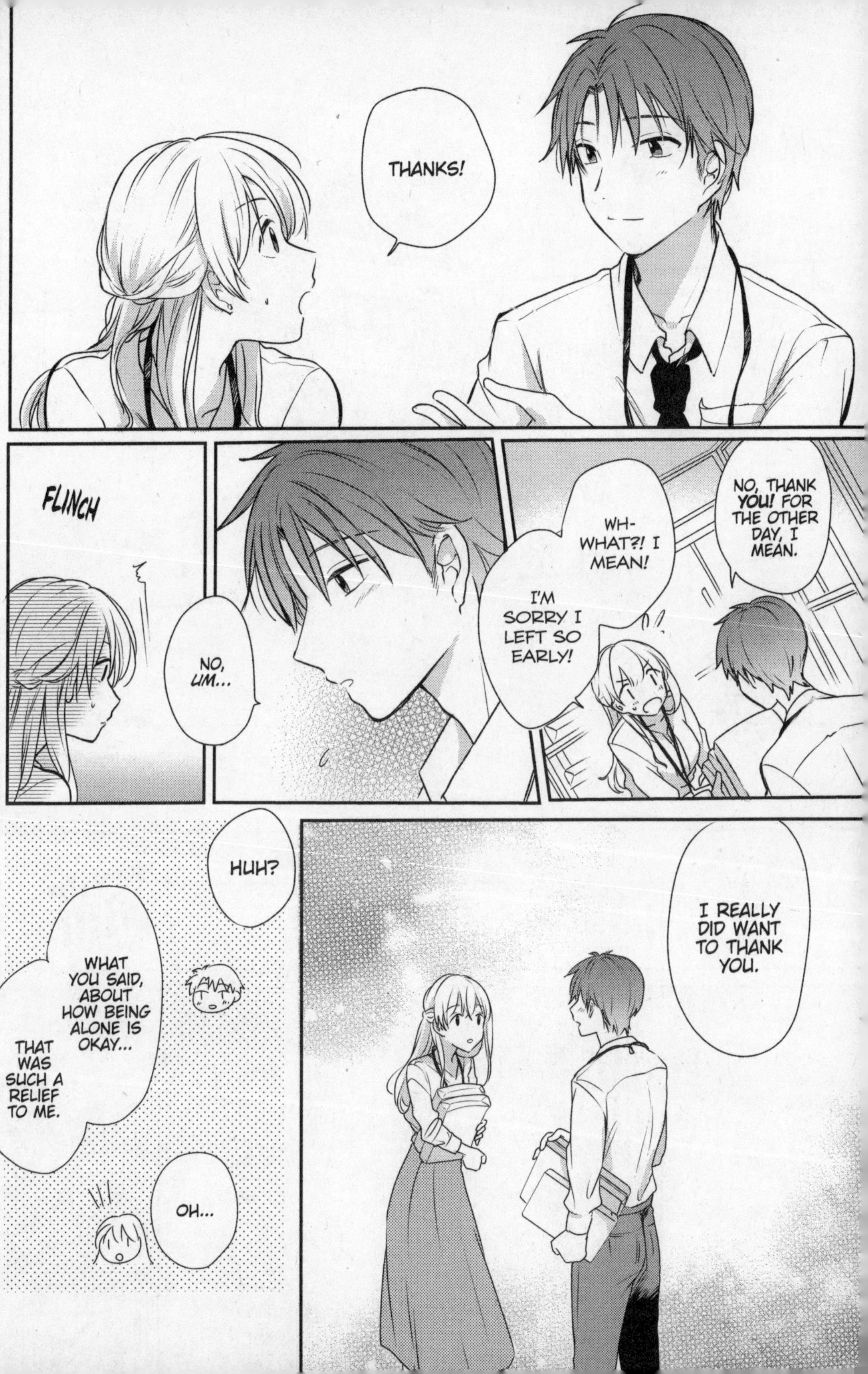
THANKS!
NO, THANK YOU! FOR THE OTHER DAY, I MEAN.
WH-WHAT?! I MEAN!
I'M SORRY I LEFT SO EARLY!
NO, UM...
FLINCH
I REALLY DID WANT TO THANK YOU.
HUH?
WHAT YOU SAID, ABOUT HOW BEING ALONE IS OKAY...
THAT WAS SUCH A RELIEF TO ME.
OH...

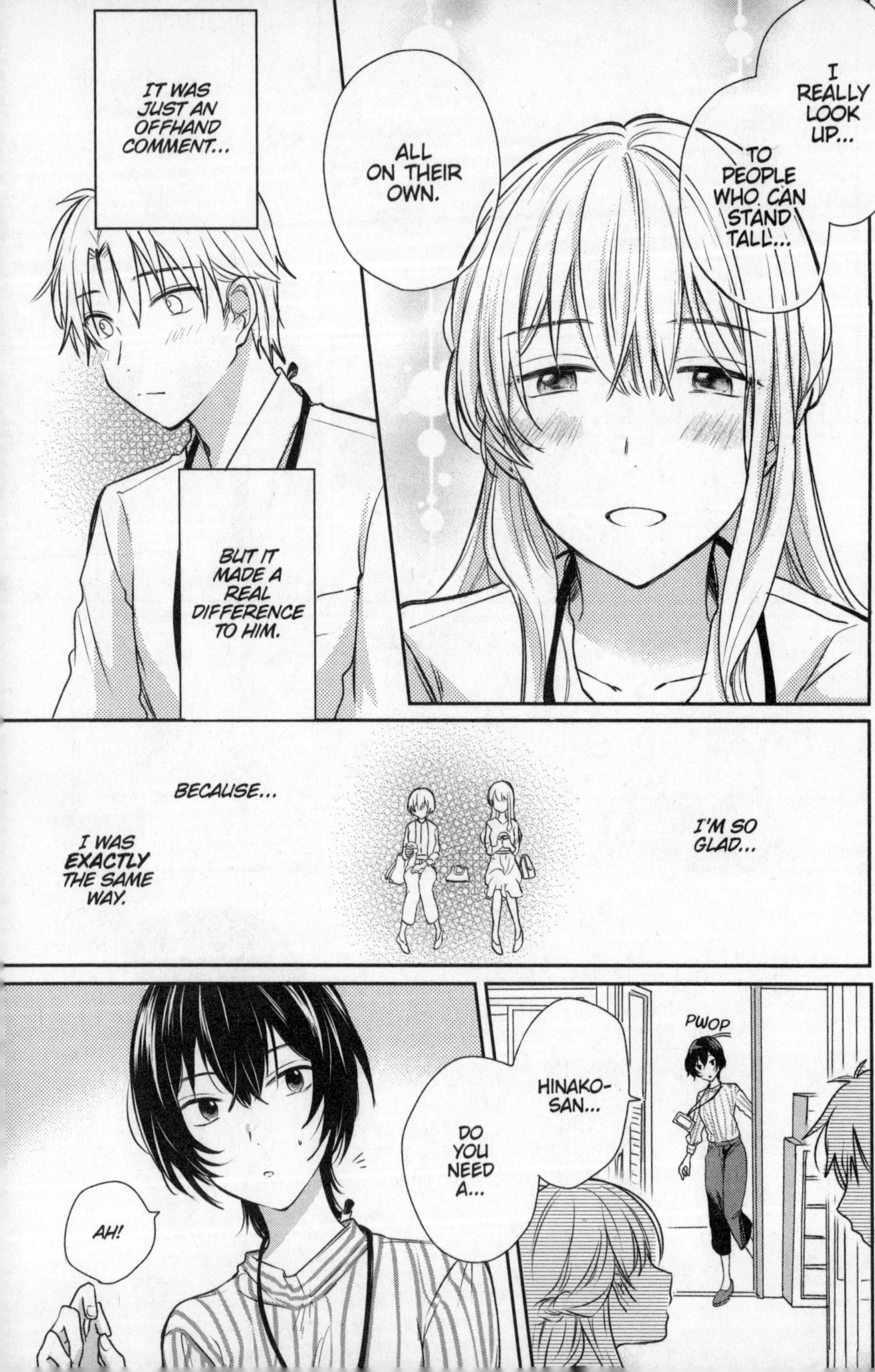
I REALLY LOOK UP...
TO PEOPLE WHO CAN STAND TALL...
ALL ON THEIR OWN.
IT WAS JUST AN OFFHAND COMMENT...
BUT IT MADE A REAL DIFFERENCE TO HIM.
I'M SO GLAD...
BECAUSE...
I WAS EXACTLY THE SAME WAY.
PWOP
HINAKO-SAN...
DO YOU NEED A...
AH!

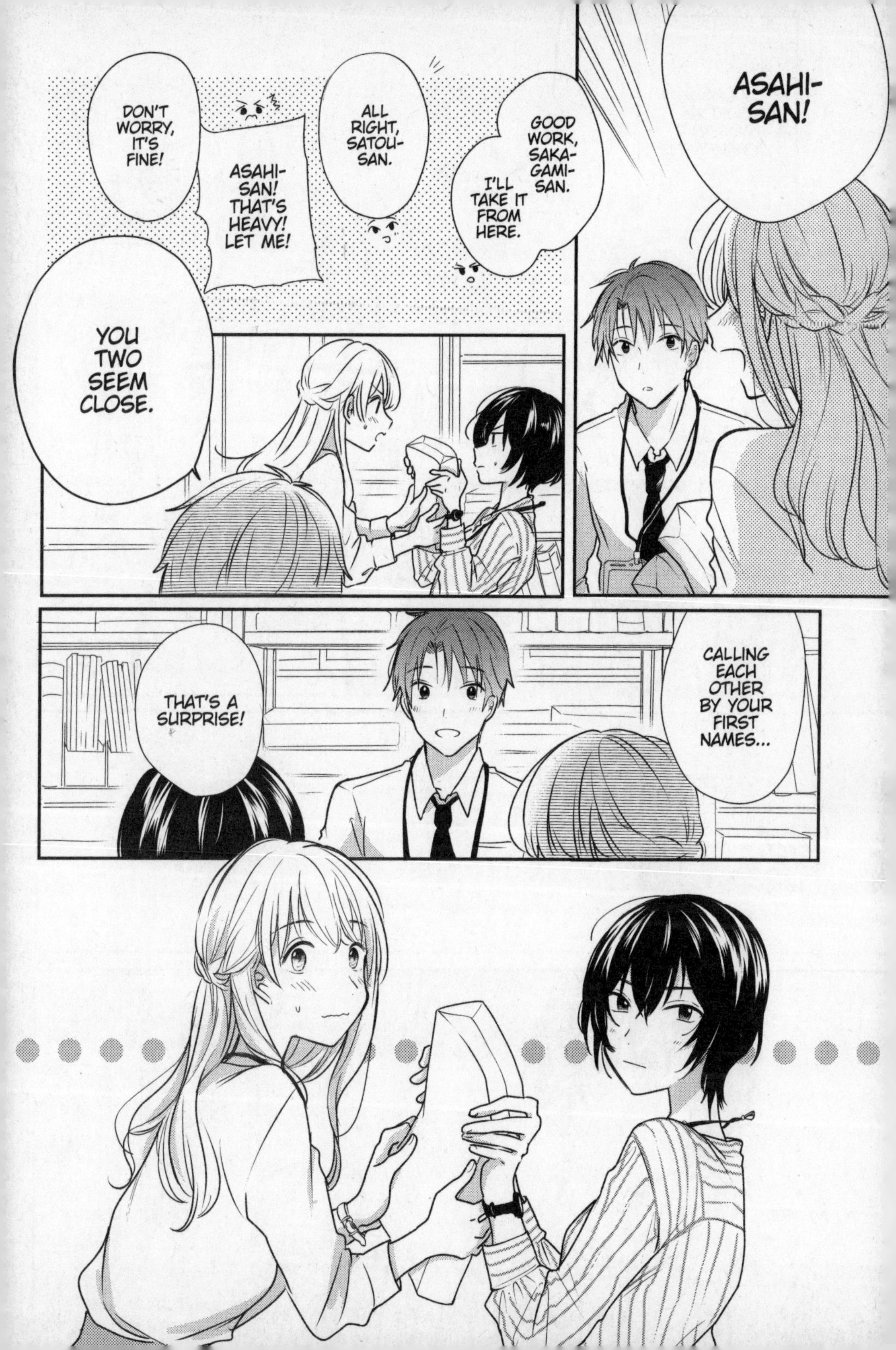
ASAHI-SAN!
GOOD WORK, SAKAGAMI-SAN.
I'LL TAKE IT FROM HERE.
ALL RIGHT, SATOU-SAN.
ASAHI-SAN! THAT'S HEAVY! LET ME!
DON'T WORRY, IT'S FINE!
YOU TWO SEEM CLOSE.
CALLING EACH OTHER BY YOUR FIRST NAMES...
THAT'S A SURPRISE!

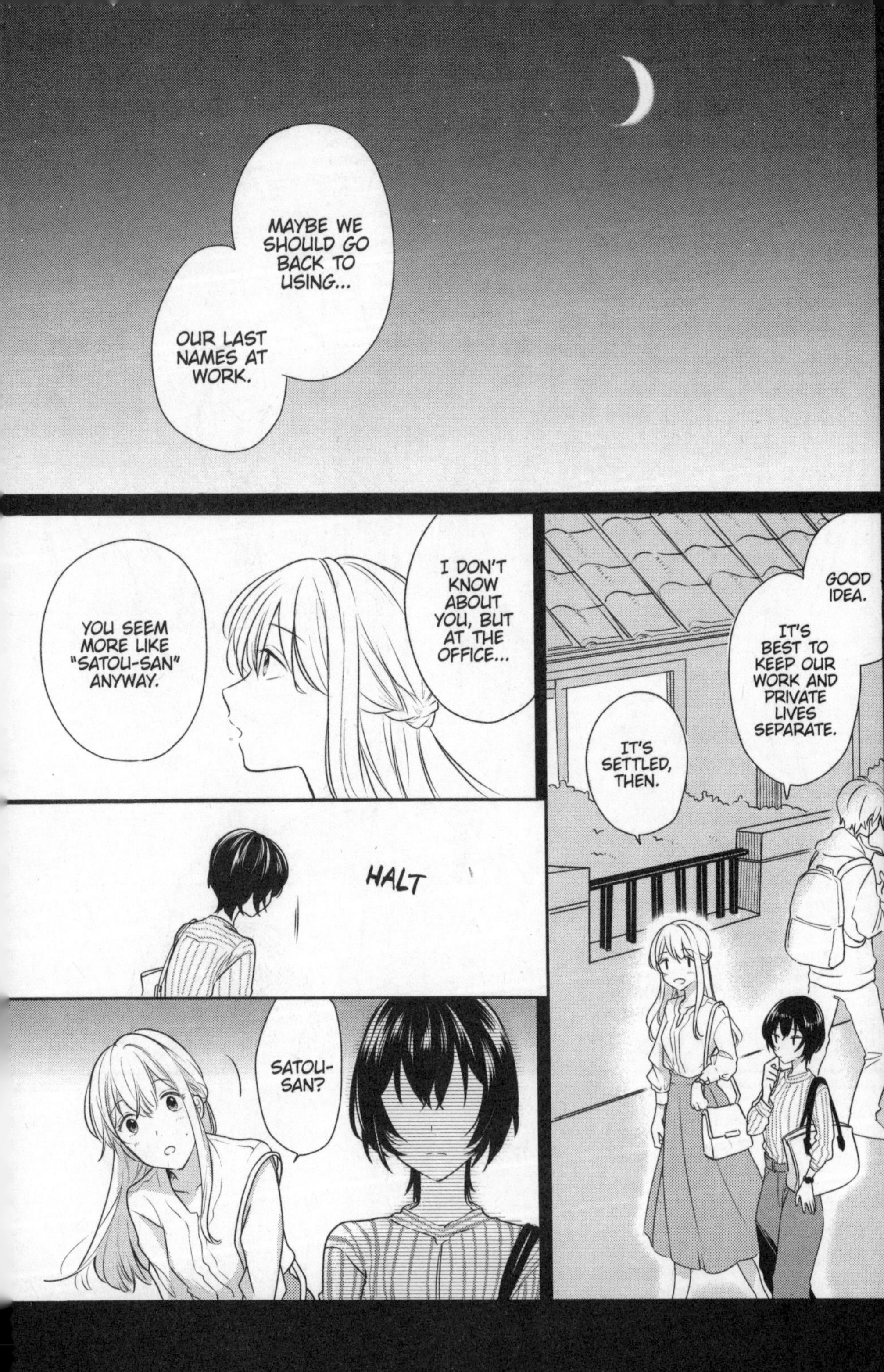
MAYBE WE SHOULD GO BACK TO USING...
OUR LAST NAMES AT WORK.
GOOD IDEA.
IT'S BEST TO KEEP OUR WORK AND PRIVATE LIVES SEPARATE.
IT'S SETTLED, THEN.
I DON'T KNOW ABOUT YOU, BUT AT THE OFFICE...
YOU SEEM MORE LIKE "SATOU-SAN" ANYWAY.
HALT
SATOU-SAN?

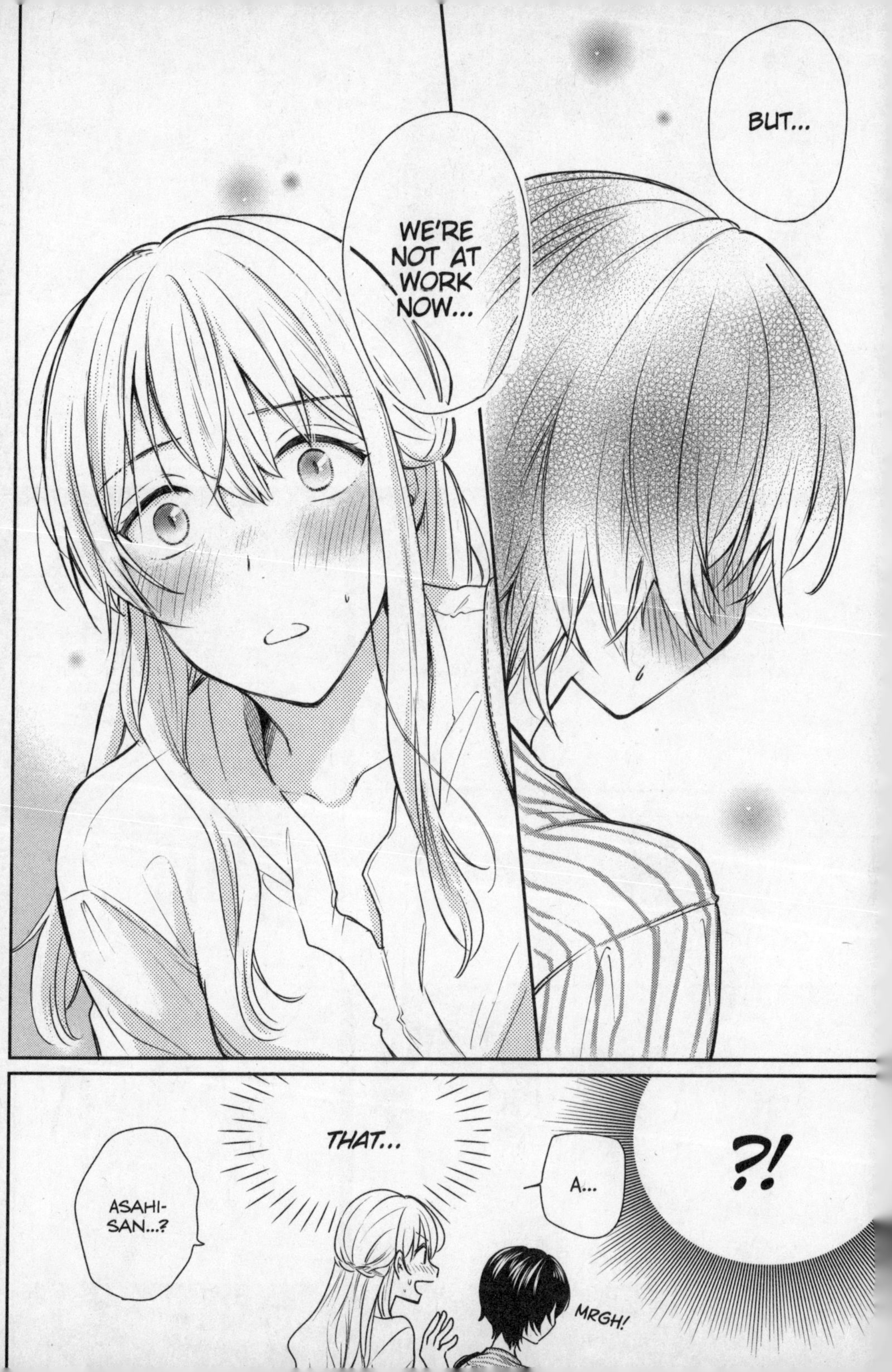
BUT...
WE'RE NOT AT WORK NOW...
?!
A...
THAT...
ASAHI-SAN...?
MRGH!

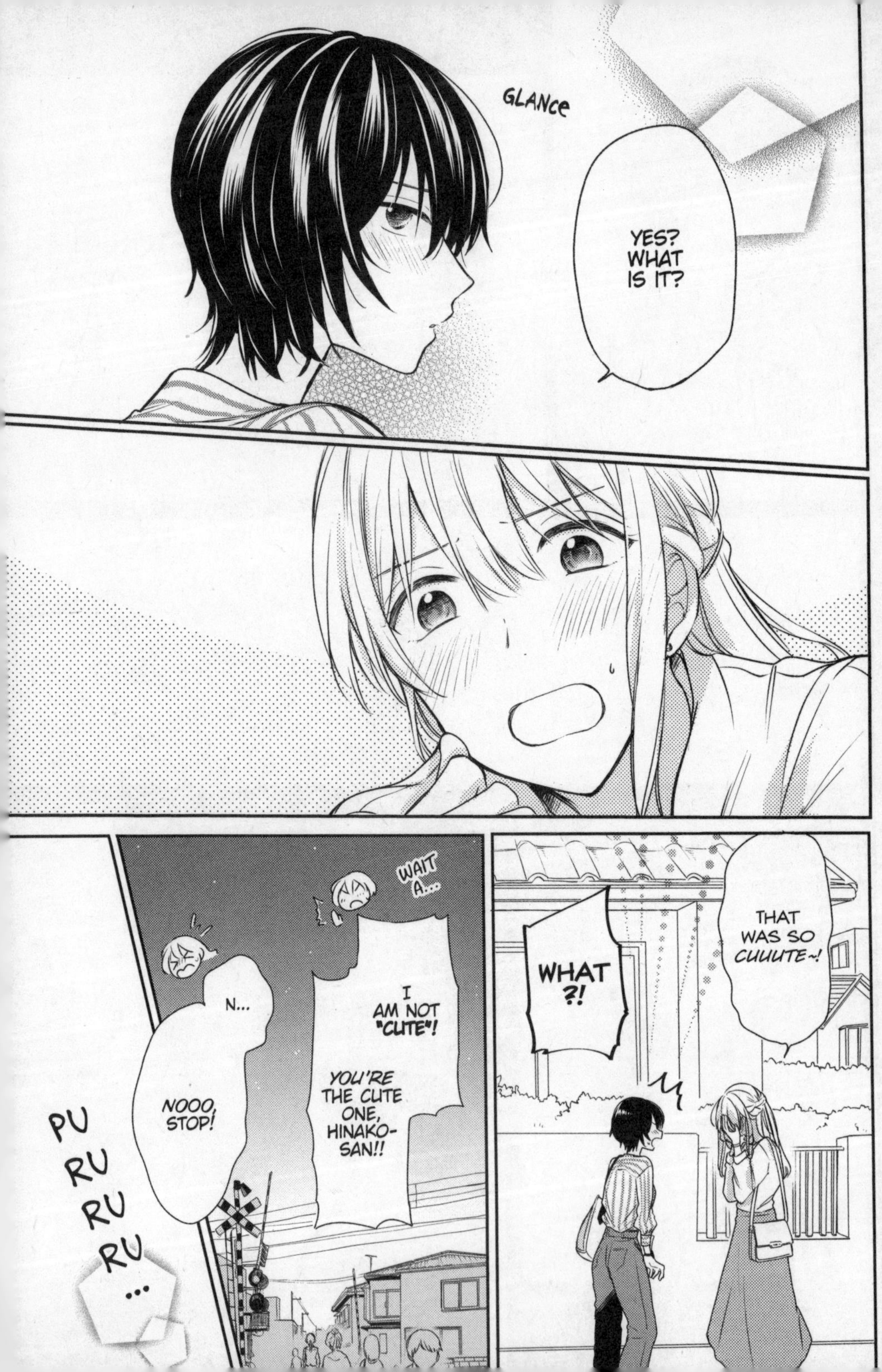
GLANCE
YES? WHAT IS IT?
THAT WAS SO CUUUTE~!
WHAT ?!
WAIT A...
I AM NOT "CUTE"!
YOU'RE THE CUTE ONE, HINAKO-SAN!!
N...
NOOO, STOP!
PU RU RU RU ...

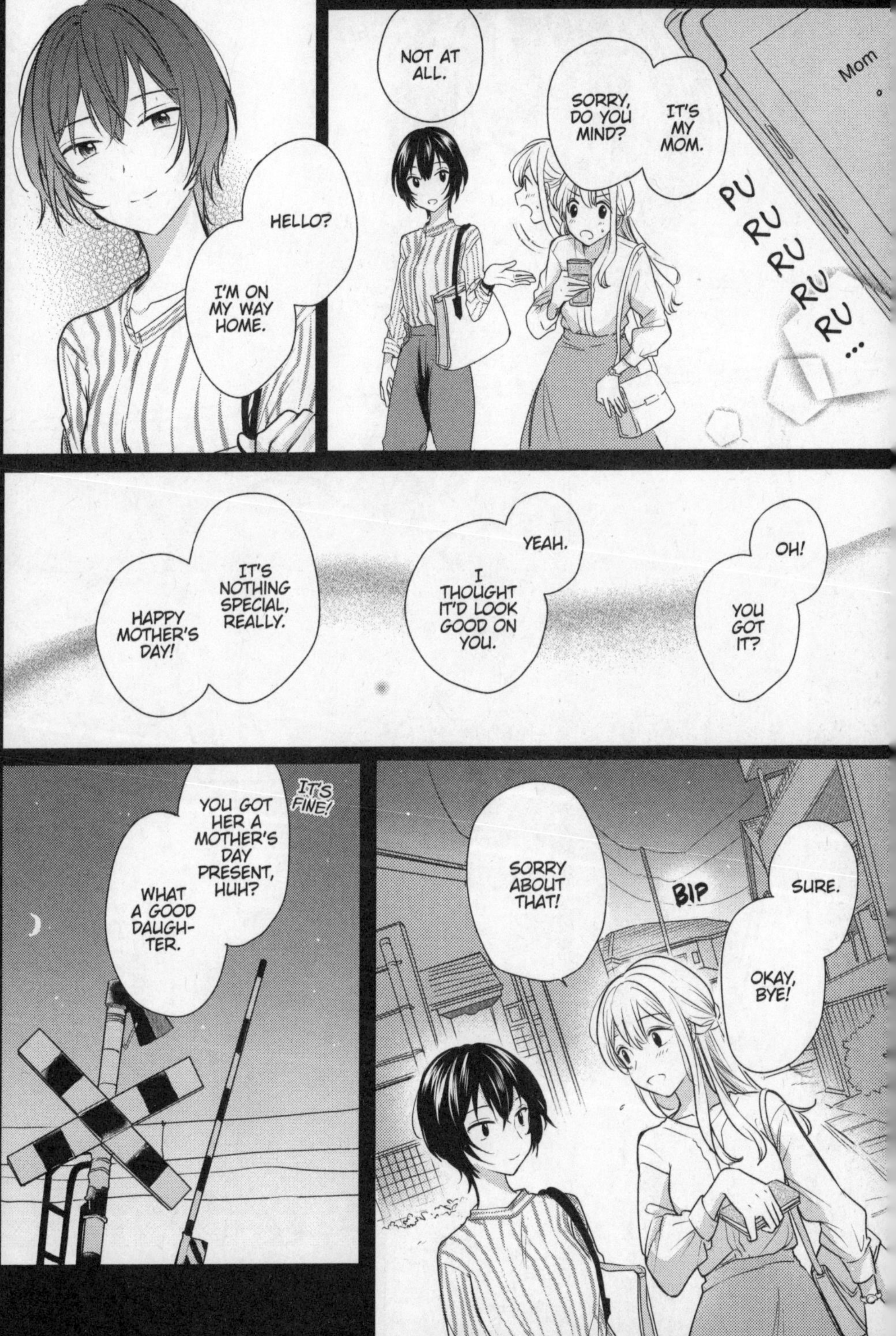
Mom
PU RU RU RU RU ...
IT'S MY MOM.
SORRY, DO YOU MIND?
NOT AT ALL.
HELLO?
I'M ON MY WAY HOME.
OH!
YOU GOT IT?
YEAH.
I THOUGHT IT'D LOOK GOOD ON YOU.
IT'S NOTHING SPECIAL, REALLY.
HAPPY MOTHER'S DAY!
SURE.
OKAY, BYE!
BIP
SORRY ABOUT THAT!
IT'S FINE!
YOU GOT HER A MOTHER'S DAY PRESENT, HUH?
WHAT A GOOD DAUGH-TER.

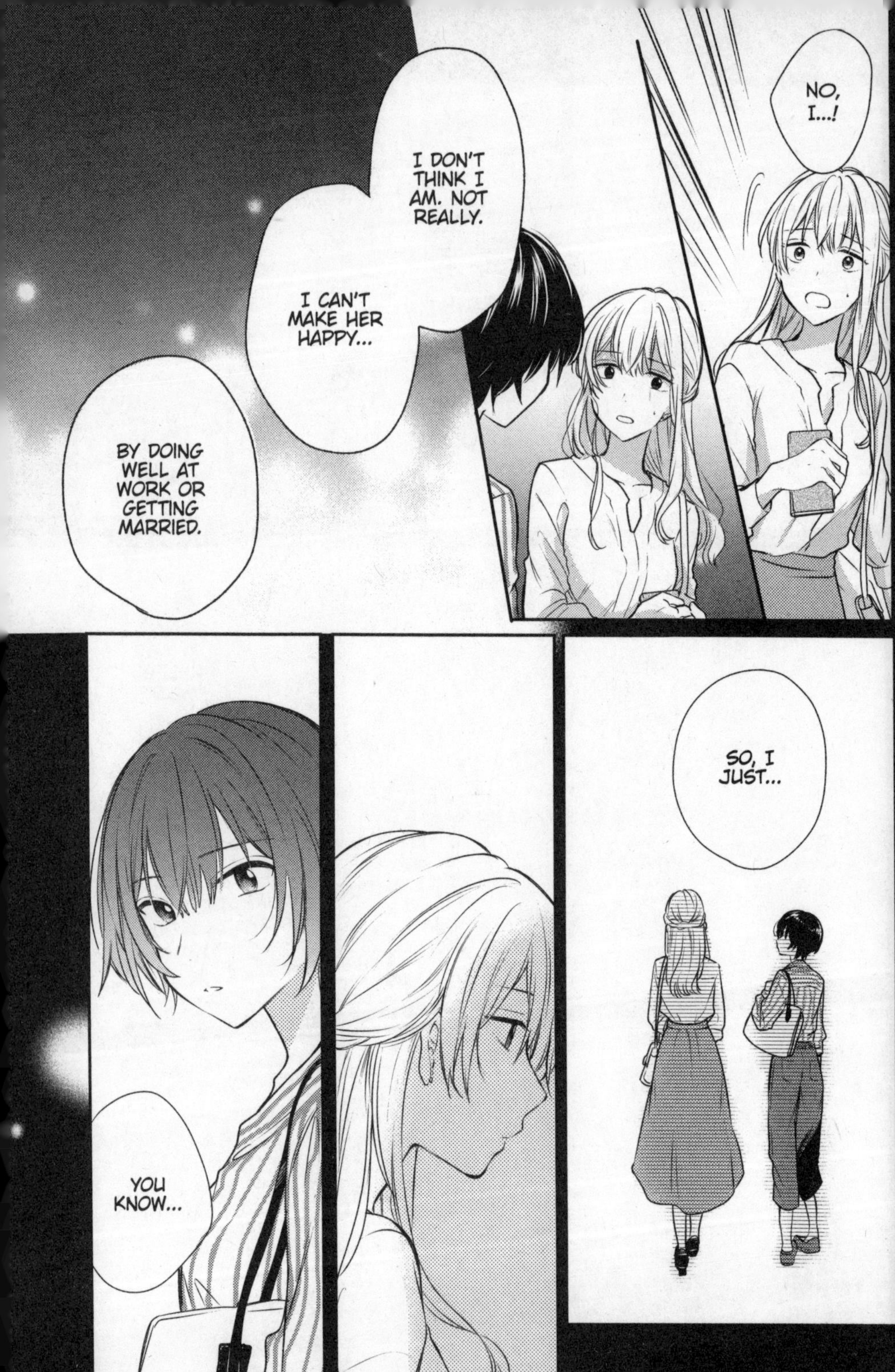
NO, I...!
I DON'T THINK I AM. NOT REALLY.
I CAN'T MAKE HER HAPPY...
BY DOING WELL AT WORK OR GETTING MARRIED.
SO, I JUST...
YOU KNOW...

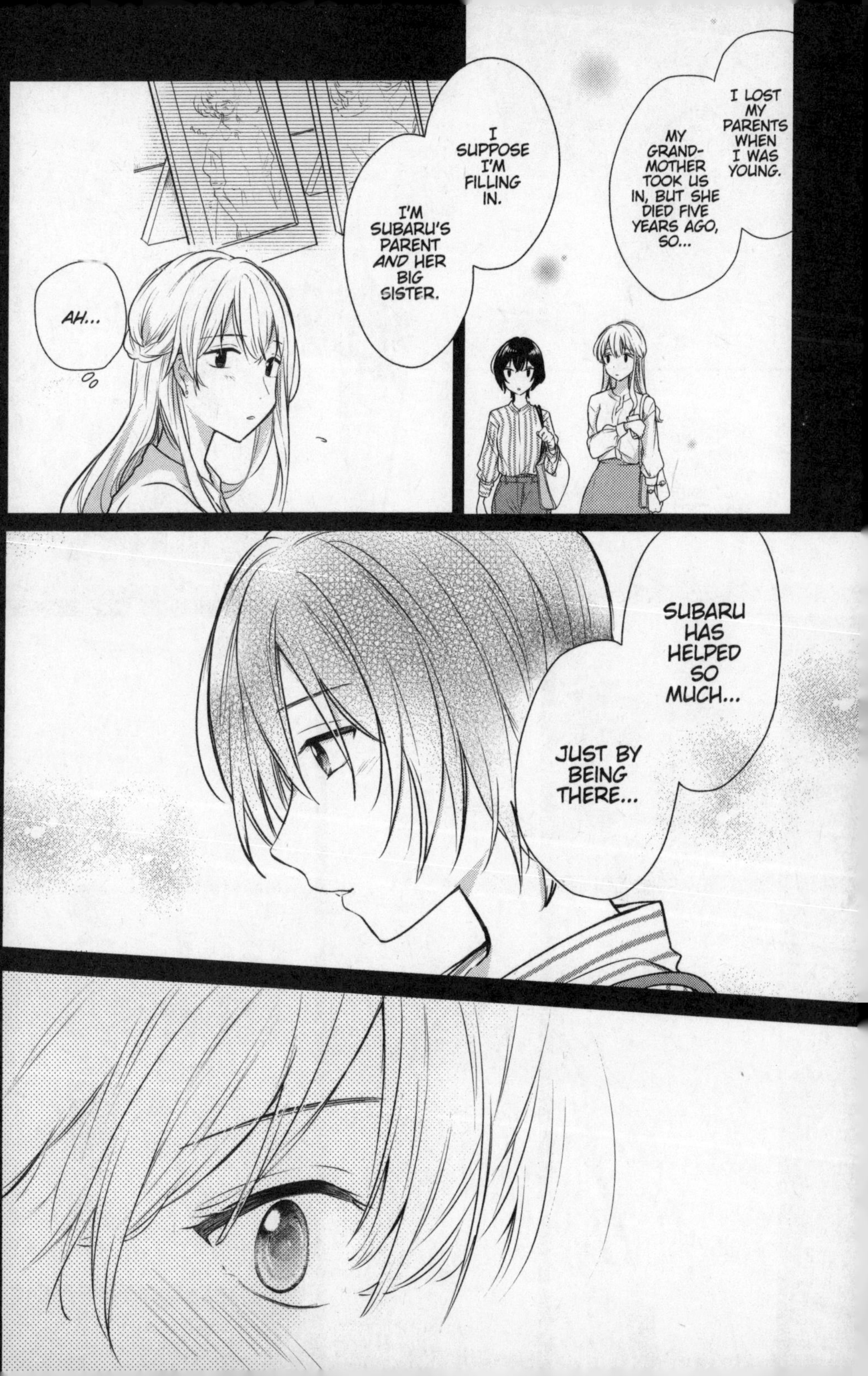
I LOST MY PARENTS WHEN I WAS YOUNG.
MY GRANDMOTHER TOOK US IN, BUT SHE DIED FIVE YEARS AGO, SO...
I SUPPOSE I'M FILLING IN.
I'M SUBARU'S PARENT AND HER BIG SISTER.
AH...
SUBARU HAS HELPED SO MUCH...
JUST BY BEING THERE...

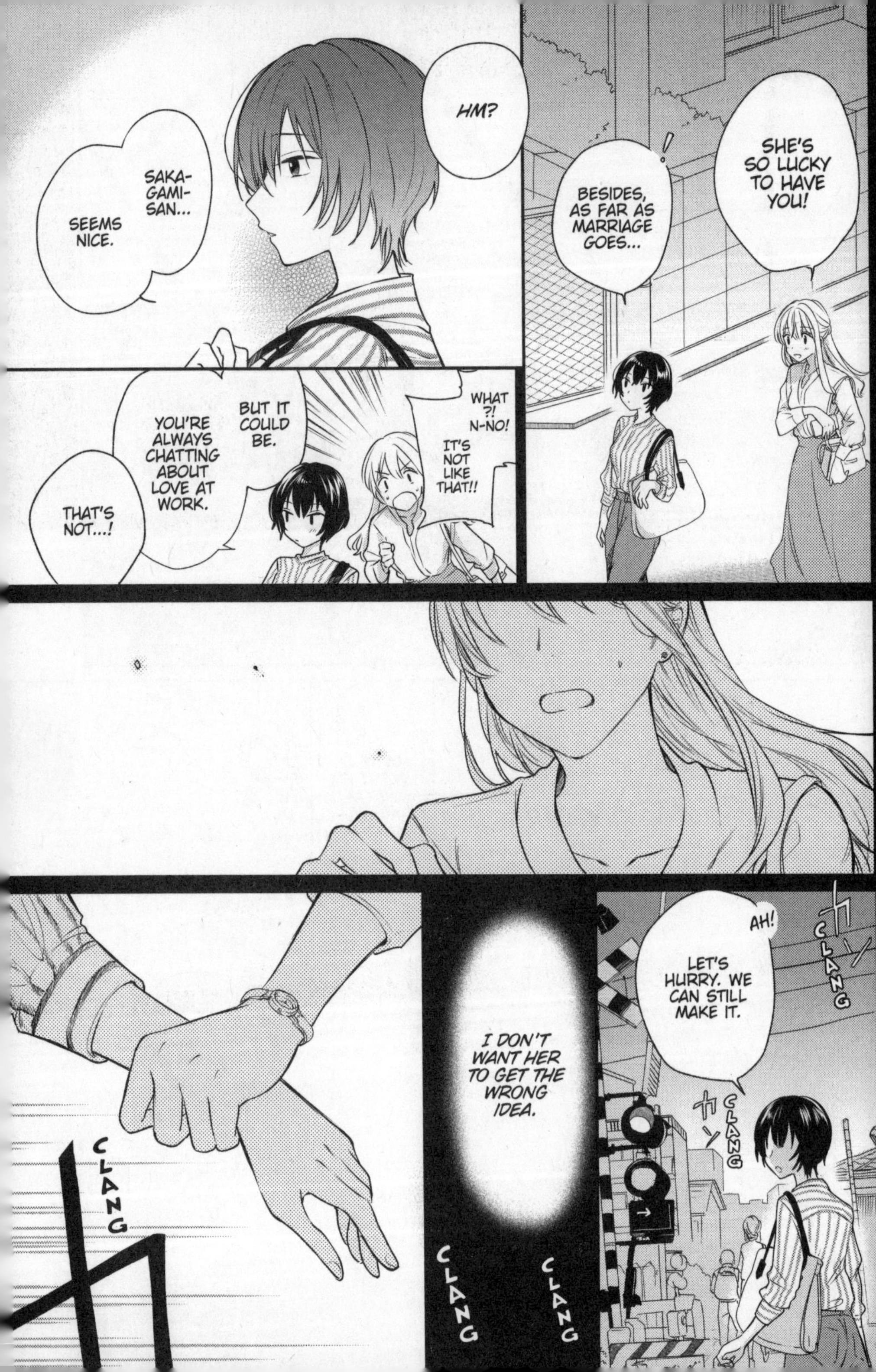
SHE'S SO LUCKY TO HAVE YOU!
!
BESIDES, AS FAR AS MARRIAGE GOES...
HM?
SAKA-GAMI-SAN...
SEEMS NICE.
WHAT?! N-NO!
IT'S NOT LIKE THAT!!
BUT IT COULD BE.
YOU'RE ALWAYS CHATTING ABOUT LOVE AT WORK.
THAT'S NOT...!
CLANG
AH!
LET'S HURRY. WE CAN STILL MAKE IT.
CLANG
I DON'T WANT HER TO GET THE WRONG IDEA.
CLANG
CLANG
CLANG

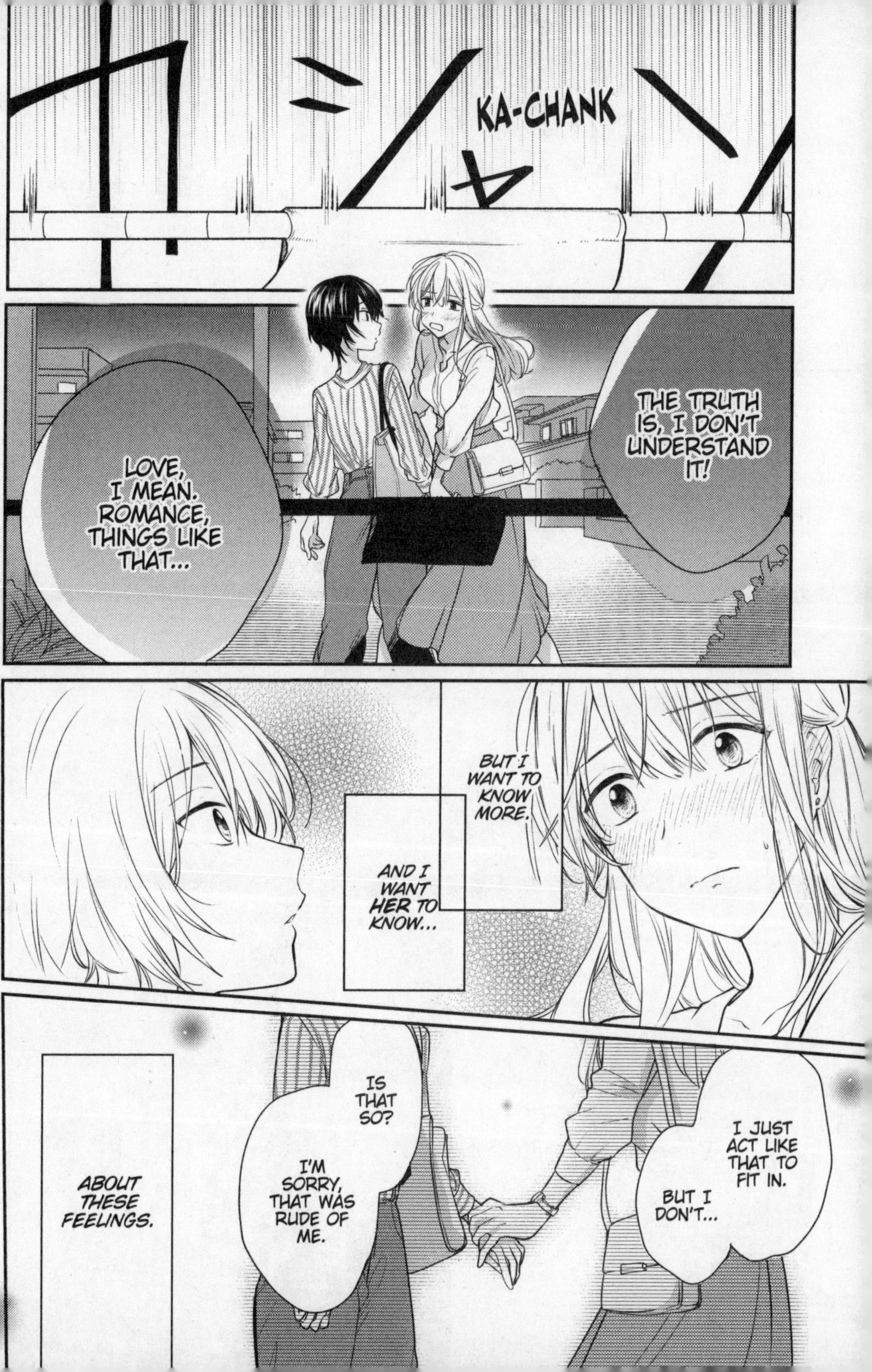
KA-CHANK
THE TRUTH IS, I DON'T UNDERSTAND IT!
LOVE, I MEAN. ROMANCE, THINGS LIKE THAT...
BUT I WANT TO KNOW MORE.
AND I WANT *HER* TO KNOW...
I JUST ACT LIKE THAT TO FIT IN.
BUT I DON'T...
IS THAT SO?
I'M SORRY, THAT WAS RUDE OF ME.
ABOUT THESE FEELINGS.

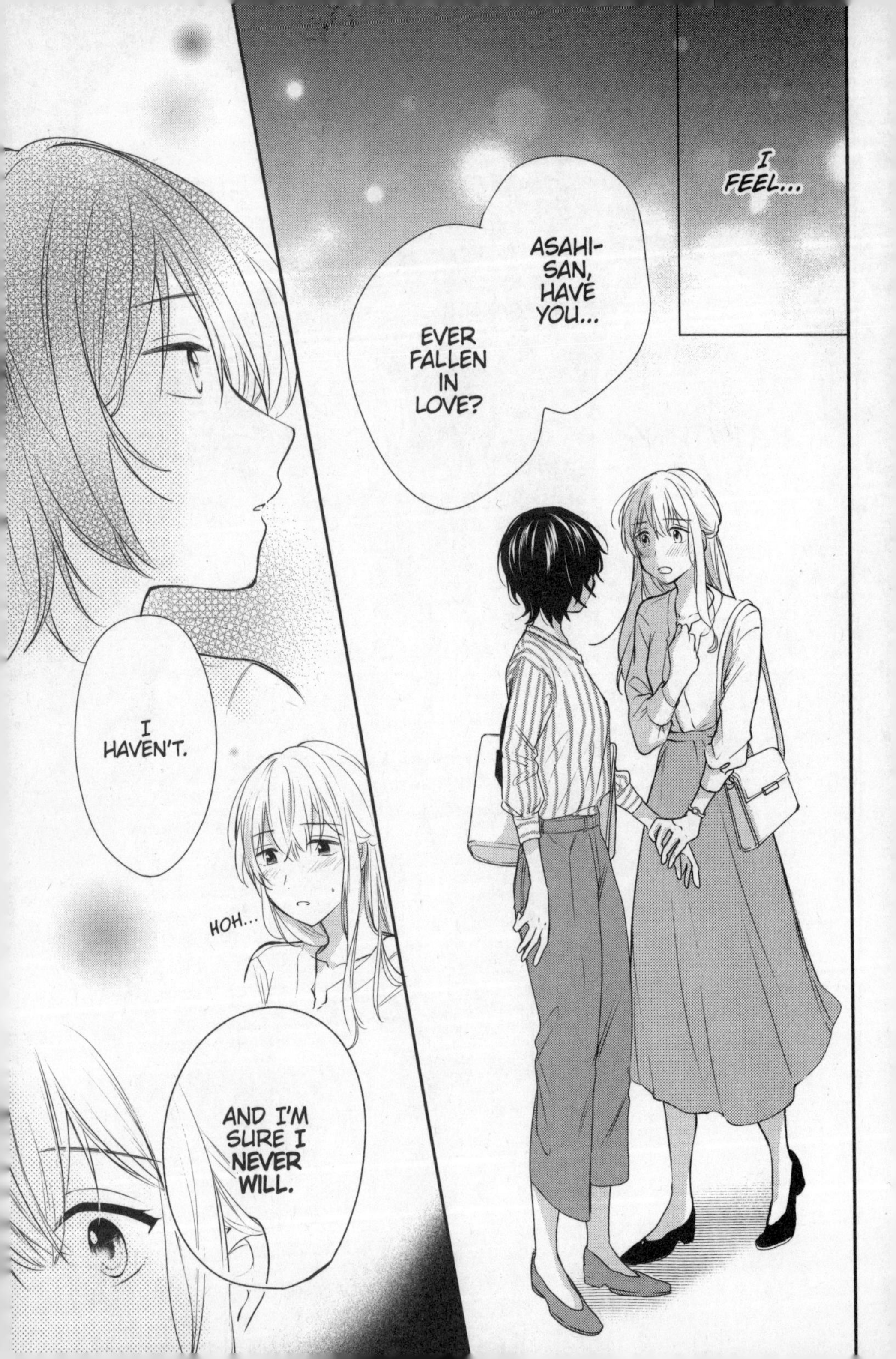
I FEEL...
ASAHI-SAN, HAVE YOU...
EVER FALLEN IN LOVE?
I HAVEN'T.
HOH...
AND I'M SURE I NEVER WILL.

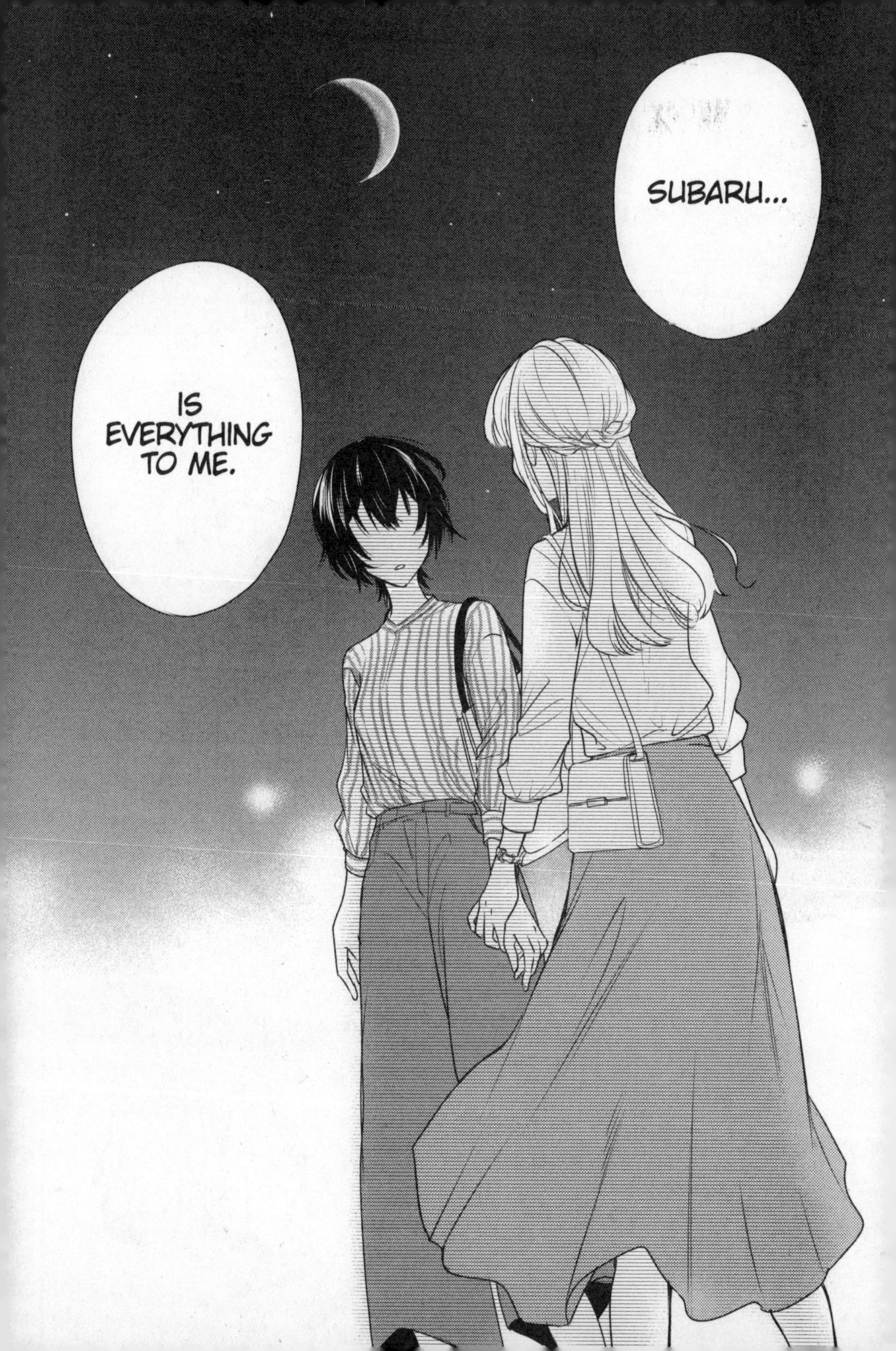
SUBARU...
IS EVERYTHING TO ME.

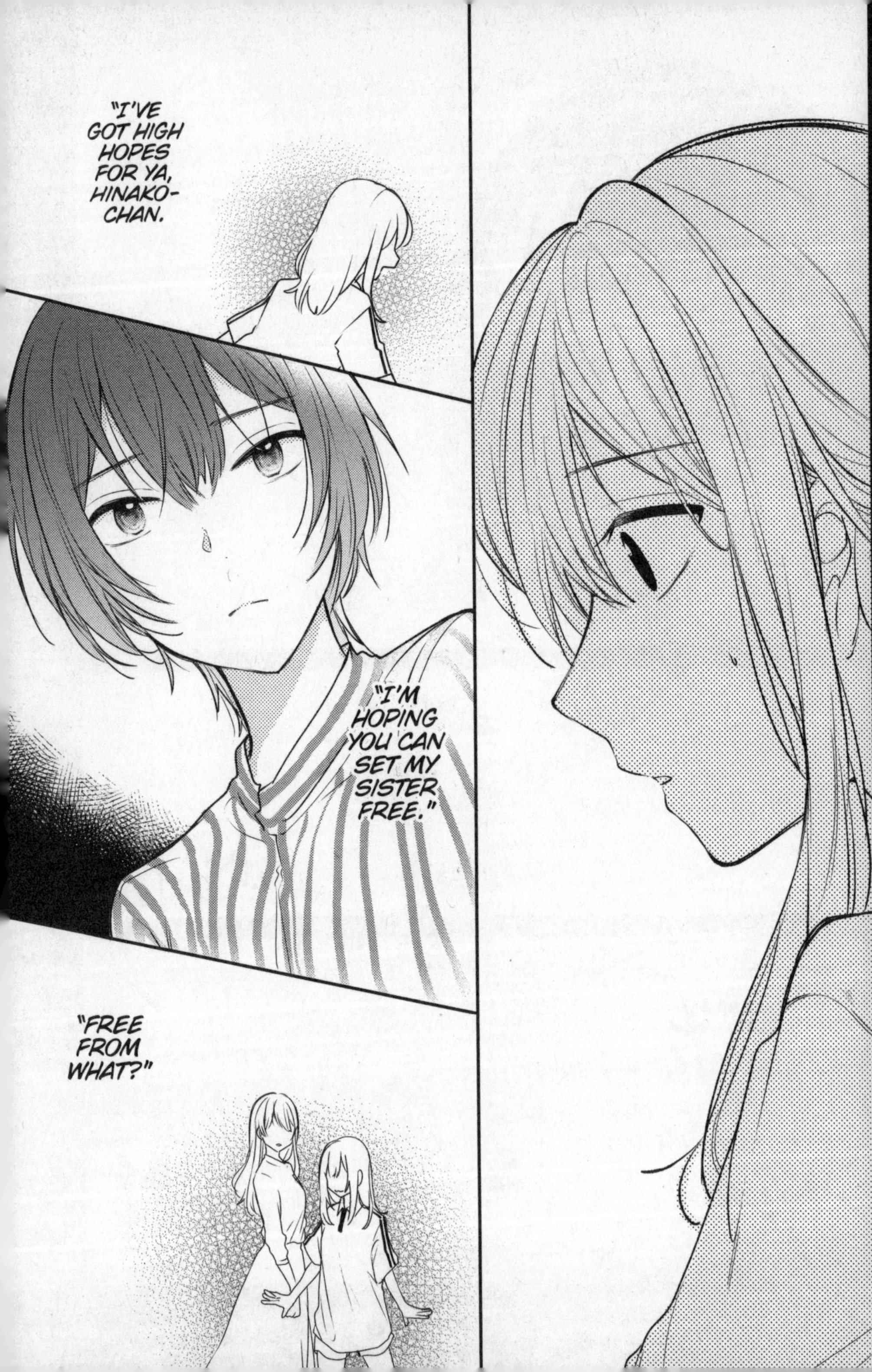
"I'VE GOT HIGH HOPES FOR YA, HINAKO-CHAN.
"I'M HOPING YOU CAN SET MY SISTER FREE."
"FREE FROM WHAT?"

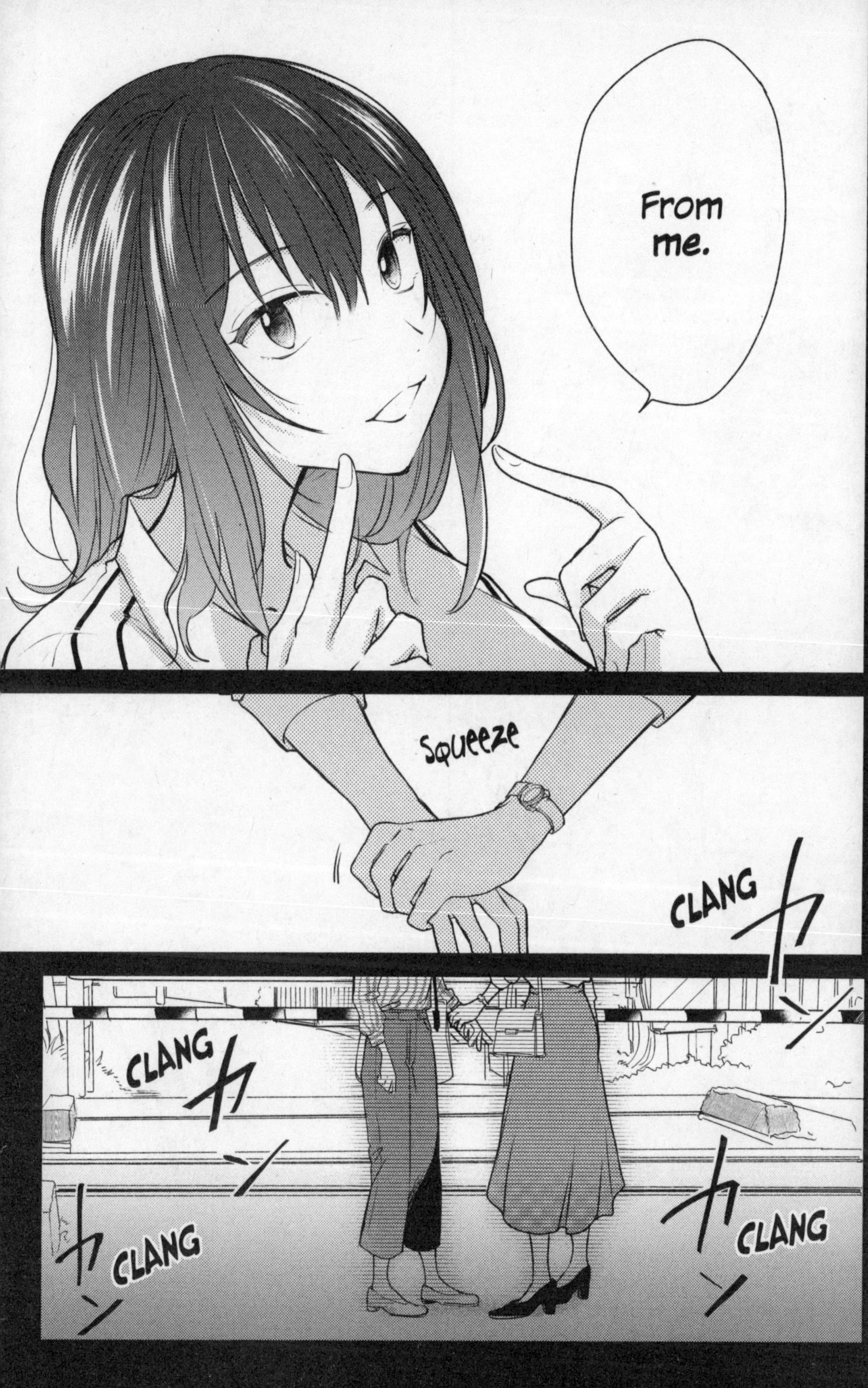
From me.
Squeeze
CLANG
CLANG
CLANG
CLANG

Doughnuts
Under a Crescent Moon

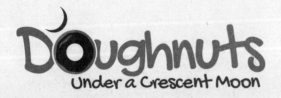

Doughnuts
Under a Crescent Moon

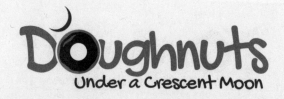

Chapter 7: Guiding Star

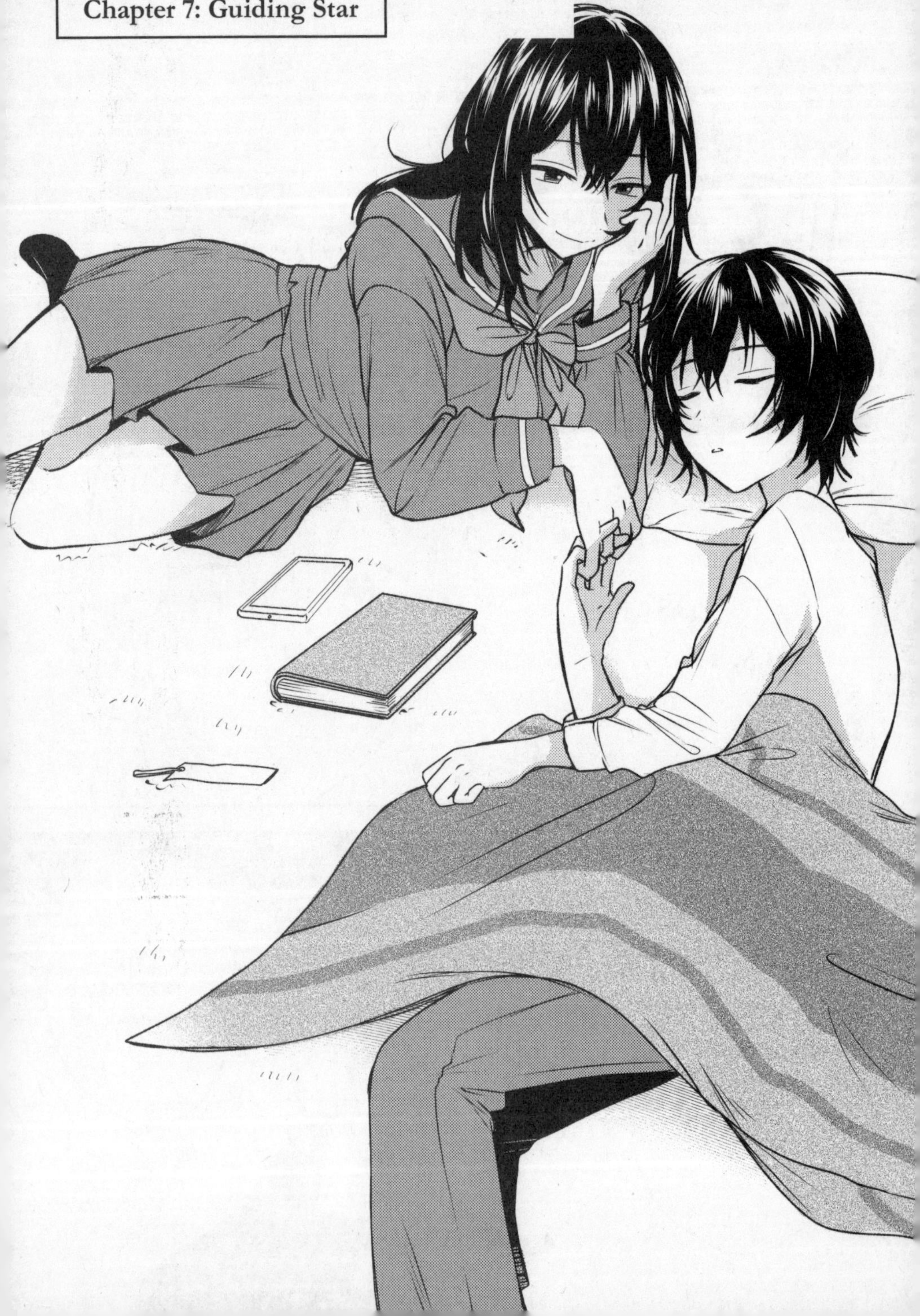

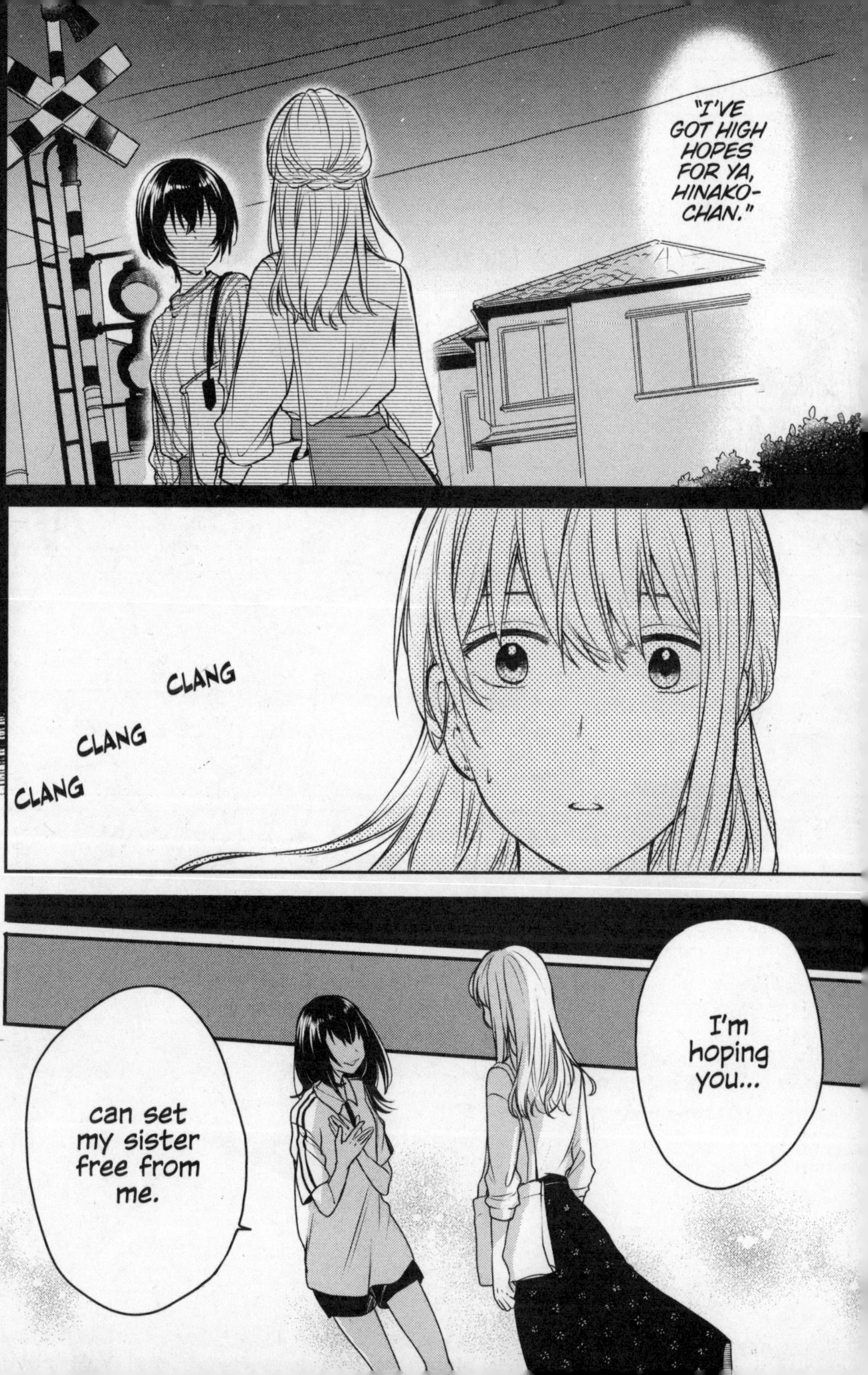
"I'VE GOT HIGH HOPES FOR YA, HINAKO-CHAN."
CLANG
CLANG
CLANG
I'm hoping you...
can set my sister free from me.

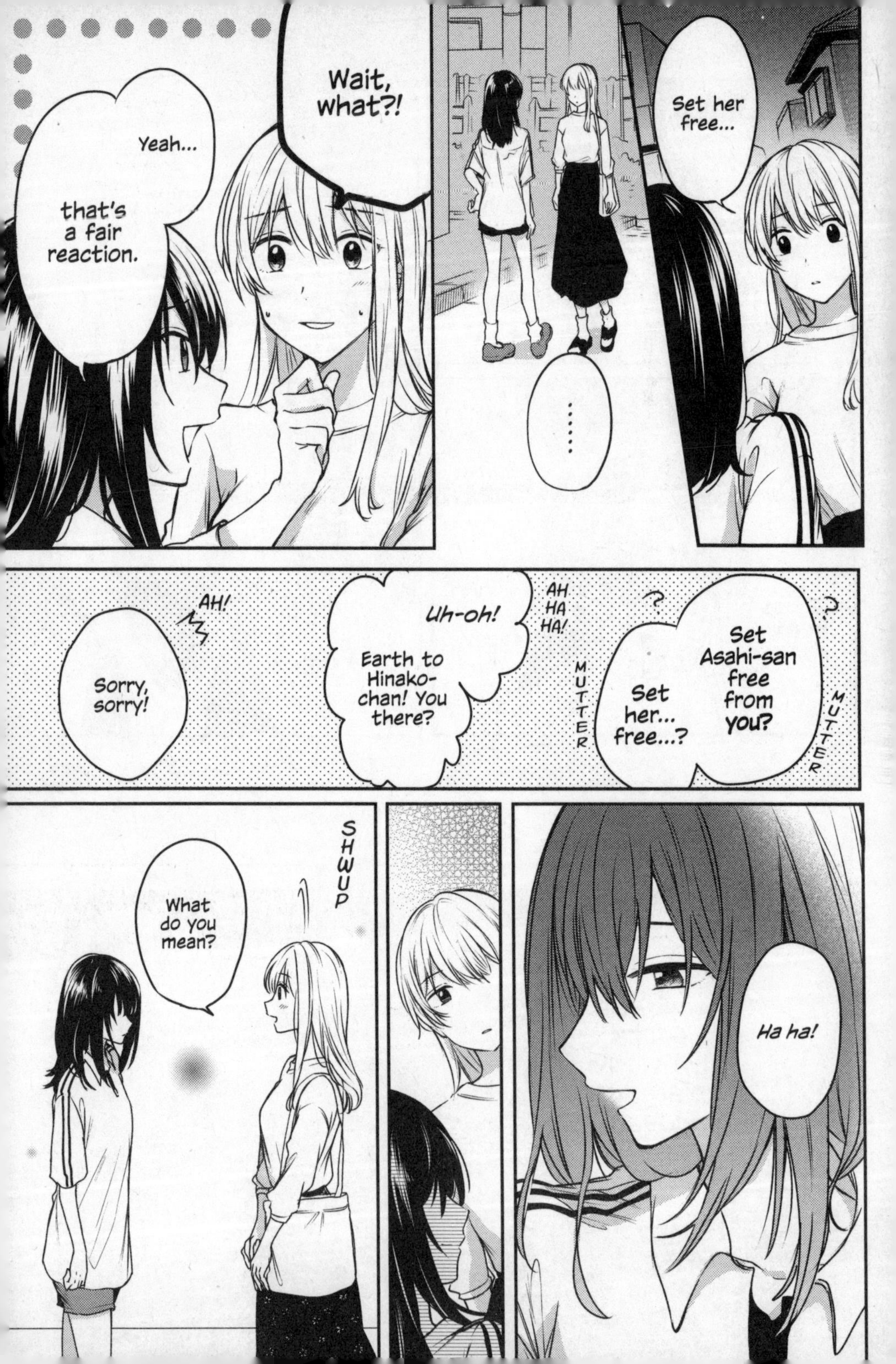
Set her free...
......
Wait, what?!
Yeah...
that's a fair reaction.
MUTTER
Set Asahi-san free from you?
Set her... free...?
MUTTER
AH HA HA!
Uh-oh!
Earth to Hinako-chan! You there?
AH!
Sorry, sorry!
Ha ha!
SHWUP
What do you mean?

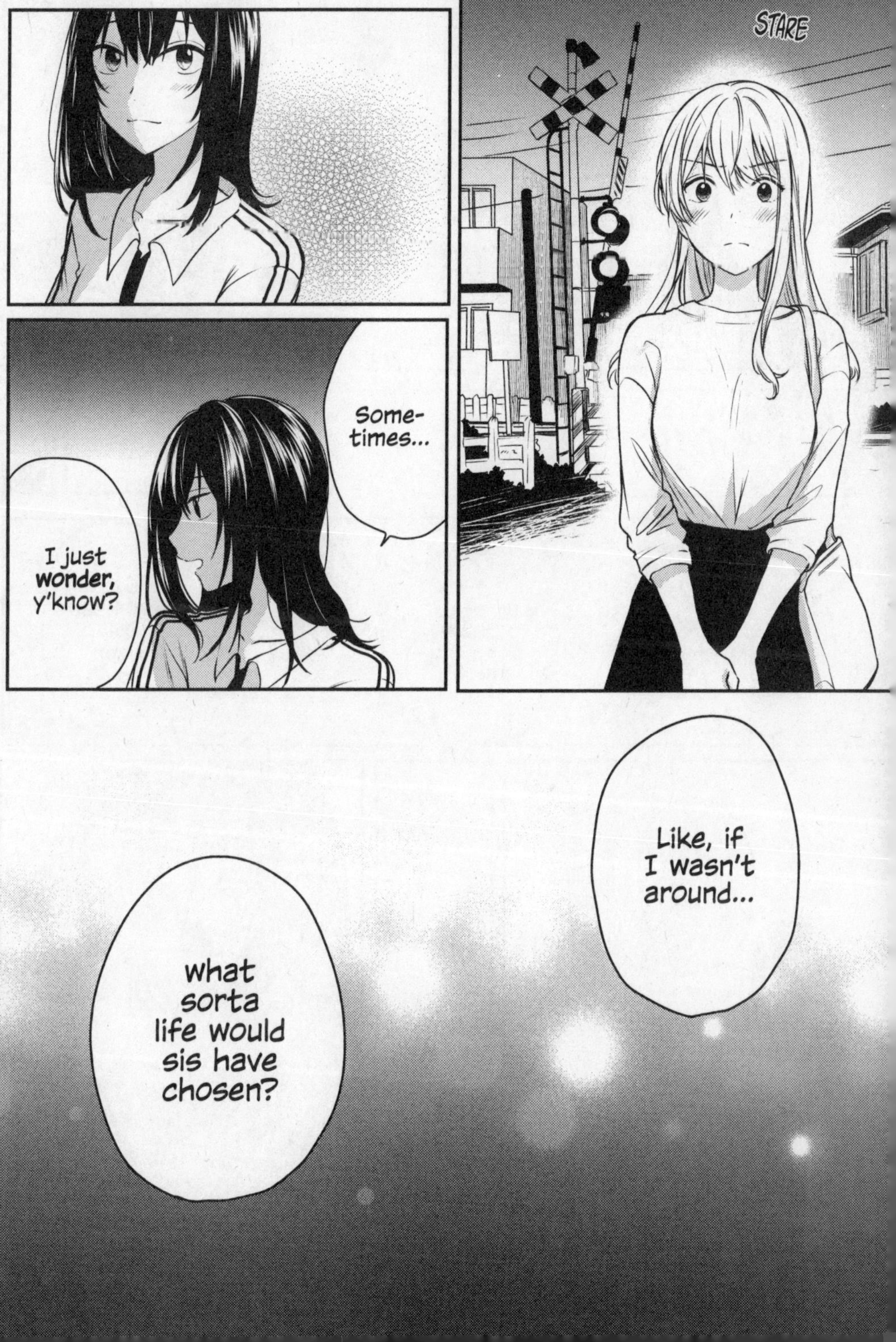
STARE
Some-times...
I just wonder, y'know?
Like, if I wasn't around...
what sorta life would sis have chosen?

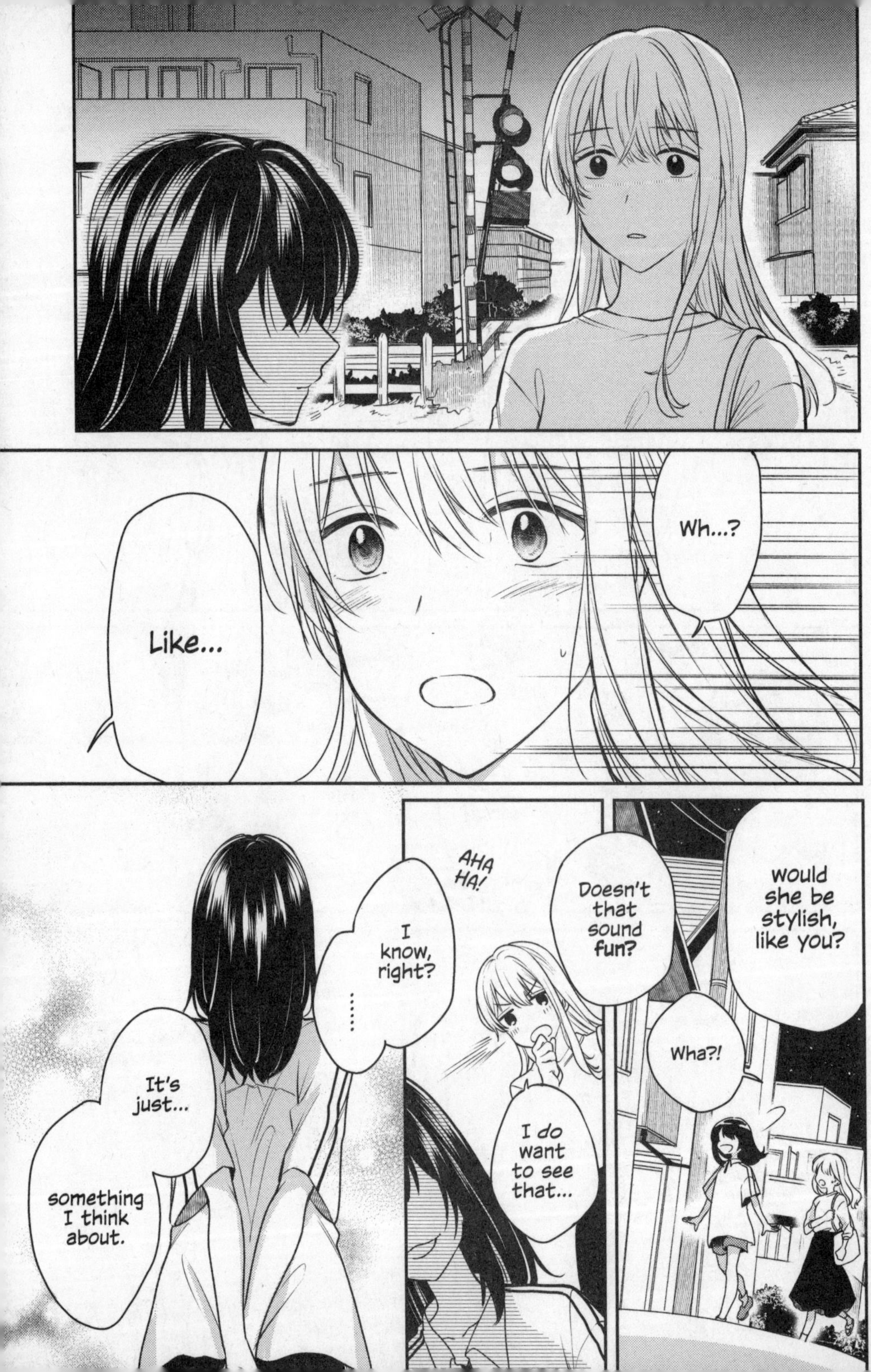
Wh...?
Like...
would she be stylish, like you?
Wha?!
Doesn't that sound fun?
AHA HA!
I know, right?
......
I do want to see that...
It's just...
something I think about.

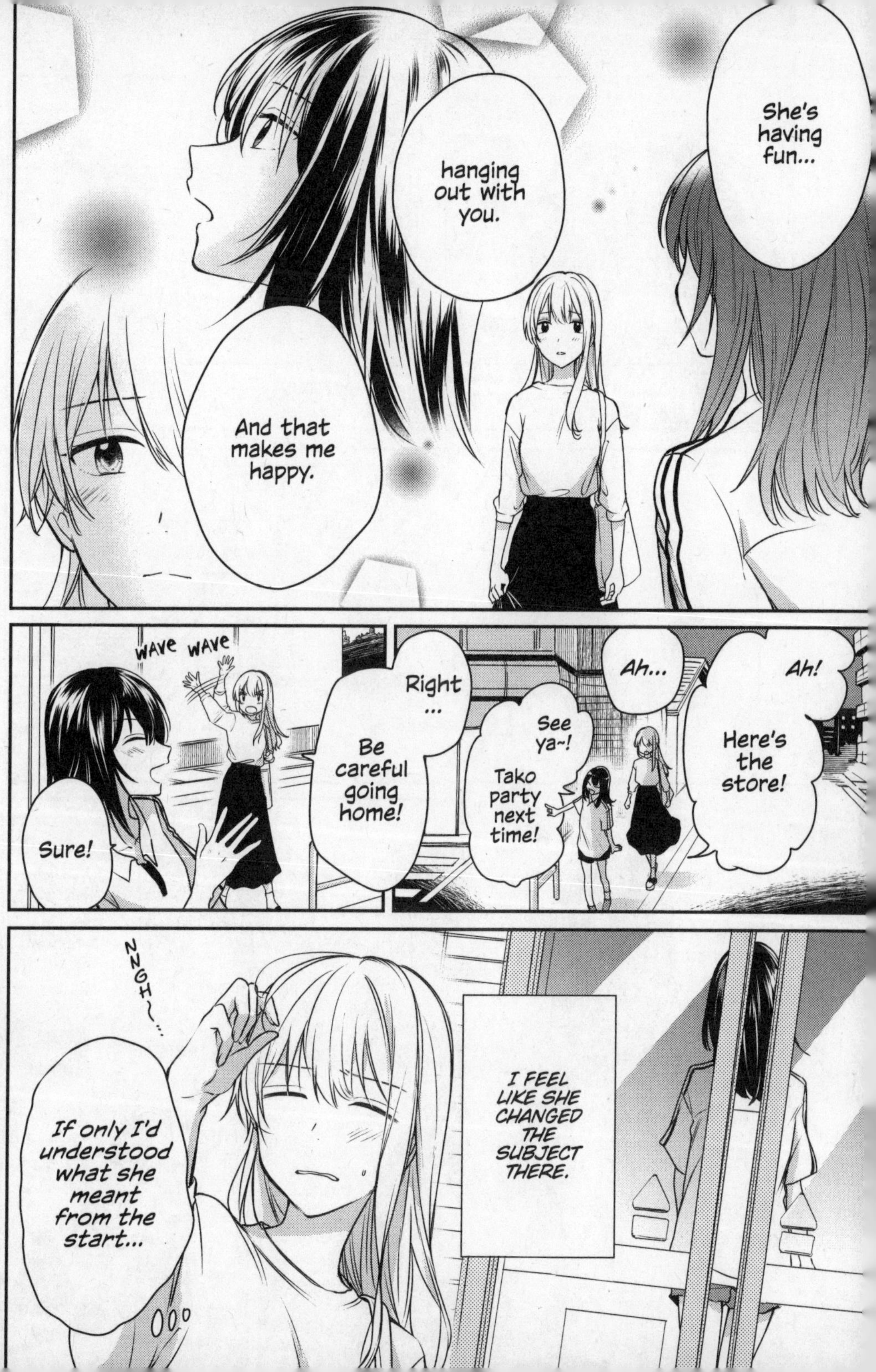
She's having fun...
hanging out with you.
And that makes me happy.
Ah!
Here's the store!
Ah...
See ya~!
Tako party next time!
Right ...
Be careful going home!
WAVE WAVE
Sure!
I FEEL LIKE SHE CHANGED THE SUBJECT THERE.
NNGH~...
If only I'd understood what she meant from the start...

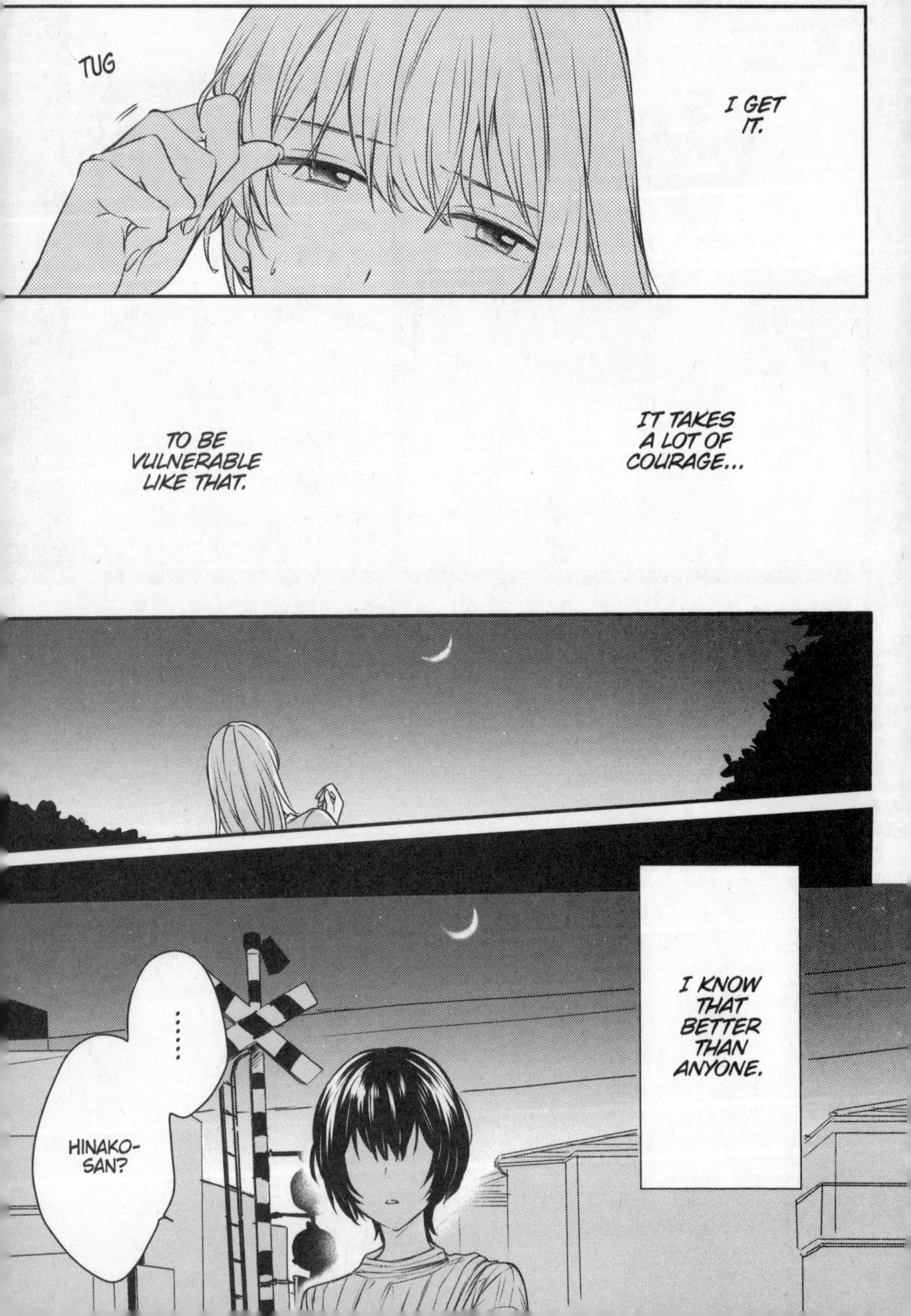
I GET IT.
TUG
IT TAKES A LOT OF COURAGE...
TO BE VULNERABLE LIKE THAT.
I KNOW THAT BETTER THAN ANYONE.
......
HINAKO-SAN?

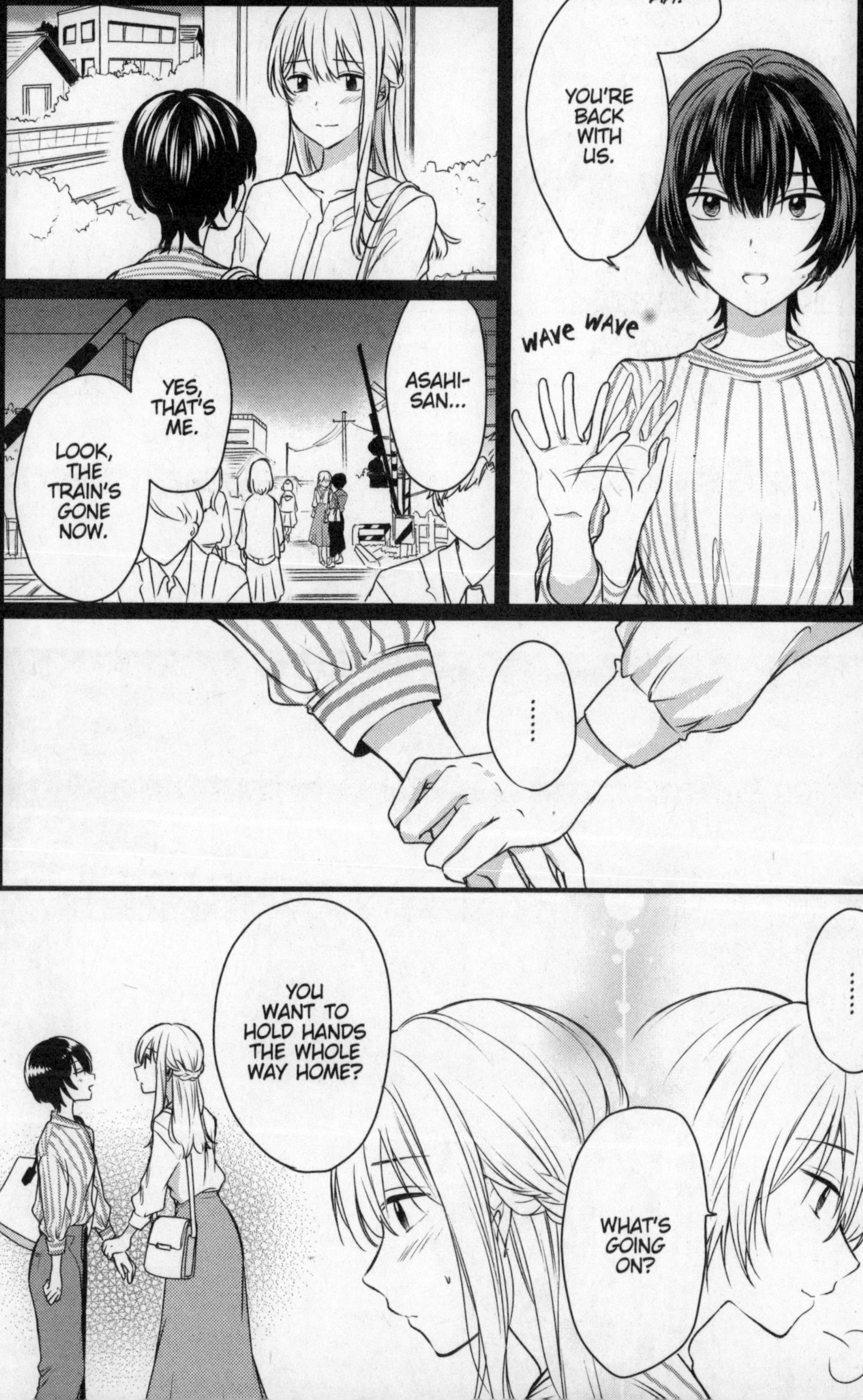
AH!
YOU'RE BACK WITH US.
wave wave
ASAHI-SAN...
YES, THAT'S ME.
LOOK, THE TRAIN'S GONE NOW.
......
......
WHAT'S GOING ON?
YOU WANT TO HOLD HANDS THE WHOLE WAY HOME?

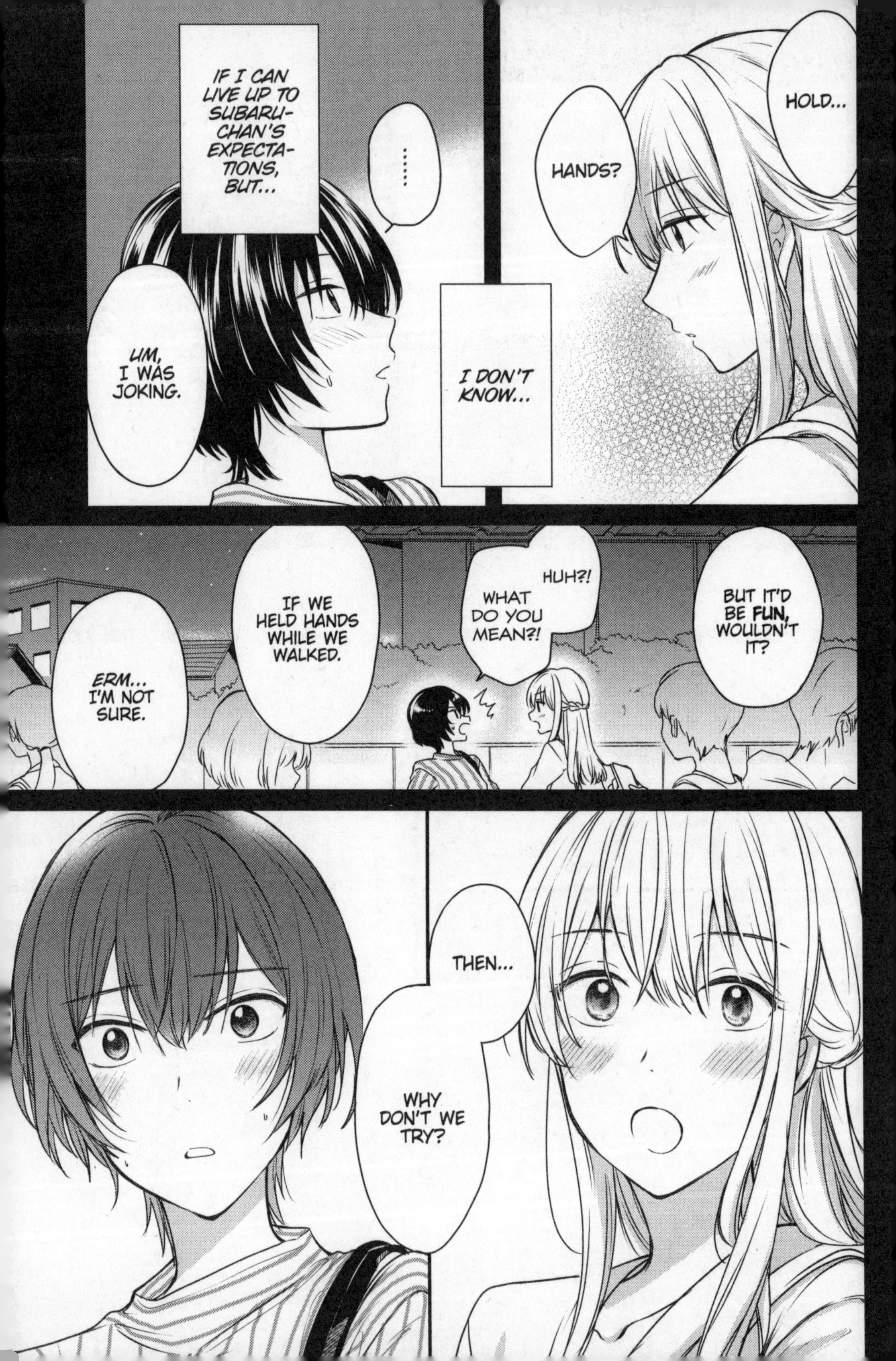
HOLD...
HANDS?
IF I CAN LIVE UP TO SUBARU-CHAN'S EXPECTATIONS, BUT...
......
I DON'T KNOW...
UM, I WAS JOKING.
BUT IT'D BE **FUN,** WOULDN'T IT?
HUH?! WHAT DO YOU MEAN?!
IF WE HELD HANDS WHILE WE WALKED.
ERM... I'M NOT SURE.
THEN...
WHY DON'T WE TRY?

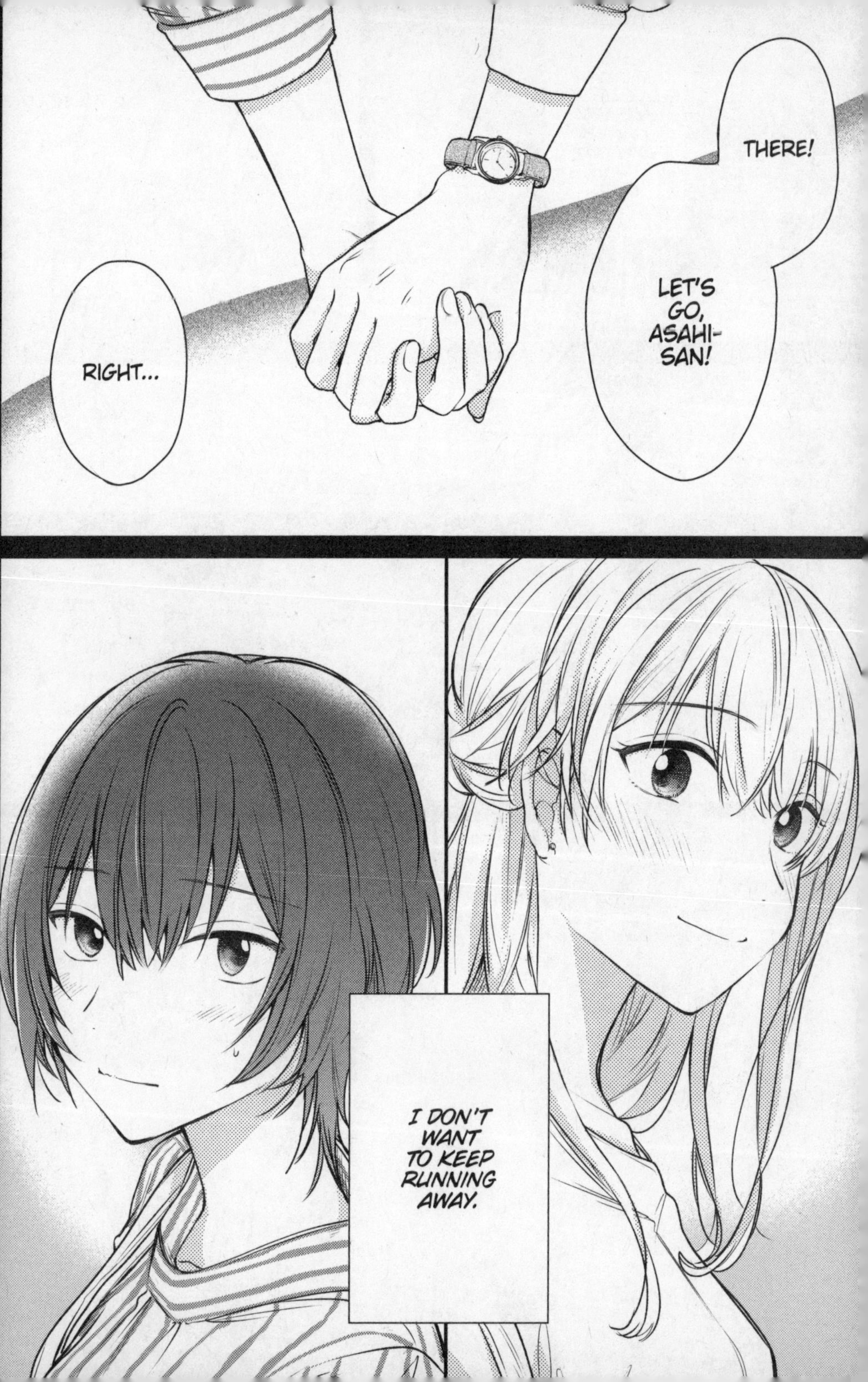
THERE!
LET'S GO, ASAHI-SAN!
RIGHT...
I DON'T WANT TO KEEP RUNNING AWAY.

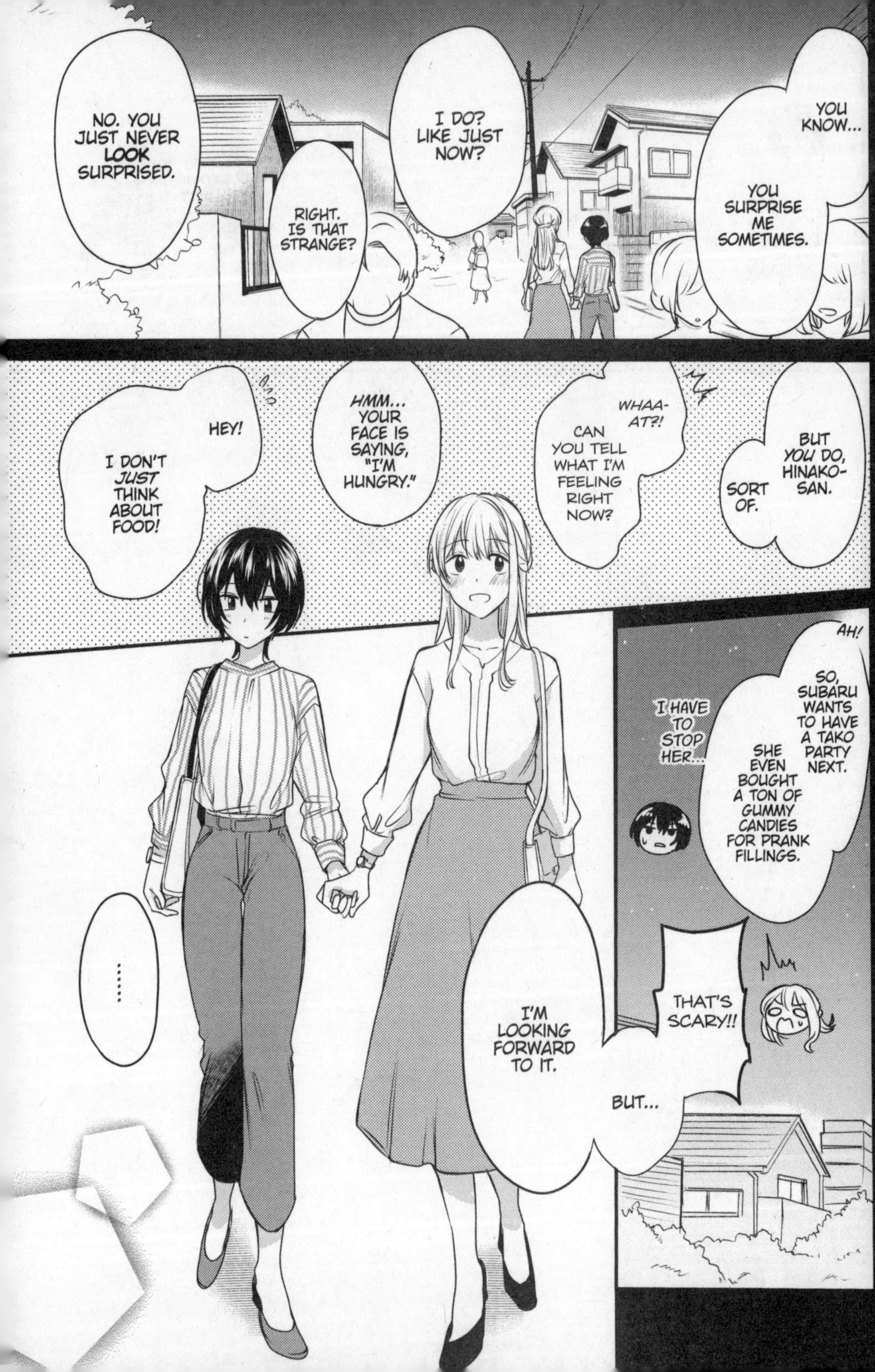
YOU KNOW...
YOU SURPRISE ME SOMETIMES.
I DO? LIKE JUST NOW?
RIGHT. IS THAT STRANGE?
NO. YOU JUST NEVER **LOOK** SURPRISED.
BUT *YOU* DO, HINAKO-SAN.
SORT OF.
WHAA-AT?!
CAN YOU TELL WHAT I'M FEELING RIGHT NOW?
HMM... YOUR FACE IS SAYING, "I'M HUNGRY."
HEY!
I DON'T *JUST* THINK ABOUT FOOD!
AH!
SO, SUBARU WANTS TO HAVE A TAKO PARTY NEXT.
SHE EVEN BOUGHT A TON OF GUMMY CANDIES FOR PRANK FILLINGS.
I HAVE TO STOP HER...
THAT'S SCARY!!
BUT...
I'M LOOKING FORWARD TO IT.
......

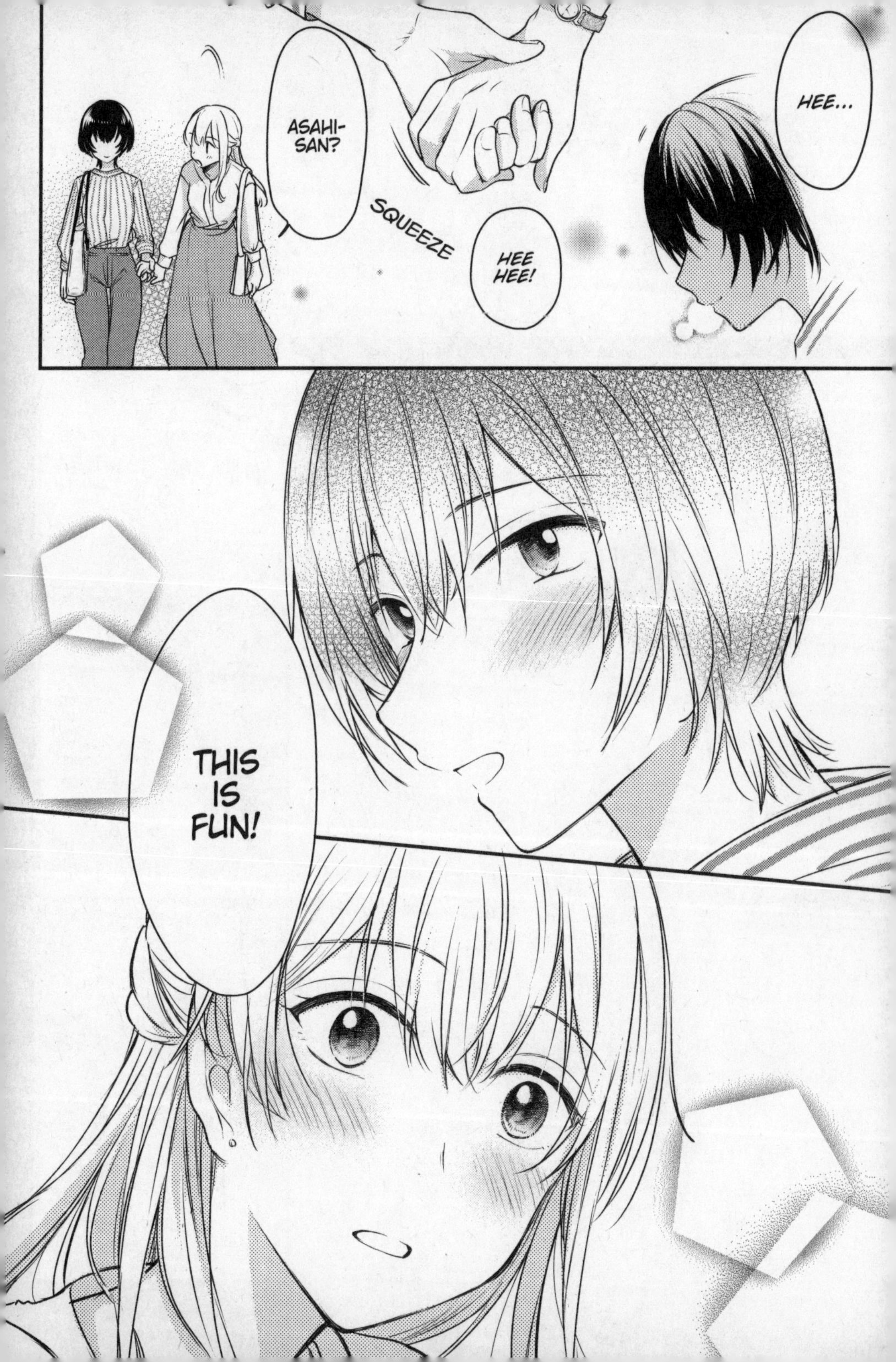
HEE...
HEE HEE!
SQUEEZE
ASAHI-SAN?
THIS IS FUN!

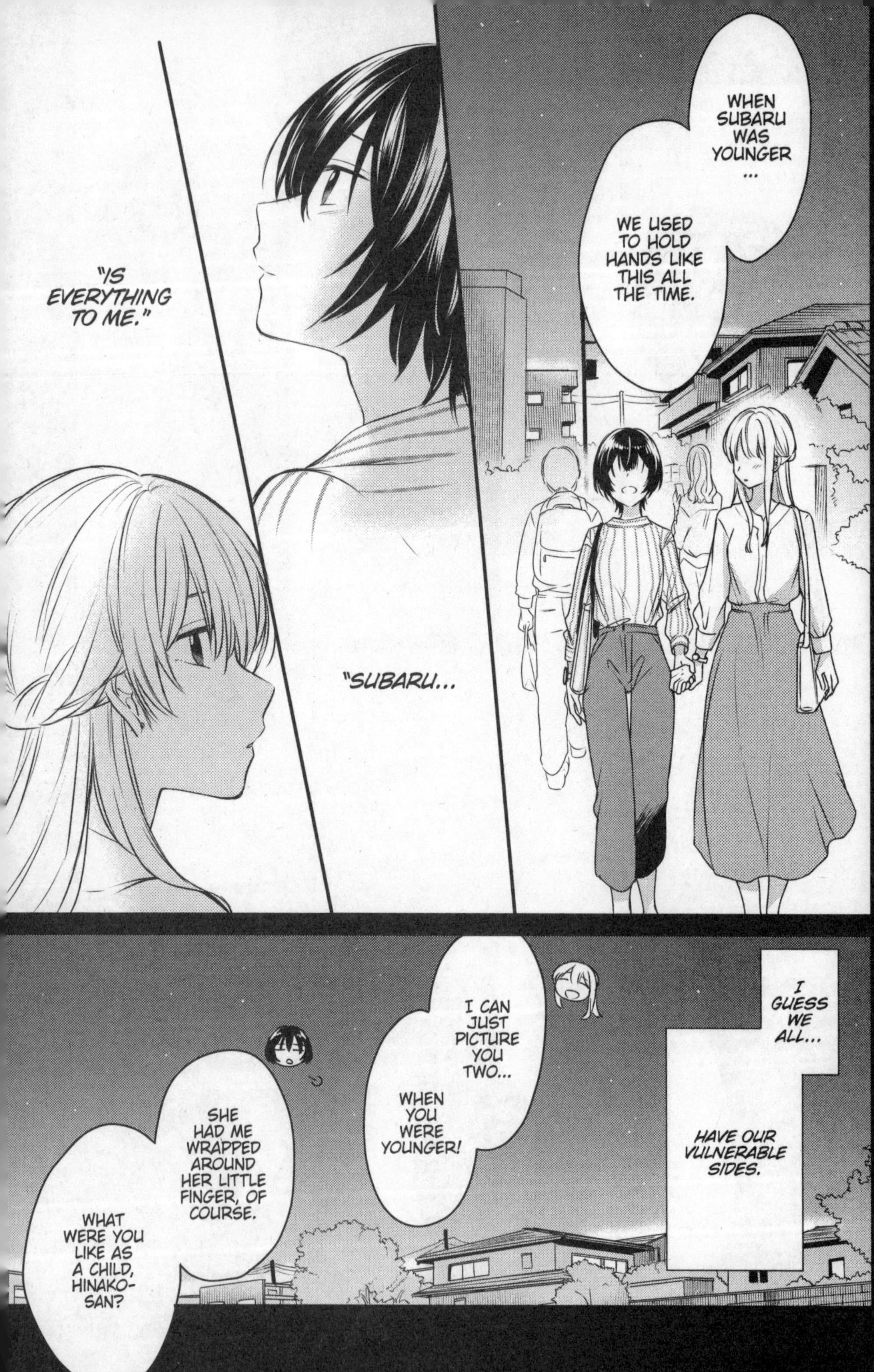

WHEN SUBARU WAS YOUNGER...
WE USED TO HOLD HANDS LIKE THIS ALL THE TIME.
"SUBARU...
"IS EVERYTHING TO ME."
I GUESS WE ALL...
HAVE OUR VULNERABLE SIDES.
I CAN JUST PICTURE YOU TWO...
WHEN YOU WERE YOUNGER!
SHE HAD ME WRAPPED AROUND HER LITTLE FINGER, OF COURSE.
WHAT WERE YOU LIKE AS A CHILD, HINAKO-SAN?

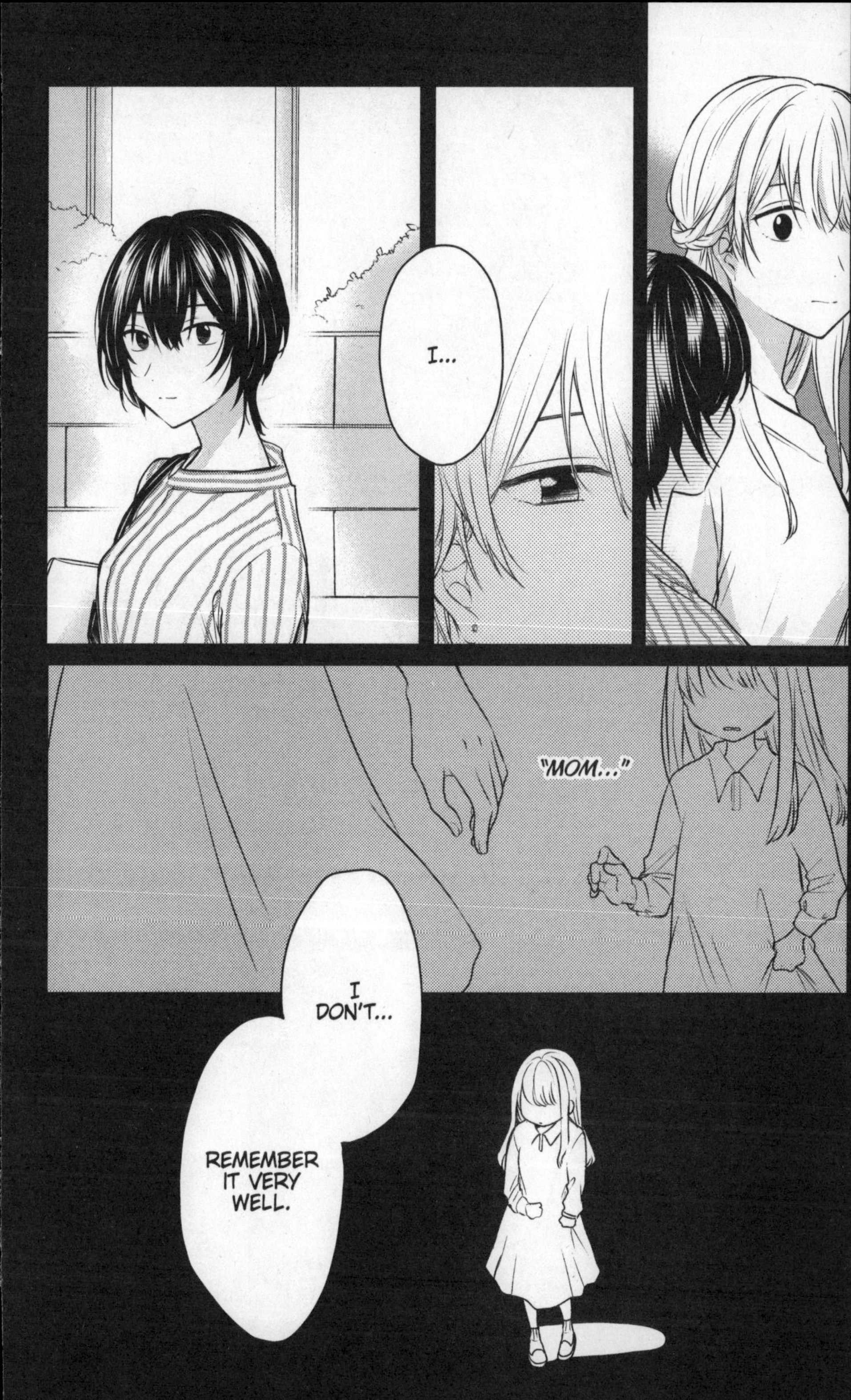
I...
"MOM..."
I DON'T...
REMEMBER IT VERY WELL.

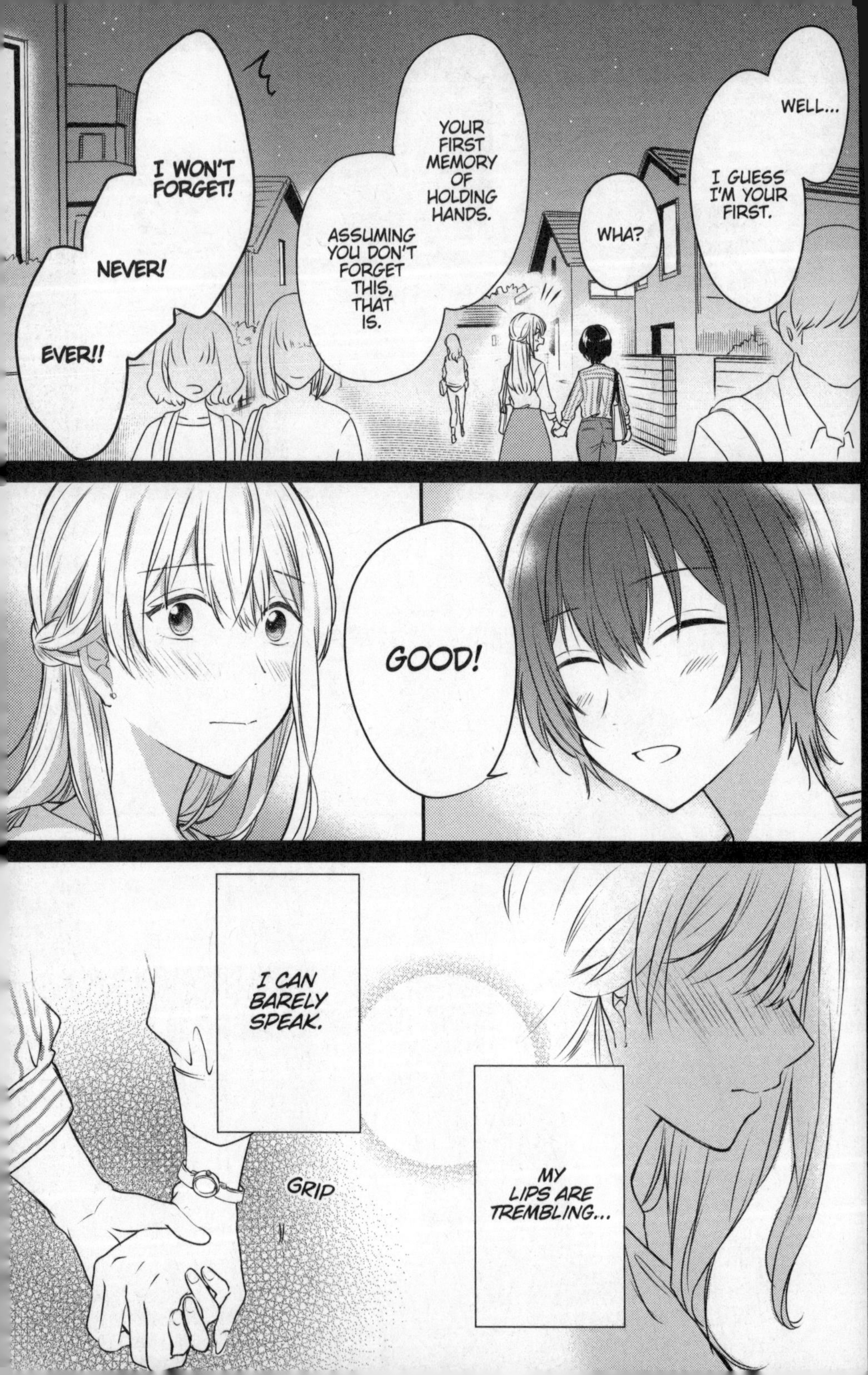
WELL...
I GUESS I'M YOUR FIRST.
WHA?
YOUR FIRST MEMORY OF HOLDING HANDS.
ASSUMING YOU DON'T FORGET THIS, THAT IS.
I WON'T FORGET!
NEVER!
EVER!!
GOOD!
I CAN BARELY SPEAK.
MY LIPS ARE TREMBLING...
GRIP

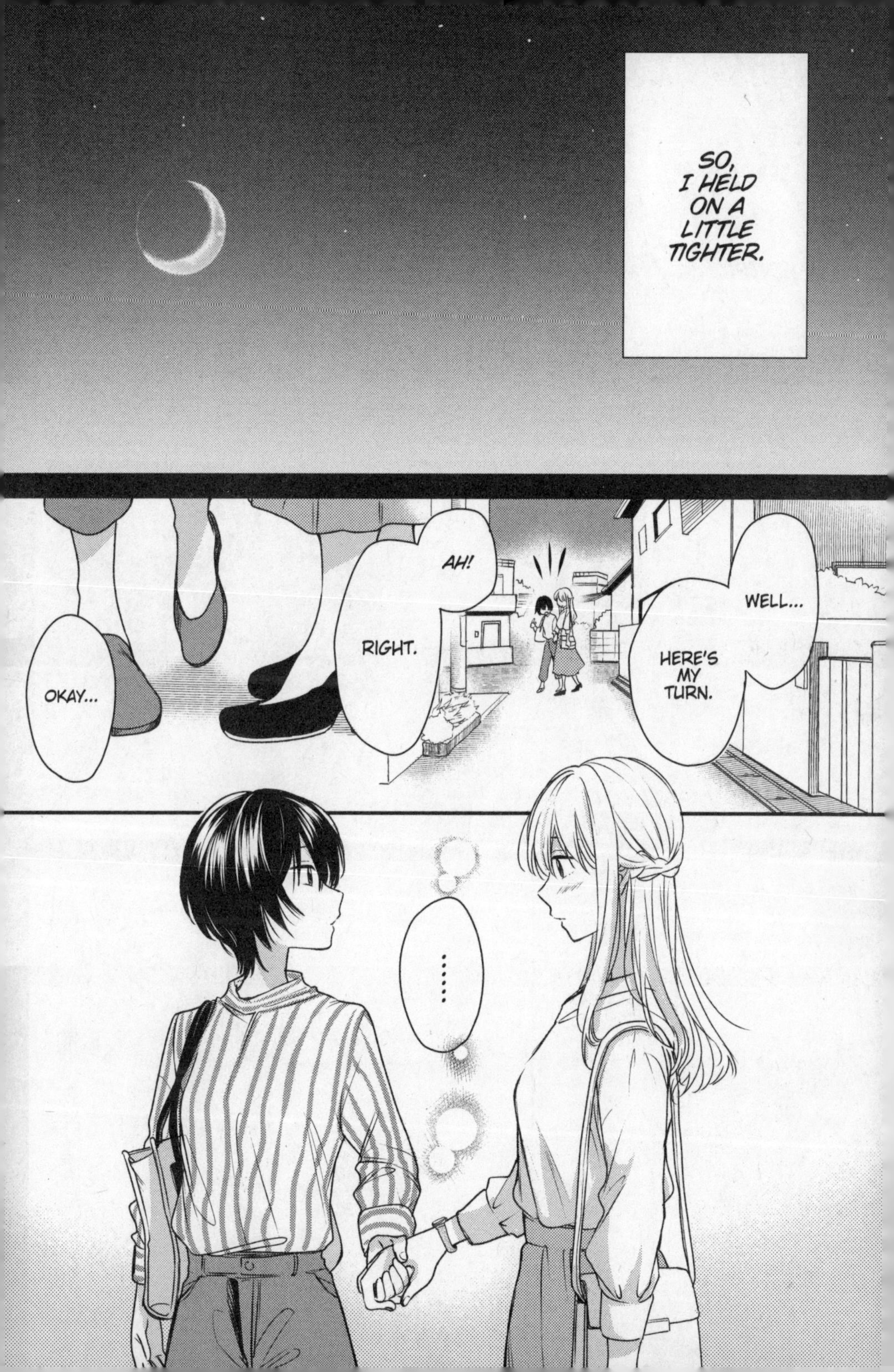
SO, I HELD ON A LITTLE TIGHTER.
WELL... HERE'S MY TURN.
AH! RIGHT.
OKAY...
......

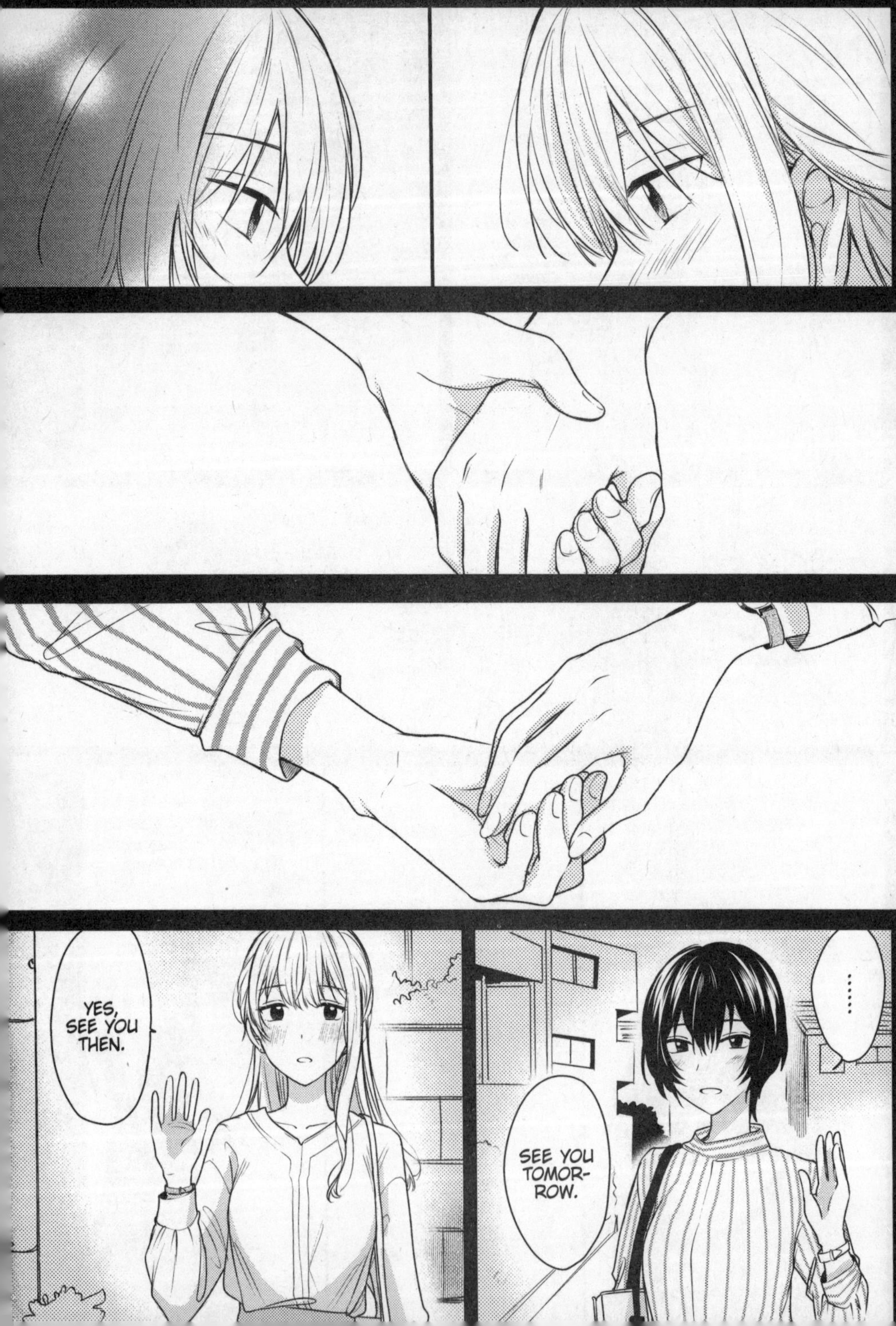
......
SEE YOU TOMORROW.
YES, SEE YOU THEN.

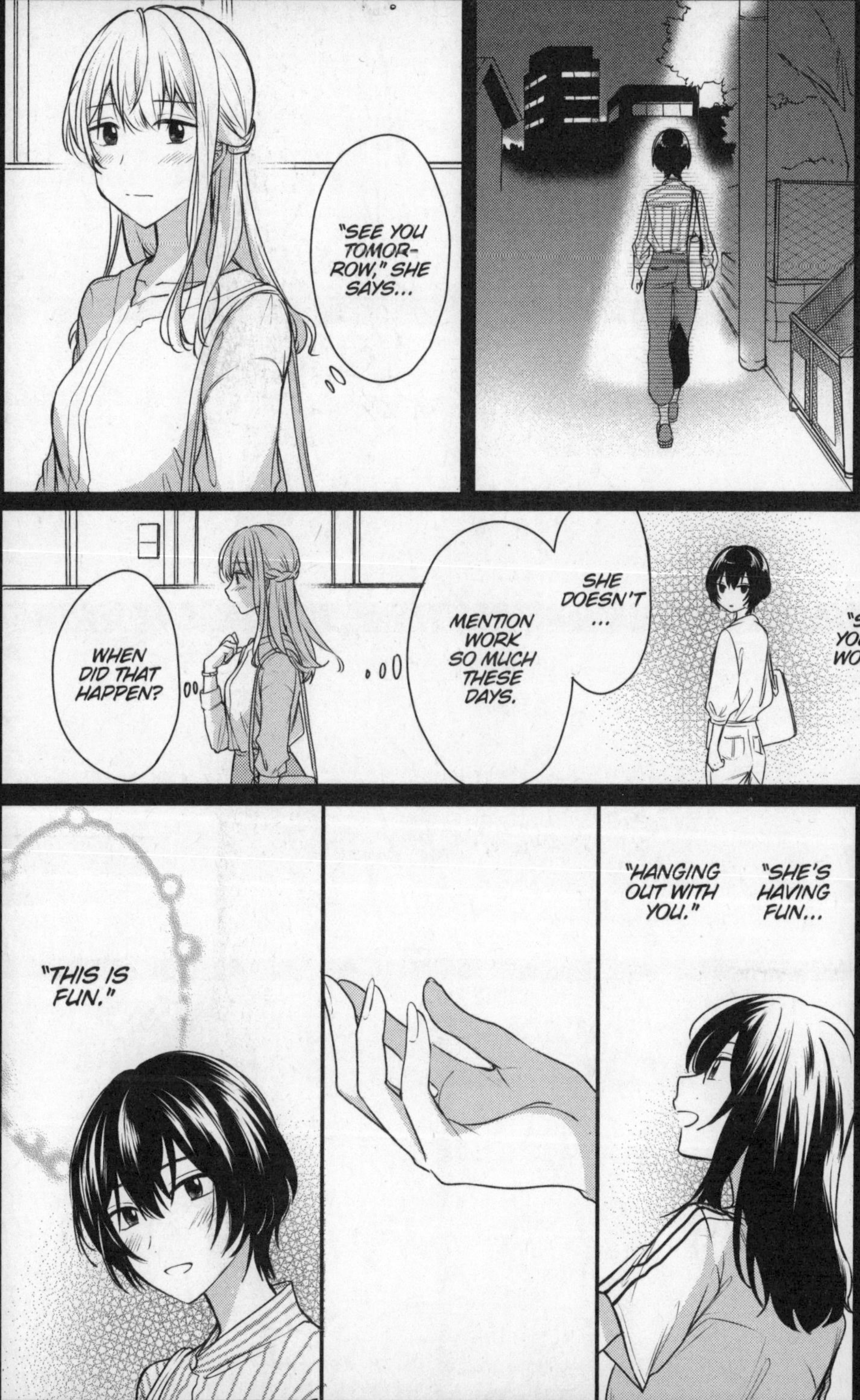
"SEE YOU TOMORROW," SHE SAYS...
"SEE YOU AT WORK."
SHE DOESN'T ...
MENTION WORK SO MUCH THESE DAYS.
WHEN DID THAT HAPPEN?
"SHE'S HAVING FUN...
"HANGING OUT WITH YOU."
"THIS IS FUN."

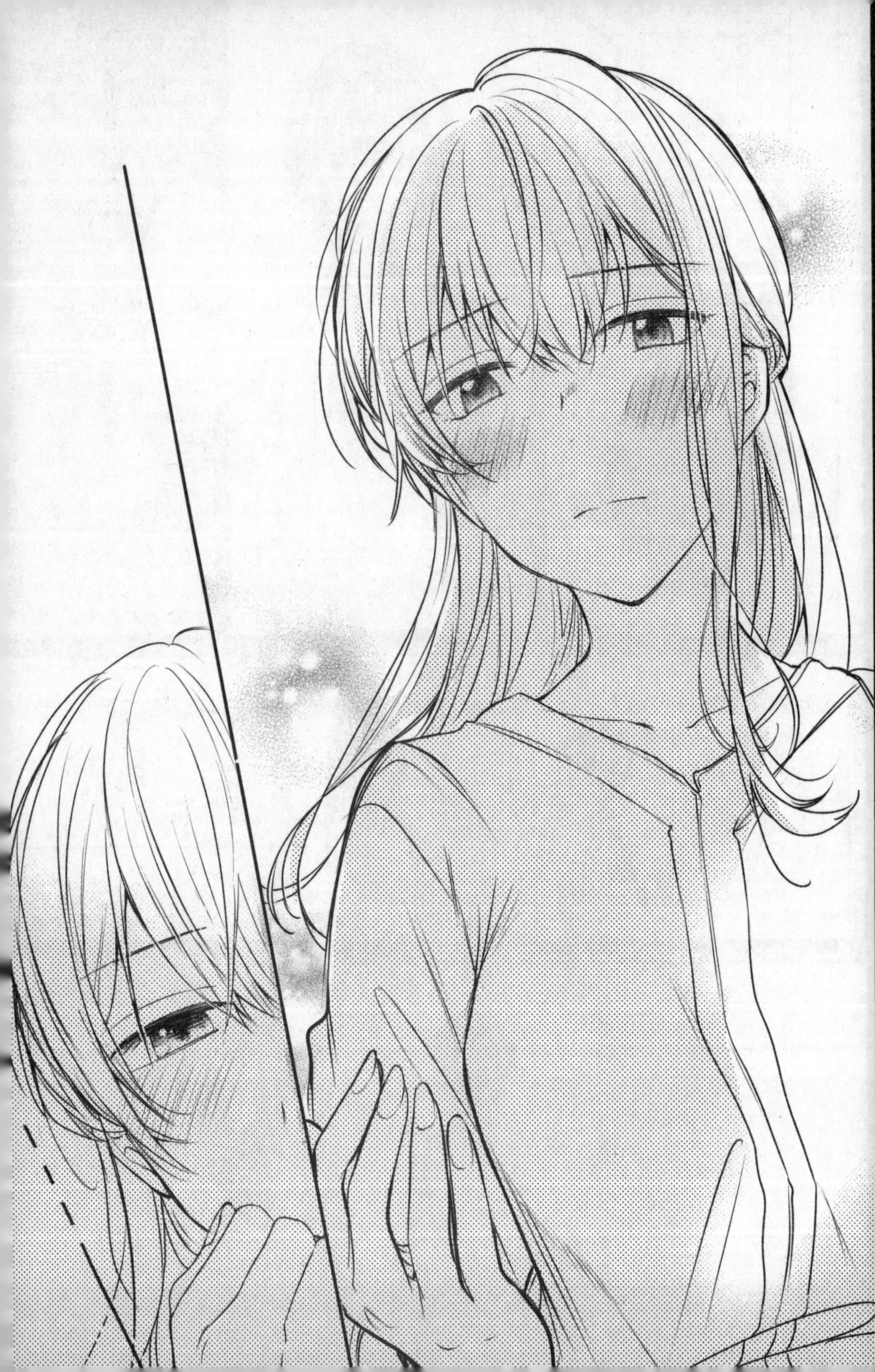

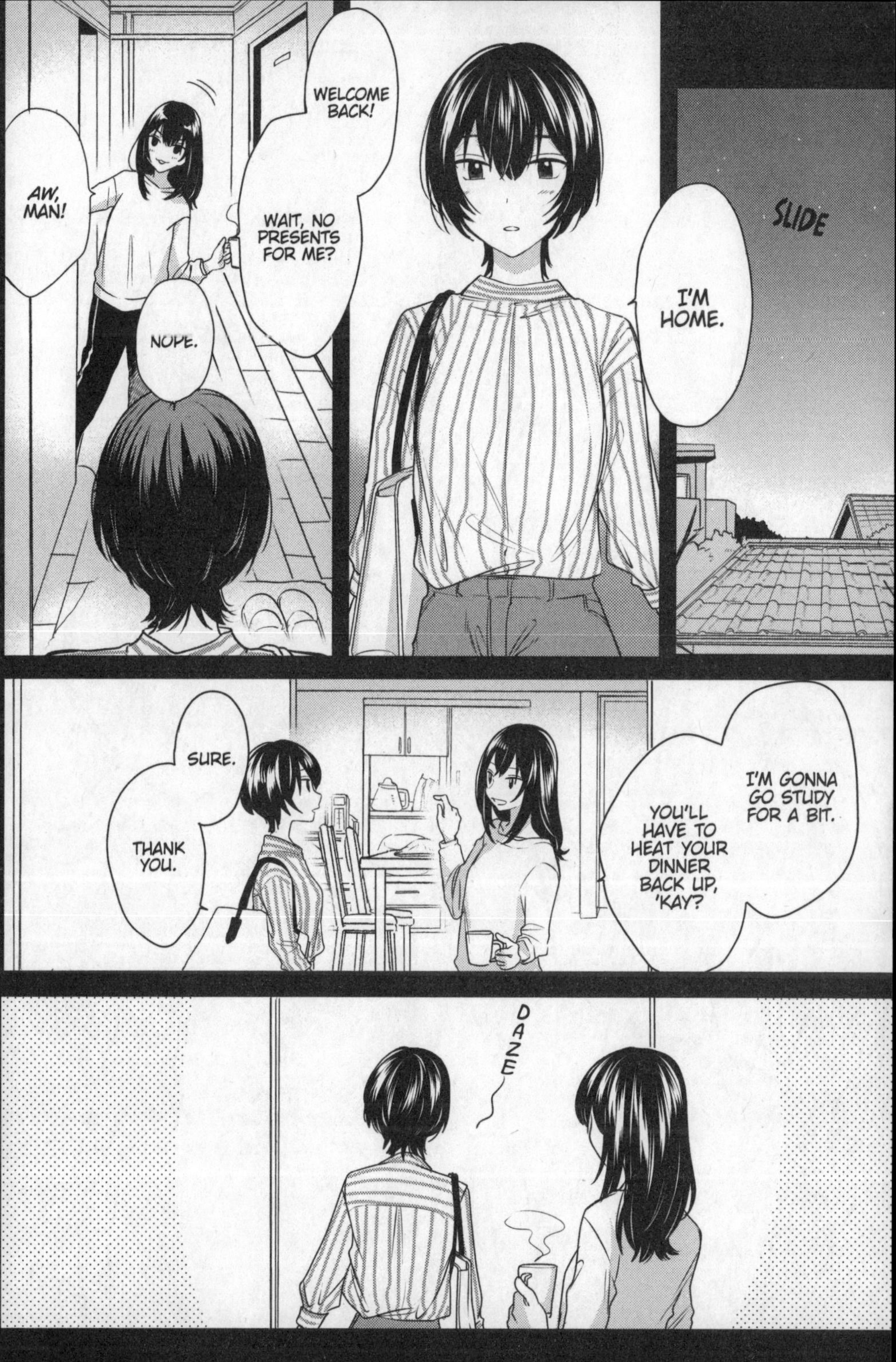
SLIDE
I'M HOME.
WELCOME BACK!
WAIT, NO PRESENTS FOR ME?
NOPE.
AW, MAN!
I'M GONNA GO STUDY FOR A BIT.
YOU'LL HAVE TO HEAT YOUR DINNER BACK UP, 'KAY?
SURE.
THANK YOU.
DAZE

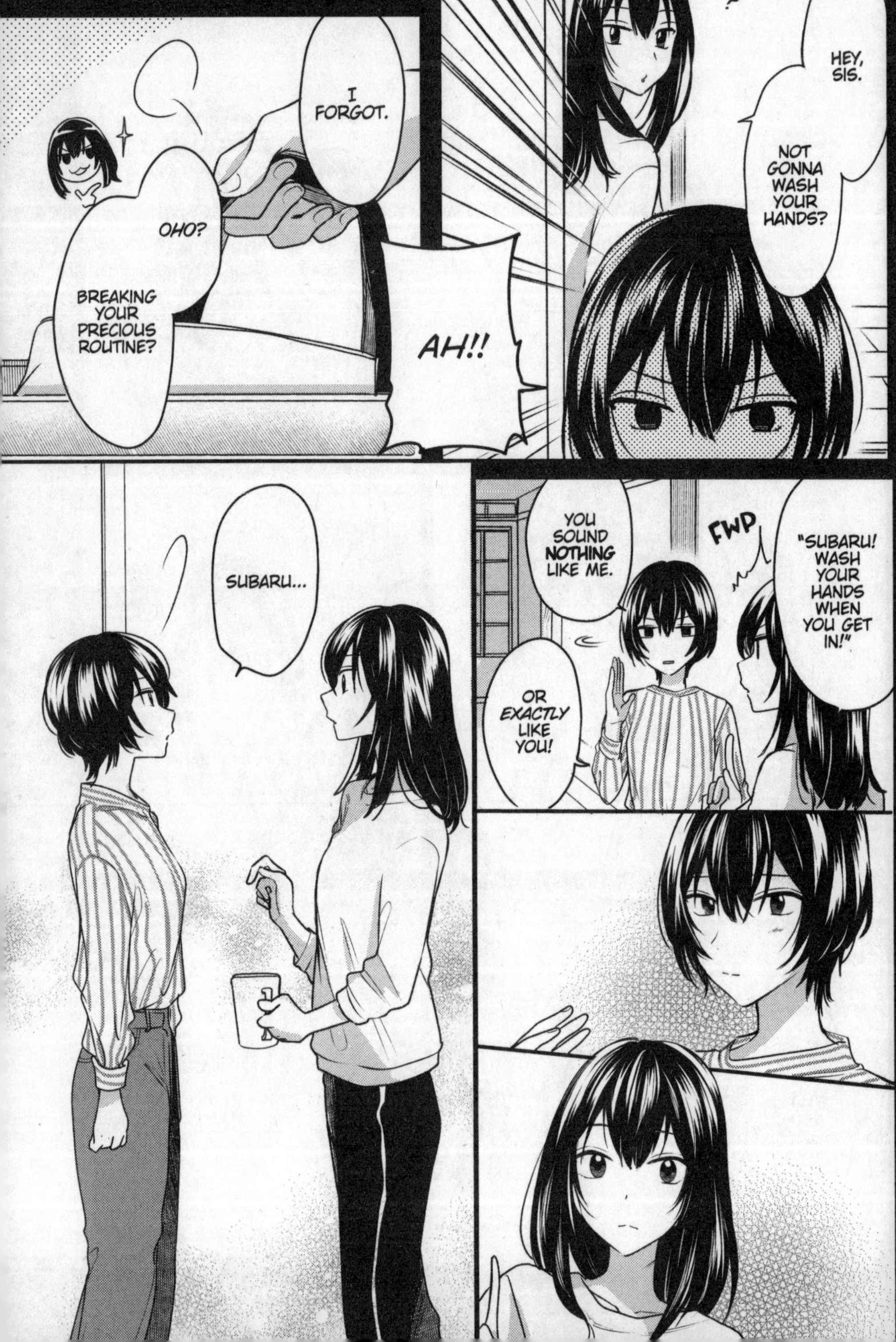
HEY, SIS.
NOT GONNA WASH YOUR HANDS?
AH!!
I FORGOT.
OHO?
BREAKING YOUR PRECIOUS ROUTINE?
"SUBARU! WASH YOUR HANDS WHEN YOU GET IN!"
FWP
YOU SOUND **NOTHING** LIKE ME.
OR *EXACTLY* LIKE YOU!
SUBARU...

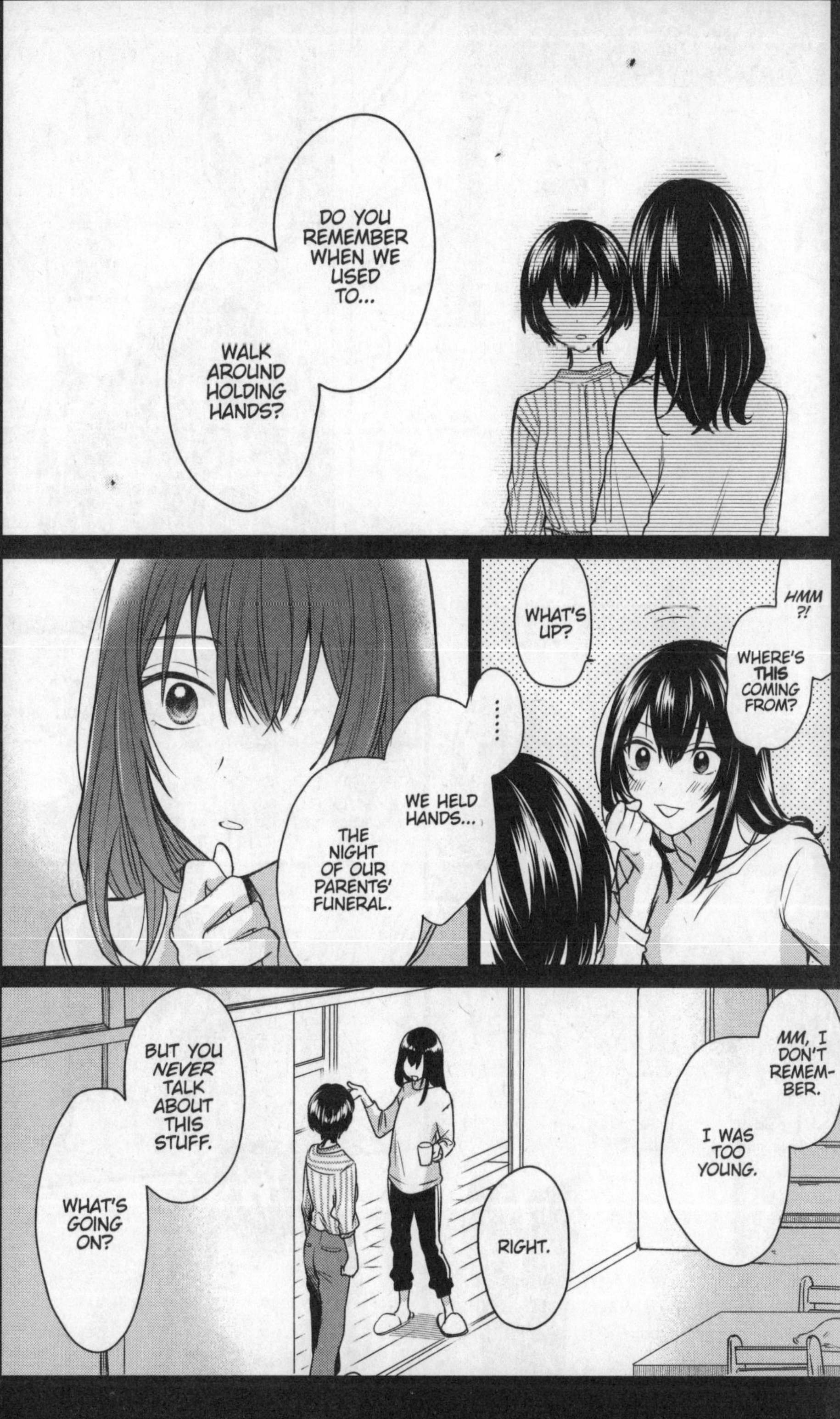
DO YOU REMEMBER WHEN WE USED TO...
WALK AROUND HOLDING HANDS?
HMM ?!
WHERE'S THIS COMING FROM?
WHAT'S UP?
......
WE HELD HANDS...
THE NIGHT OF OUR PARENTS' FUNERAL.
MM, I DON'T REMEM-BER.
I WAS TOO YOUNG.
RIGHT.
BUT YOU *NEVER* TALK ABOUT THIS STUFF.
WHAT'S GOING ON?

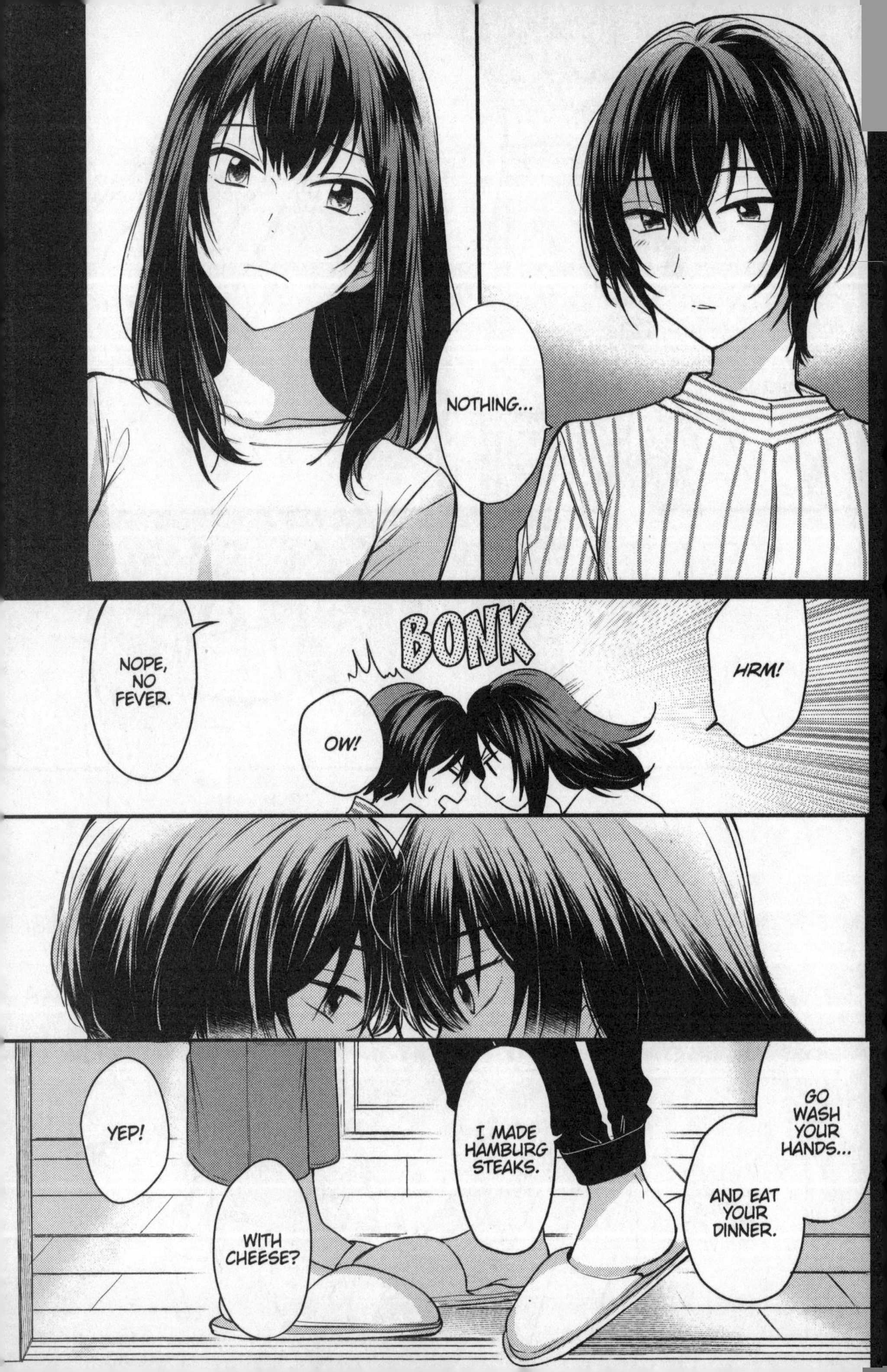
NOTHING...
HRM!
BONK
OW!
NOPE, NO FEVER.
GO WASH YOUR HANDS...
AND EAT YOUR DINNER.
I MADE HAMBURG STEAKS.
WITH CHEESE?
YEP!

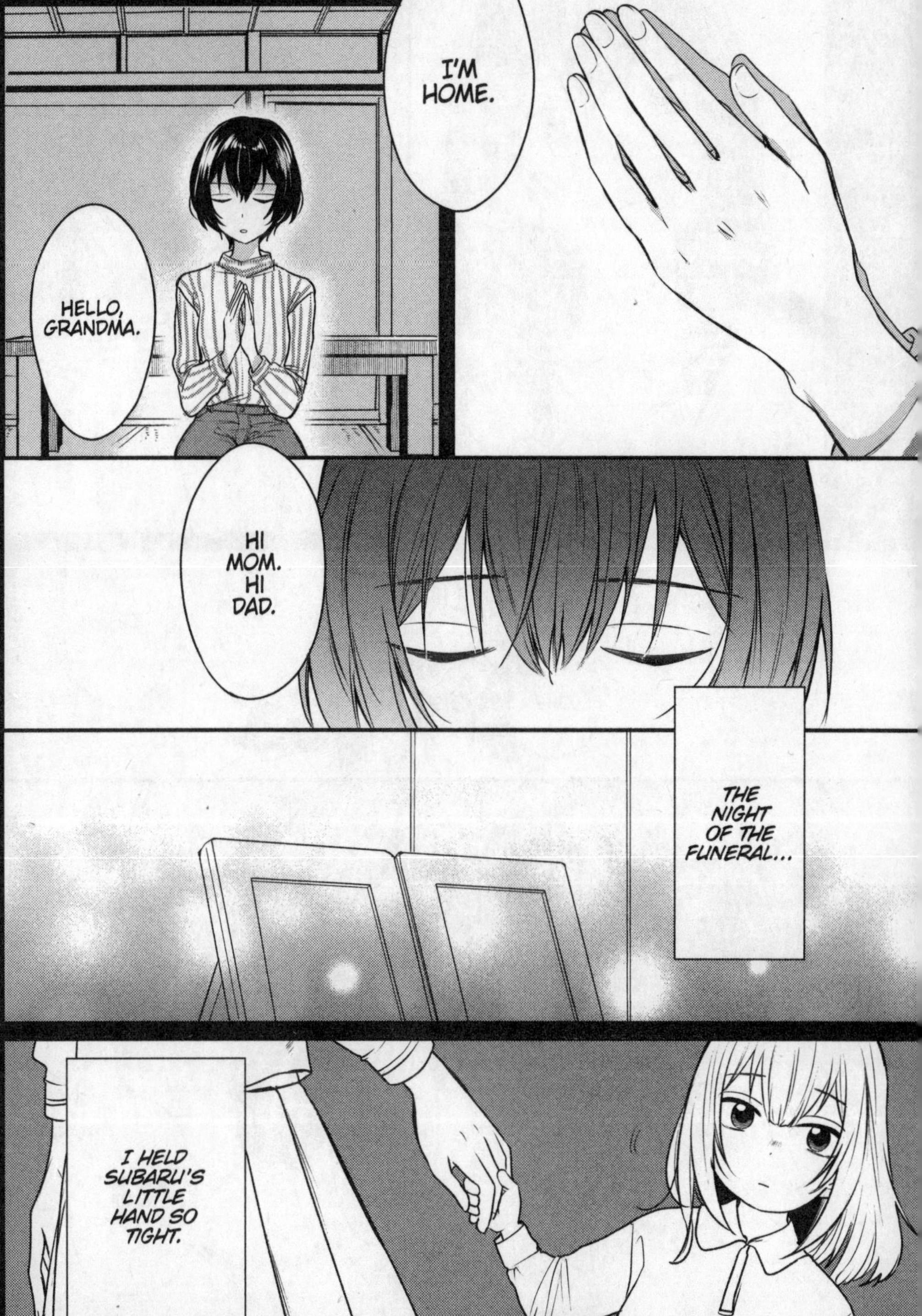
I'M HOME.
HELLO, GRANDMA.
HI MOM. HI DAD.
THE NIGHT OF THE FUNERAL...
I HELD SUBARU'S LITTLE HAND SO TIGHT.

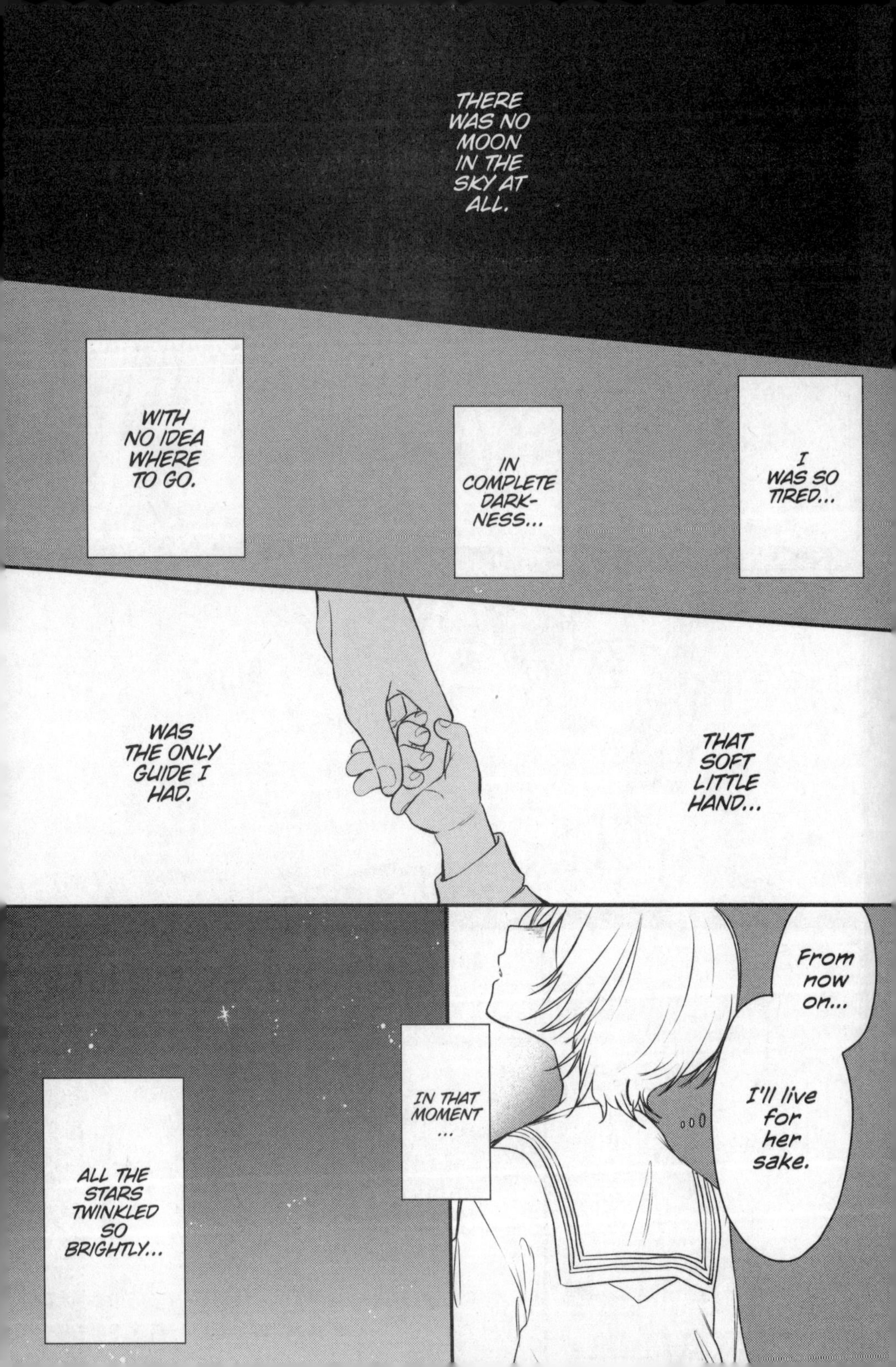
THERE WAS NO MOON IN THE SKY AT ALL.
I WAS SO TIRED...
IN COMPLETE DARKNESS...
WITH NO IDEA WHERE TO GO.
THAT SOFT LITTLE HAND...
WAS THE ONLY GUIDE I HAD.
From now on...
I'll live for her sake.
IN THAT MOMENT...
ALL THE STARS TWINKLED SO BRIGHTLY...

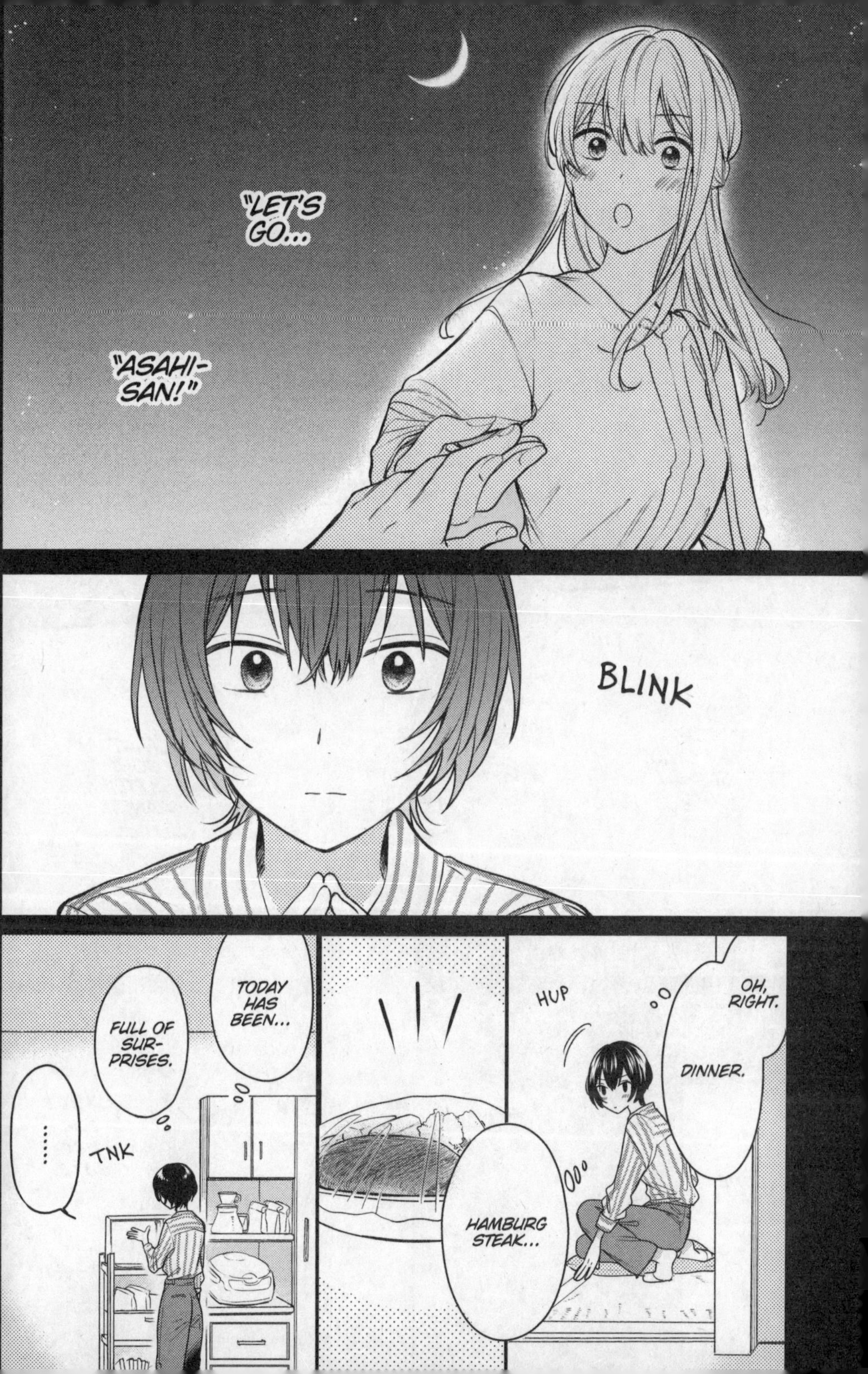
"LET'S GO...
"ASAHI-SAN!"
BLINK
OH, RIGHT.
HUP
DINNER.
HAMBURG STEAK...
TODAY HAS BEEN...
FULL OF SUR-PRISES.
TNK
......

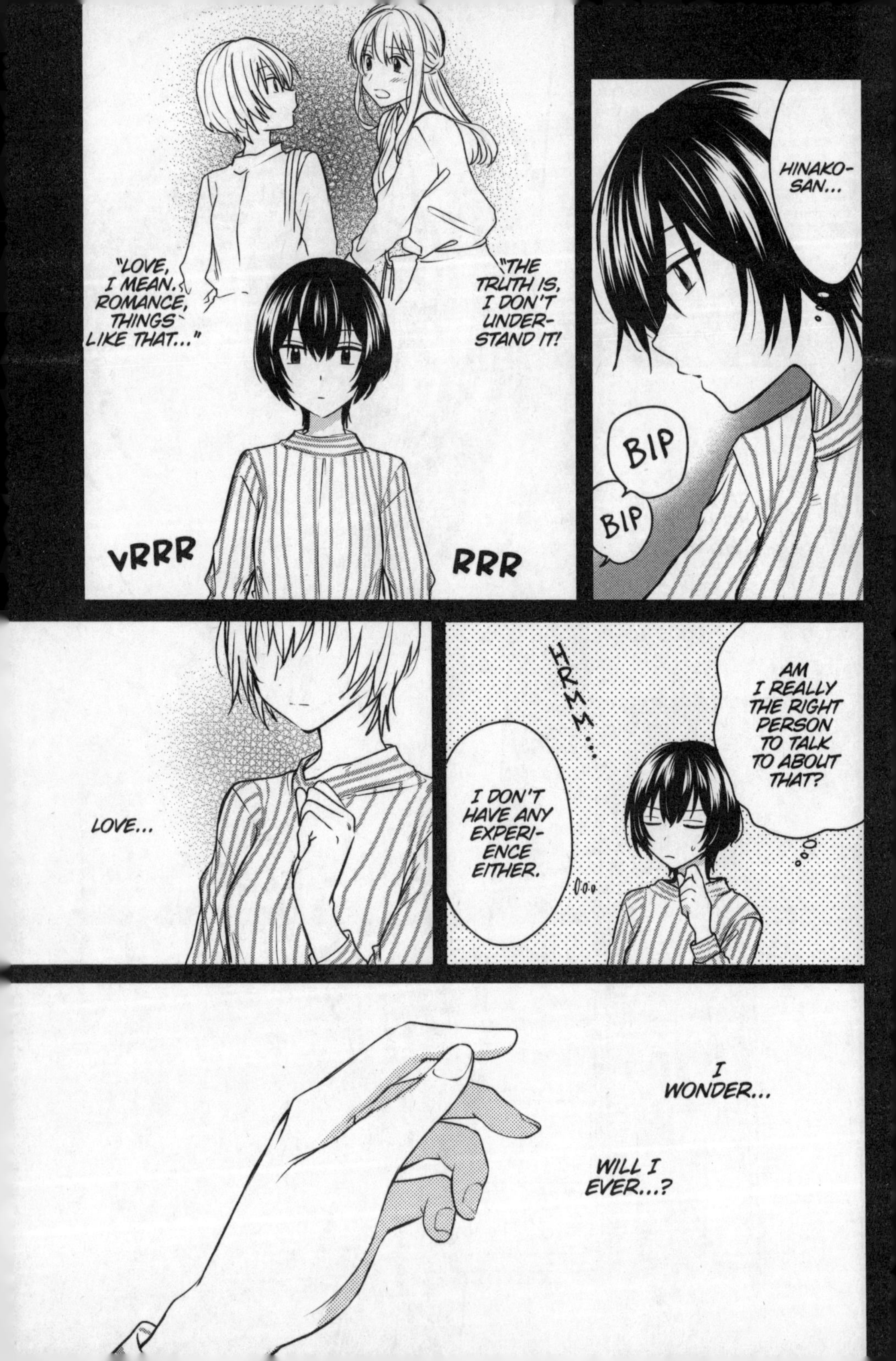
HINAKO-SAN...
BIP
BIP
"THE TRUTH IS, I DON'T UNDERSTAND IT!
"LOVE, I MEAN. ROMANCE, THINGS LIKE THAT..."
VRRR RRR
AM I REALLY THE RIGHT PERSON TO TALK TO ABOUT THAT?
HRMM...
I DON'T HAVE ANY EXPERIENCE EITHER.
LOVE...
I WONDER...
WILL I EVER...?

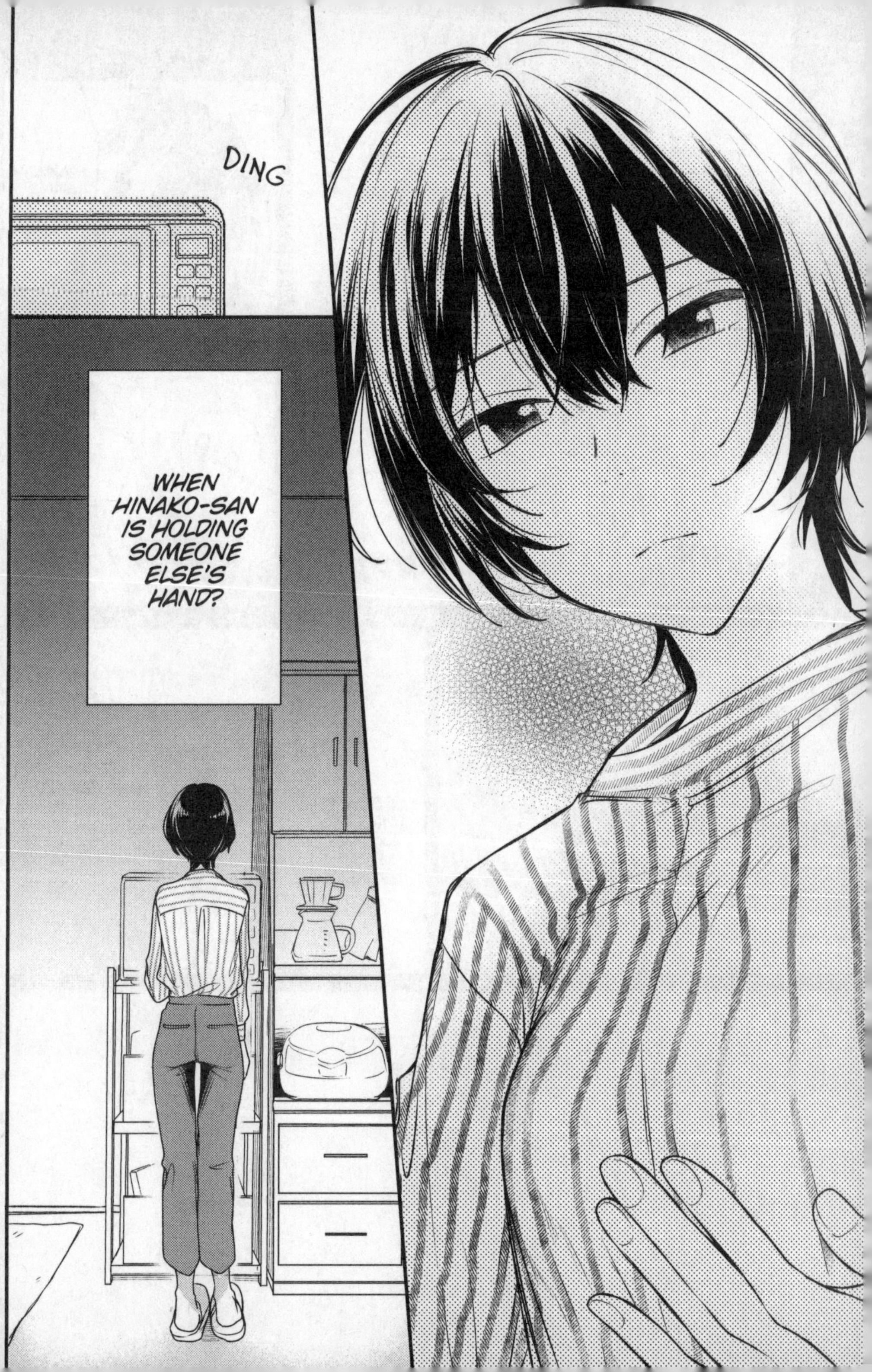
DING
WHEN HINAKO-SAN IS HOLDING SOMEONE ELSE'S HAND?

Doughnuts

Under a Crescent Moon

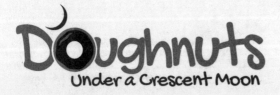

Doughnuts Under a Crescent Moon

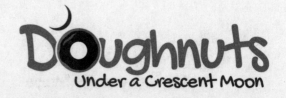

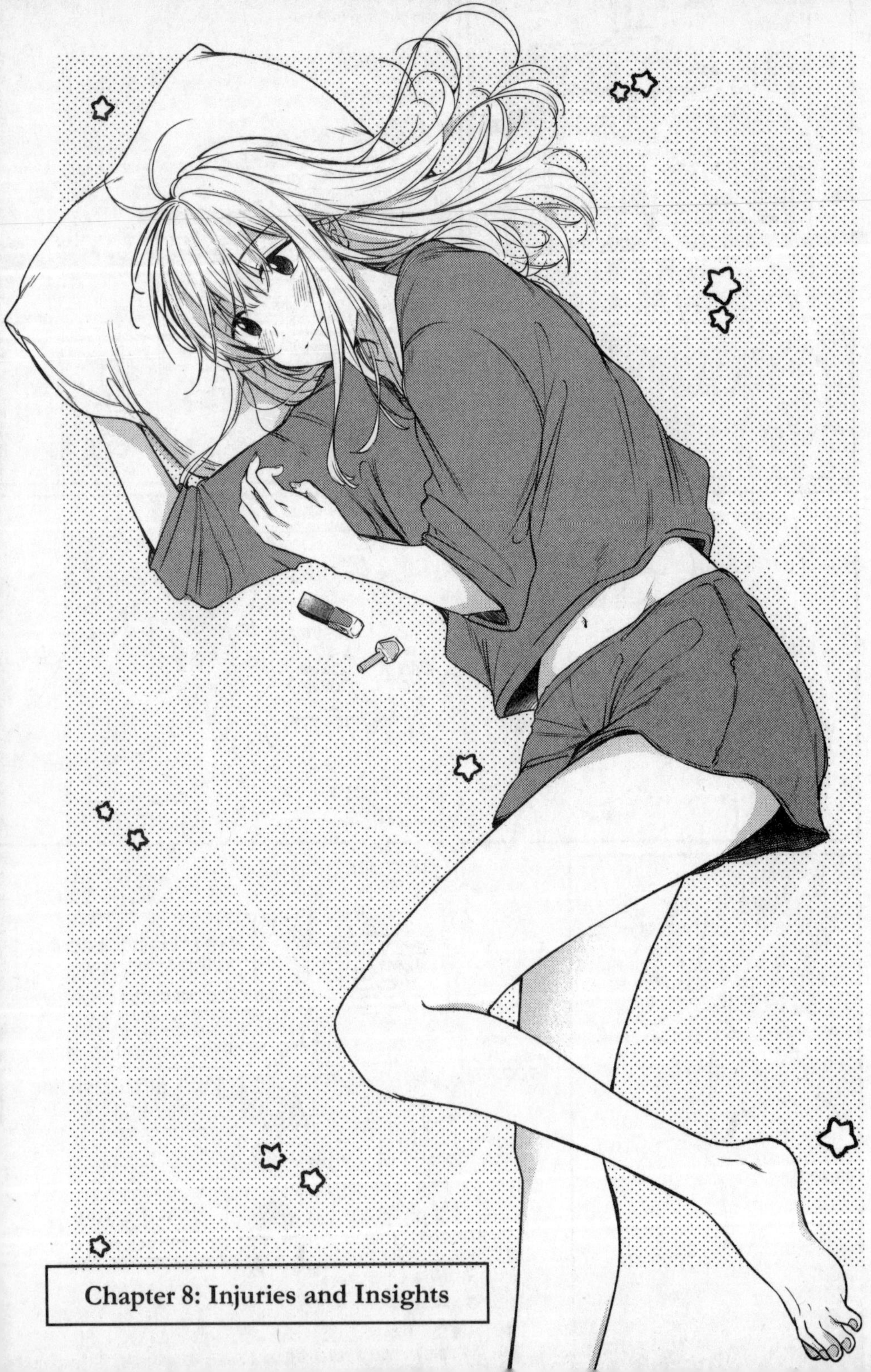

Chapter 8: Injuries and Insights

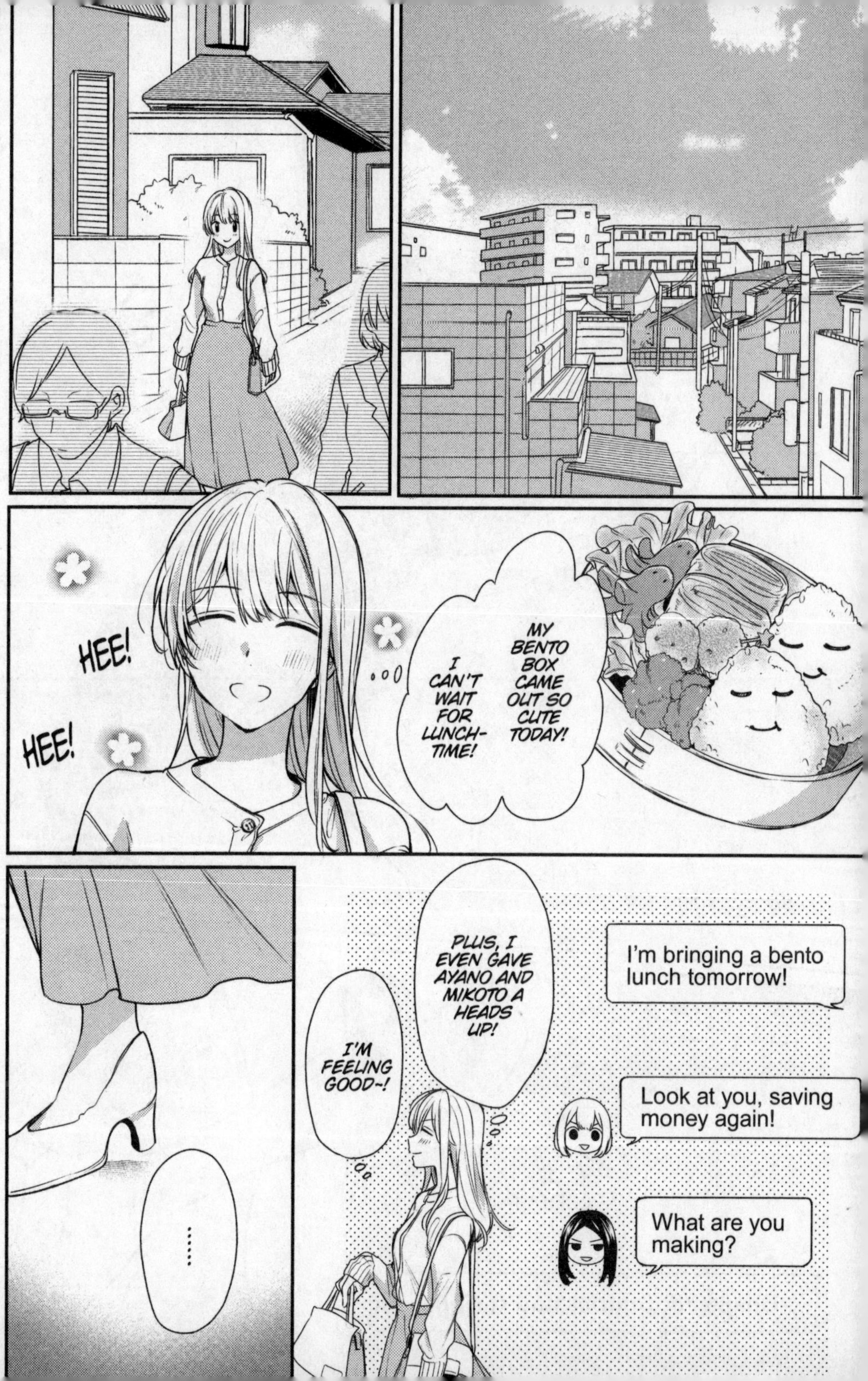
MY BENTO BOX CAME OUT SO CUTE TODAY!
I CAN'T WAIT FOR LUNCH-TIME!
HEE!
HEE!
I'm bringing a bento lunch tomorrow!
Look at you, saving money again!
What are you making?
PLUS, I EVEN GAVE AYANO AND MIKOTO A HEADS UP!
I'M FEELING GOOD~!
......

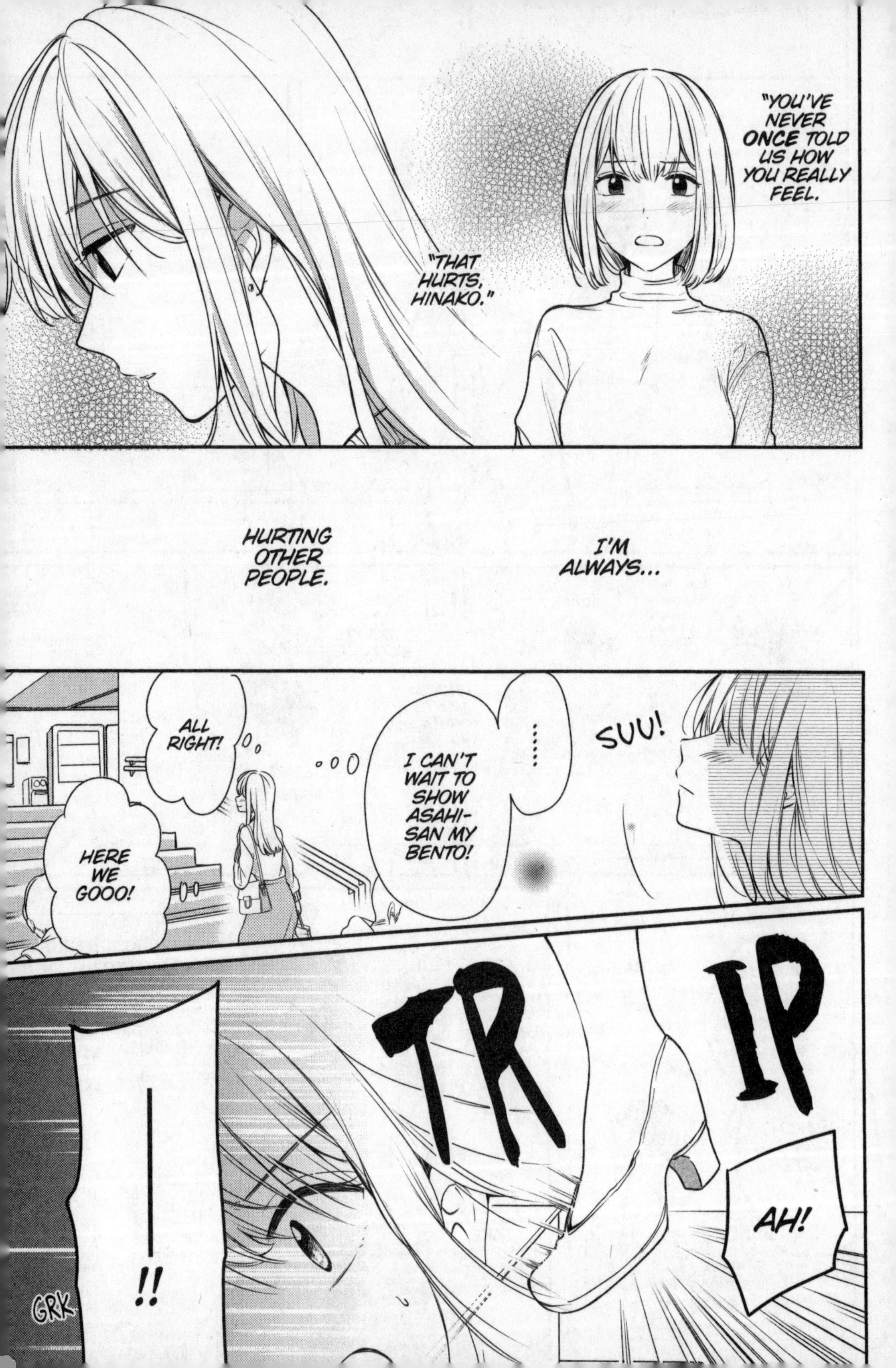

"YOU'VE NEVER ONCE TOLD US HOW YOU REALLY FEEL.
"THAT HURTS, HINAKO."
I'M ALWAYS...
HURTING OTHER PEOPLE.
SUU!
......
I CAN'T WAIT TO SHOW ASAHI-SAN MY BENTO!
ALL RIGHT!
HERE WE GOOO!
TRIP
AH!
——!!
GRK

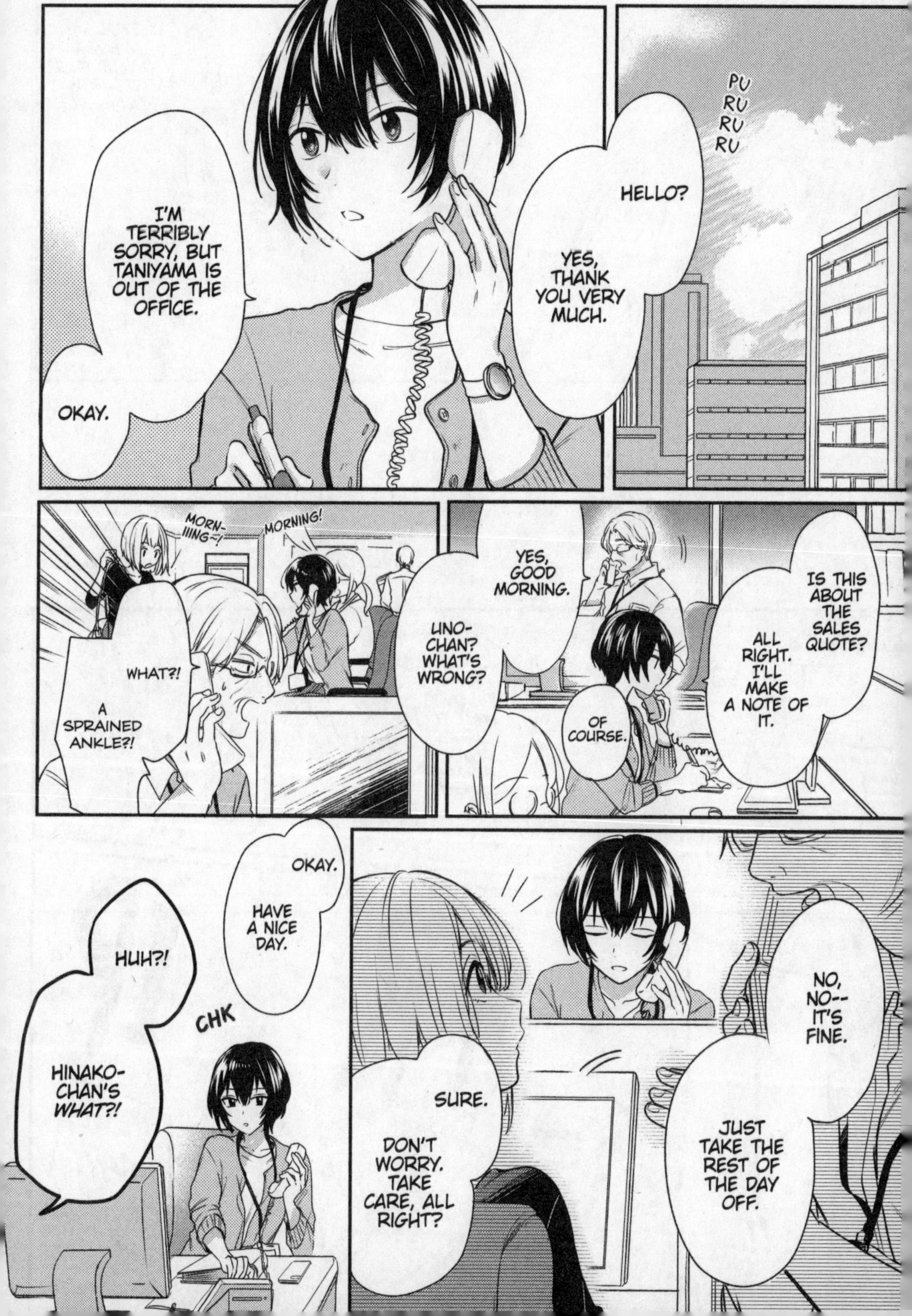
PU RU RU RU
HELLO?
YES, THANK YOU VERY MUCH.
I'M TERRIBLY SORRY, BUT TANIYAMA IS OUT OF THE OFFICE.
OKAY.
IS THIS ABOUT THE SALES QUOTE?
ALL RIGHT. I'LL MAKE A NOTE OF IT.
YES, GOOD MORNING.
OF COURSE.
UNO-CHAN? WHAT'S WRONG?
MORNING!
MORN-IIING~!
WHAT?!
A SPRAINED ANKLE?!
NO, NO-- IT'S FINE.
JUST TAKE THE REST OF THE DAY OFF.
SURE.
DON'T WORRY. TAKE CARE, ALL RIGHT?
OKAY.
HAVE A NICE DAY.
CHK
HUH?!
HINAKO-CHAN'S WHAT?!

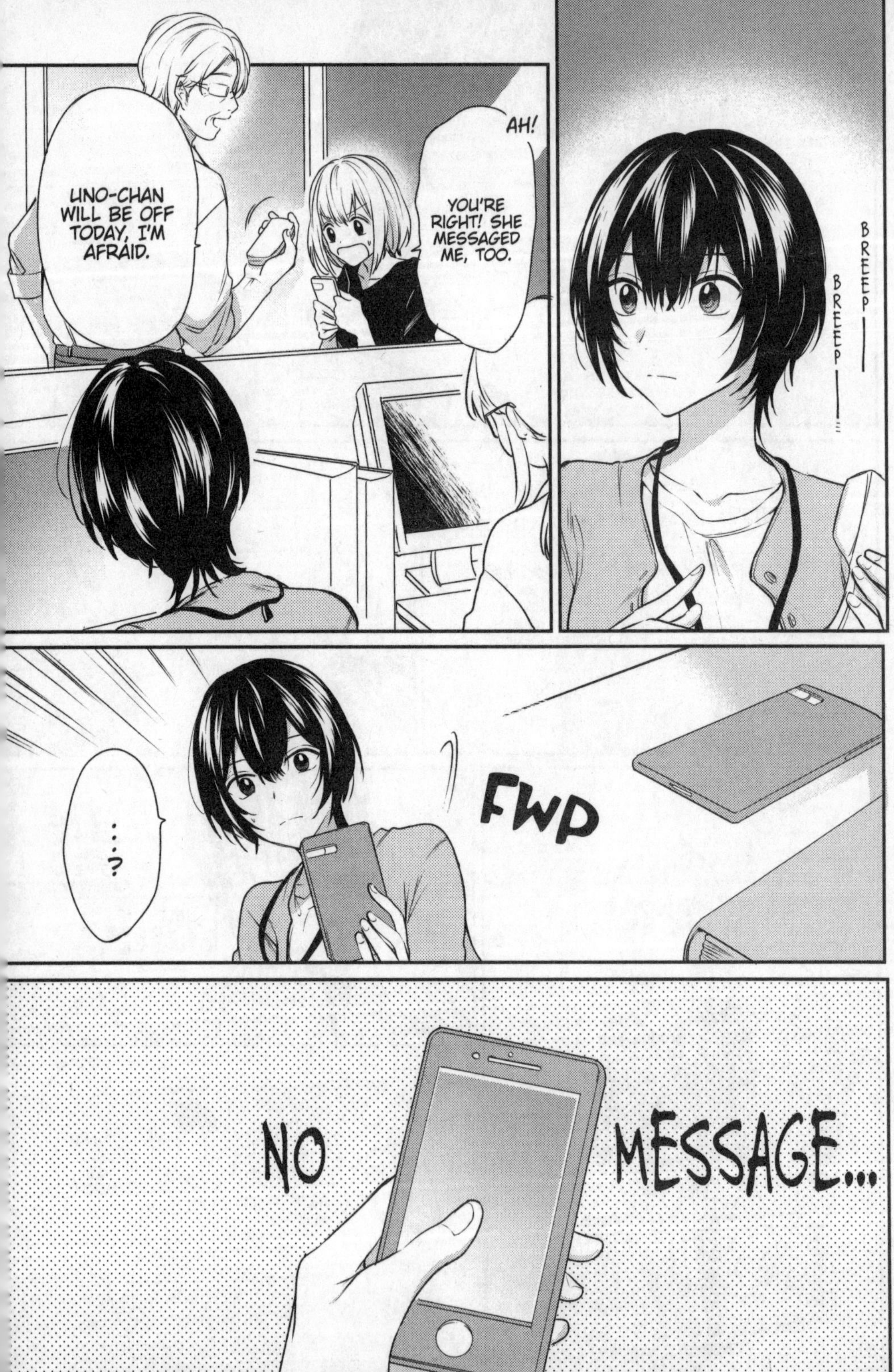
BREEP BREEP
UNO-CHAN WILL BE OFF TODAY, I'M AFRAID.
AH!
YOU'RE RIGHT! SHE MESSAGED ME, TOO.
FWP
...?
NO MESSAGE...

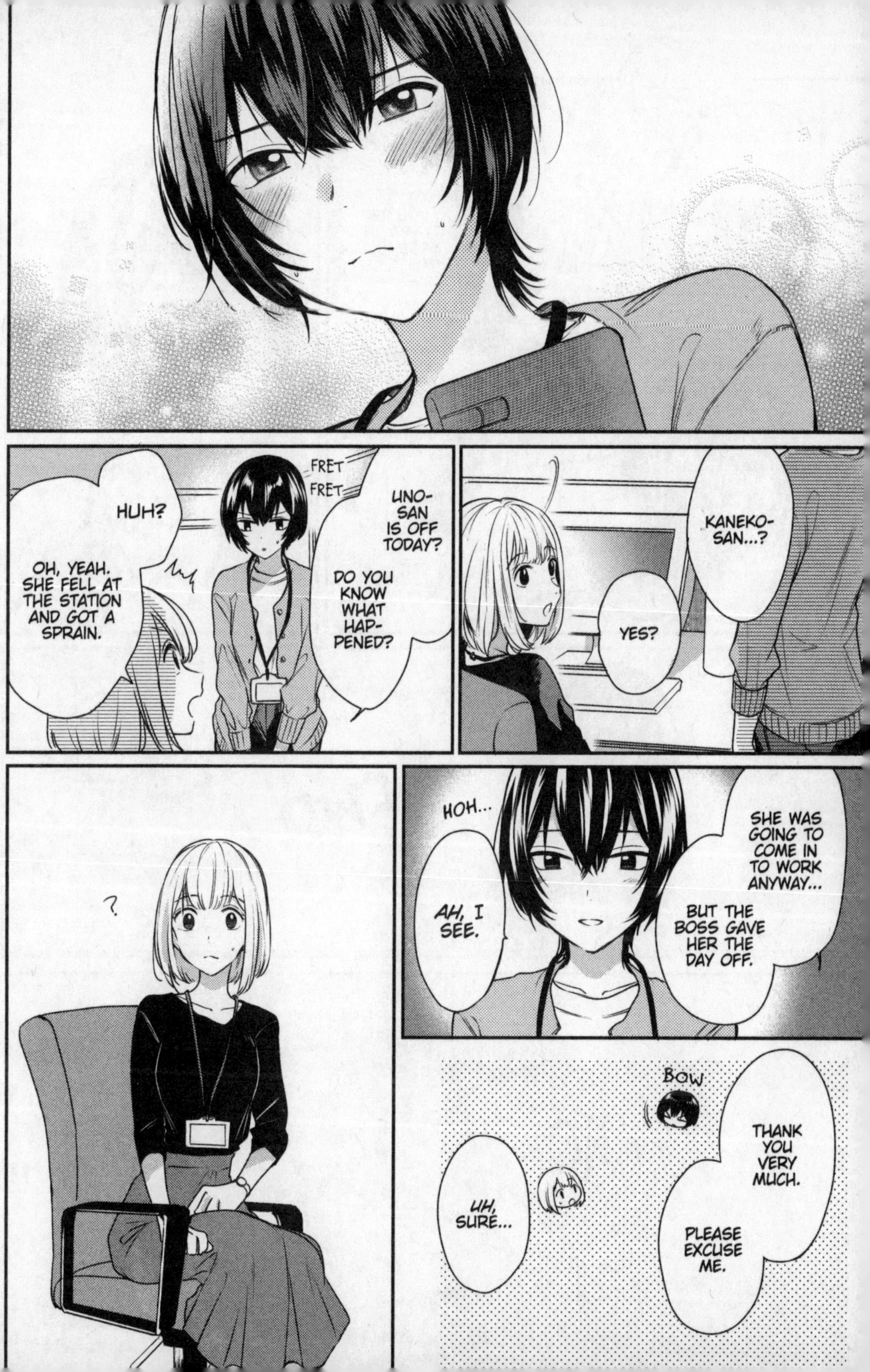
KANEKO-SAN...?
YES?
FRET FRET
UNO-SAN IS OFF TODAY?
DO YOU KNOW WHAT HAP-PENED?
HUH?
OH, YEAH. SHE FELL AT THE STATION AND GOT A SPRAIN.
SHE WAS GOING TO COME IN TO WORK ANYWAY...
BUT THE BOSS GAVE HER THE DAY OFF.
HOH...
AH, I SEE.
BOW
THANK YOU VERY MUCH.
PLEASE EXCUSE ME.
UH, SURE...
?

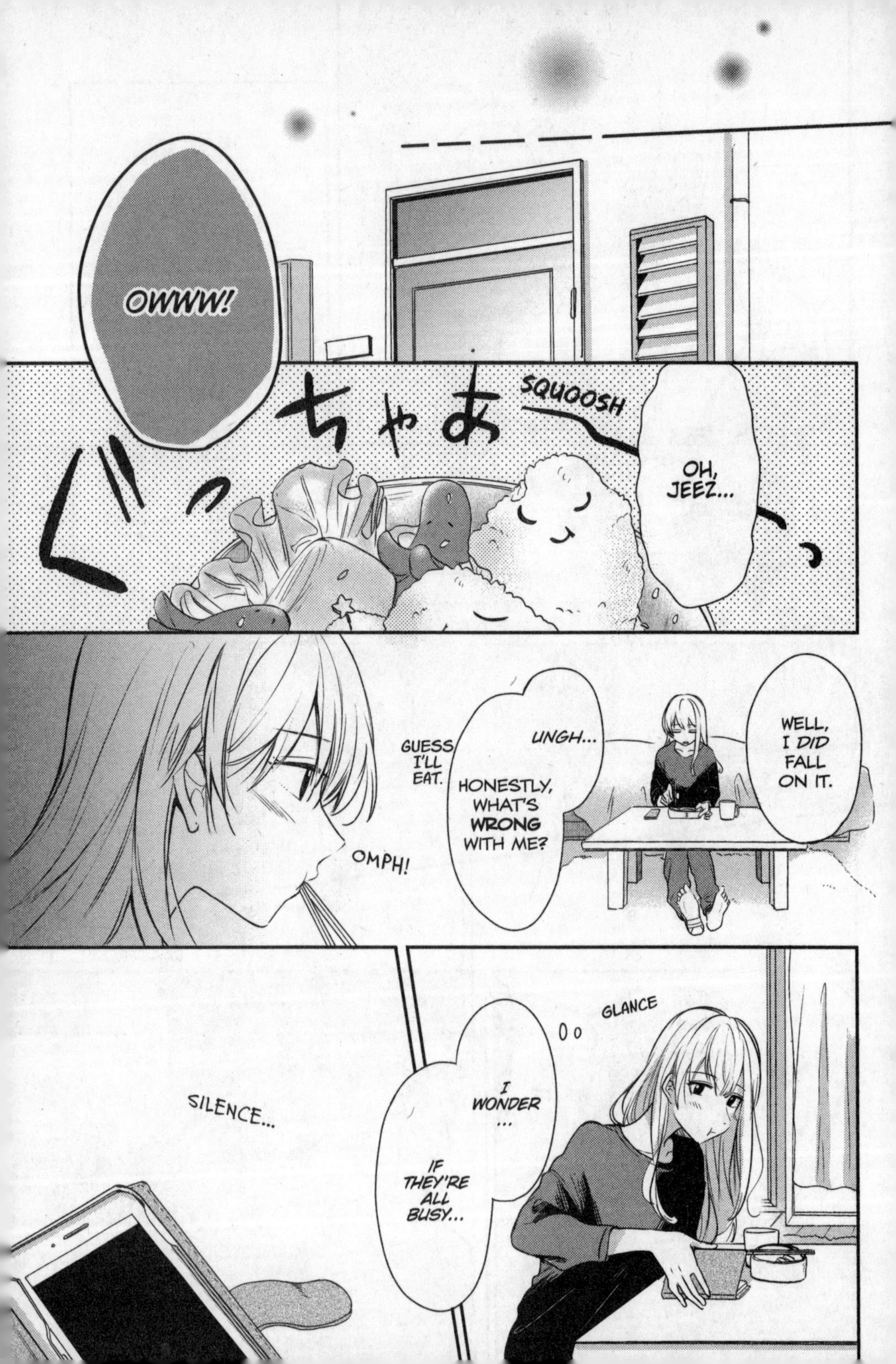

OWWW!
OH, JEEZ...
SQUOOSH
ぐっちゃあ
WELL, I DID FALL ON IT.
UNGH...
HONESTLY, WHAT'S WRONG WITH ME?
GUESS I'LL EAT.
OMPH!
GLANCE
I WONDER...
IF THEY'RE ALL BUSY...
SILENCE...

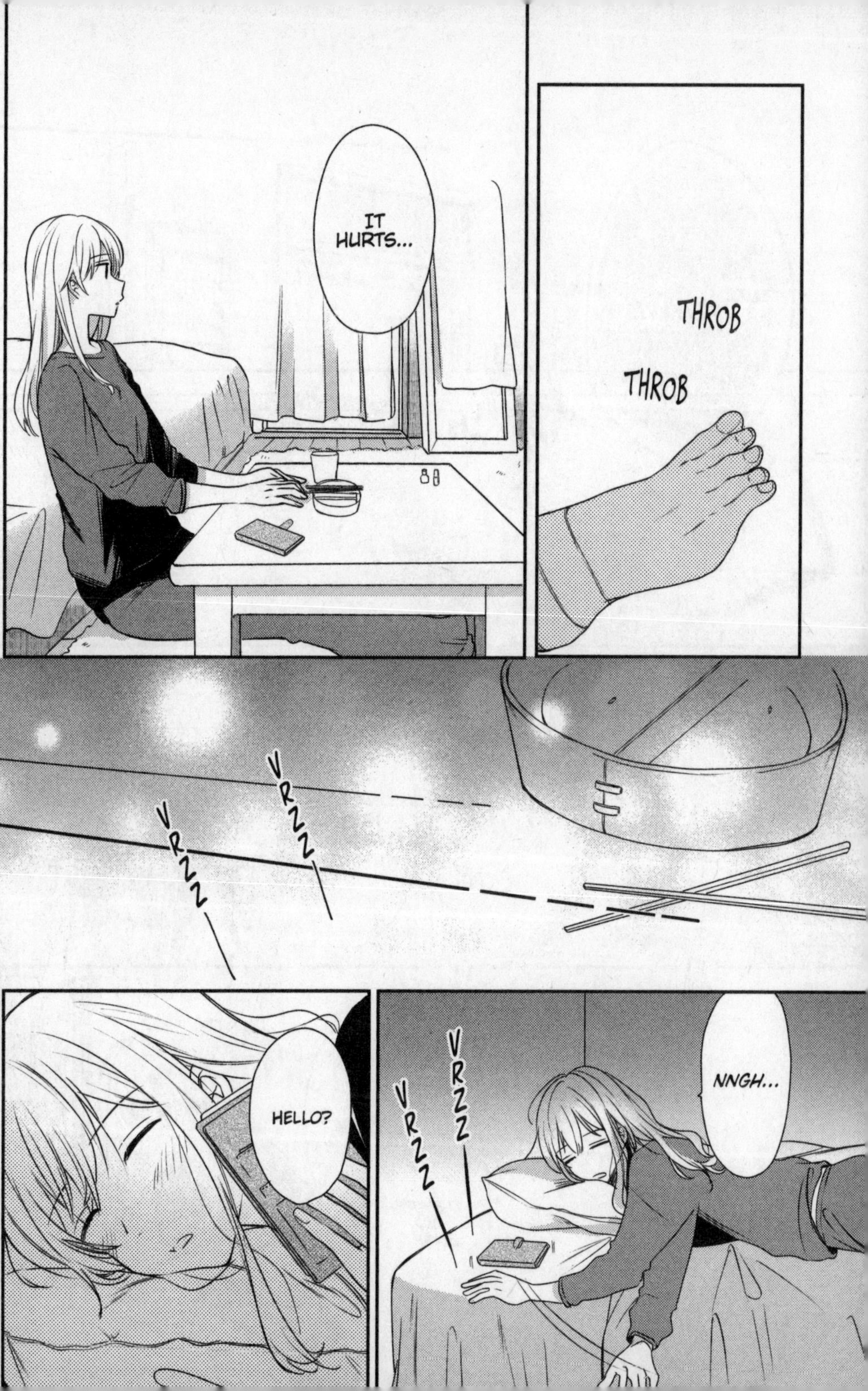
THROB
THROB
IT HURTS...
VRZZZ
VRZZZ
NNGH...
VRZZZ
VRZZZ
HELLO?

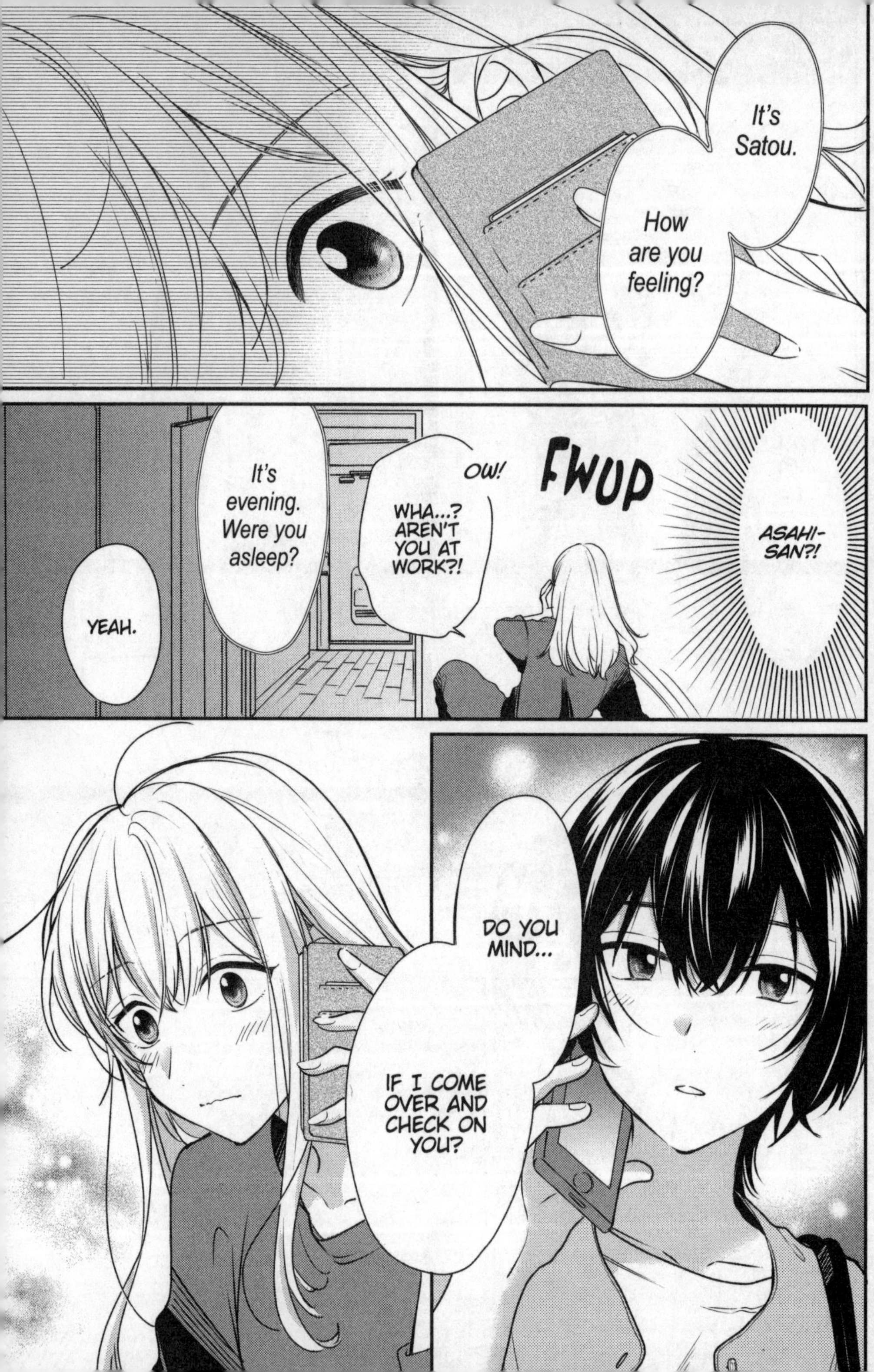

It's Satou.
How are you feeling?
ASAHI-SAN?!
FWUP
OW!
WHA...? AREN'T YOU AT WORK?!
It's evening. Were you asleep?
YEAH.
DO YOU MIND...
IF I COME OVER AND CHECK ON YOU?

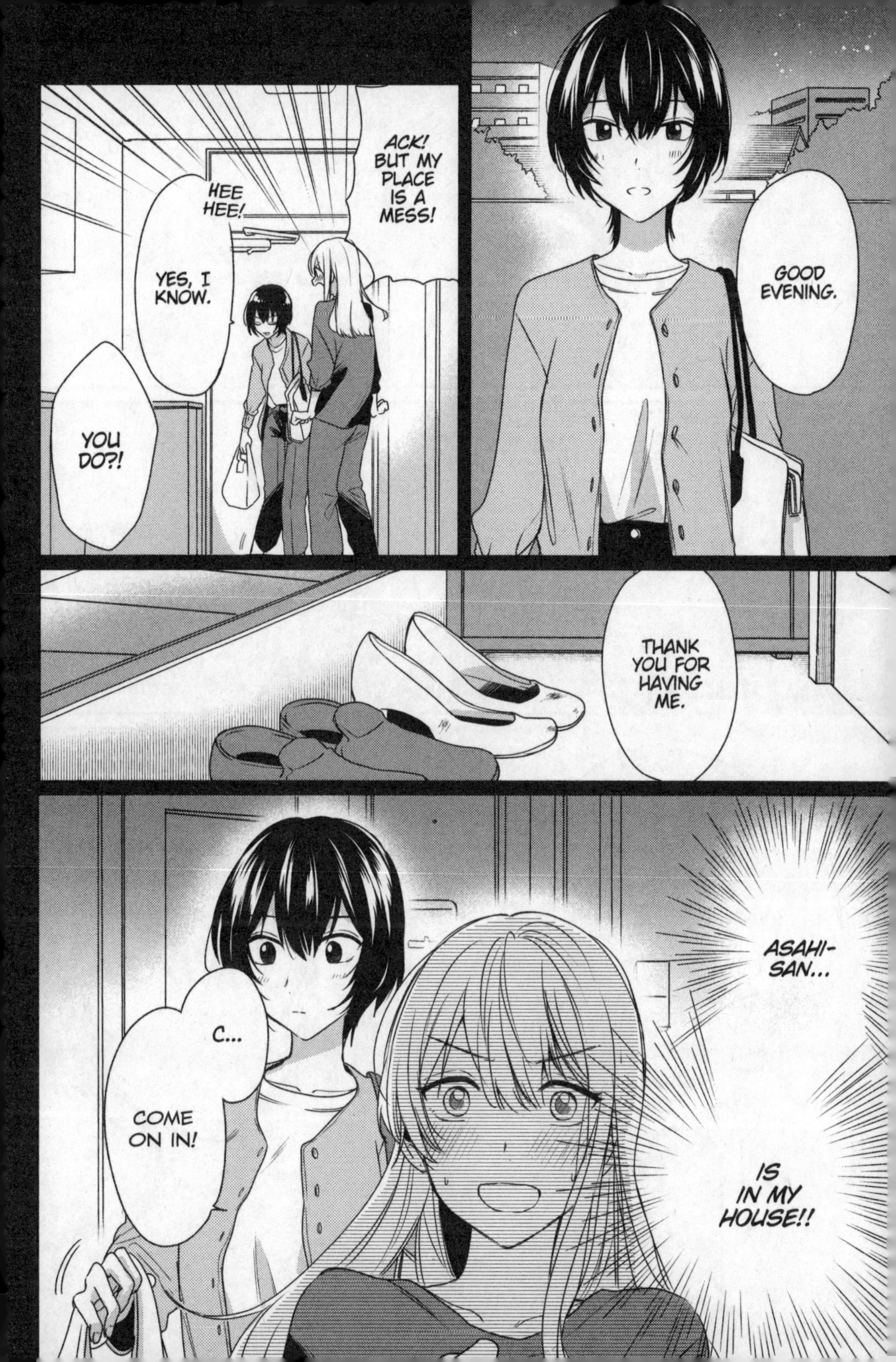
GOOD EVENING.
ACK! BUT MY PLACE IS A MESS!
HEE HEE!
YES, I KNOW.
YOU DO?!
THANK YOU FOR HAVING ME.
ASAHI-SAN...
IS IN MY HOUSE!!
C...
COME ON IN!

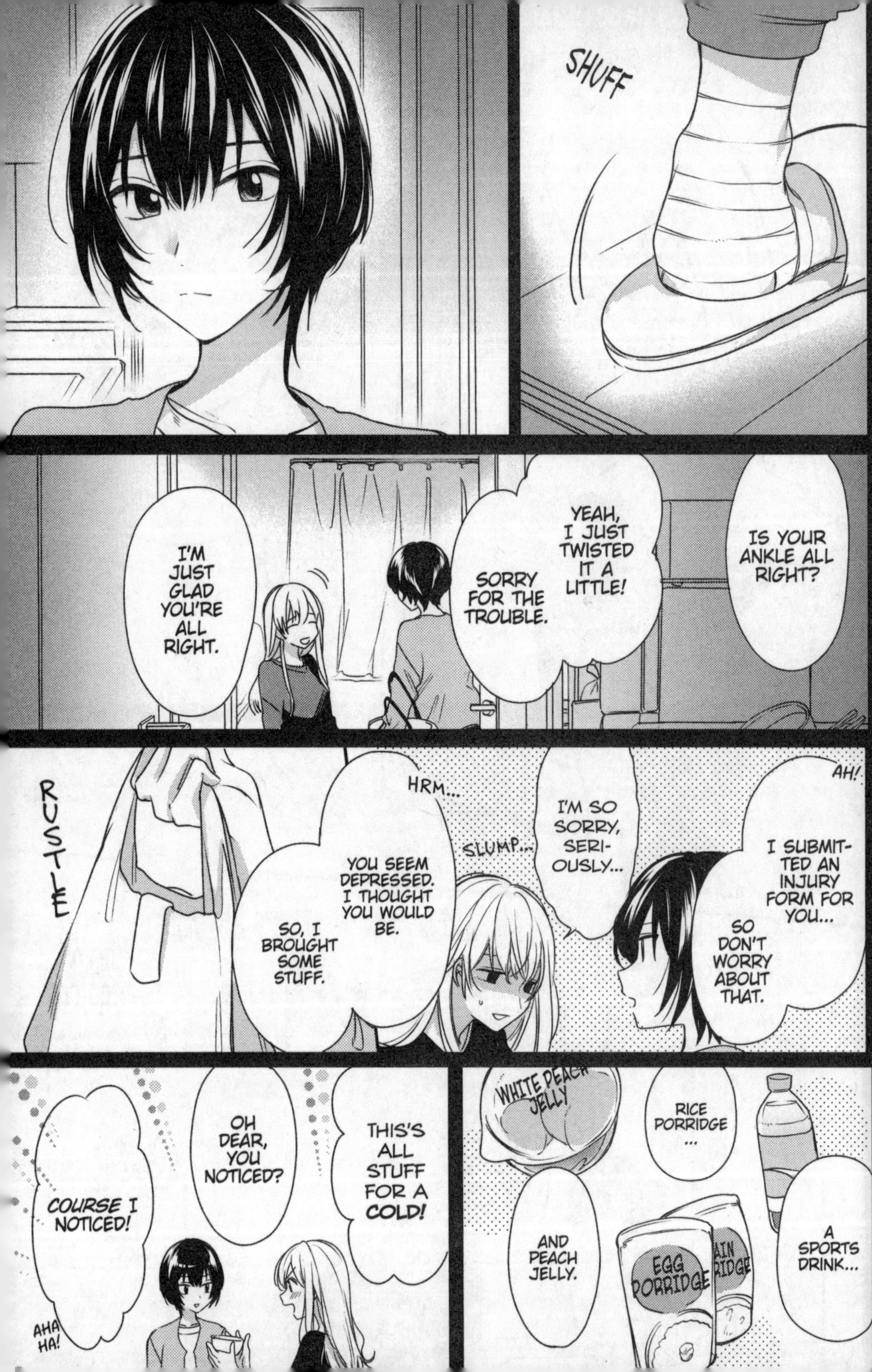
SHUFF
IS YOUR ANKLE ALL RIGHT?
YEAH, I JUST TWISTED IT A LITTLE!
SORRY FOR THE TROUBLE.
I'M JUST GLAD YOU'RE ALL RIGHT.
AH!
I SUBMIT-TED AN INJURY FORM FOR YOU...
SO DON'T WORRY ABOUT THAT.
I'M SO SORRY, SERI-OUSLY...
SLUMP...
HRM...
YOU SEEM DEPRESSED. I THOUGHT YOU WOULD BE.
SO, I BROUGHT SOME STUFF.
RUSTLE
RICE PORRIDGE ...
WHITE PEACH JELLY
A SPORTS DRINK...
AND PEACH JELLY.
EGG PORRIDGE
THIS'S ALL STUFF FOR A COLD!
OH DEAR, YOU NOTICED?
COURSE I NOTICED!
AHA HA!

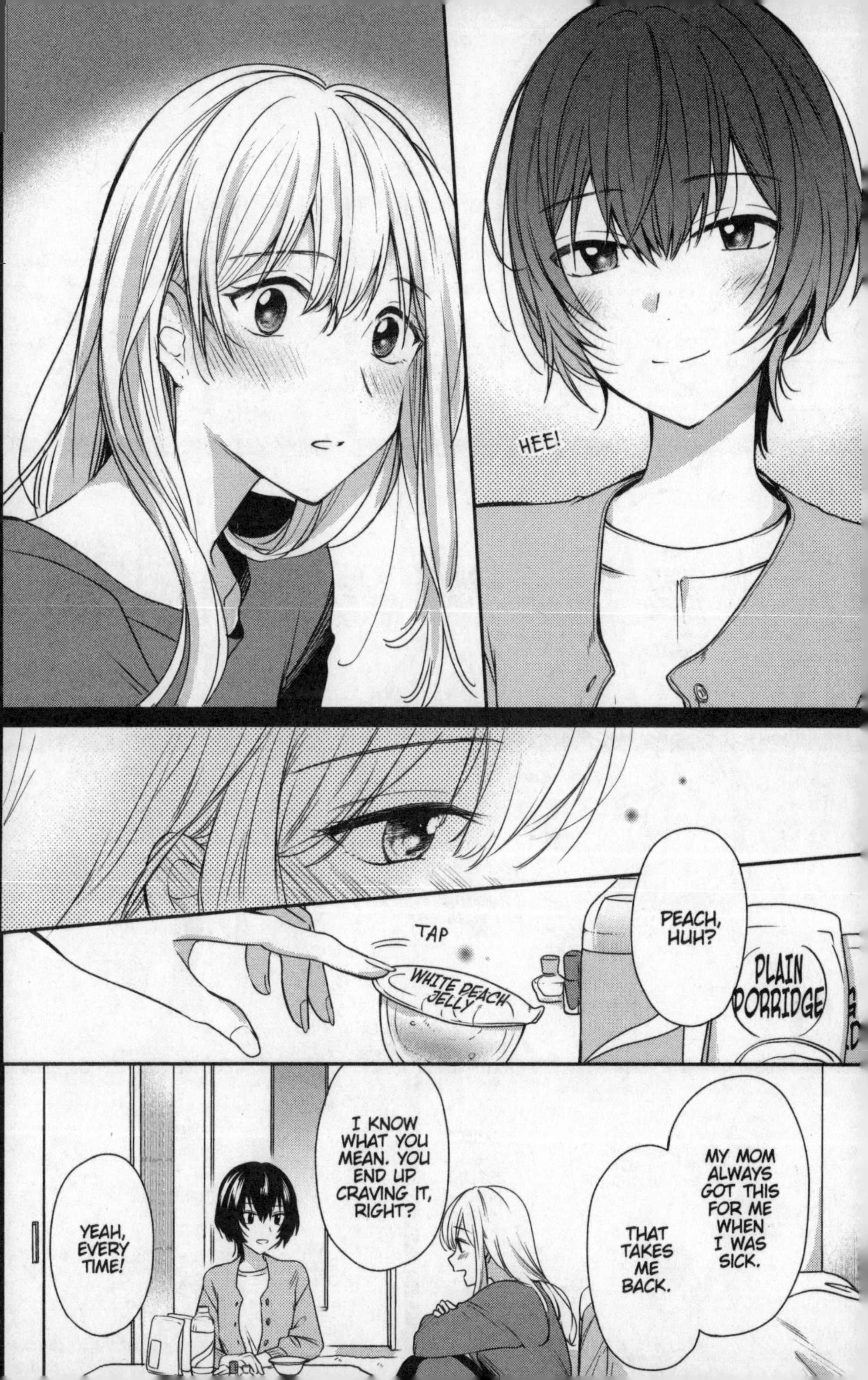
HEE!
PEACH, HUH?
PLAIN PORRIDGE
TAP
WHITE PEACH JELLY
MY MOM ALWAYS GOT THIS FOR ME WHEN I WAS SICK.
THAT TAKES ME BACK.
I KNOW WHAT YOU MEAN. YOU END UP CRAVING IT, RIGHT?
YEAH, EVERY TIME!

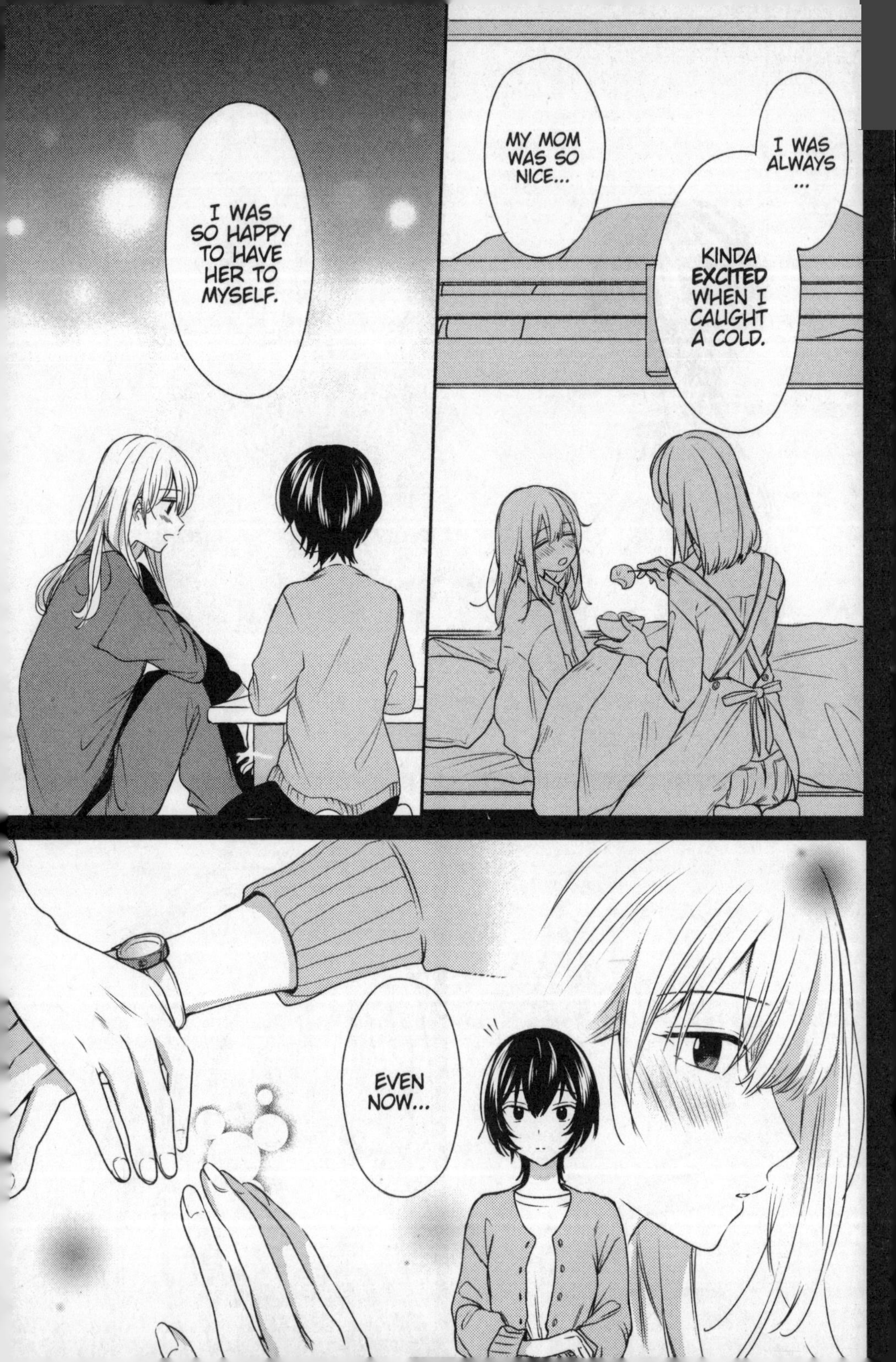
I WAS ALWAYS ... KINDA EXCITED WHEN I CAUGHT A COLD.
MY MOM WAS SO NICE...
I WAS SO HAPPY TO HAVE HER TO MYSELF.
EVEN NOW...

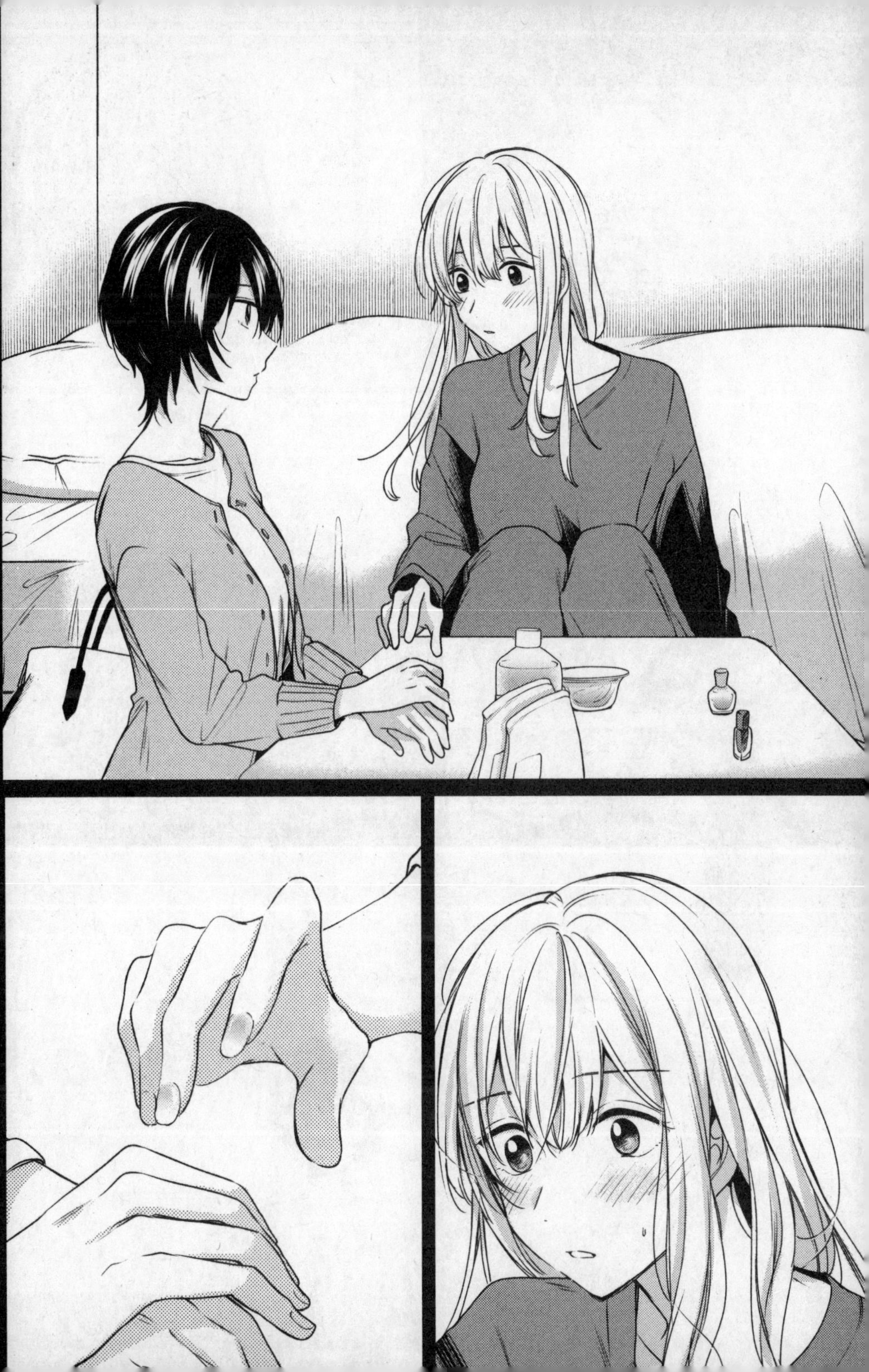

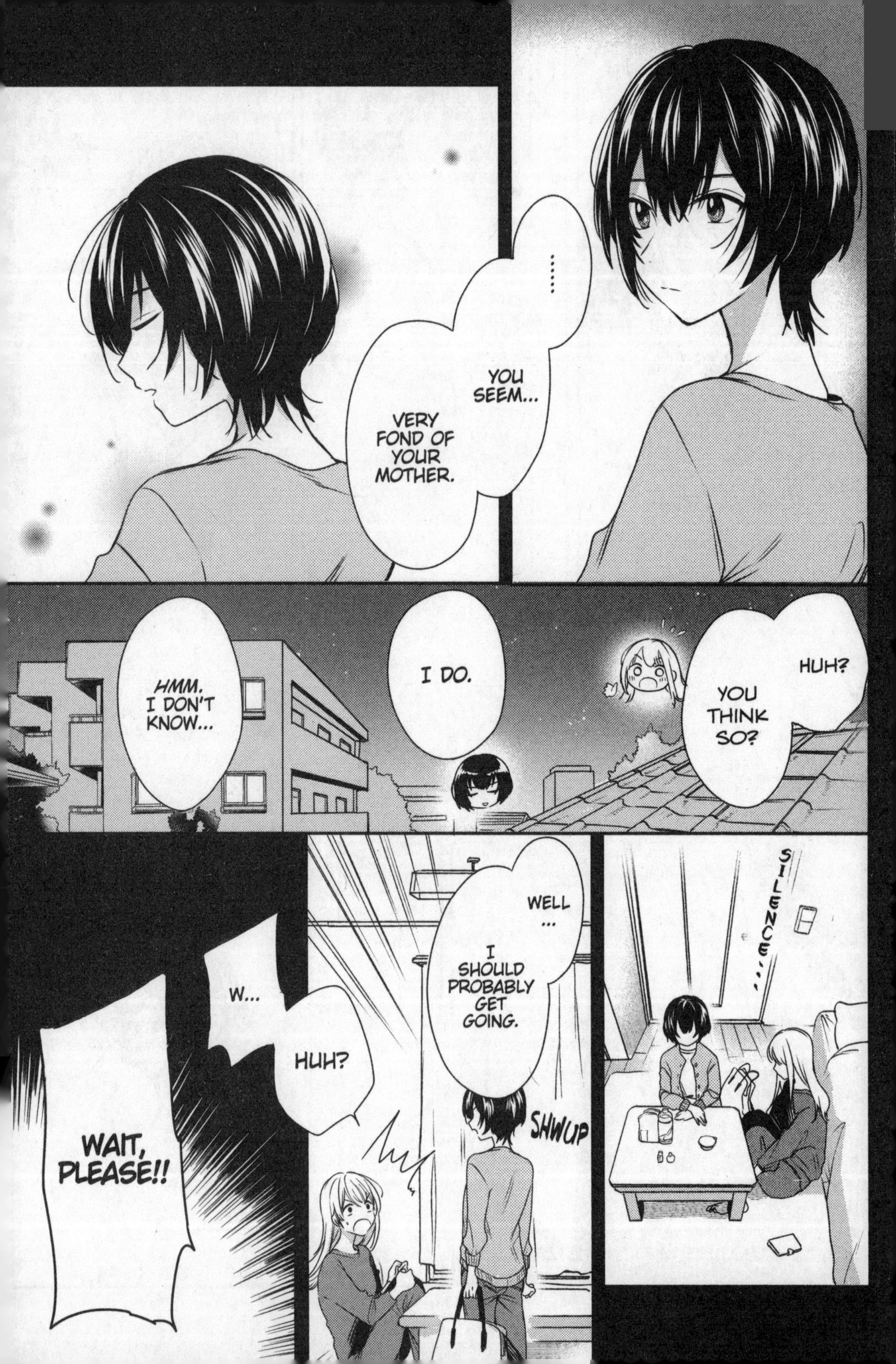
......
YOU SEEM... VERY FOND OF YOUR MOTHER.
HUH? YOU THINK SO?
I DO.
HMM. I DON'T KNOW...
SILENCE...
WELL ... I SHOULD PROBABLY GET GOING.
SHWUP
HUH?
W...
WAIT, PLEASE!!

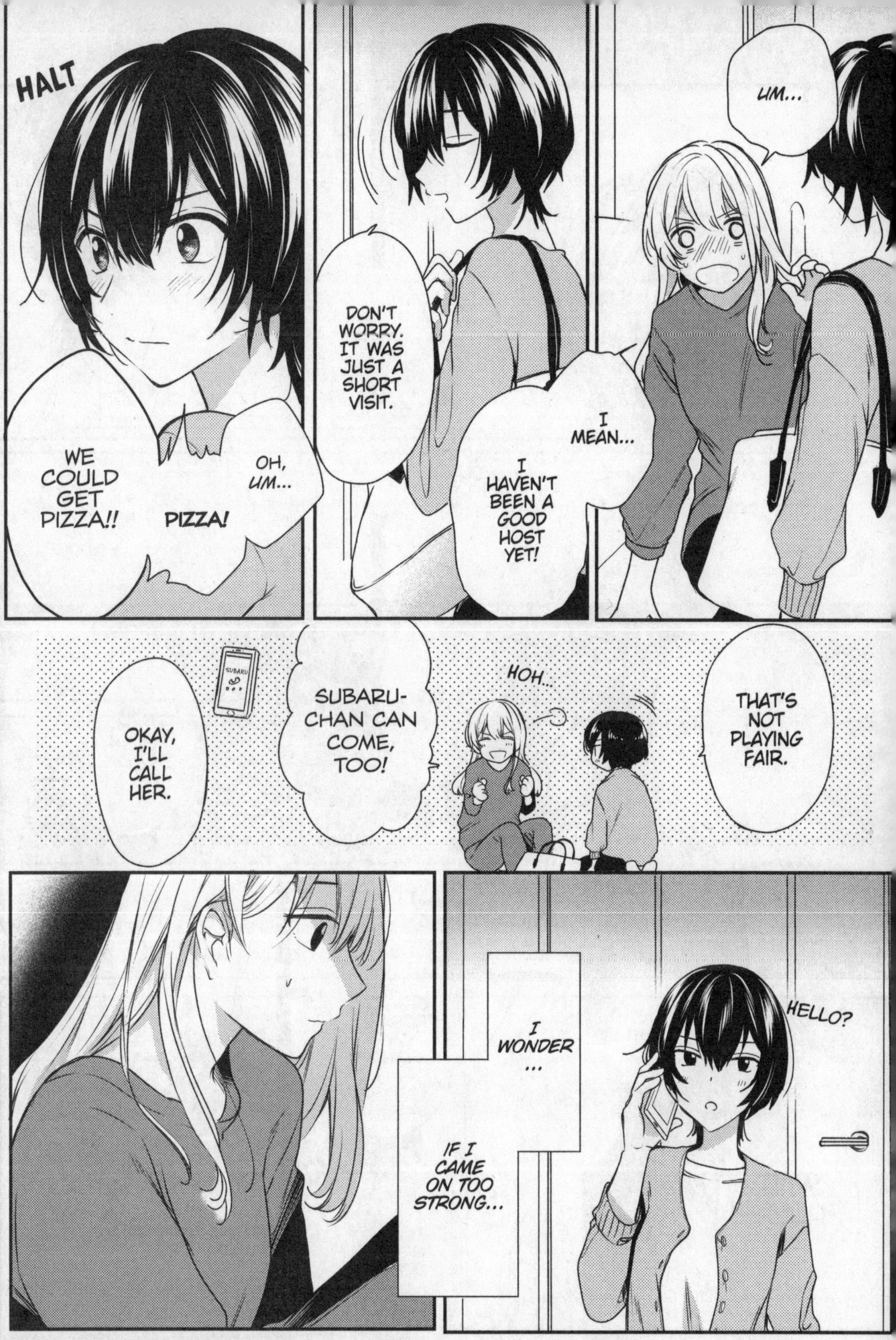
UM...
I MEAN...
I HAVEN'T BEEN A GOOD HOST YET!
DON'T WORRY. IT WAS JUST A SHORT VISIT.
HALT
OH, UM...
WE COULD GET PIZZA!!
PIZZA!
THAT'S NOT PLAYING FAIR.
HOH...
SUBARU-CHAN CAN COME, TOO!
SUBARU
OKAY, I'LL CALL HER.
HELLO?
I WONDER...
IF I CAME ON TOO STRONG...

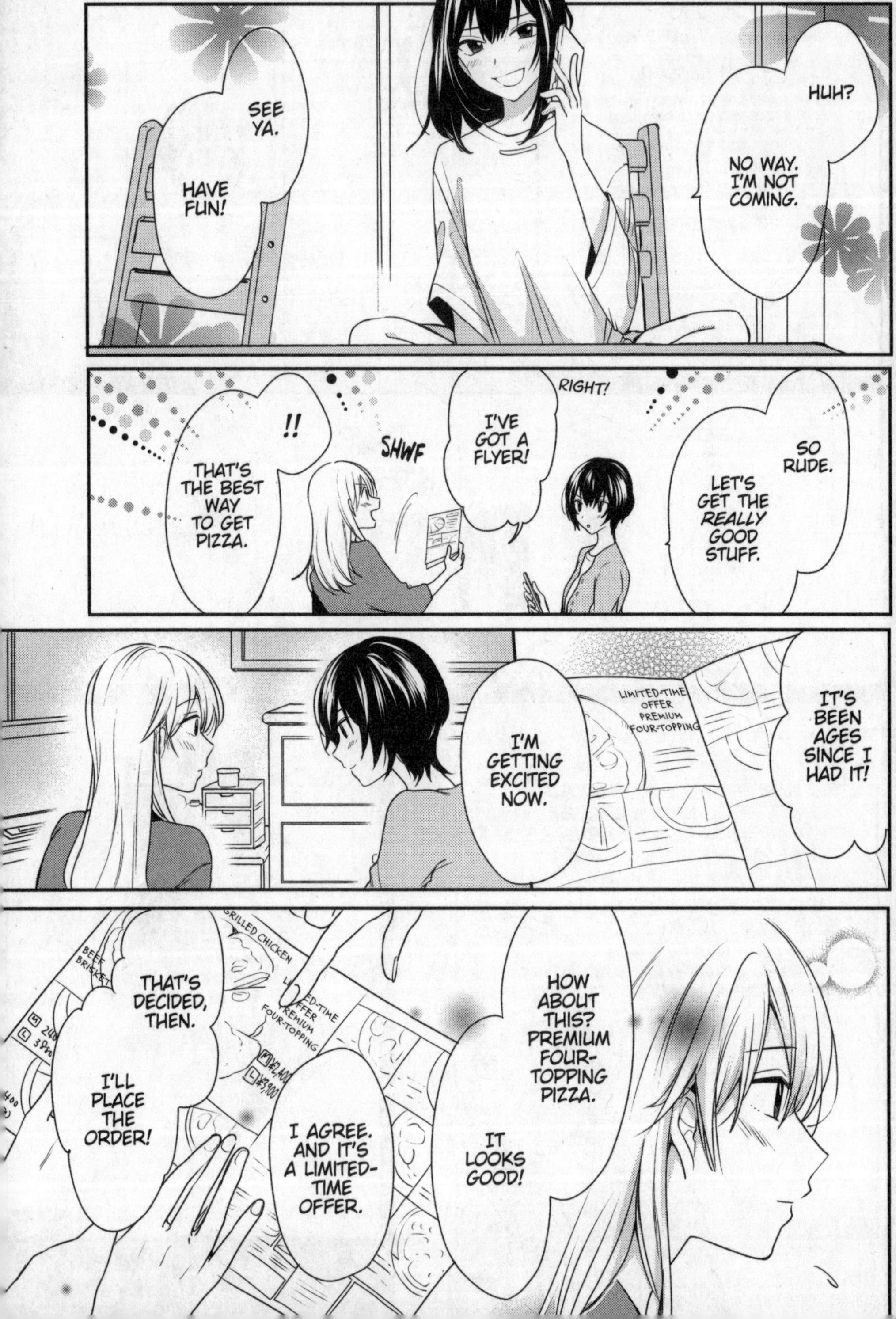

HUH?
NO WAY. I'M NOT COMING.
SEE YA.
HAVE FUN!
SO RUDE.
LET'S GET THE *REALLY* GOOD STUFF.
RIGHT!
I'VE GOT A FLYER!
SHWF
!!
THAT'S THE BEST WAY TO GET PIZZA.
IT'S BEEN AGES SINCE I HAD IT!
LIMITED-TIME OFFER PREMIUM FOUR-TOPPING
I'M GETTING EXCITED NOW.
HOW ABOUT THIS? PREMIUM FOUR-TOPPING PIZZA.
IT LOOKS GOOD!
I AGREE. AND IT'S A LIMITED-TIME OFFER.
GRILLED CHICKEN
BEEF BRISKET
LIMITED-TIME OFFER PREMIUM FOUR-TOPPING
¥2,400
¥3,900
THAT'S DECIDED, THEN.
I'LL PLACE THE ORDER!

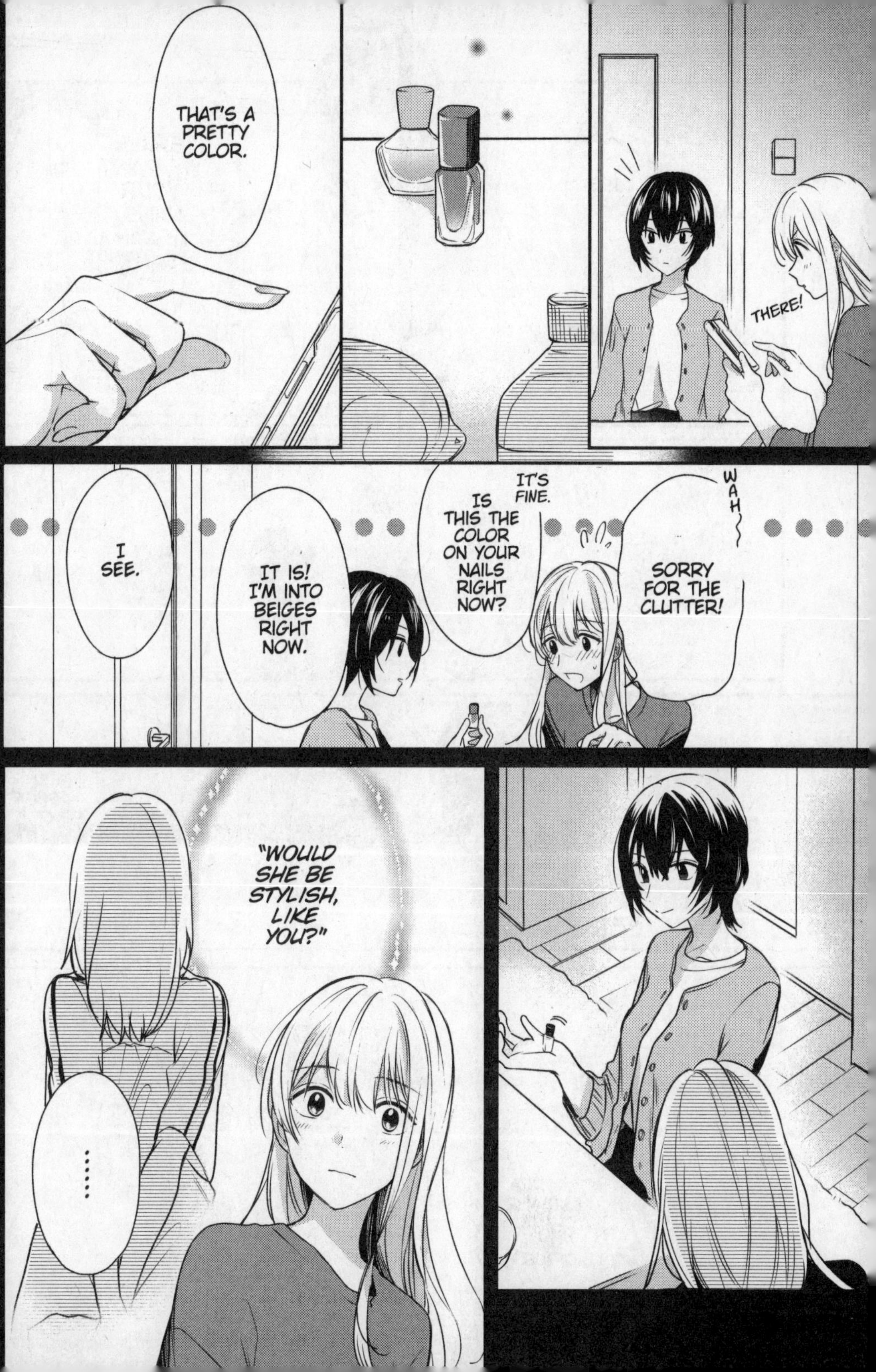
THERE!
THAT'S A PRETTY COLOR.
WAH~
SORRY FOR THE CLUTTER!
IT'S FINE.
IS THIS THE COLOR ON YOUR NAILS RIGHT NOW?
IT IS! I'M INTO BEIGES RIGHT NOW.
I SEE.
"WOULD SHE BE STYLISH, LIKE YOU?"
……

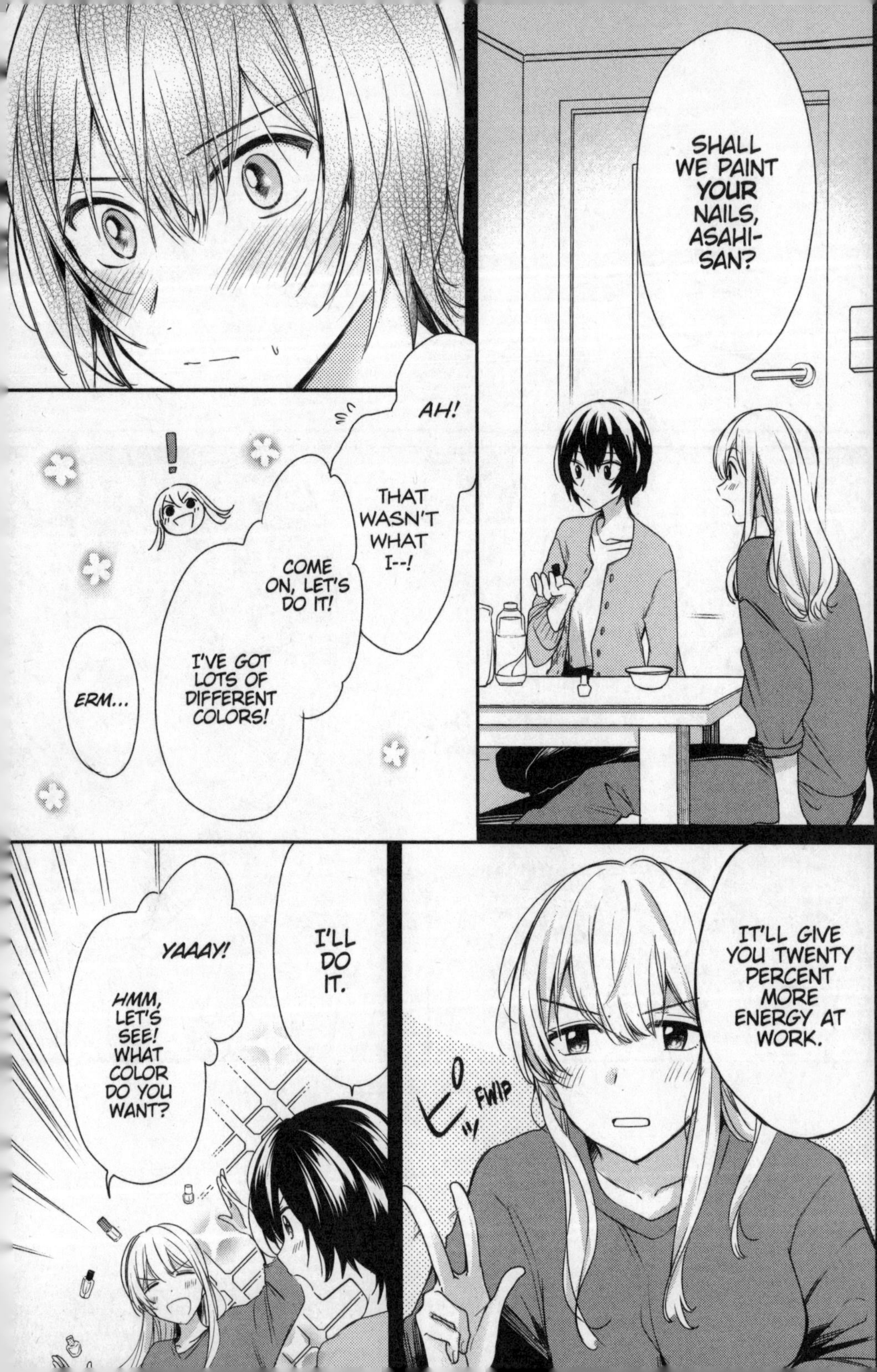
SHALL WE PAINT YOUR NAILS, ASAHI-SAN?
AH!
THAT WASN'T WHAT I--!
COME ON, LET'S DO IT!
I'VE GOT LOTS OF DIFFERENT COLORS!
ERM...
IT'LL GIVE YOU TWENTY PERCENT MORE ENERGY AT WORK.
FWIP
I'LL DO IT.
YAAAY!
HMM, LET'S SEE! WHAT COLOR DO YOU WANT?

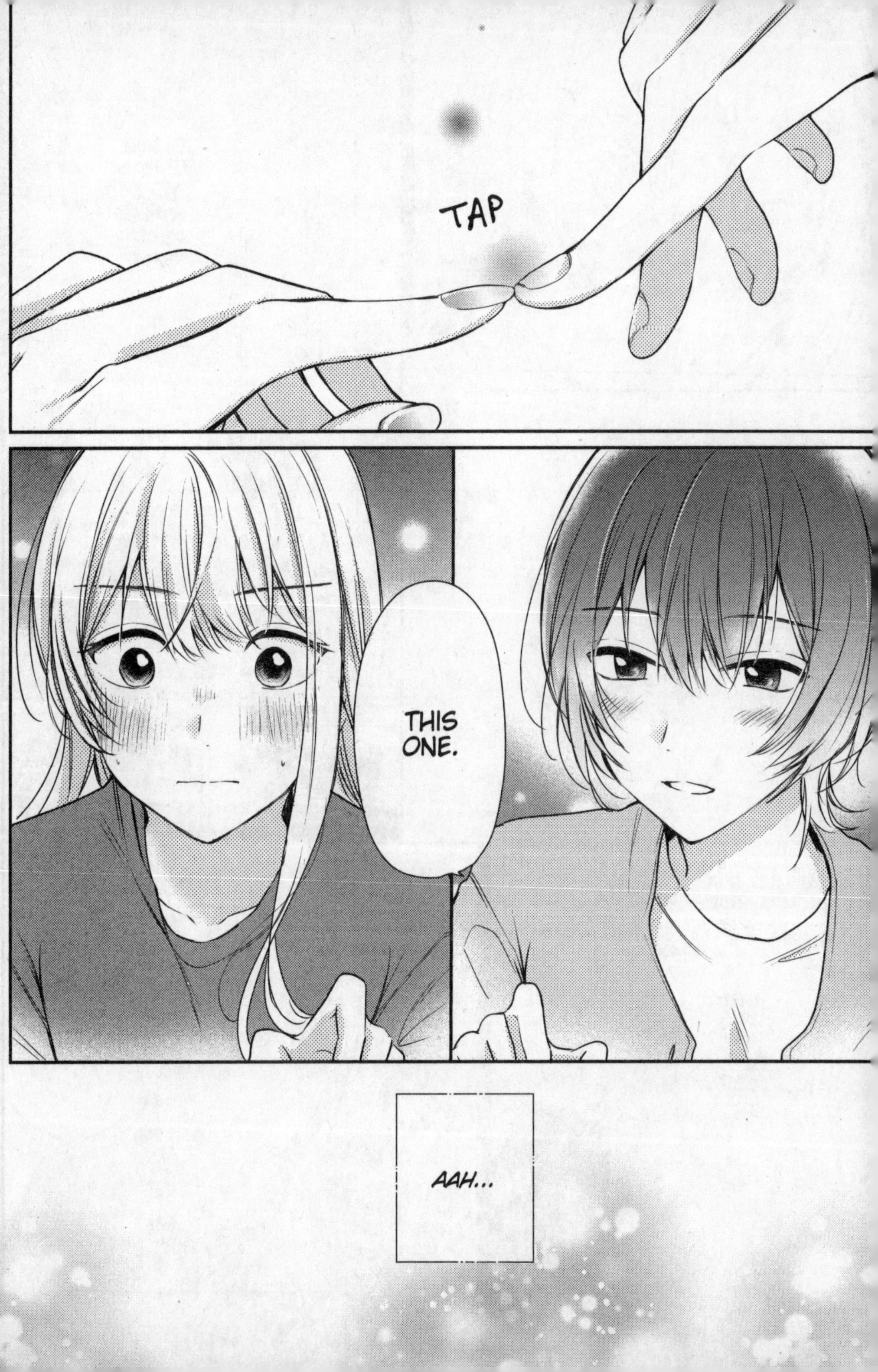
TAP
THIS ONE.
AAH...

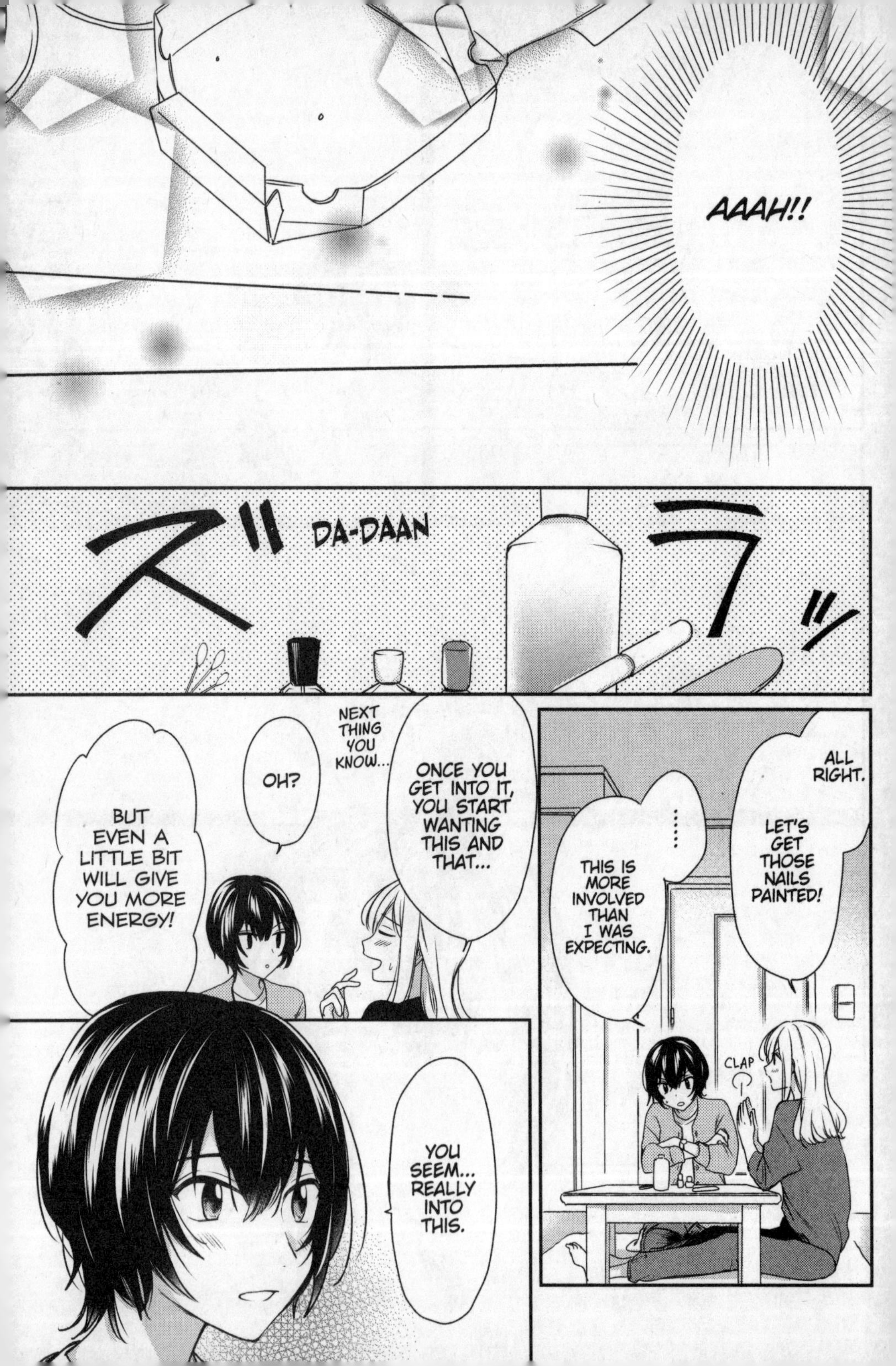
AAAH!!
ズラッ
DA-DAAN
ALL RIGHT.
LET'S GET THOSE NAILS PAINTED!
CLAP
......
THIS IS MORE INVOLVED THAN I WAS EXPECTING.
ONCE YOU GET INTO IT, YOU START WANTING THIS AND THAT...
NEXT THING YOU KNOW...
OH?
BUT EVEN A LITTLE BIT WILL GIVE YOU MORE ENERGY!
YOU SEEM... REALLY INTO THIS.

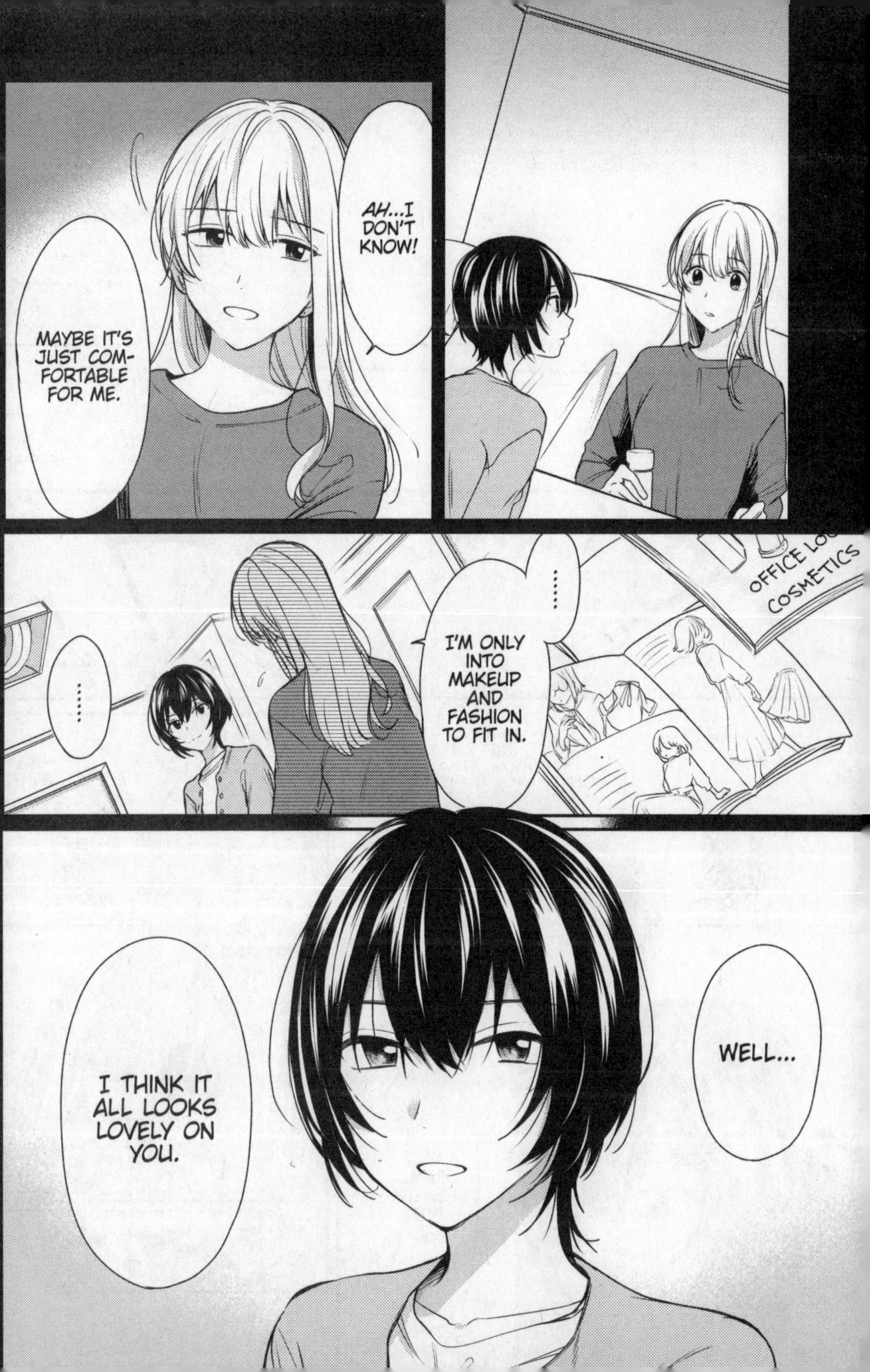
AH...I DON'T KNOW!
MAYBE IT'S JUST COMFORTABLE FOR ME.
OFFICE
COSMETICS
......
I'M ONLY INTO MAKEUP AND FASHION TO FIT IN.
......
WELL...
I THINK IT ALL LOOKS LOVELY ON YOU.

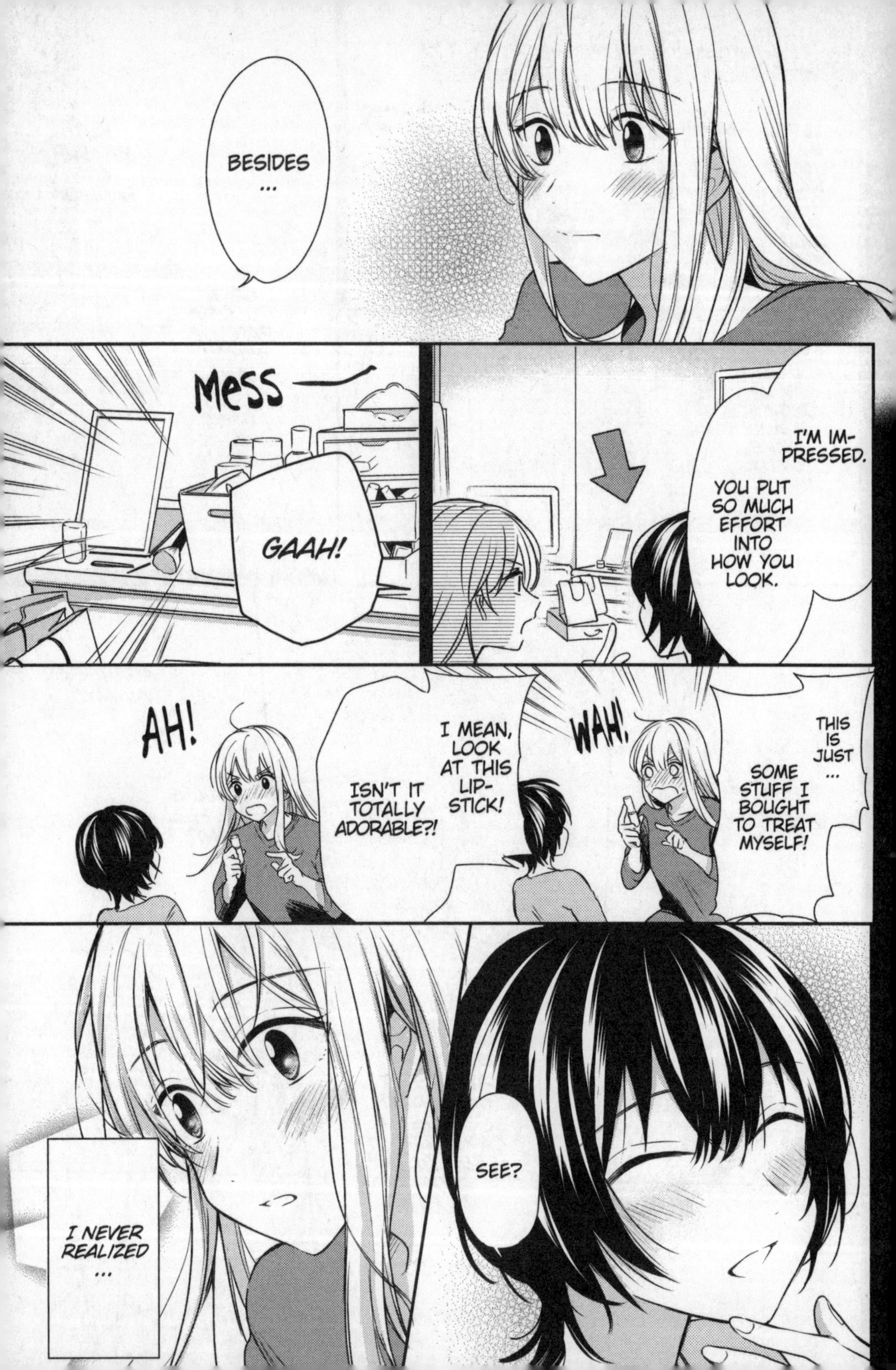
BESIDES ...
I'M IMPRESSED.
YOU PUT SO MUCH EFFORT INTO HOW YOU LOOK.
Mess—
GAAH!
THIS IS JUST ...
SOME STUFF I BOUGHT TO TREAT MYSELF!
WAH!
I MEAN, LOOK AT THIS LIP-STICK!
ISN'T IT TOTALLY ADORABLE?!
AH!
SEE?
I NEVER REALIZED ...

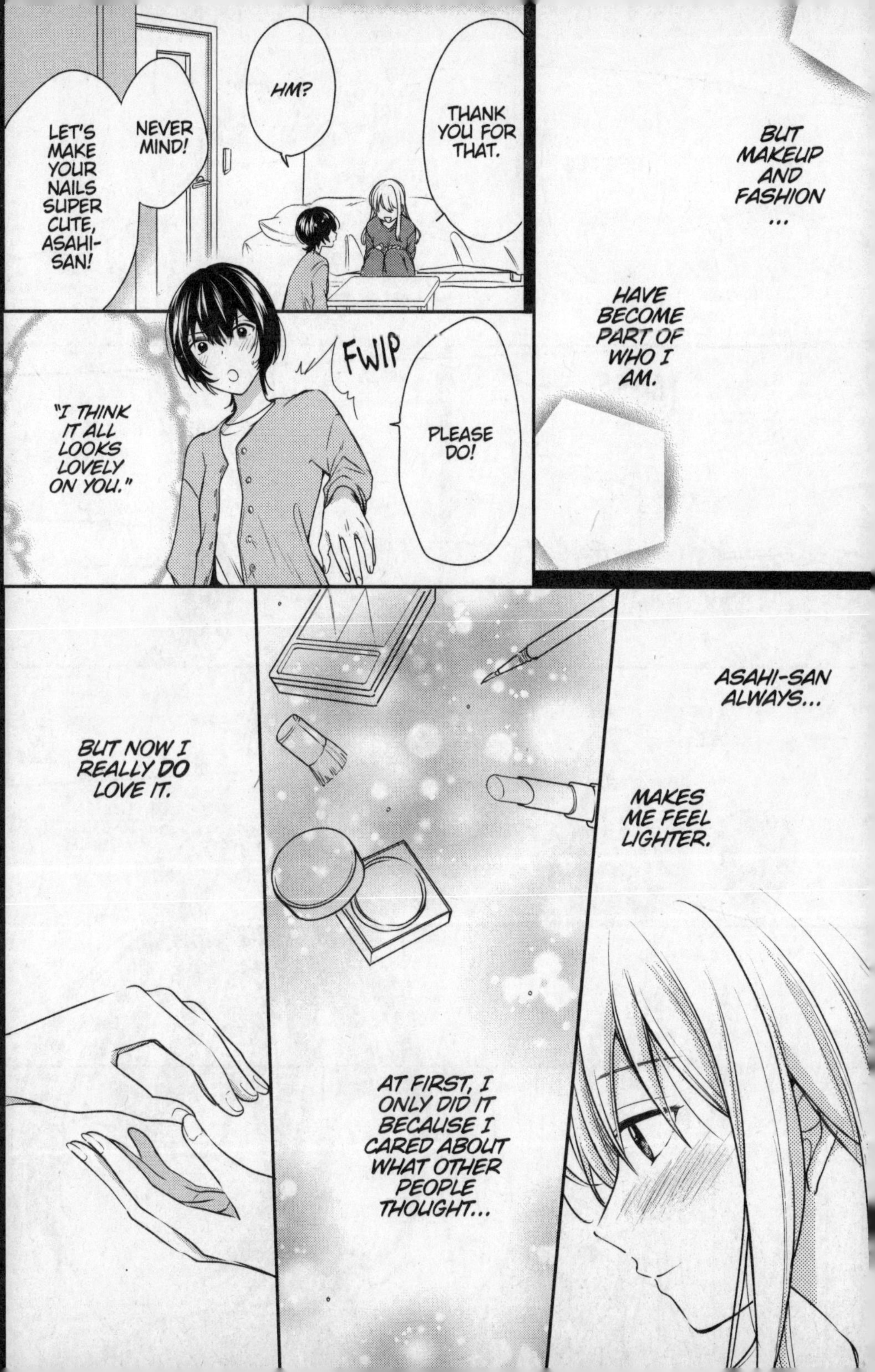
BUT MAKEUP AND FASHION...
HAVE BECOME PART OF WHO I AM.
THANK YOU FOR THAT.
HM?
NEVER MIND!
LET'S MAKE YOUR NAILS SUPER CUTE, ASAHI-SAN!
PLEASE DO!
FWIP
"I THINK IT ALL LOOKS LOVELY ON YOU."
ASAHI-SAN ALWAYS...
MAKES ME FEEL LIGHTER.
AT FIRST, I ONLY DID IT BECAUSE I CARED ABOUT WHAT OTHER PEOPLE THOUGHT...
BUT NOW I REALLY DO LOVE IT.

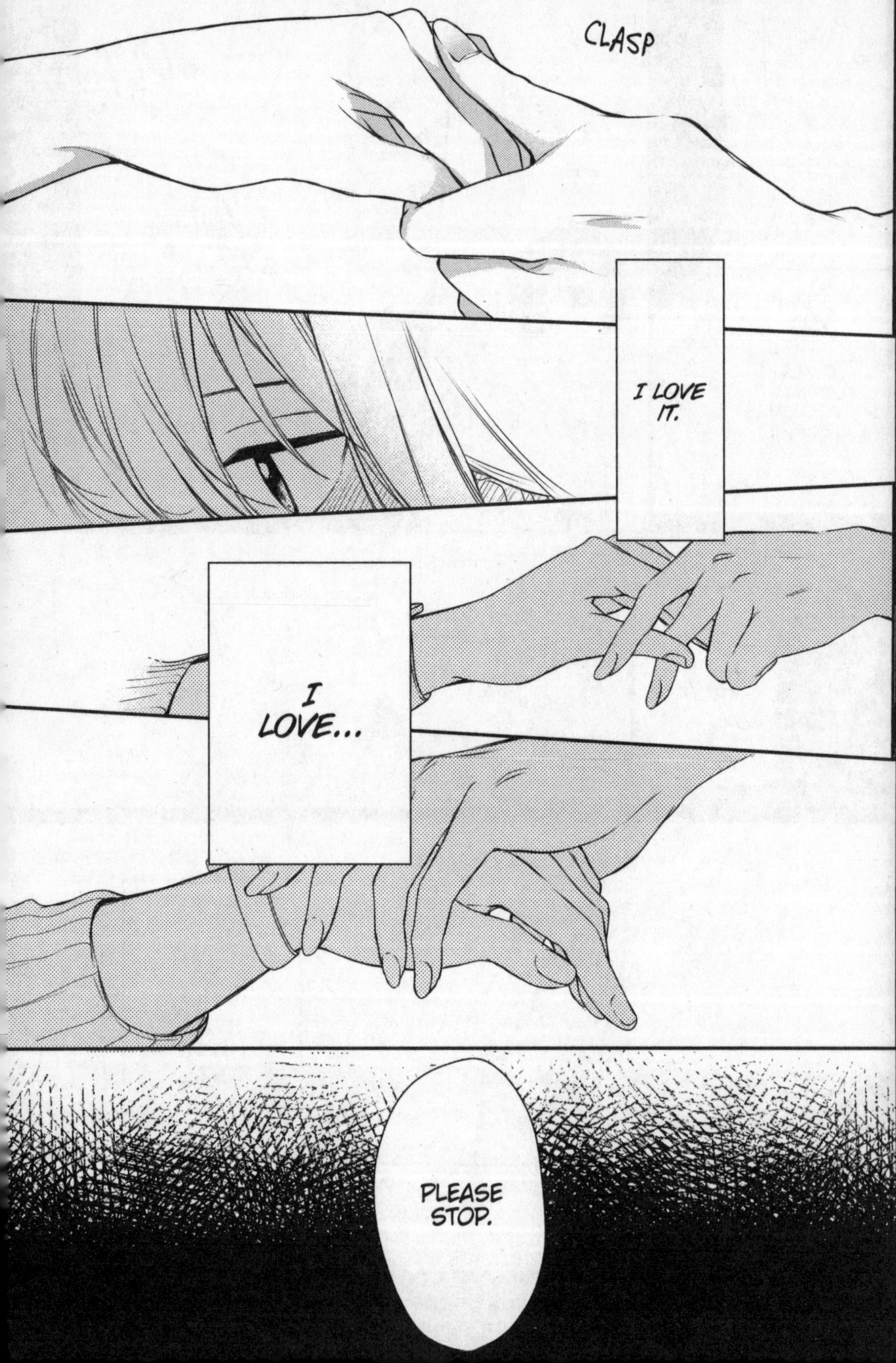
CLASP
I LOVE IT.
I LOVE...
PLEASE STOP.

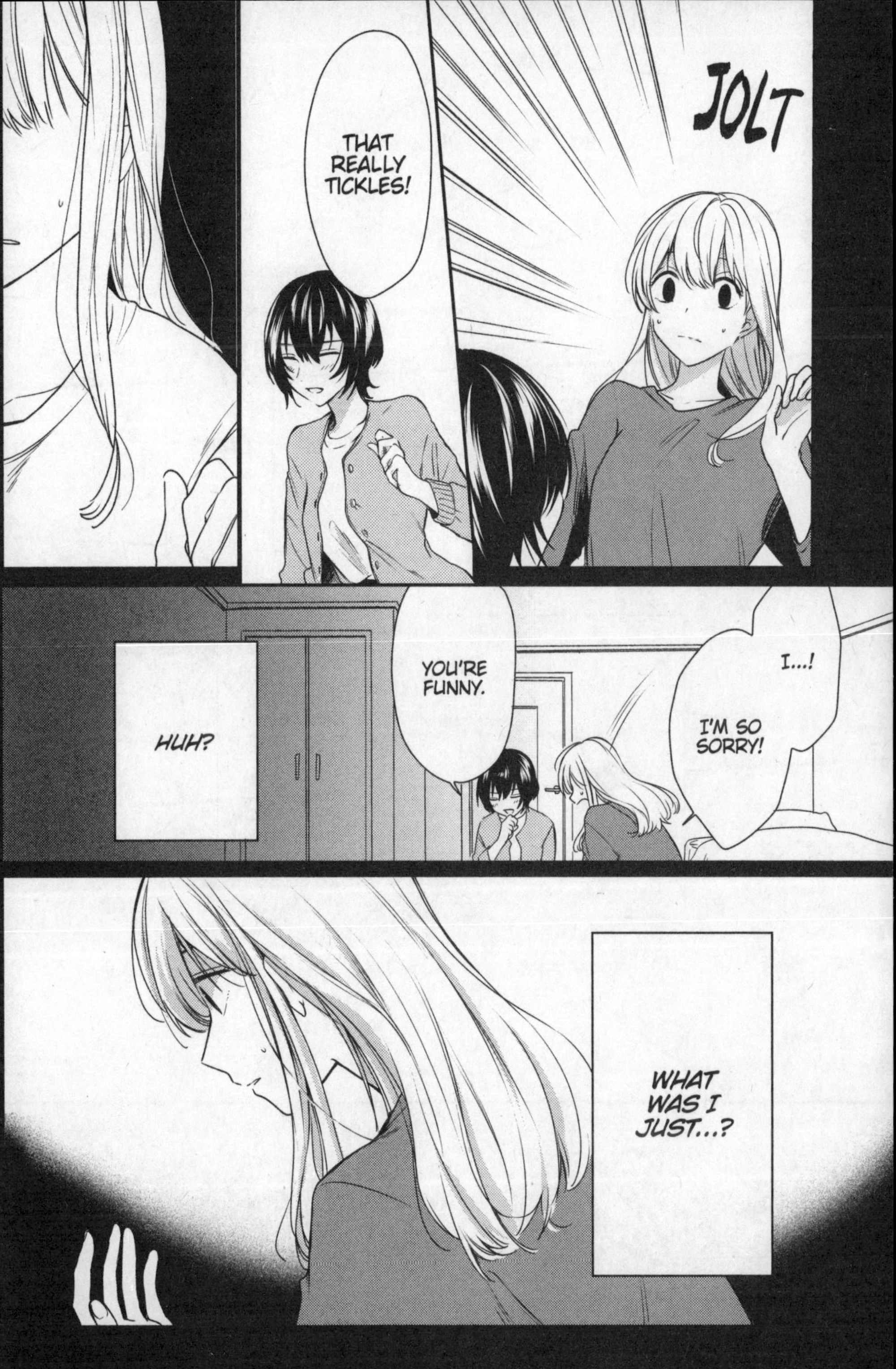
JOLT
THAT REALLY TICKLES!
I...!
I'M SO SORRY!
YOU'RE FUNNY.
HUH?
WHAT WAS I JUST...?

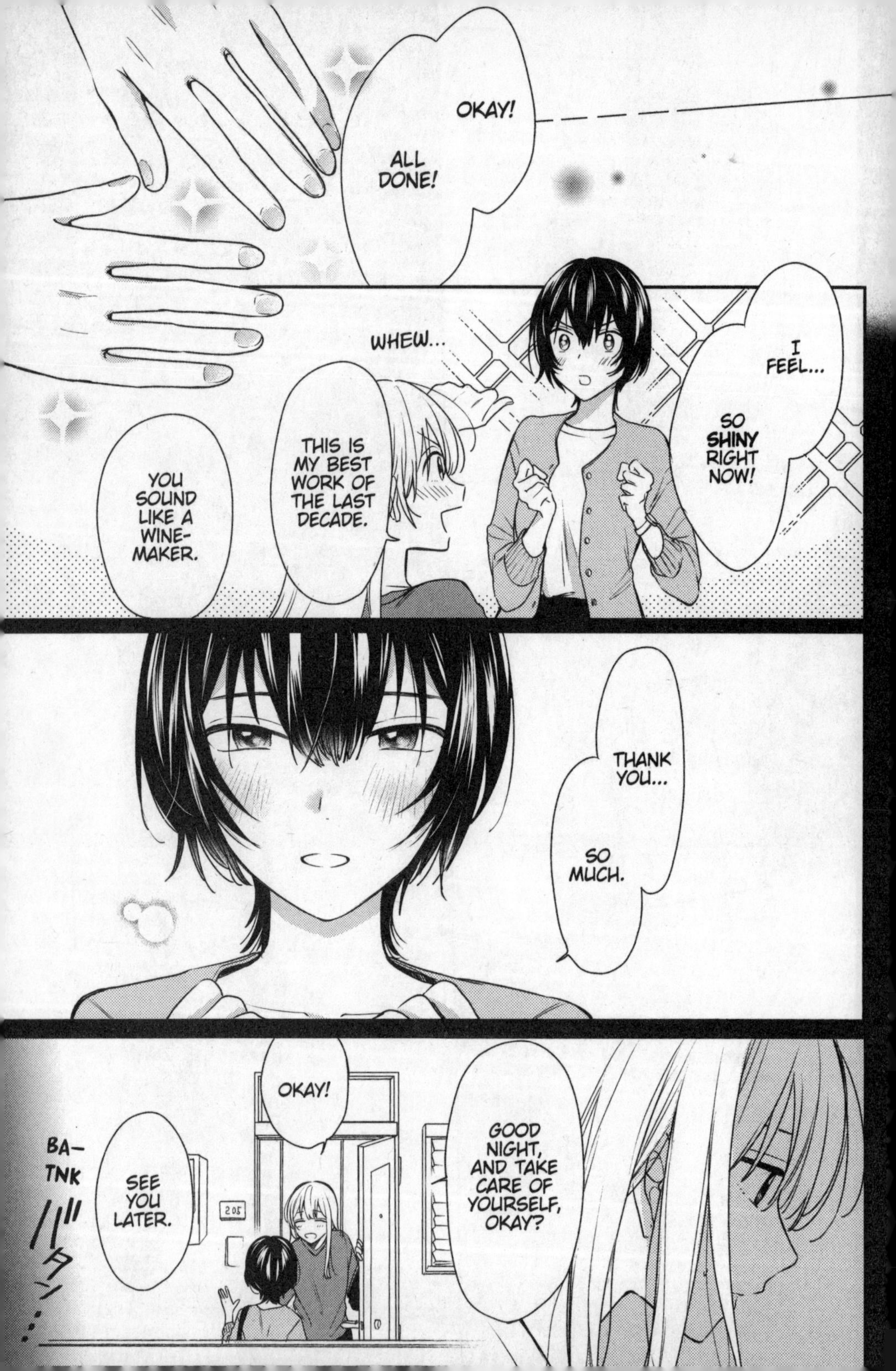

OKAY! ALL DONE!
I FEEL... SO SHINY RIGHT NOW!
WHEW...
THIS IS MY BEST WORK OF THE LAST DECADE.
YOU SOUND LIKE A WINE-MAKER.
THANK YOU... SO MUCH.
GOOD NIGHT, AND TAKE CARE OF YOURSELF, OKAY?
OKAY!
205
SEE YOU LATER.
BA-TNK
バタン…

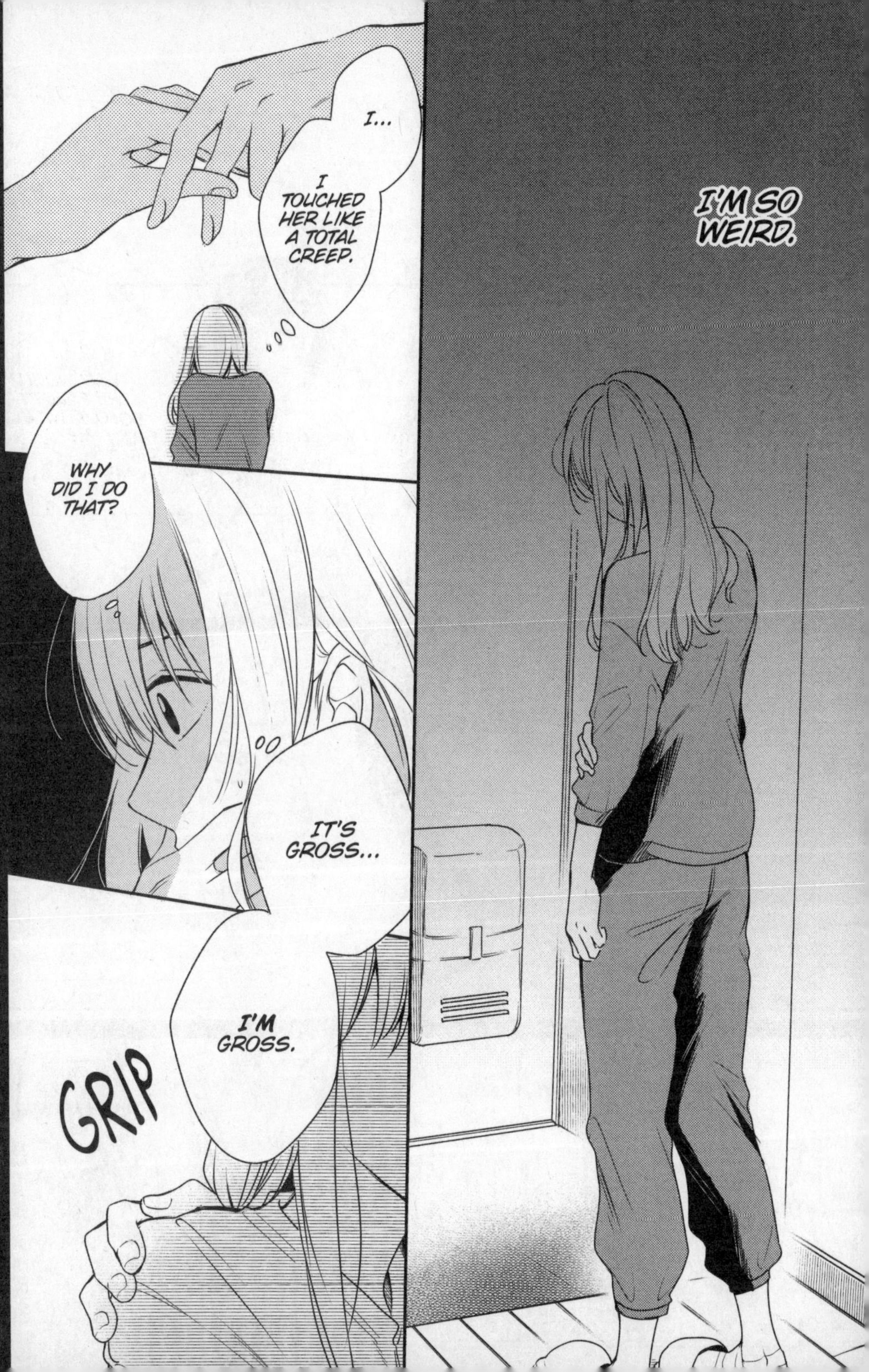
I'M SO WEIRD.
I...
I TOUCHED HER LIKE A TOTAL CREEP.
WHY DID I DO THAT?
IT'S GROSS...
I'M GROSS.
GRIP

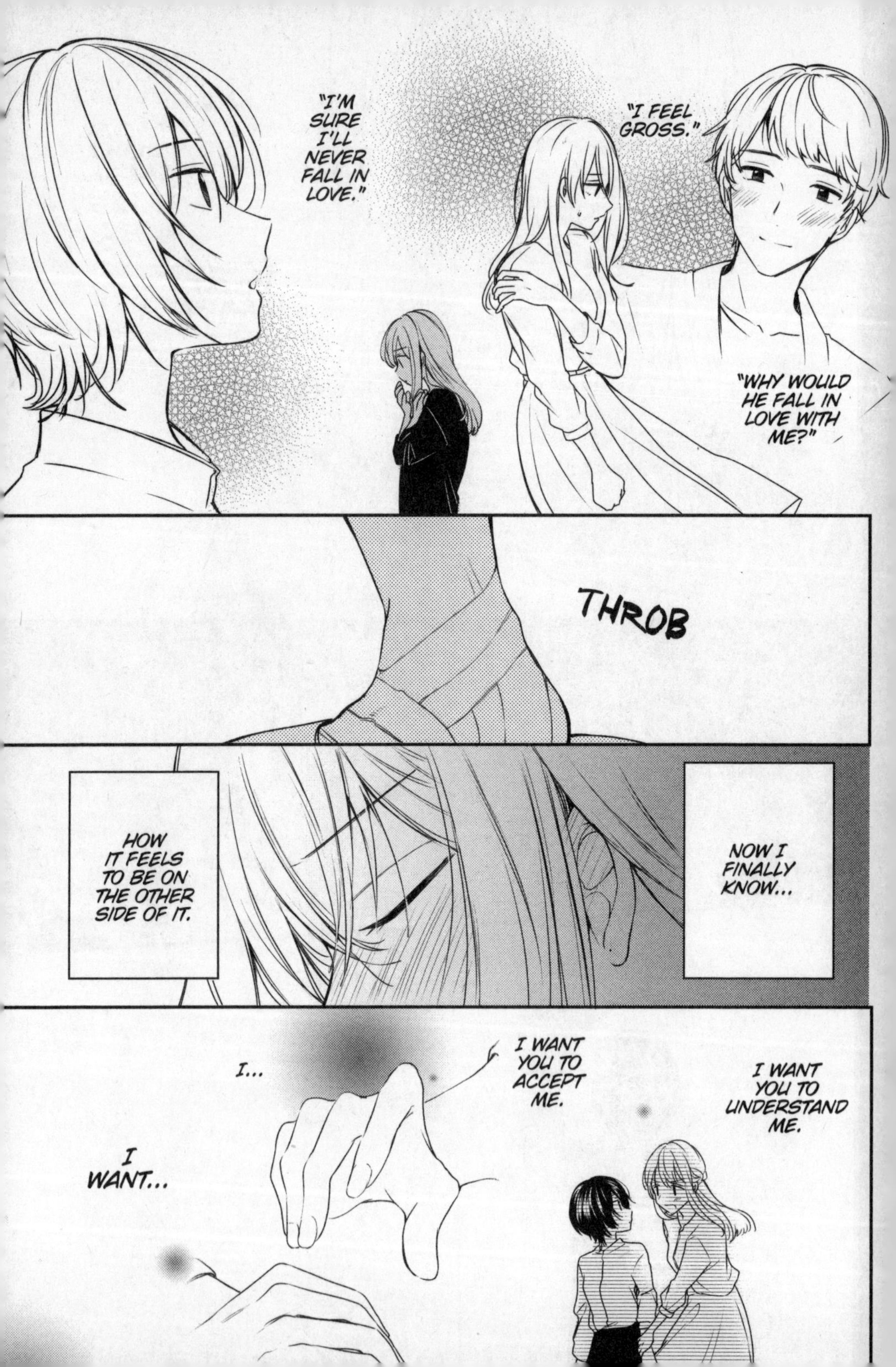
"I FEEL GROSS."
"I'M SURE I'LL NEVER FALL IN LOVE."
"WHY WOULD HE FALL IN LOVE WITH ME?"
THROB
NOW I FINALLY KNOW...
HOW IT FEELS TO BE ON THE OTHER SIDE OF IT.
I WANT YOU TO UNDERSTAND ME.
I WANT YOU TO ACCEPT ME.
I...
I WANT...

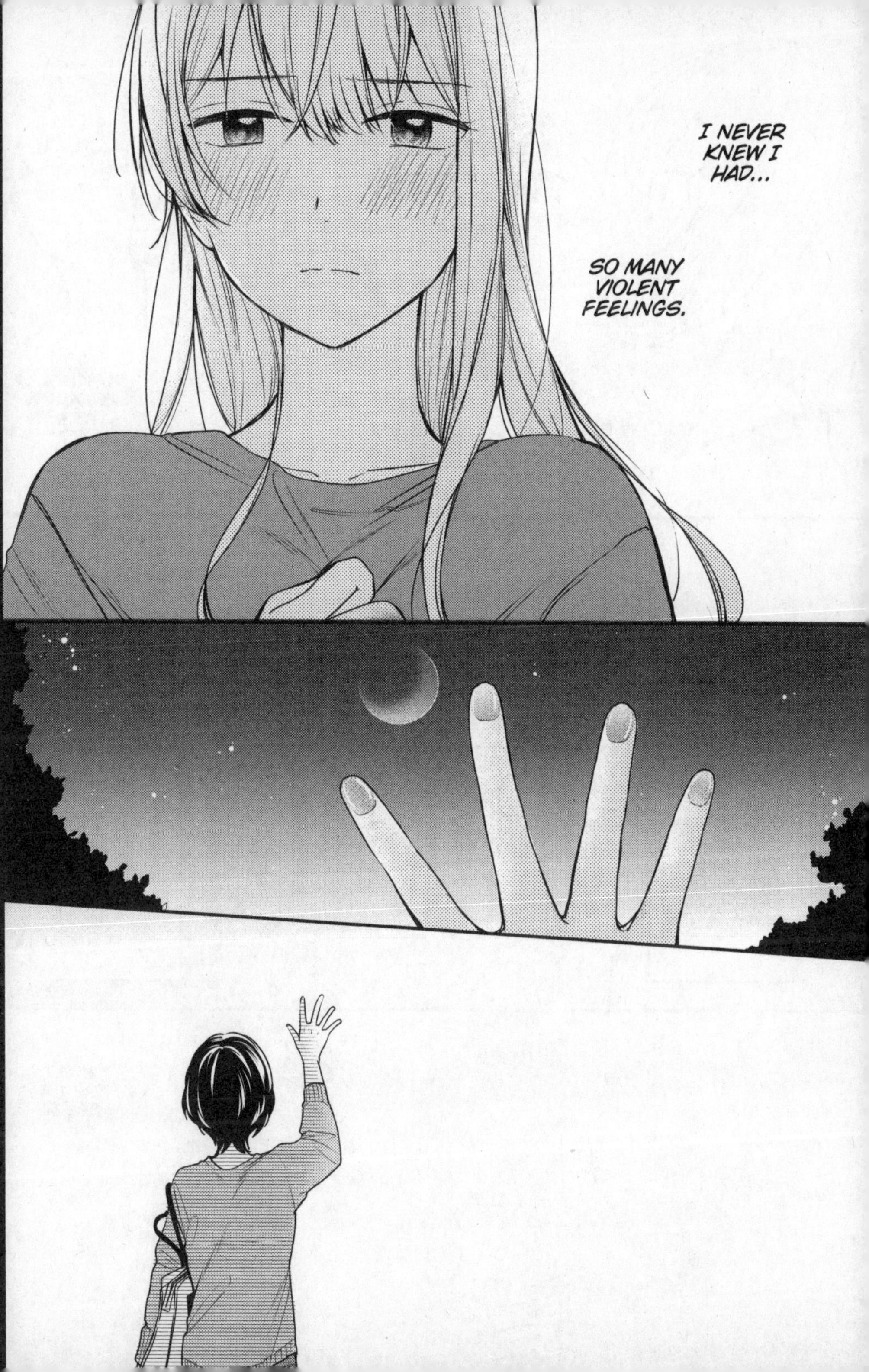
I NEVER KNEW I HAD...
SO MANY VIOLENT FEELINGS.

Doughnuts
Under a Crescent Moon

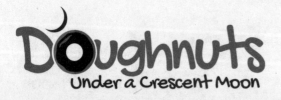

Doughnuts Under a Crescent Moon

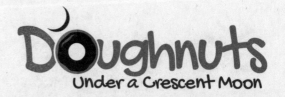

Chapter 9: Hands That Pull Away, Hands That Hold

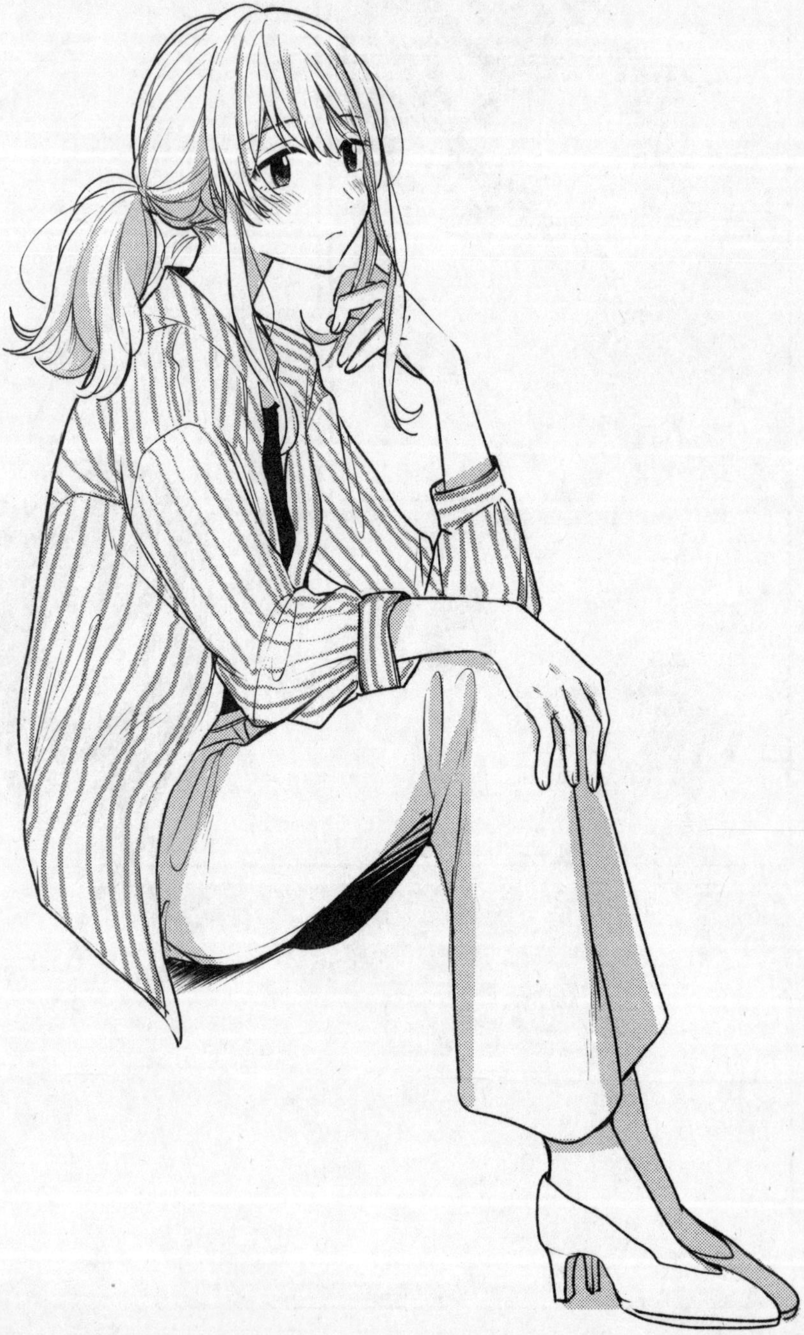

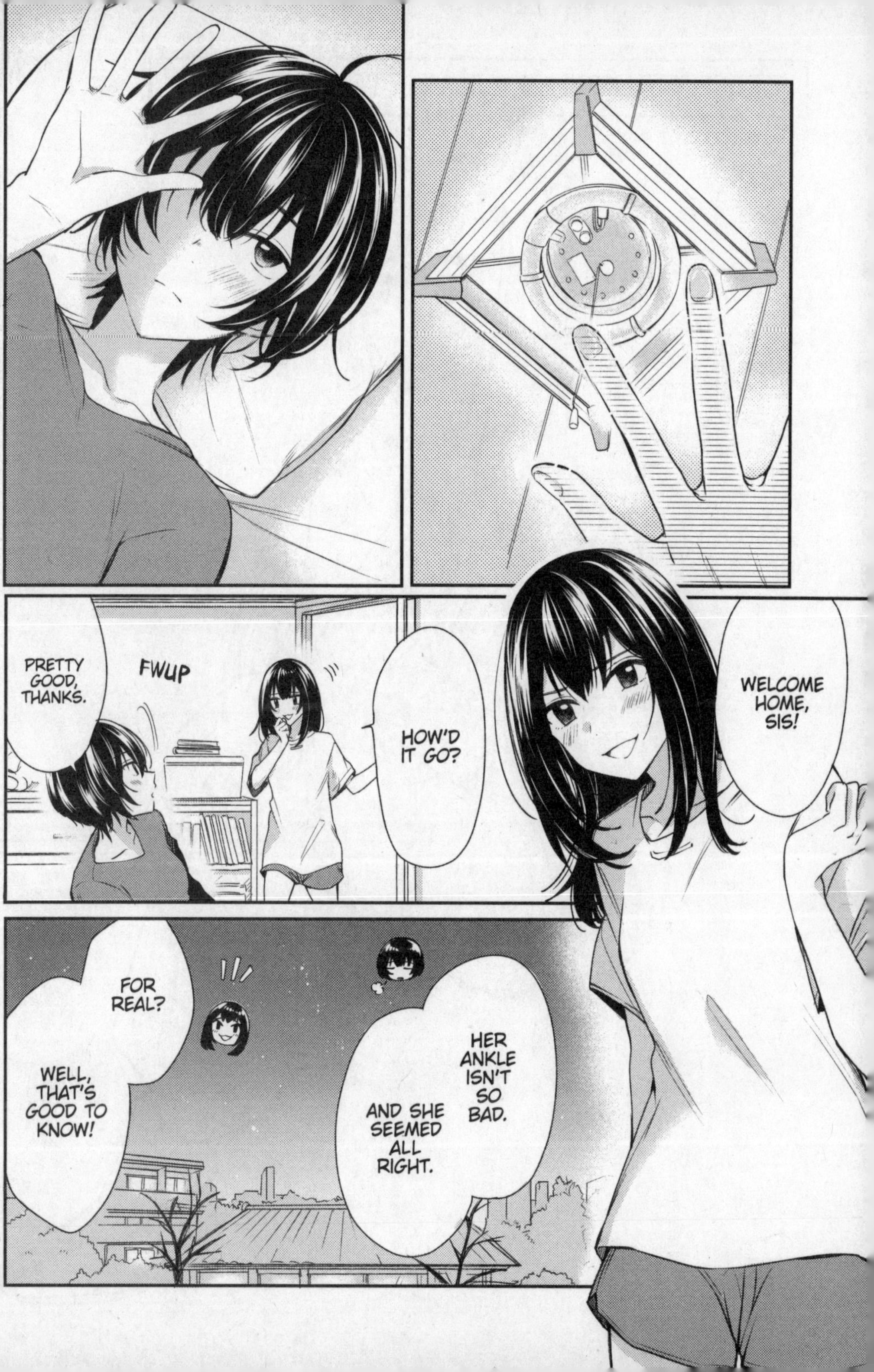
WELCOME HOME, SIS!
HOW'D IT GO?
FWUP
PRETTY GOOD, THANKS.
HER ANKLE ISN'T SO BAD.
AND SHE SEEMED ALL RIGHT.
FOR REAL?
WELL, THAT'S GOOD TO KNOW!

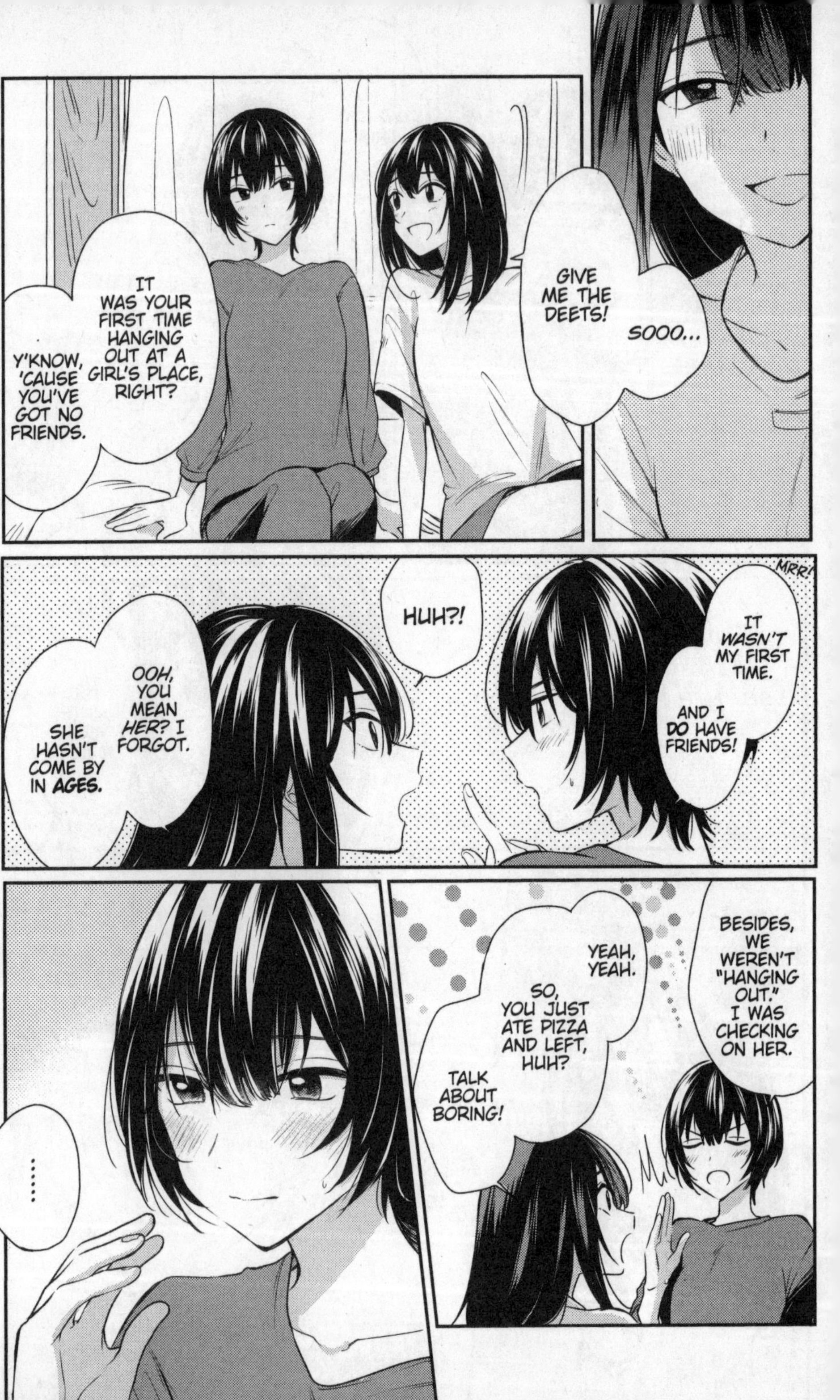
SOOO...
GIVE ME THE DEETS!
IT WAS YOUR FIRST TIME HANGING OUT AT A GIRL'S PLACE, RIGHT?
Y'KNOW, 'CAUSE YOU'VE GOT NO FRIENDS.
MRR!
IT *WASN'T* MY FIRST TIME.
AND I **DO** HAVE FRIENDS!
HUH?!
OOH, YOU MEAN *HER*? I FORGOT.
SHE HASN'T COME BY IN **AGES.**
BESIDES, WE WEREN'T "HANGING OUT." I WAS CHECKING ON HER.
YEAH, YEAH.
SO, YOU JUST ATE PIZZA AND LEFT, HUH?
TALK ABOUT BORING!
......

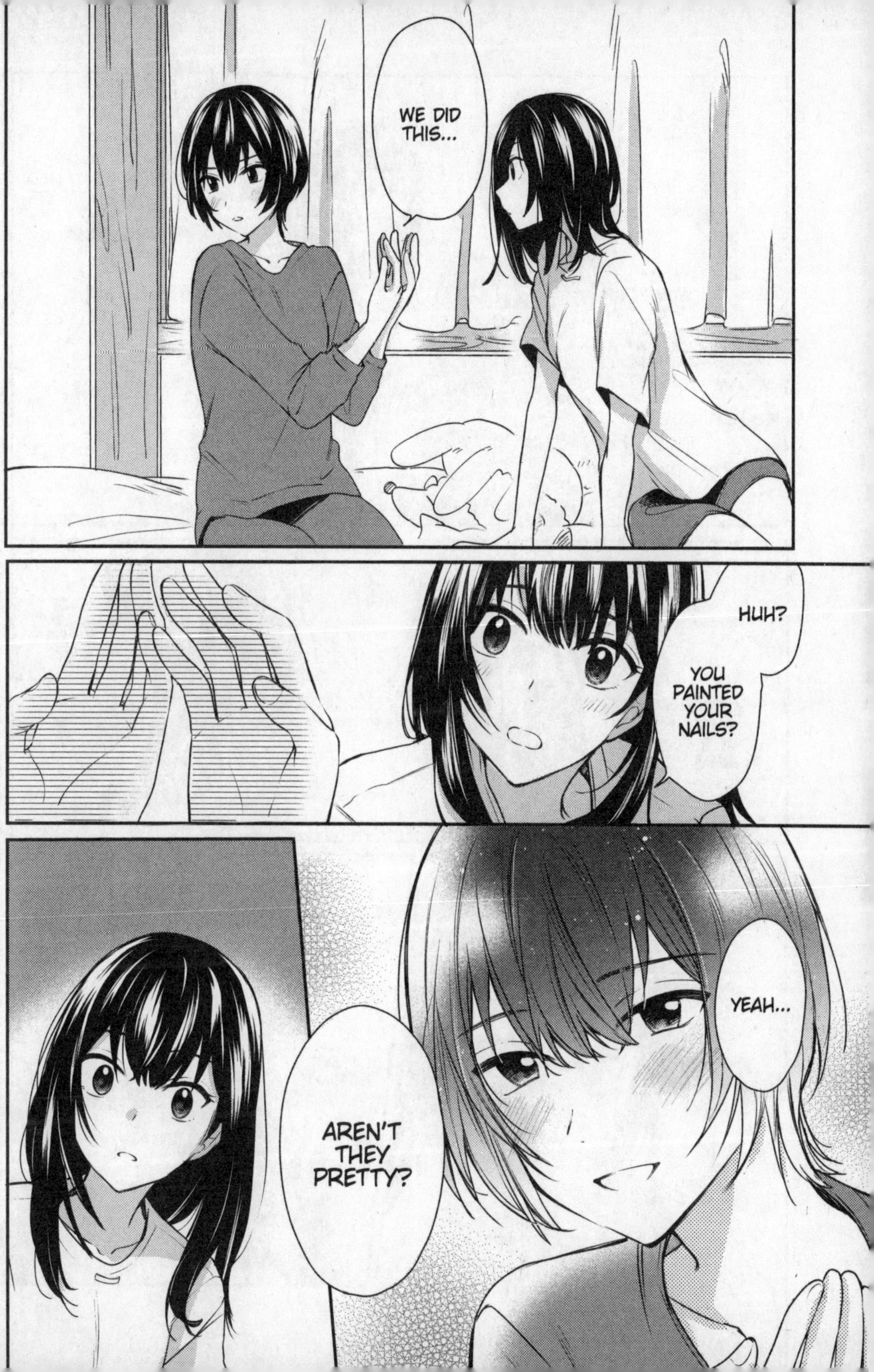
WE DID THIS...
HUH?
YOU PAINTED YOUR NAILS?
YEAH...
AREN'T THEY PRETTY?

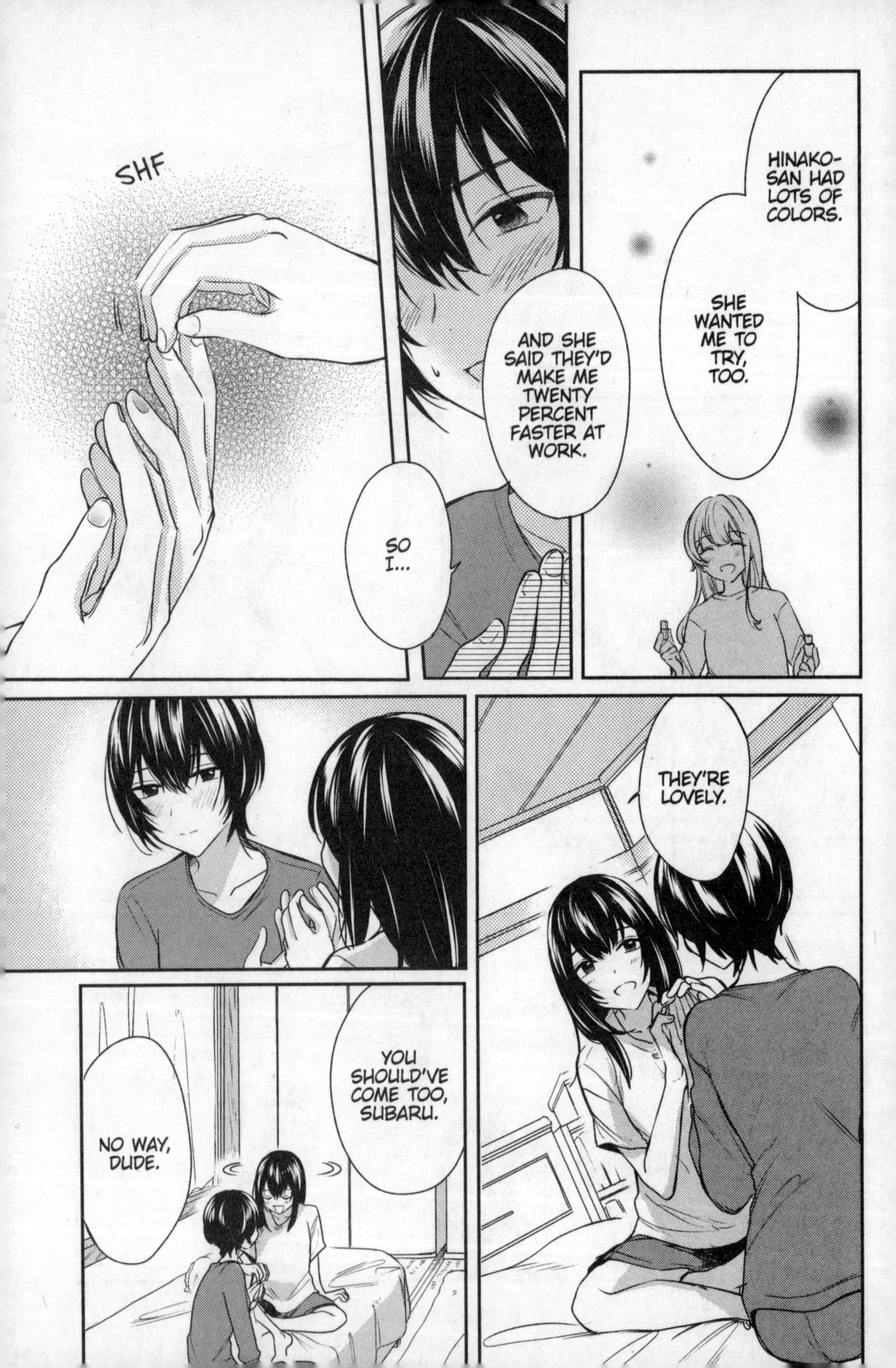
HINAKO-SAN HAD LOTS OF COLORS.
SHE WANTED ME TO TRY, TOO.
AND SHE SAID THEY'D MAKE ME TWENTY PERCENT FASTER AT WORK.
SO I...
SHF
THEY'RE LOVELY.
YOU SHOULD'VE COME TOO, SUBARU.
NO WAY, DUDE.

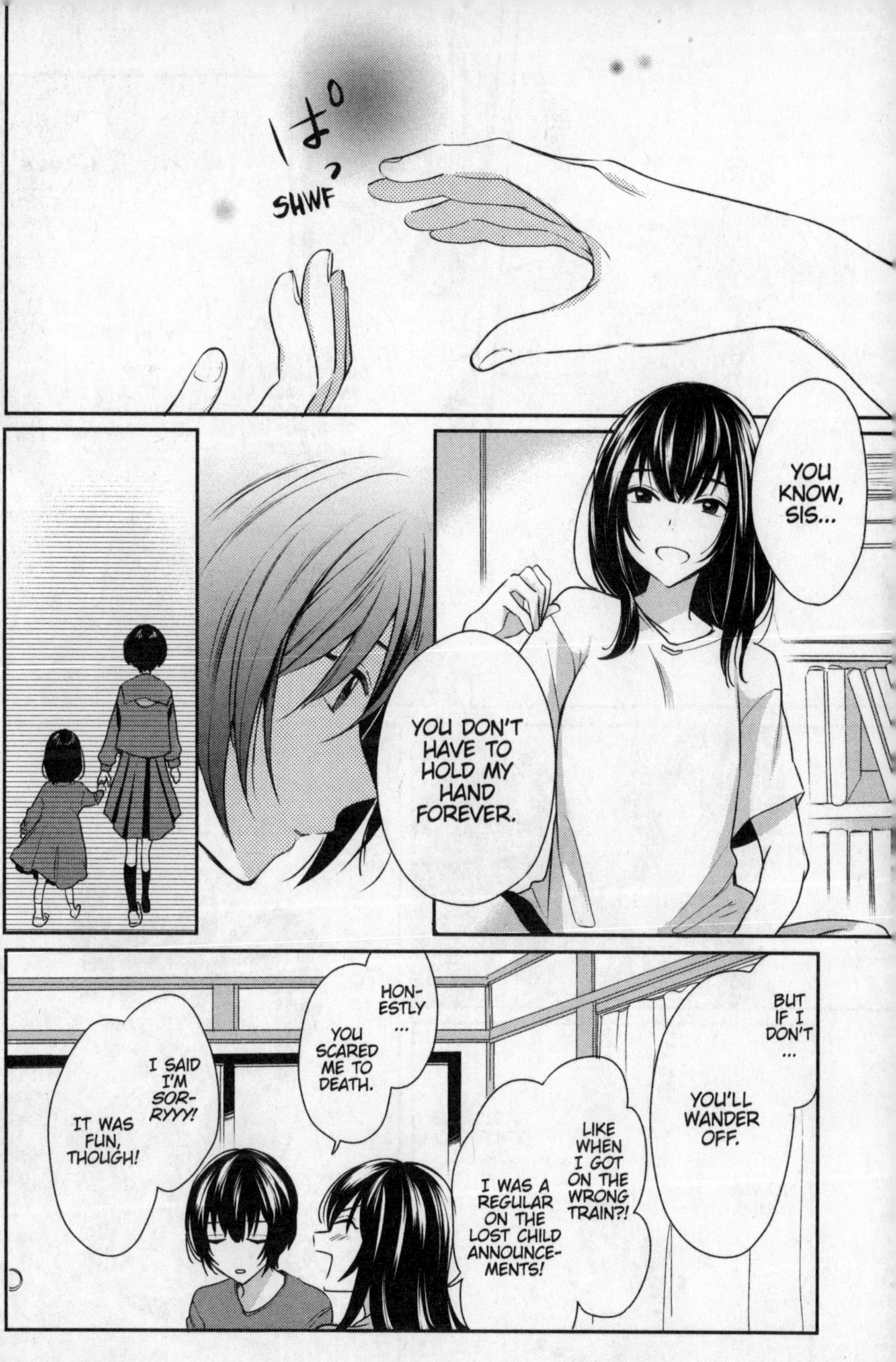
ぱっ
SHWF
YOU KNOW, SIS...
YOU DON'T HAVE TO HOLD MY HAND FOREVER.
BUT IF I DON'T...
YOU'LL WANDER OFF.
LIKE WHEN I GOT ON THE WRONG TRAIN?!
I WAS A REGULAR ON THE LOST CHILD ANNOUNCEMENTS!
HONESTLY...
YOU SCARED ME TO DEATH.
I SAID I'M SORRYYY!
IT WAS FUN, THOUGH!

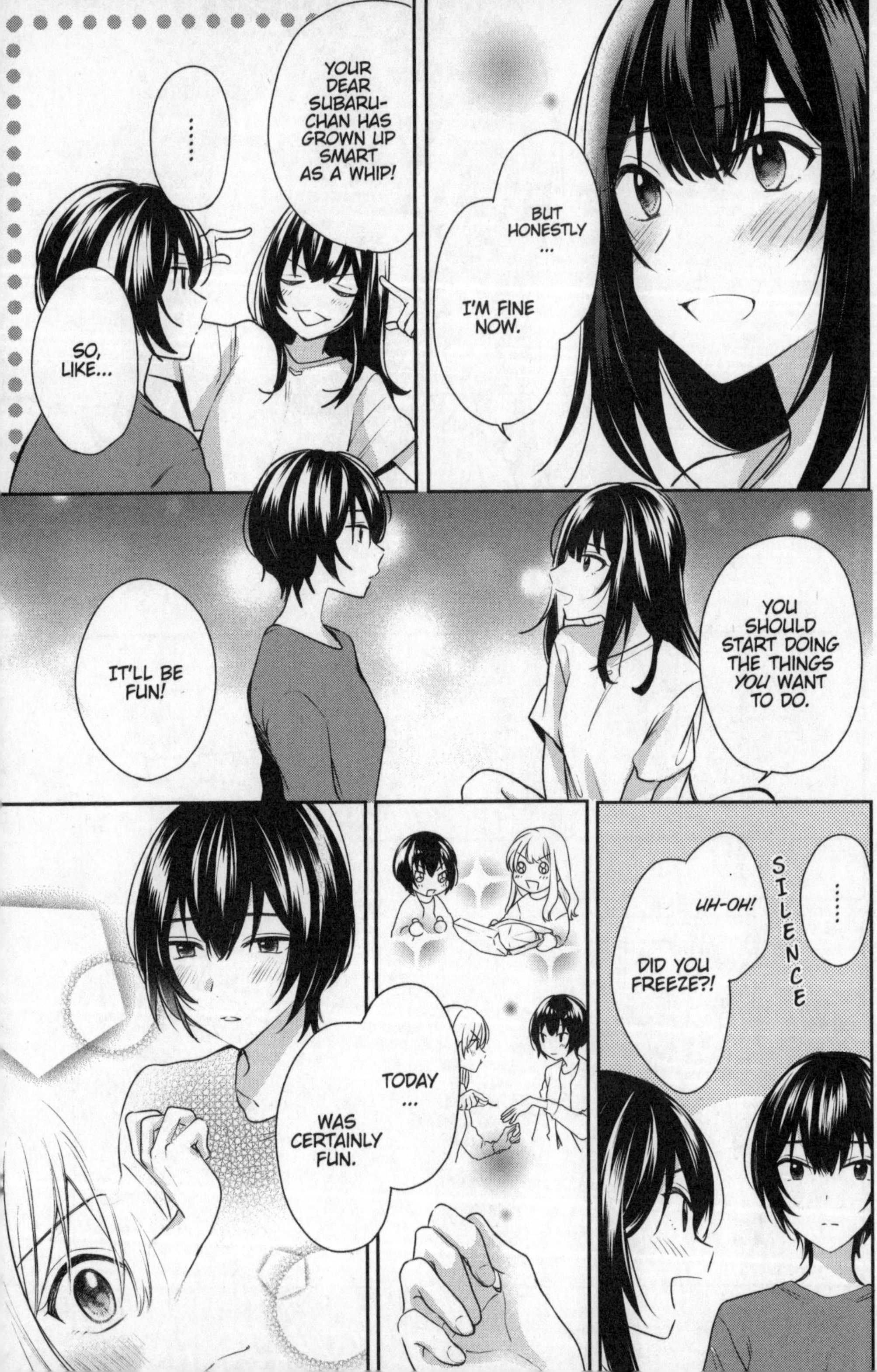
BUT HONESTLY ...
I'M FINE NOW.
YOUR DEAR SUBARU-CHAN HAS GROWN UP SMART AS A WHIP!
......
SO, LIKE...
YOU SHOULD START DOING THE THINGS *YOU* WANT TO DO.
IT'LL BE FUN!
......
SILENCE
UH-OH!
DID YOU FREEZE?!
TODAY ...
WAS CERTAINLY FUN.

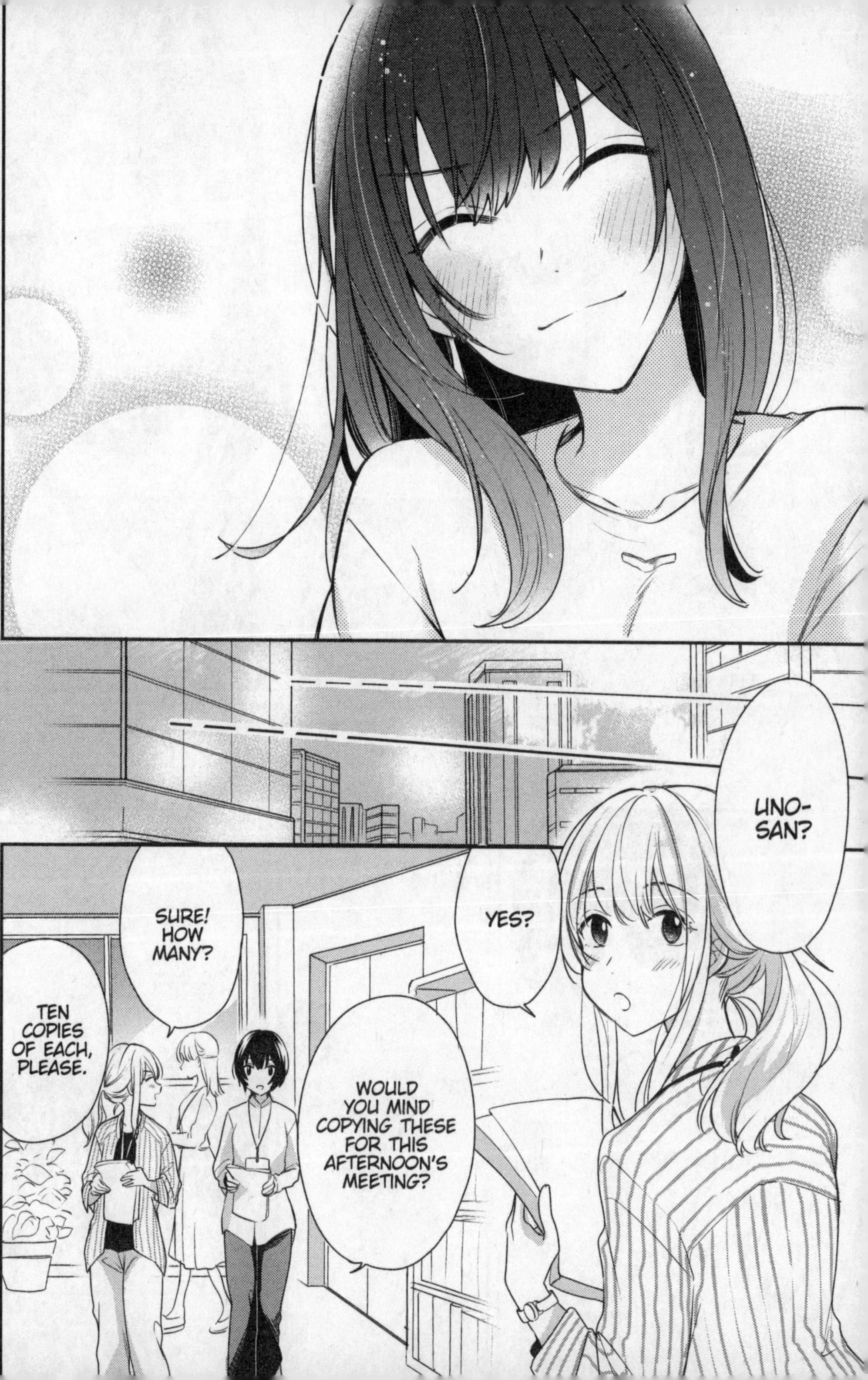
UNO-SAN?
YES?
WOULD YOU MIND COPYING THESE FOR THIS AFTERNOON'S MEETING?
SURE! HOW MANY?
TEN COPIES OF EACH, PLEASE.

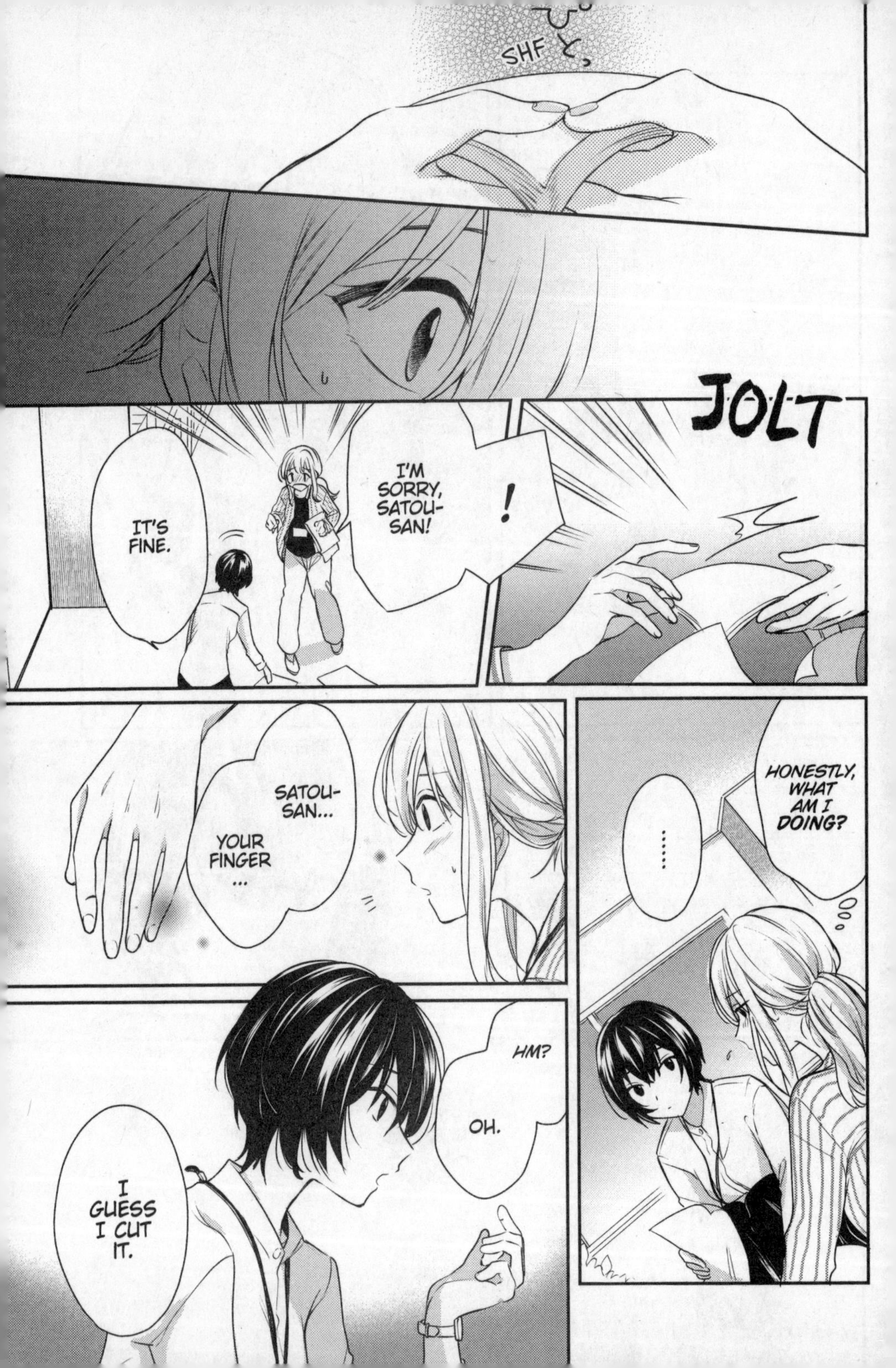
SHF
JOLT
!
I'M SORRY, SATOU-SAN!
IT'S FINE.
HONESTLY, WHAT AM I DOING?
......
SATOU-SAN...
YOUR FINGER ...
HM?
OH.
I GUESS I CUT IT.

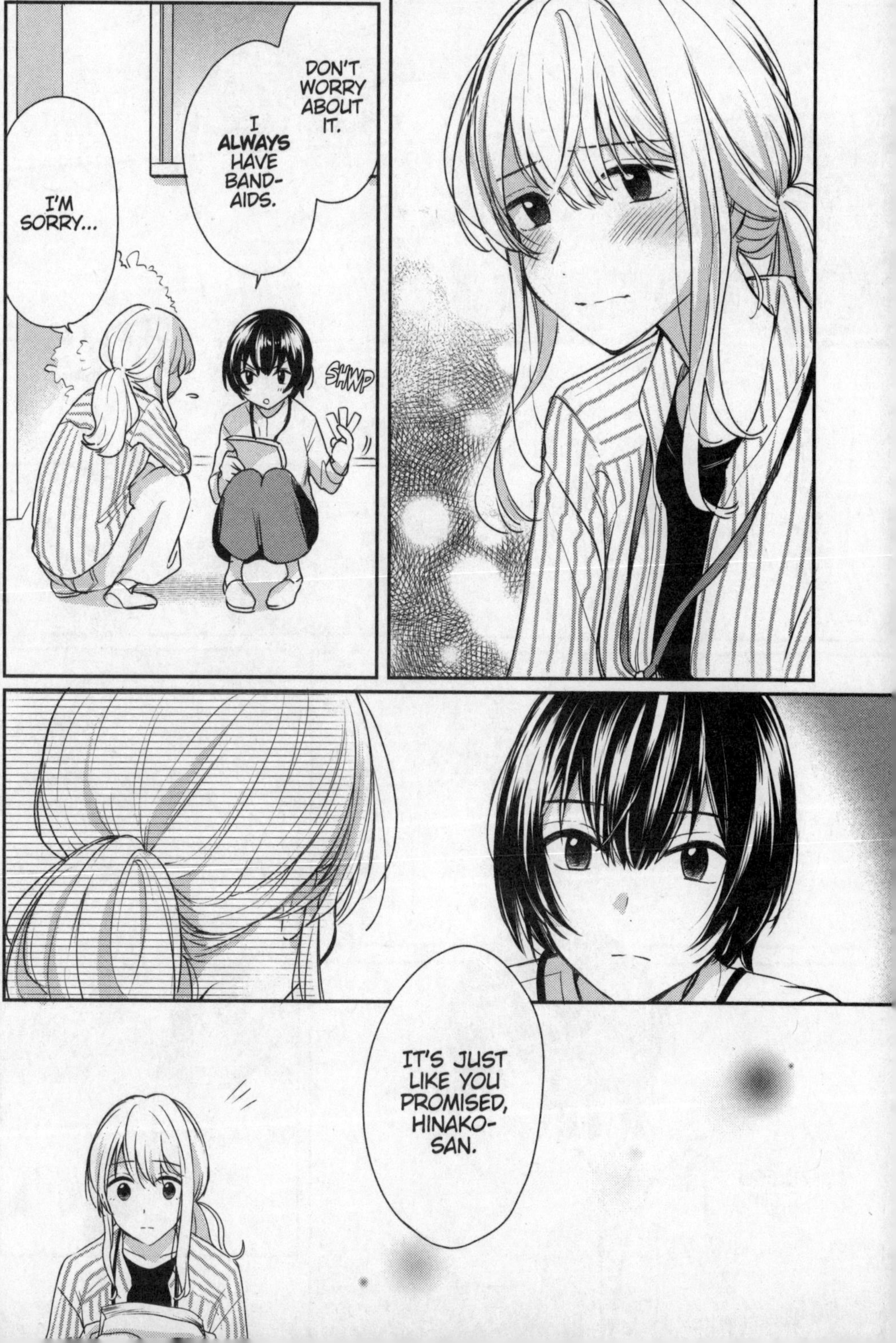
DON'T WORRY ABOUT IT.
I ALWAYS HAVE BAND-AIDS.
I'M SORRY...
SHWP
IT'S JUST LIKE YOU PROMISED, HINAKO-SAN.

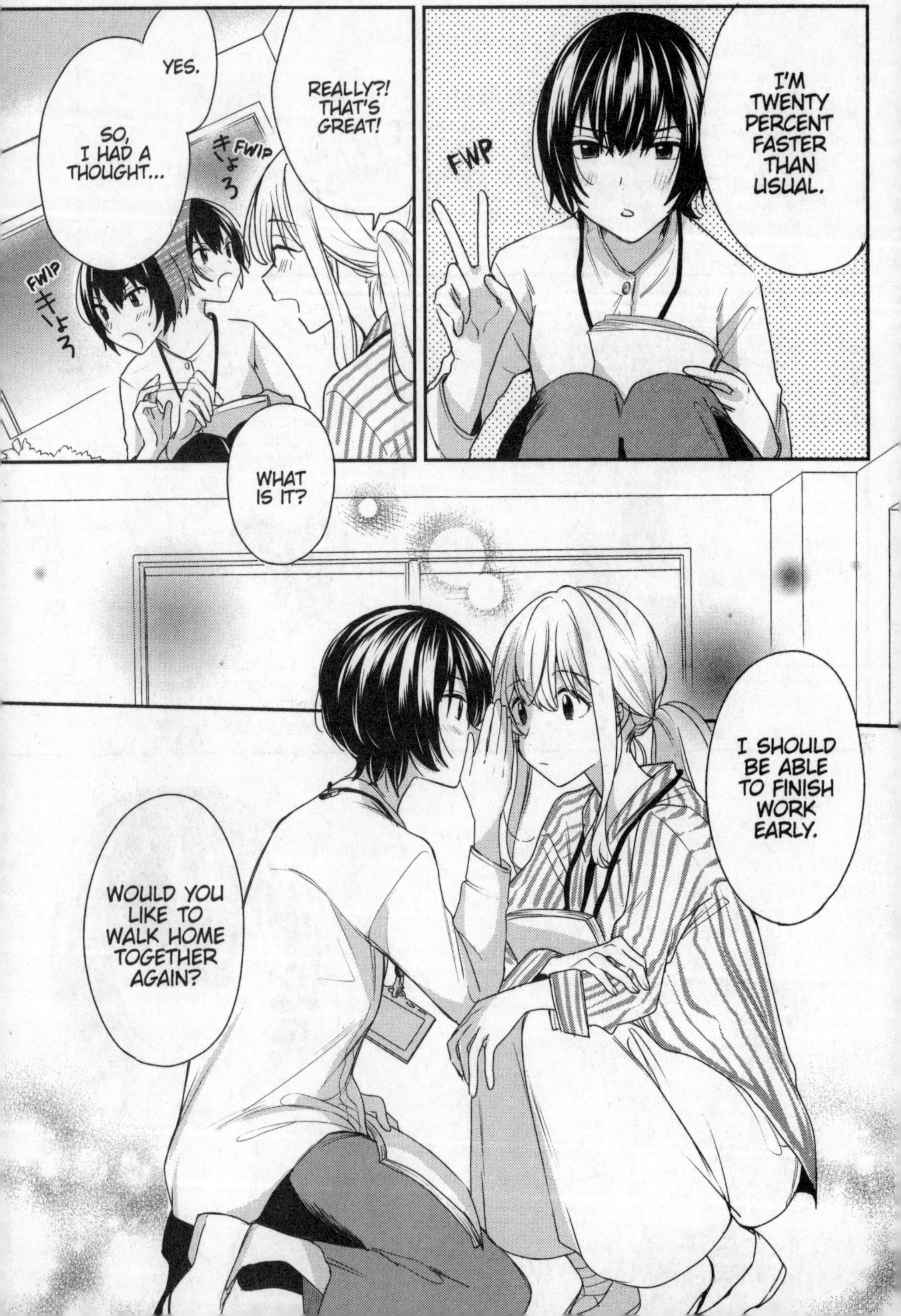
FWP
I'M TWENTY PERCENT FASTER THAN USUAL.
REALLY?! THAT'S GREAT!
YES.
SO, I HAD A THOUGHT...
FWIP きょろ
FWIP キょろ
WHAT IS IT?
I SHOULD BE ABLE TO FINISH WORK EARLY.
WOULD YOU LIKE TO WALK HOME TOGETHER AGAIN?

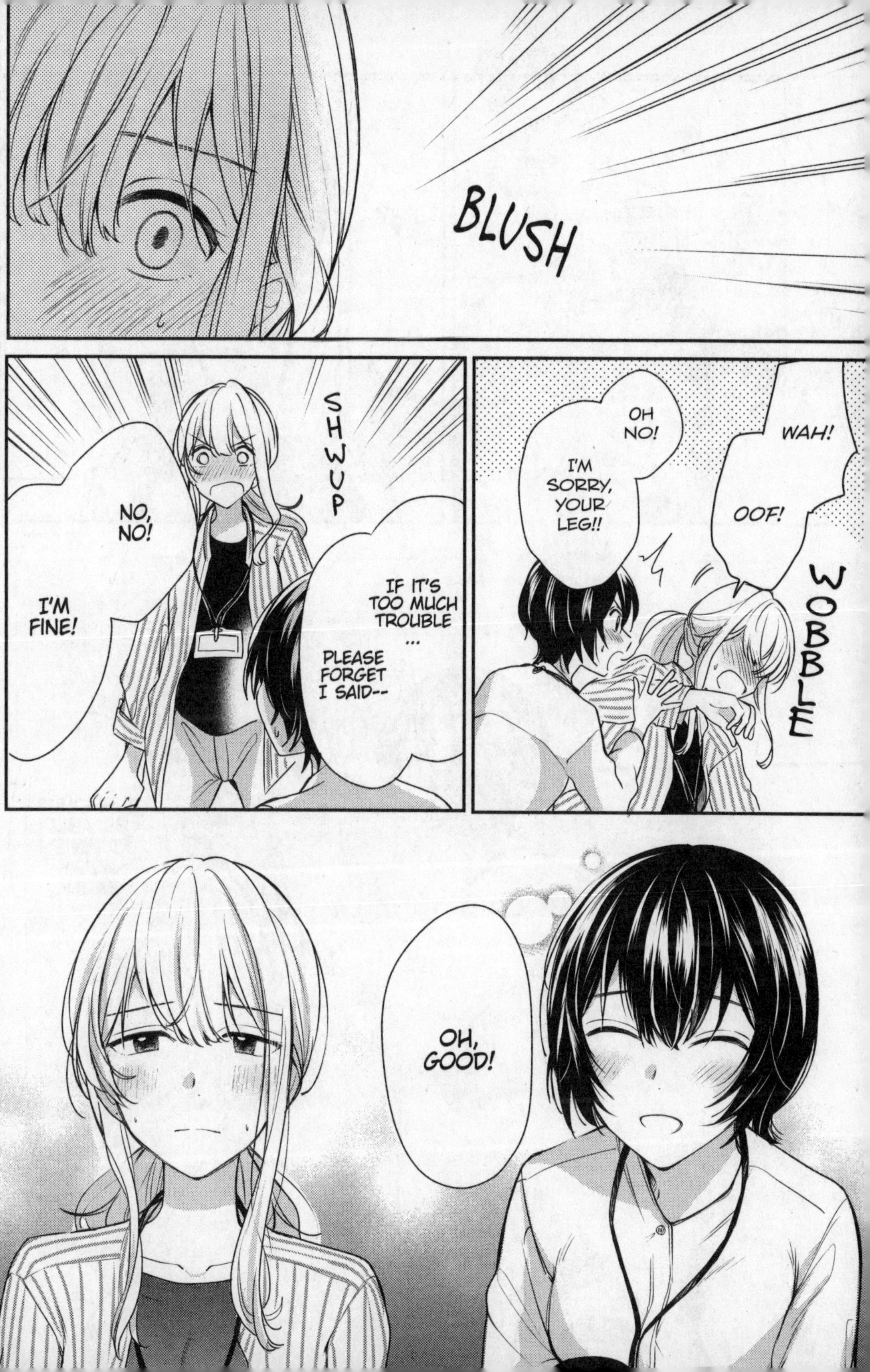
BLUSH
WAH!
OOF!
OH NO!
I'M SORRY, YOUR LEG!!
WOBBLE
SHWUP
IF IT'S TOO MUCH TROUBLE ...
PLEASE FORGET I SAID--
NO, NO!
I'M FINE!
OH, GOOD!

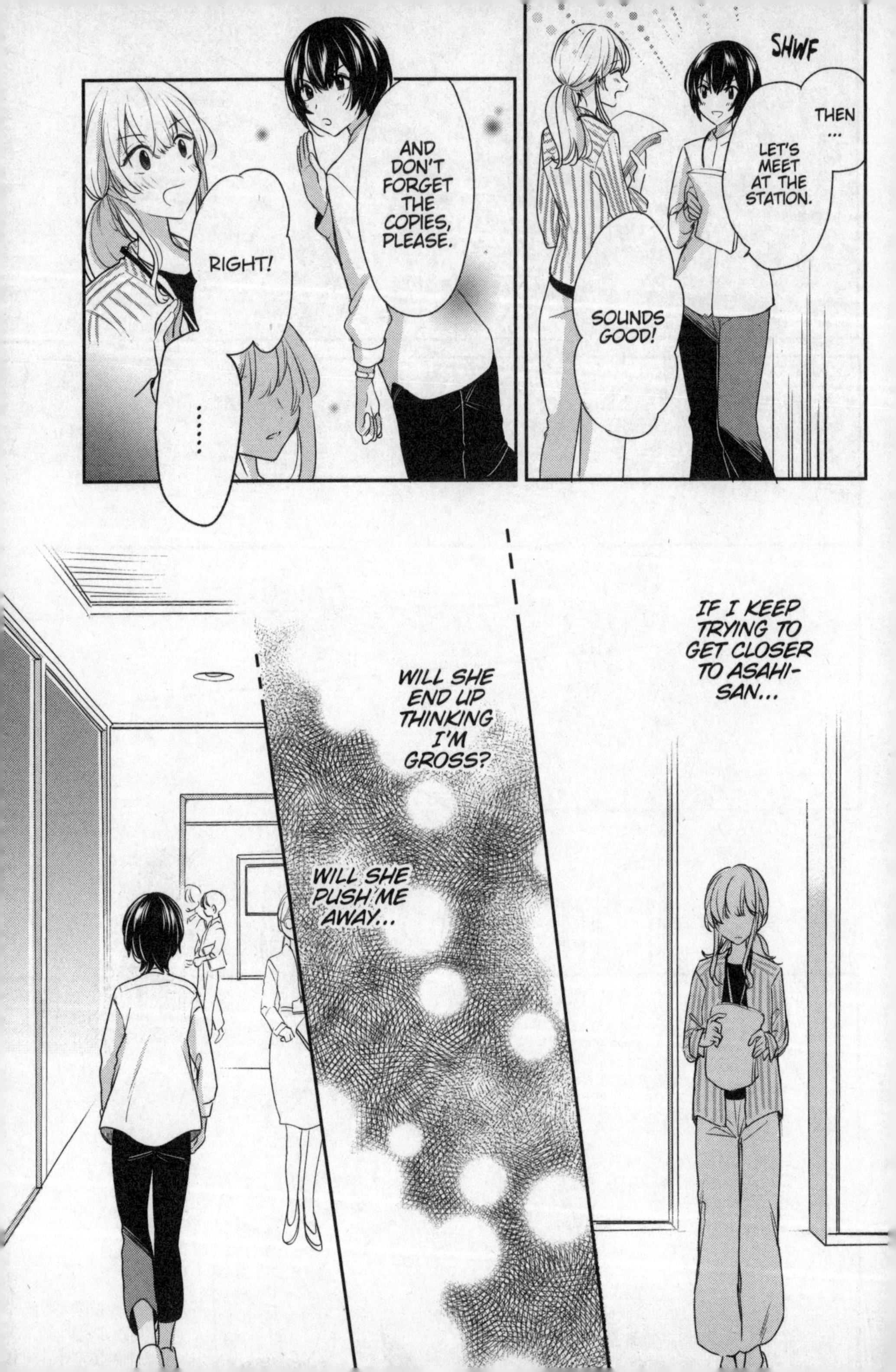
SHWF
THEN... LET'S MEET AT THE STATION.
SOUNDS GOOD!
AND DON'T FORGET THE COPIES, PLEASE.
RIGHT!
......
IF I KEEP TRYING TO GET CLOSER TO ASAHI-SAN...
WILL SHE END UP THINKING I'M GROSS?
WILL SHE PUSH ME AWAY...

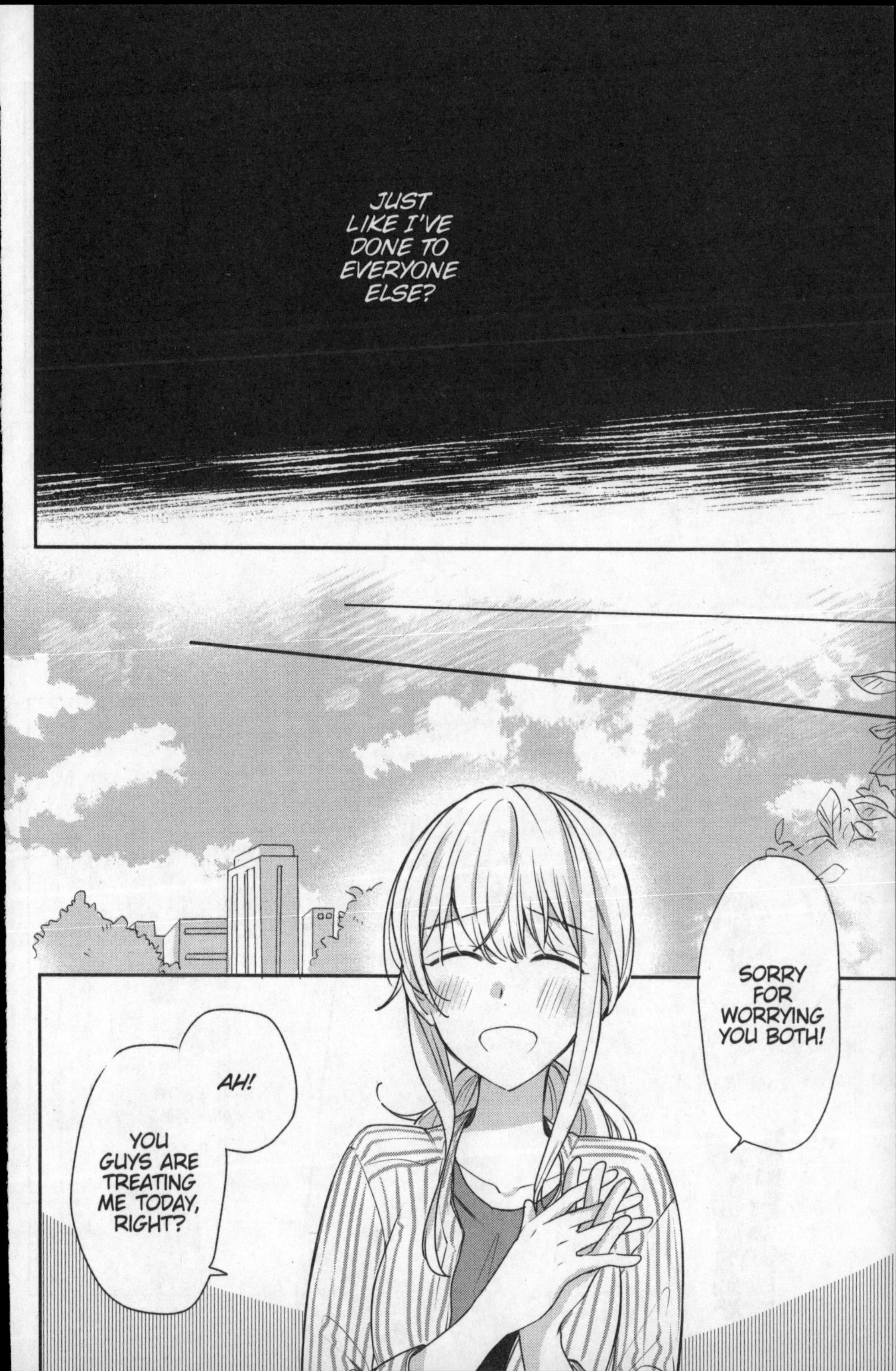

JUST LIKE I'VE DONE TO EVERYONE ELSE?
SORRY FOR WORRYING YOU BOTH!
AH!
YOU GUYS ARE TREATING ME TODAY, RIGHT?

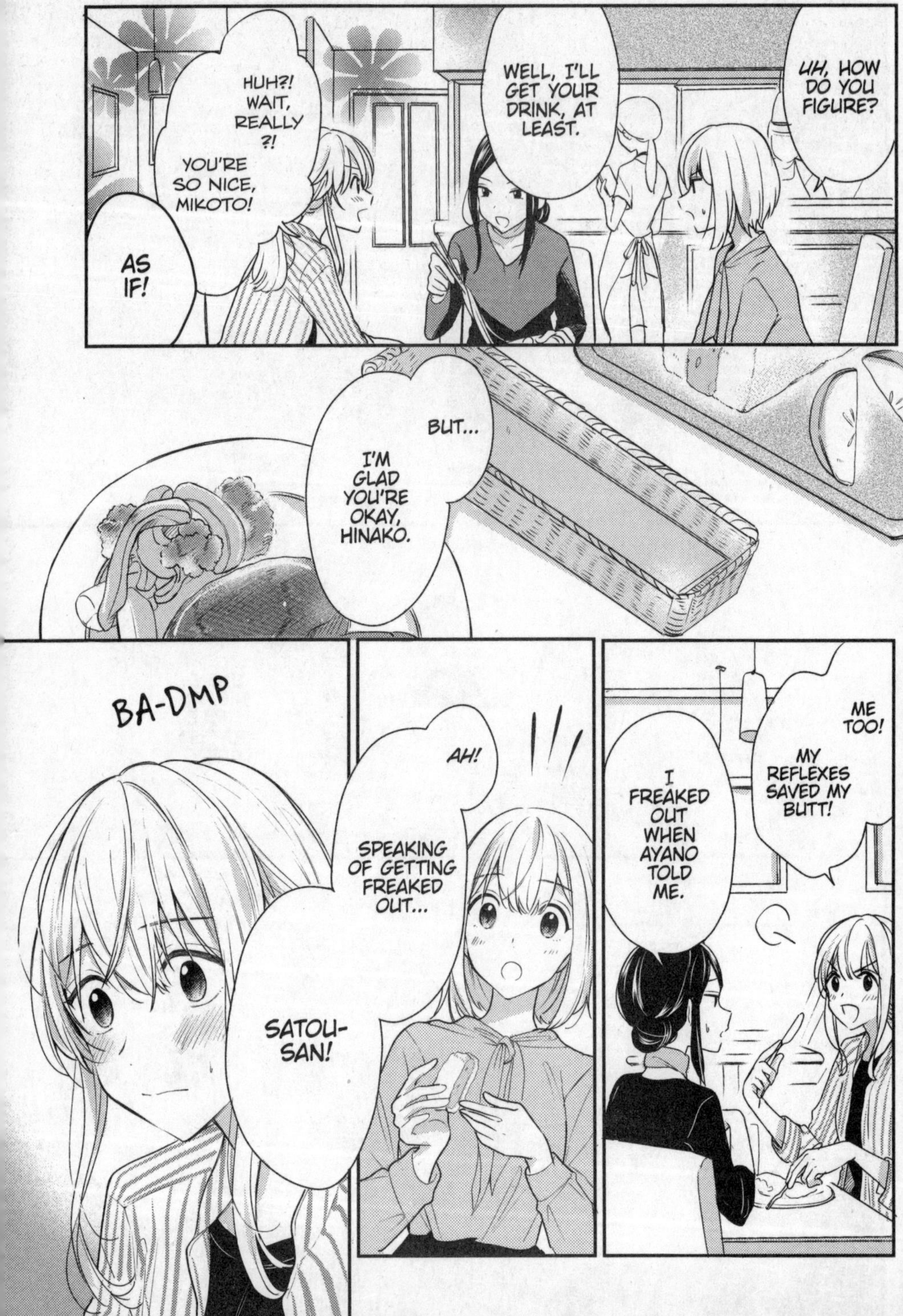
UH, HOW DO YOU FIGURE?
WELL, I'LL GET YOUR DRINK, AT LEAST.
HUH?! WAIT, REALLY?!
YOU'RE SO NICE, MIKOTO!
AS IF!
BUT...
I'M GLAD YOU'RE OKAY, HINAKO.
ME TOO!
MY REFLEXES SAVED MY BUTT!
I FREAKED OUT WHEN AYANO TOLD ME.
AH!
SPEAKING OF GETTING FREAKED OUT...
SATOU-SAN!
BA-DMP

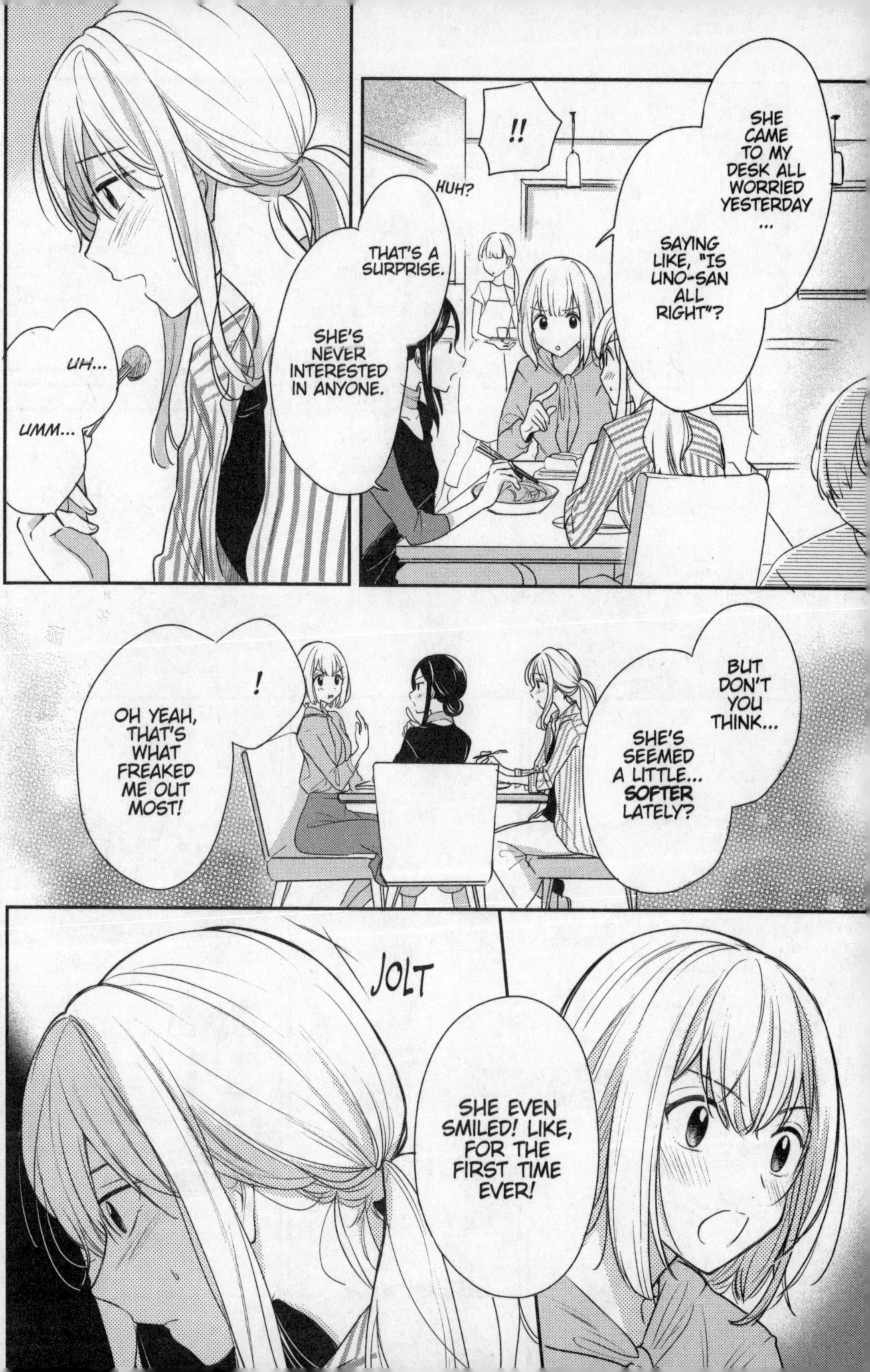
SHE CAME TO MY DESK ALL WORRIED YESTERDAY...
SAYING LIKE, "IS UNO-SAN ALL RIGHT"?
!!
HUH?
THAT'S A SURPRISE.
SHE'S NEVER INTERESTED IN ANYONE.
UH...
UMM...
BUT DON'T YOU THINK...
SHE'S SEEMED A LITTLE... SOFTER LATELY?
!
OH YEAH, THAT'S WHAT FREAKED ME OUT MOST!
JOLT
SHE EVEN SMILED! LIKE, FOR THE FIRST TIME EVER!

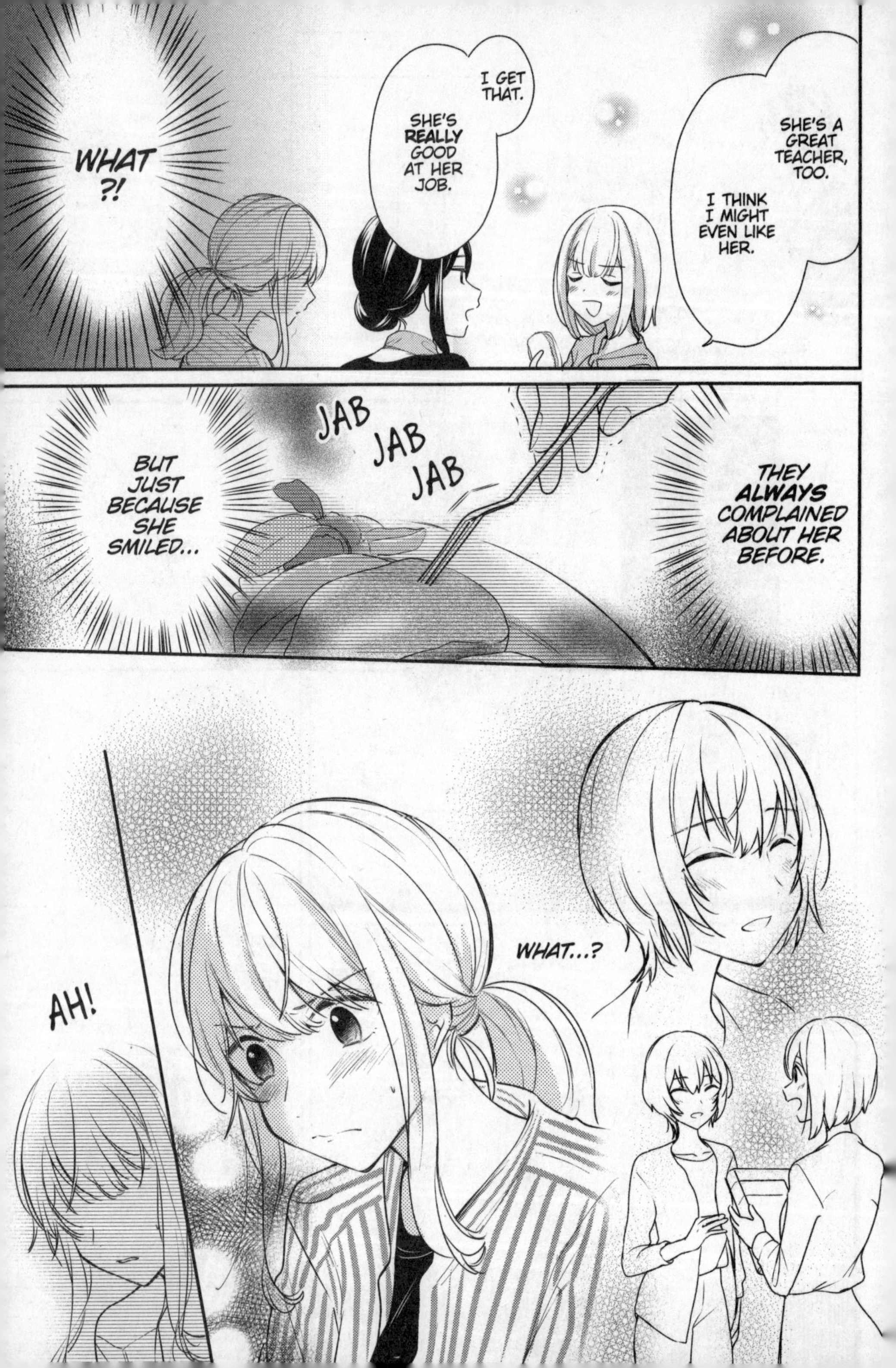
SHE'S A GREAT TEACHER, TOO.
I THINK I MIGHT EVEN LIKE HER.
I GET THAT.
SHE'S **REALLY** GOOD AT HER JOB.
WHAT?!
THEY **ALWAYS** COMPLAINED ABOUT HER BEFORE.
JAB JAB JAB
BUT JUST BECAUSE SHE SMILED...
WHAT...?
AH!

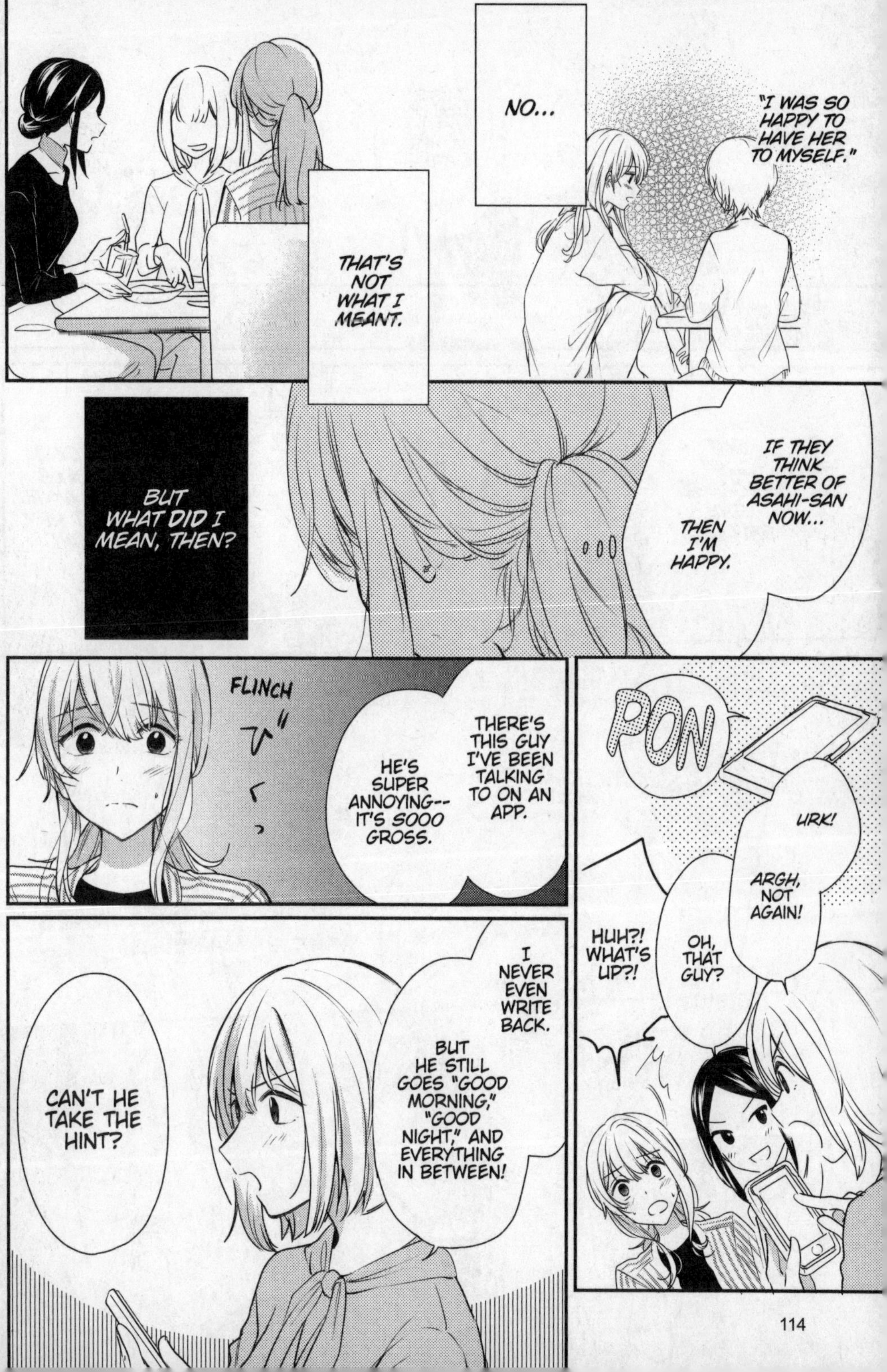
"I WAS SO HAPPY TO HAVE HER TO MYSELF."
NO...
THAT'S NOT WHAT I MEANT.
IF THEY THINK BETTER OF ASAHI-SAN NOW...
THEN I'M HAPPY.
...
BUT WHAT DID I MEAN, THEN?
PON
URK!
ARGH, NOT AGAIN!
OH, THAT GUY?
HUH?! WHAT'S UP?!
FLINCH
THERE'S THIS GUY I'VE BEEN TALKING TO ON AN APP.
HE'S SUPER ANNOYING-- IT'S SOOO GROSS.
I NEVER EVEN WRITE BACK.
BUT HE STILL GOES "GOOD MORNING," "GOOD NIGHT," AND EVERYTHING IN BETWEEN!
CAN'T HE TAKE THE HINT?

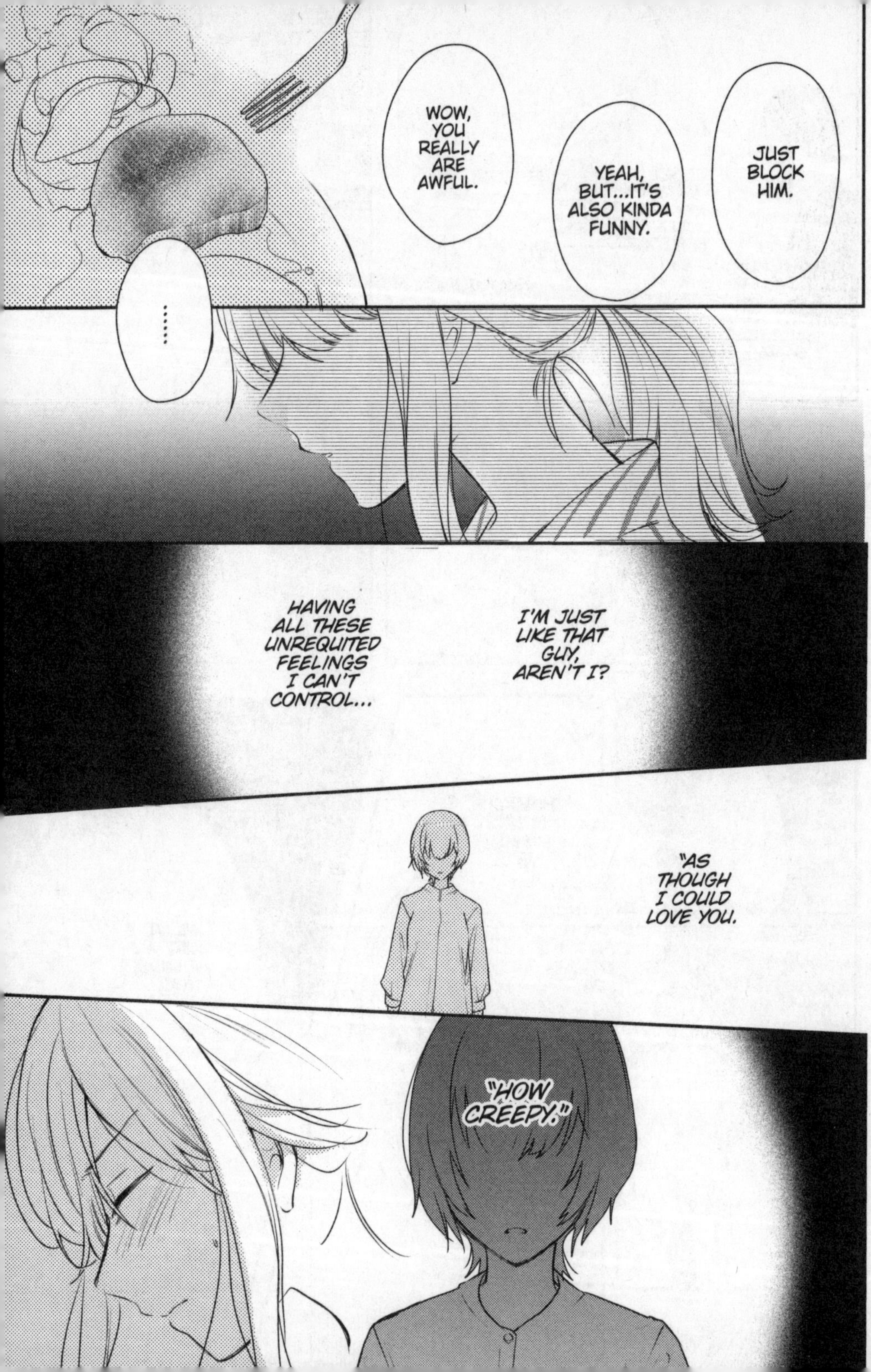
JUST BLOCK HIM.
YEAH, BUT...IT'S ALSO KINDA FUNNY.
WOW, YOU REALLY ARE AWFUL.
......
I'M JUST LIKE THAT GUY, AREN'T I?
HAVING ALL THESE UNREQUITED FEELINGS I CAN'T CONTROL...
"AS THOUGH I COULD LOVE YOU.
"HOW CREEPY."

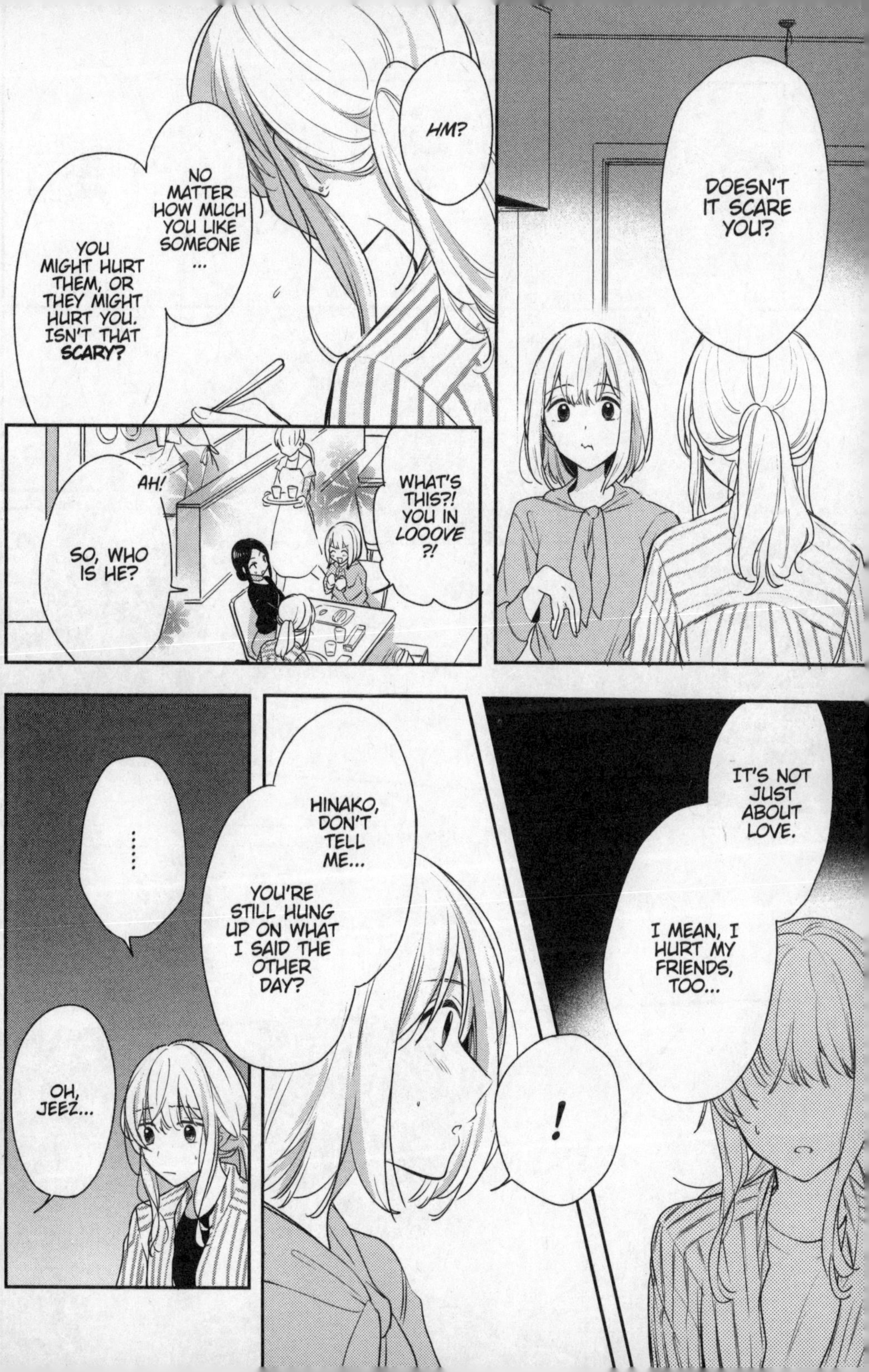
DOESN'T IT SCARE YOU?
HM?
NO MATTER HOW MUCH YOU LIKE SOMEONE ...
YOU MIGHT HURT THEM, OR THEY MIGHT HURT YOU. ISN'T THAT **SCARY?**
WHAT'S THIS?! YOU IN LOOOVE ?!
AH!
SO, WHO IS HE?
IT'S NOT JUST ABOUT LOVE.
I MEAN, I HURT MY FRIENDS, TOO...
HINAKO, DON'T TELL ME...
YOU'RE STILL HUNG UP ON WHAT I SAID THE OTHER DAY?
!
......
OH, JEEZ...

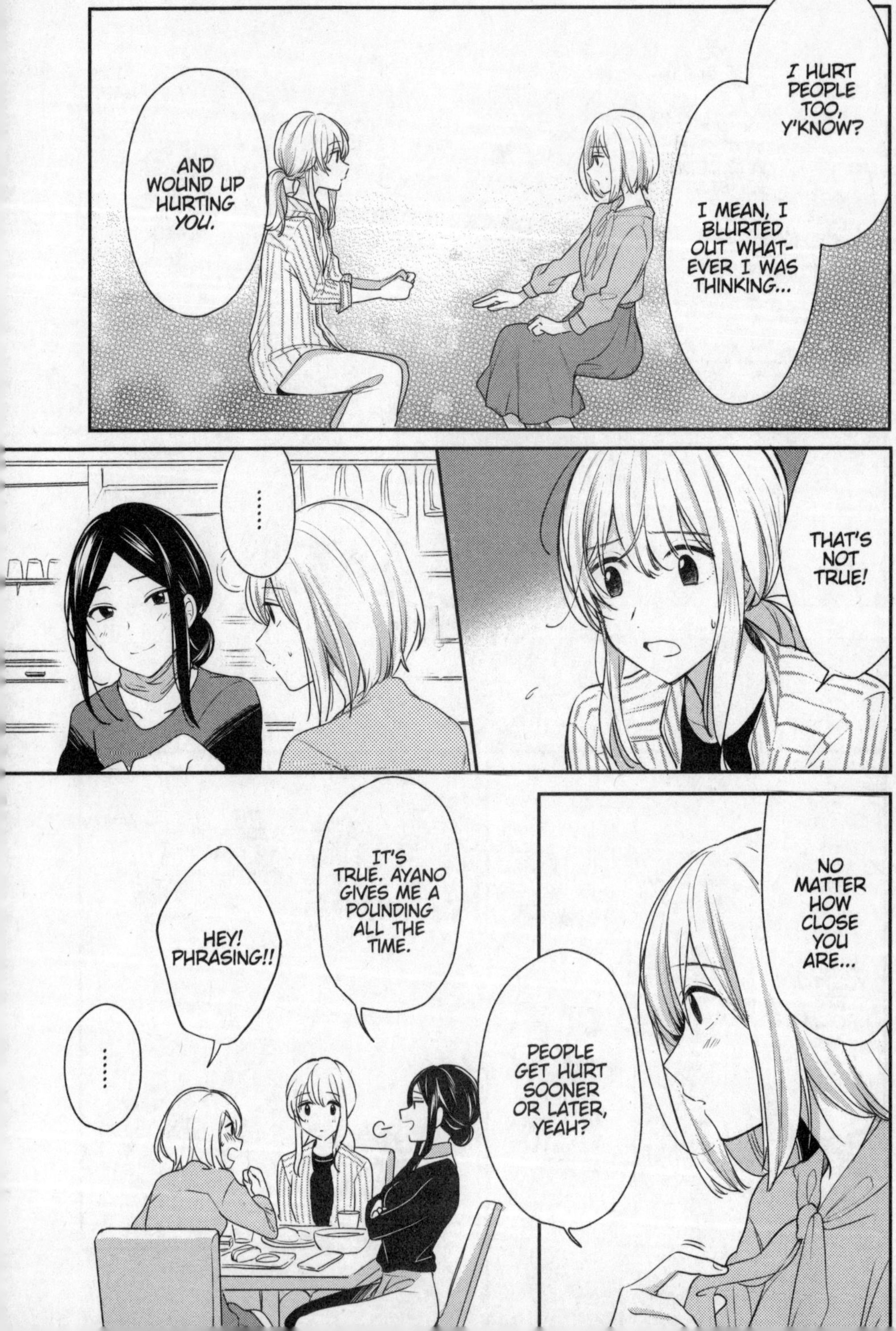
I HURT PEOPLE TOO, Y'KNOW?
I MEAN, I BLURTED OUT WHAT-EVER I WAS THINKING...
AND WOUND UP HURTING *YOU.*
THAT'S NOT TRUE!
......
NO MATTER HOW CLOSE YOU ARE...
PEOPLE GET HURT SOONER OR LATER, YEAH?
IT'S TRUE. AYANO GIVES ME A POUNDING ALL THE TIME.
HEY! PHRASING!!
......

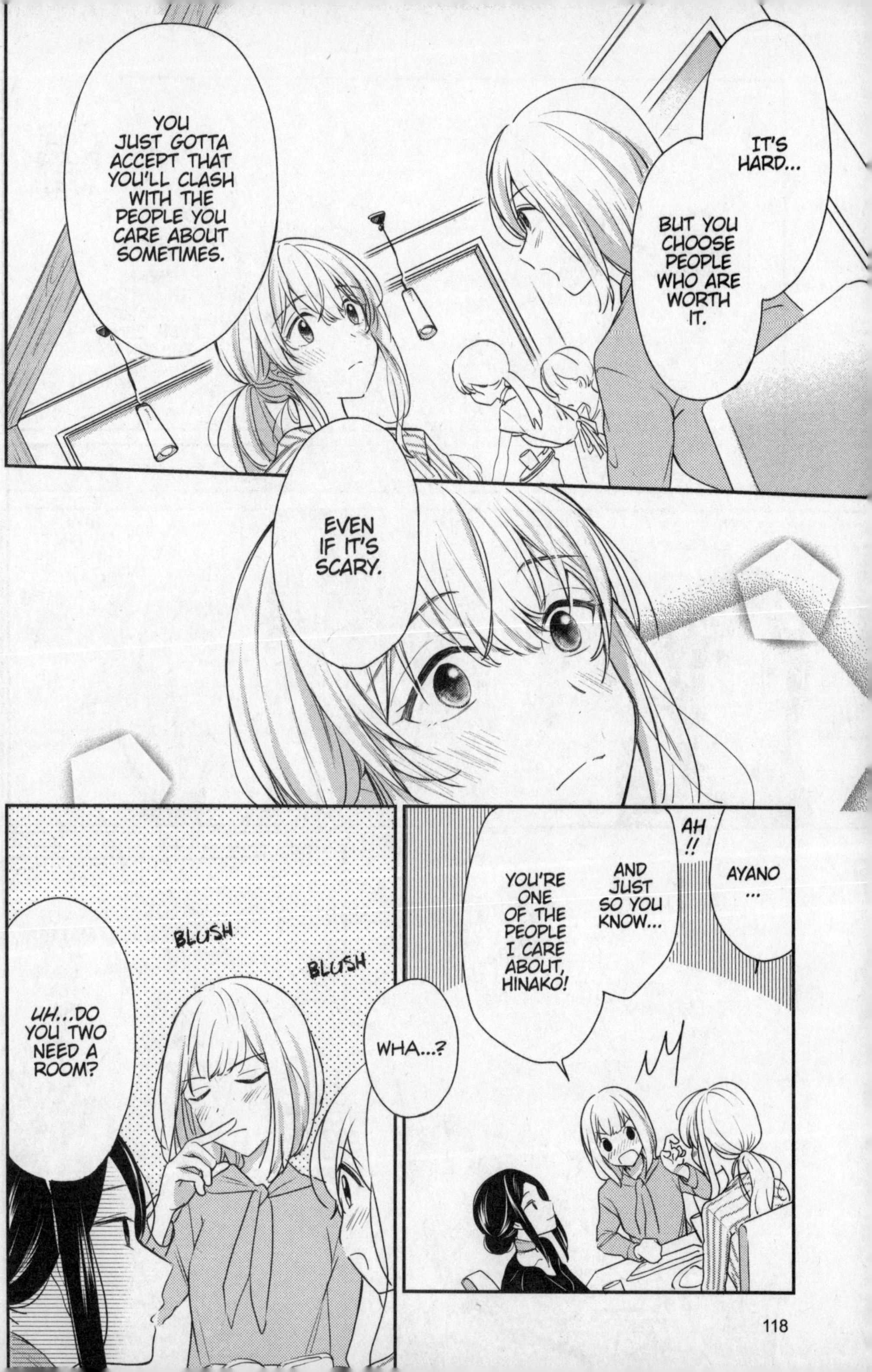

IT'S HARD...
BUT YOU CHOOSE PEOPLE WHO ARE WORTH IT.
YOU JUST GOTTA ACCEPT THAT YOU'LL CLASH WITH THE PEOPLE YOU CARE ABOUT SOMETIMES.
EVEN IF IT'S SCARY.
AYANO ...
AH !!
AND JUST SO YOU KNOW...
YOU'RE ONE OF THE PEOPLE I CARE ABOUT, HINAKO!
WHA...?
BLUSH
BLUSH
UH...DO YOU TWO NEED A ROOM?

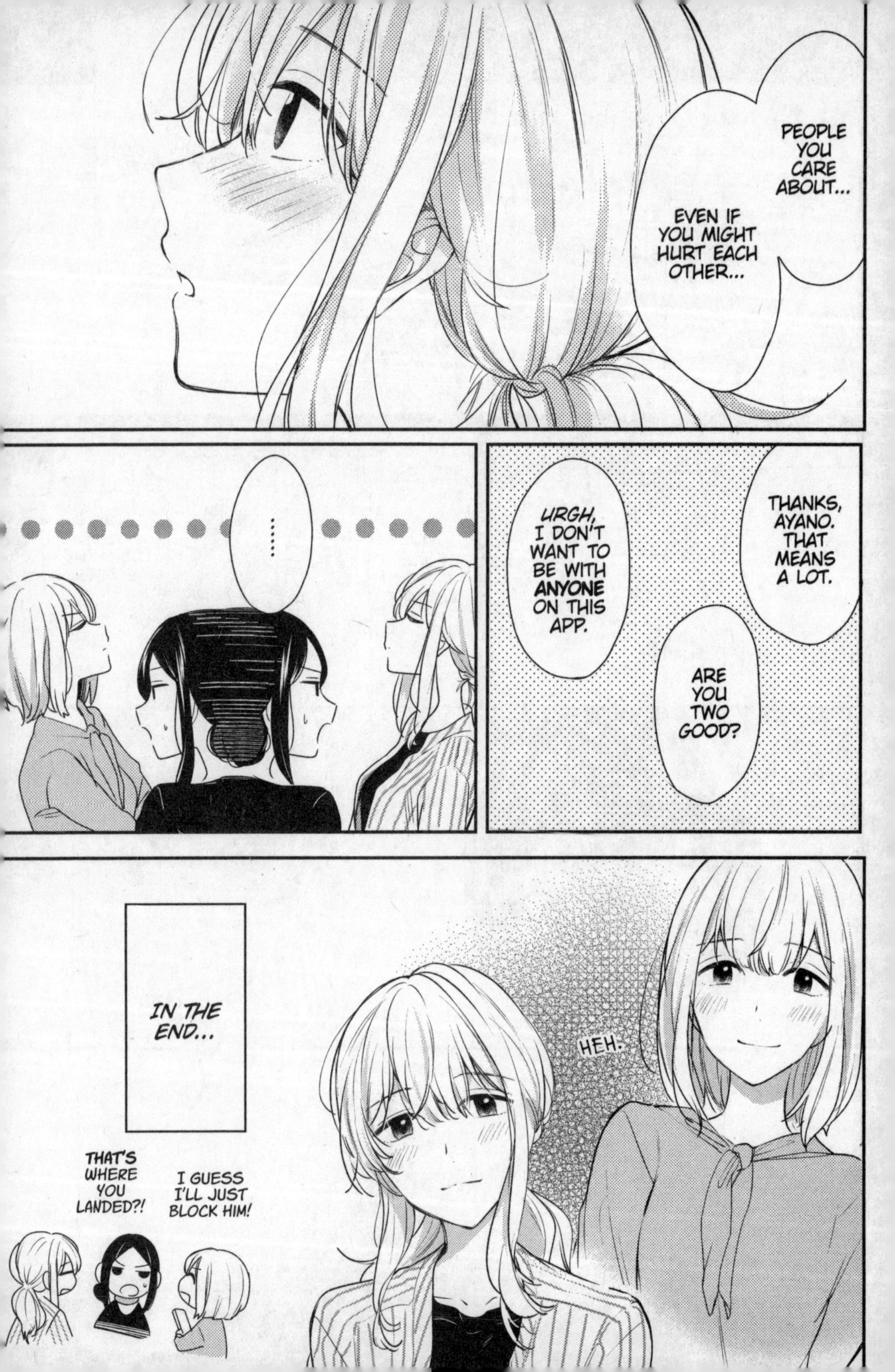
PEOPLE YOU CARE ABOUT...
EVEN IF YOU MIGHT HURT EACH OTHER...
THANKS, AYANO. THAT MEANS A LOT.
URGH, I DON'T WANT TO BE WITH **ANYONE** ON THIS APP.
ARE YOU TWO GOOD?
......
HEH.
IN THE END...
I GUESS I'LL JUST BLOCK HIM!
THAT'S WHERE YOU LANDED?!

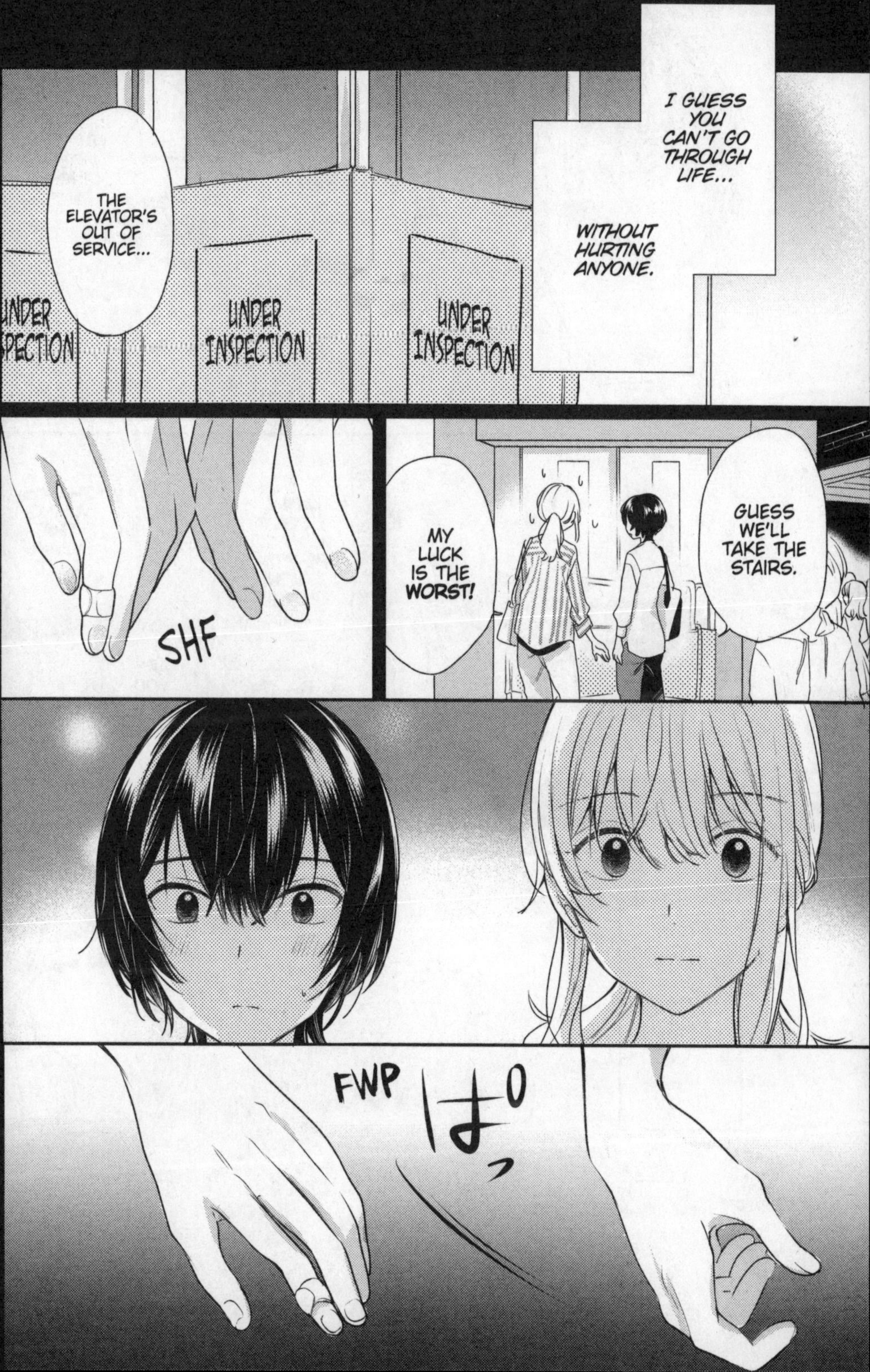
I GUESS YOU CAN'T GO THROUGH LIFE...
WITHOUT HURTING ANYONE.
THE ELEVATOR'S OUT OF SERVICE...
UNDER INSPECTION
UNDER INSPECTION
GUESS WE'LL TAKE THE STAIRS.
MY LUCK IS THE WORST!
SHF
FWP
はっ

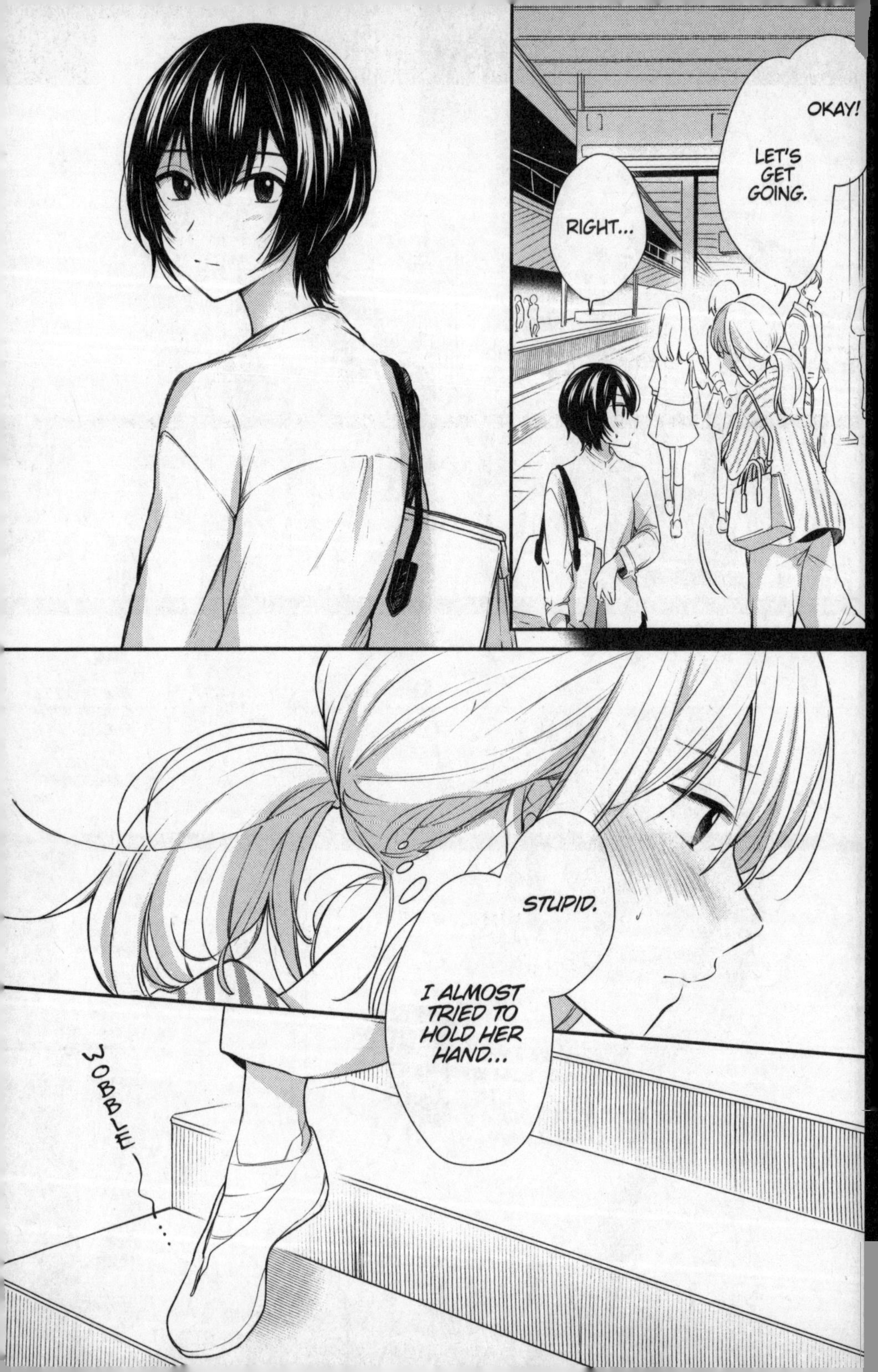
OKAY! LET'S GET GOING.
RIGHT...
STUPID.
I ALMOST TRIED TO HOLD HER HAND...
WOBBLE...

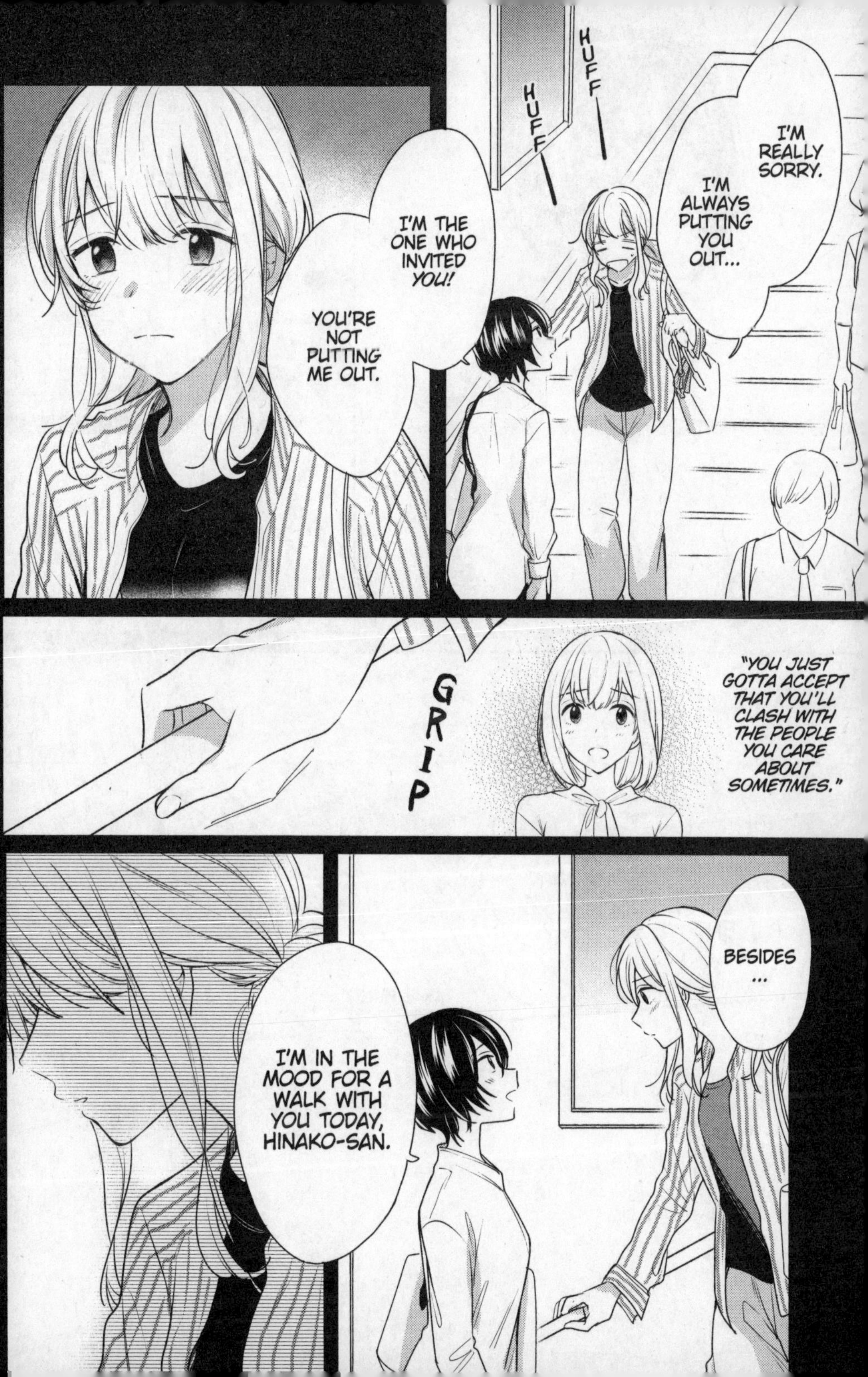
HUFF HUFF
I'M REALLY SORRY.
I'M ALWAYS PUTTING YOU OUT...
I'M THE ONE WHO INVITED YOU!
YOU'RE NOT PUTTING ME OUT.
"YOU JUST GOTTA ACCEPT THAT YOU'LL CLASH WITH THE PEOPLE YOU CARE ABOUT SOMETIMES."
GRIP
BESIDES...
I'M IN THE MOOD FOR A WALK WITH YOU TODAY, HINAKO-SAN.

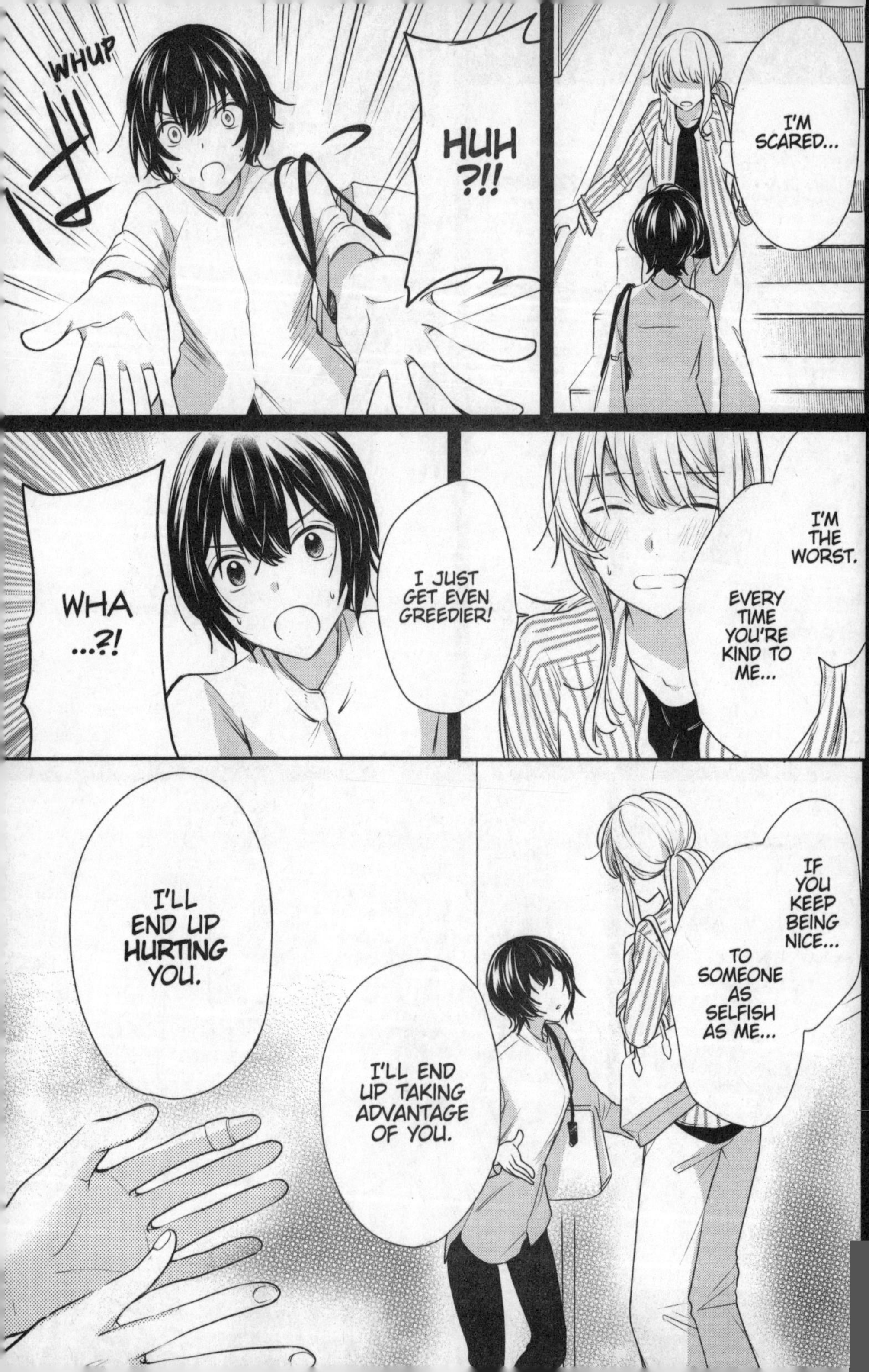
I'M SCARED...
HUH ?!!
WHUP
I'M THE WORST.
EVERY TIME YOU'RE KIND TO ME...
I JUST GET EVEN GREEDIER!
WHA ...?!
IF YOU KEEP BEING NICE...
TO SOMEONE AS SELFISH AS ME...
I'LL END UP TAKING ADVANTAGE OF YOU.
I'LL END UP HURTING YOU.

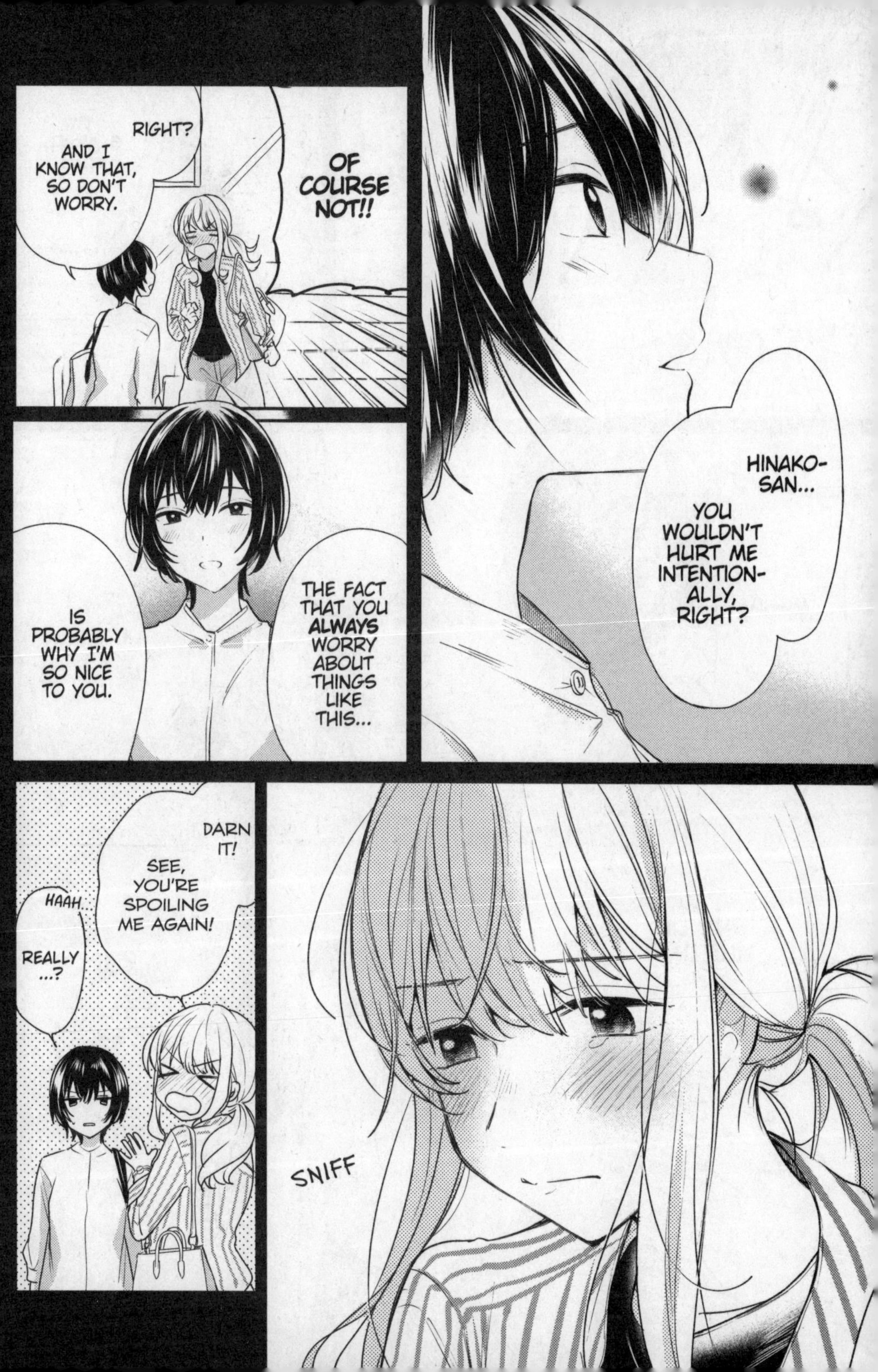
HINAKO-SAN...
YOU WOULDN'T HURT ME INTENTIONALLY, RIGHT?
OF COURSE NOT!!
RIGHT? AND I KNOW THAT, SO DON'T WORRY.
THE FACT THAT YOU ALWAYS WORRY ABOUT THINGS LIKE THIS...
IS PROBABLY WHY I'M SO NICE TO YOU.
SNIFF
DARN IT! SEE, YOU'RE SPOILING ME AGAIN!
HAAH...
REALLY...?

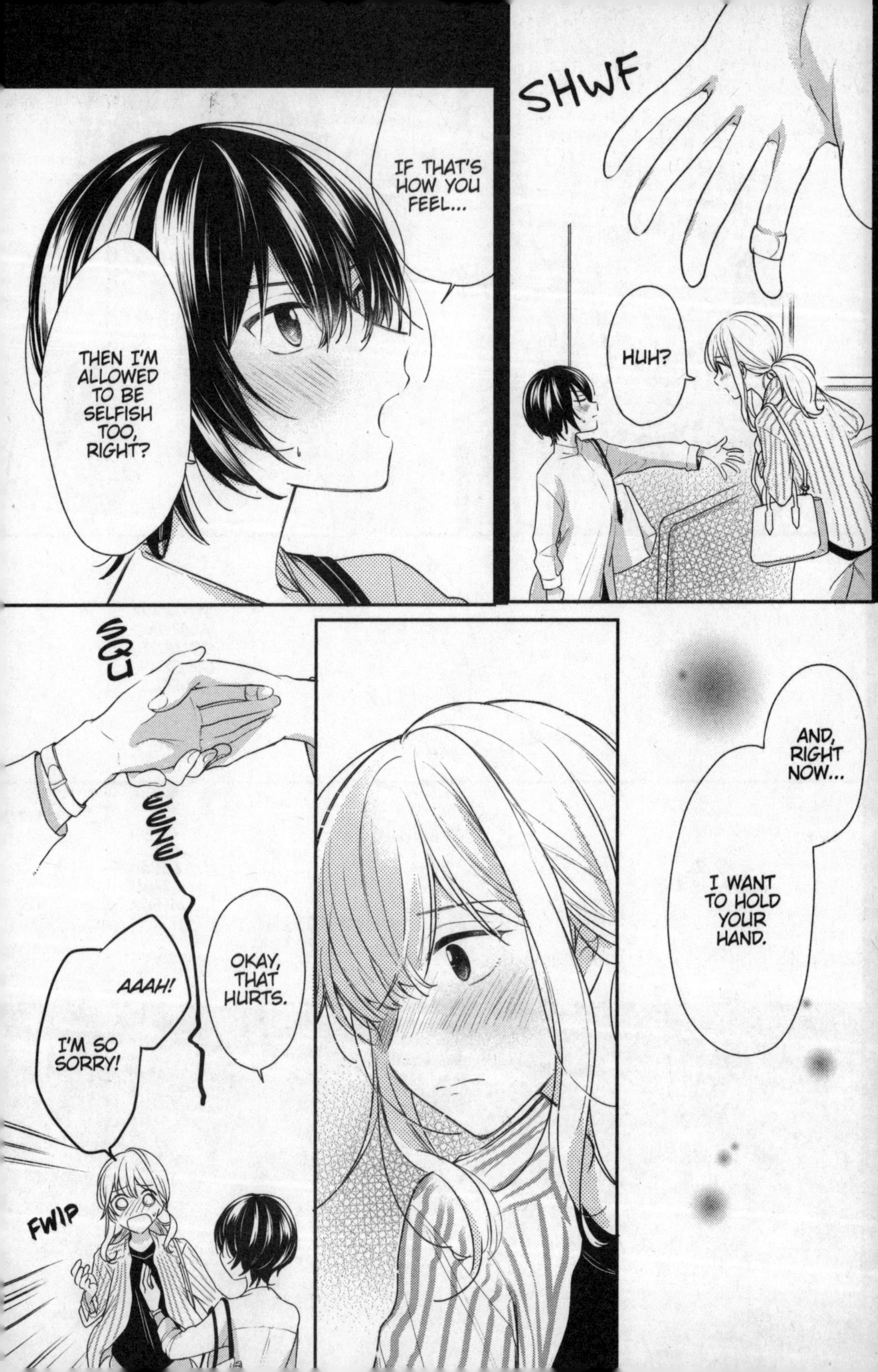
SHWF
HUH?
IF THAT'S HOW YOU FEEL...
THEN I'M ALLOWED TO BE SELFISH TOO, RIGHT?
AND, RIGHT NOW...
I WANT TO HOLD YOUR HAND.
SQUEEZE
OKAY, THAT HURTS.
AAAH!
I'M SO SORRY!
FWIP

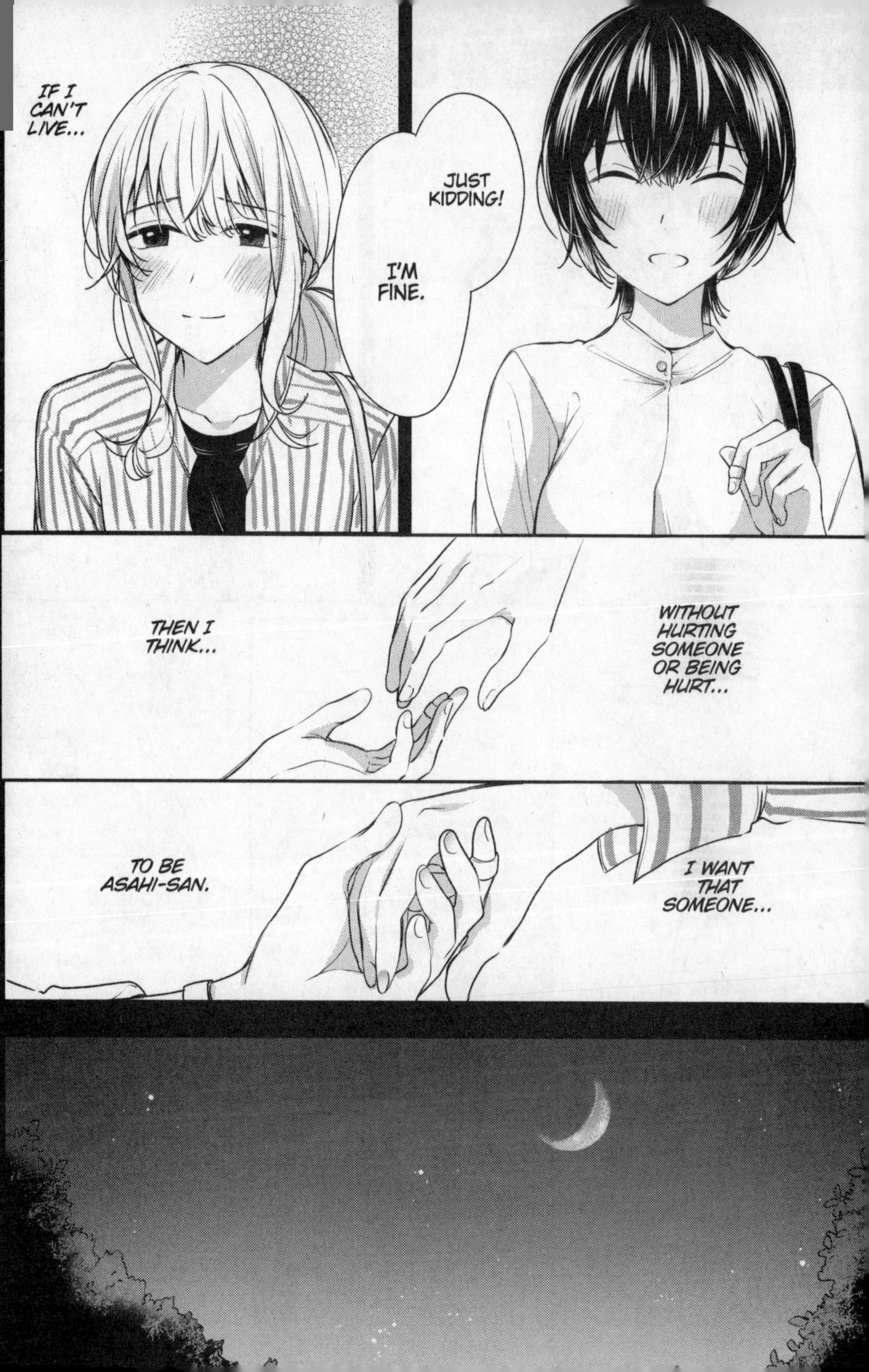
JUST KIDDING!
I'M FINE.
IF I CAN'T LIVE...
WITHOUT HURTING SOMEONE OR BEING HURT...
THEN I THINK...
I WANT THAT SOMEONE...
TO BE ASAHI-SAN.

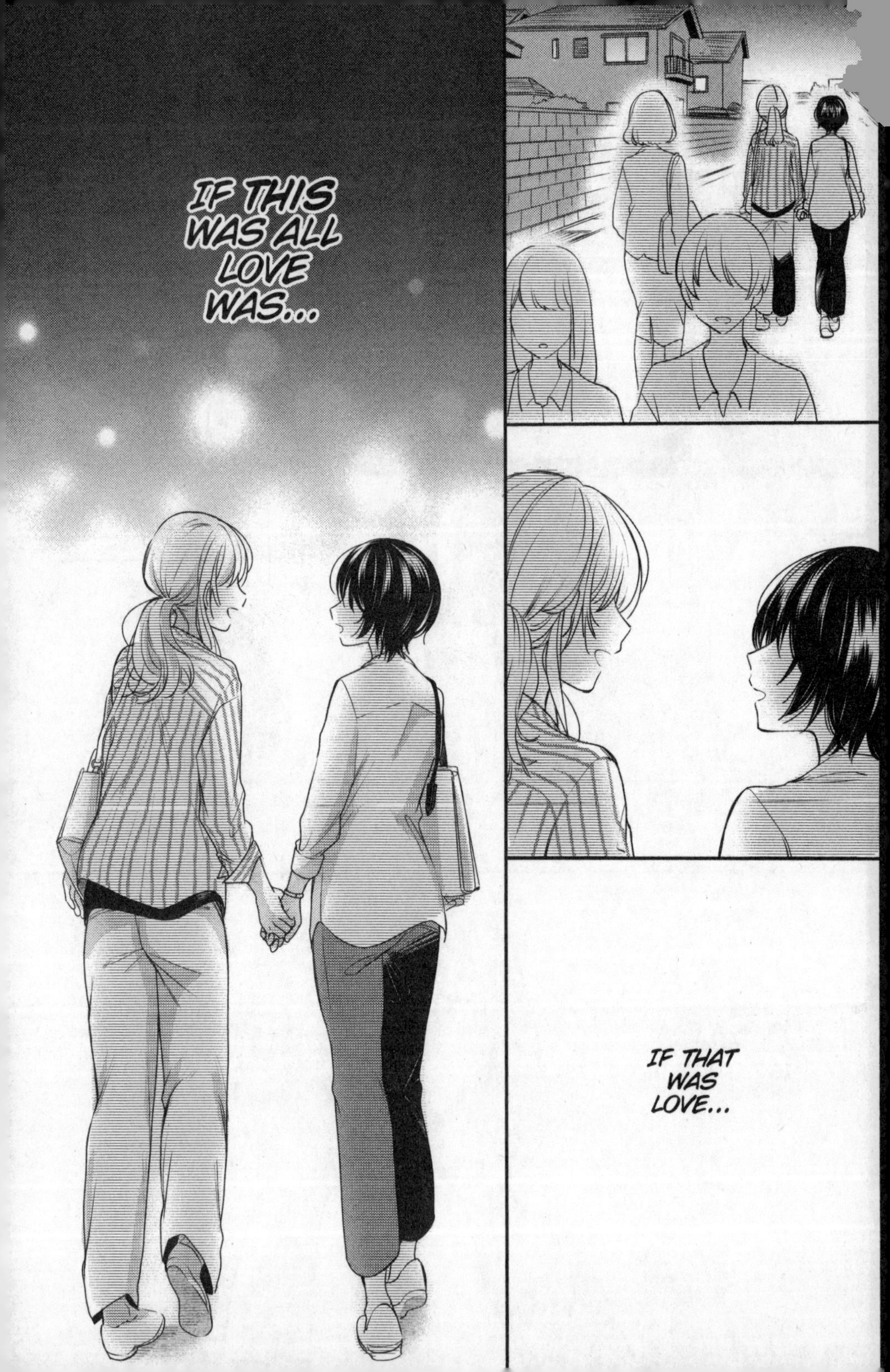
IF THAT WAS LOVE...
IF THIS WAS ALL LOVE WAS...

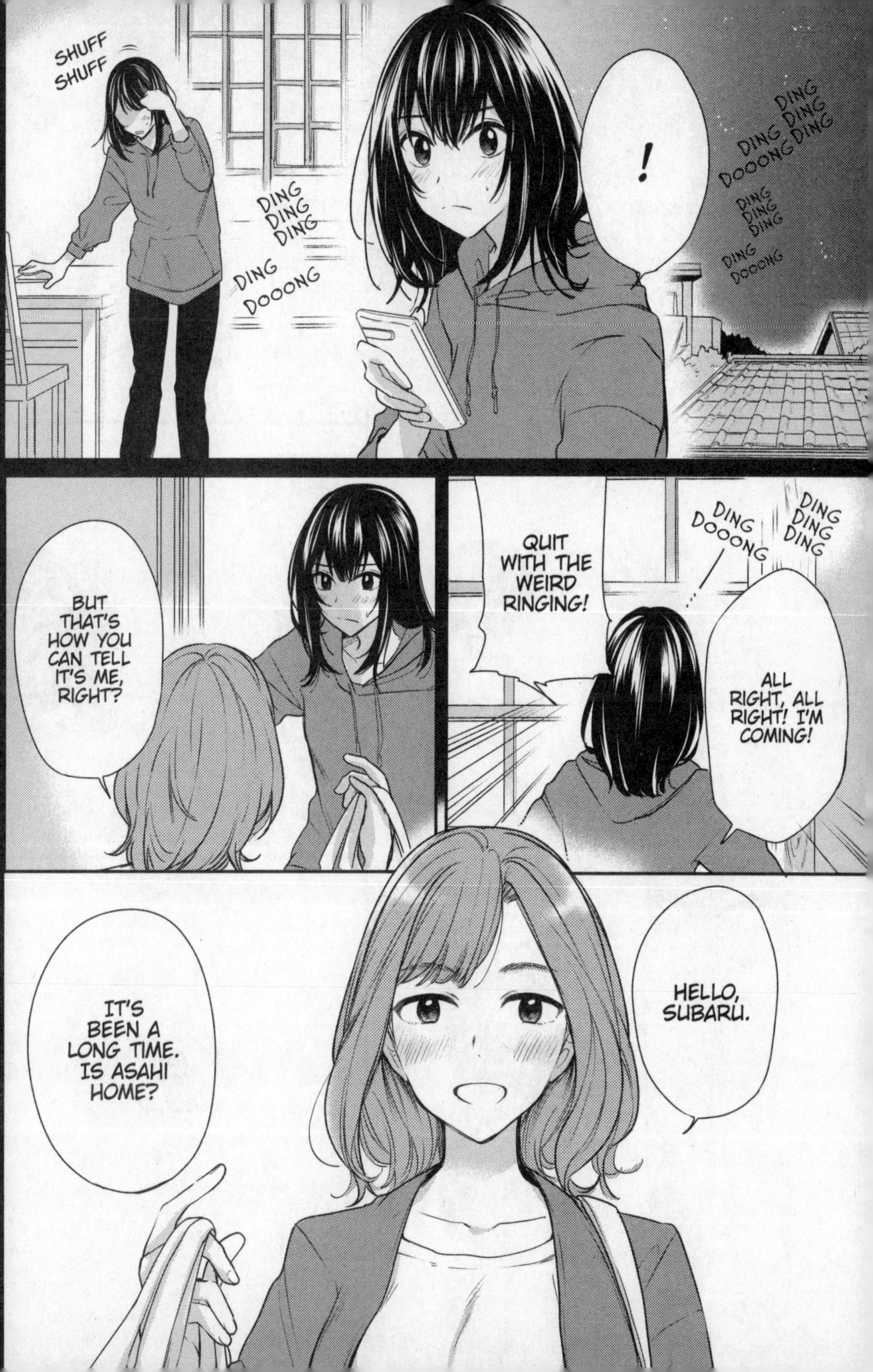
DING DING DING DOOONG DING
DING DING DING
DING DOOONG
!
DING DING DING
DING DOOONG
SHUFF SHUFF
DING DING DING
DING DOOONG
...
ALL RIGHT, ALL RIGHT! I'M COMING!
QUIT WITH THE WEIRD RINGING!
BUT THAT'S HOW YOU CAN TELL IT'S ME, RIGHT?
HELLO, SUBARU.
IT'S BEEN A LONG TIME. IS ASAHI HOME?

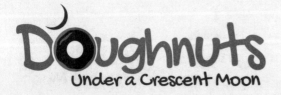
Doughnuts
Under a Crescent Moon

Doughnuts
Under a Crescent Moon

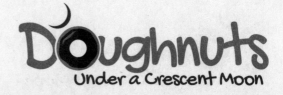

Chapter 10: A Heart with No Name

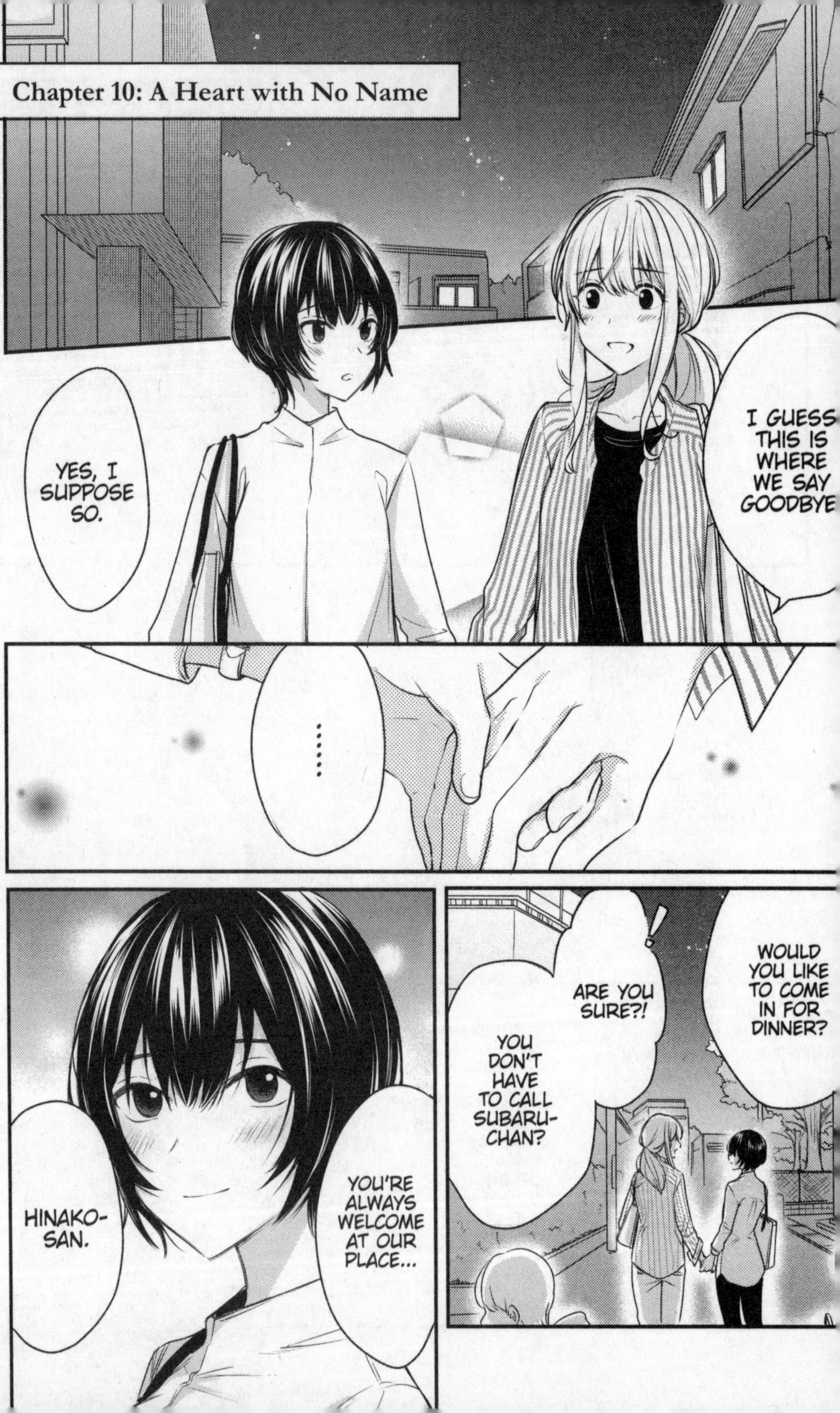

I GUESS THIS IS WHERE WE SAY GOODBYE
YES, I SUPPOSE SO.
......
WOULD YOU LIKE TO COME IN FOR DINNER?
ARE YOU SURE?!
YOU DON'T HAVE TO CALL SUBARU-CHAN?
YOU'RE ALWAYS WELCOME AT OUR PLACE...
HINAKO-SAN.

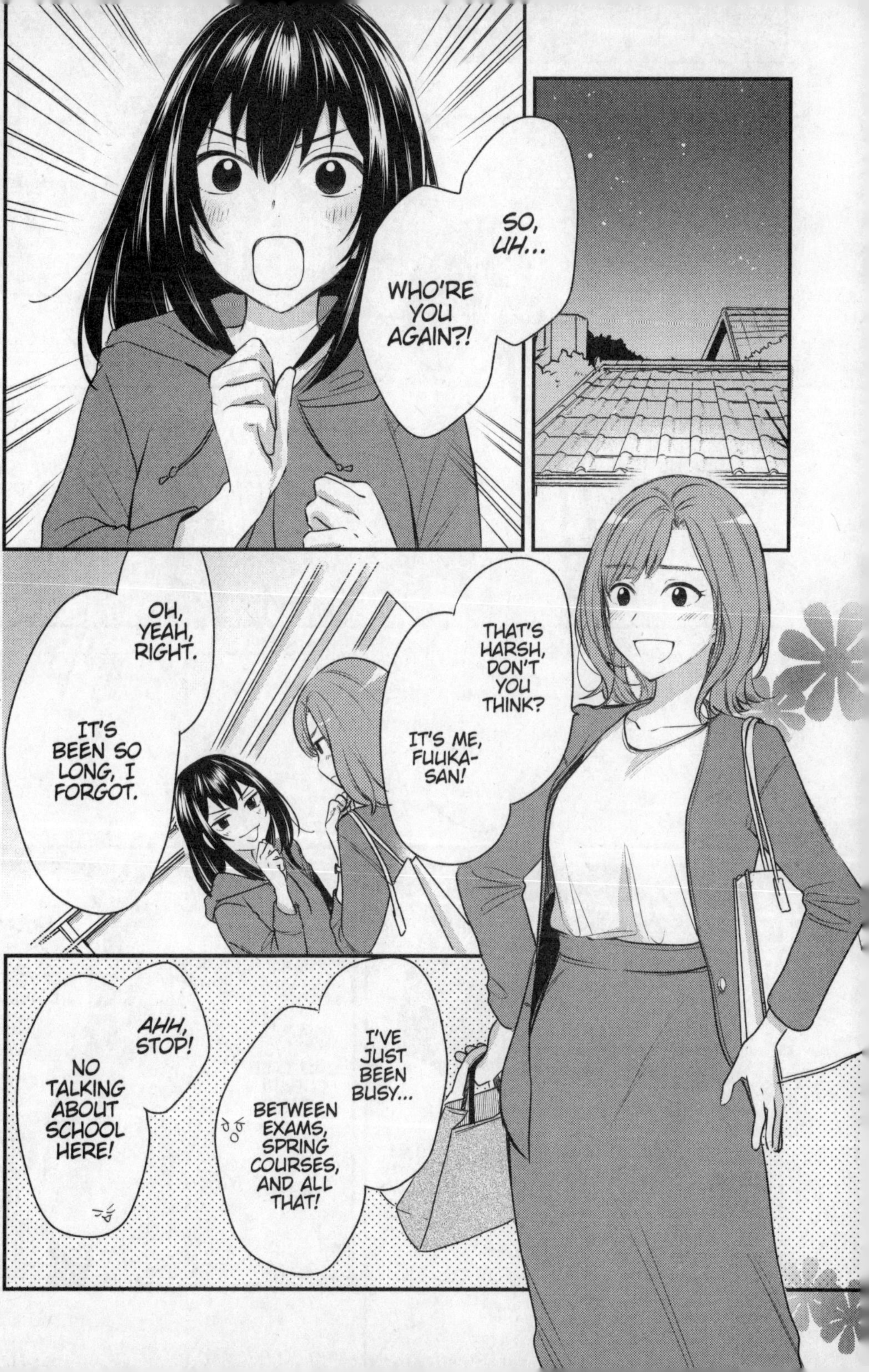
SO, UH...
WHO'RE YOU AGAIN?!
THAT'S HARSH, DON'T YOU THINK?
IT'S ME, FUUKA-SAN!
OH, YEAH, RIGHT.
IT'S BEEN SO LONG, I FORGOT.
I'VE JUST BEEN BUSY...
BETWEEN EXAMS, SPRING COURSES, AND ALL THAT!
AHH, STOP!
NO TALKING ABOUT SCHOOL HERE!

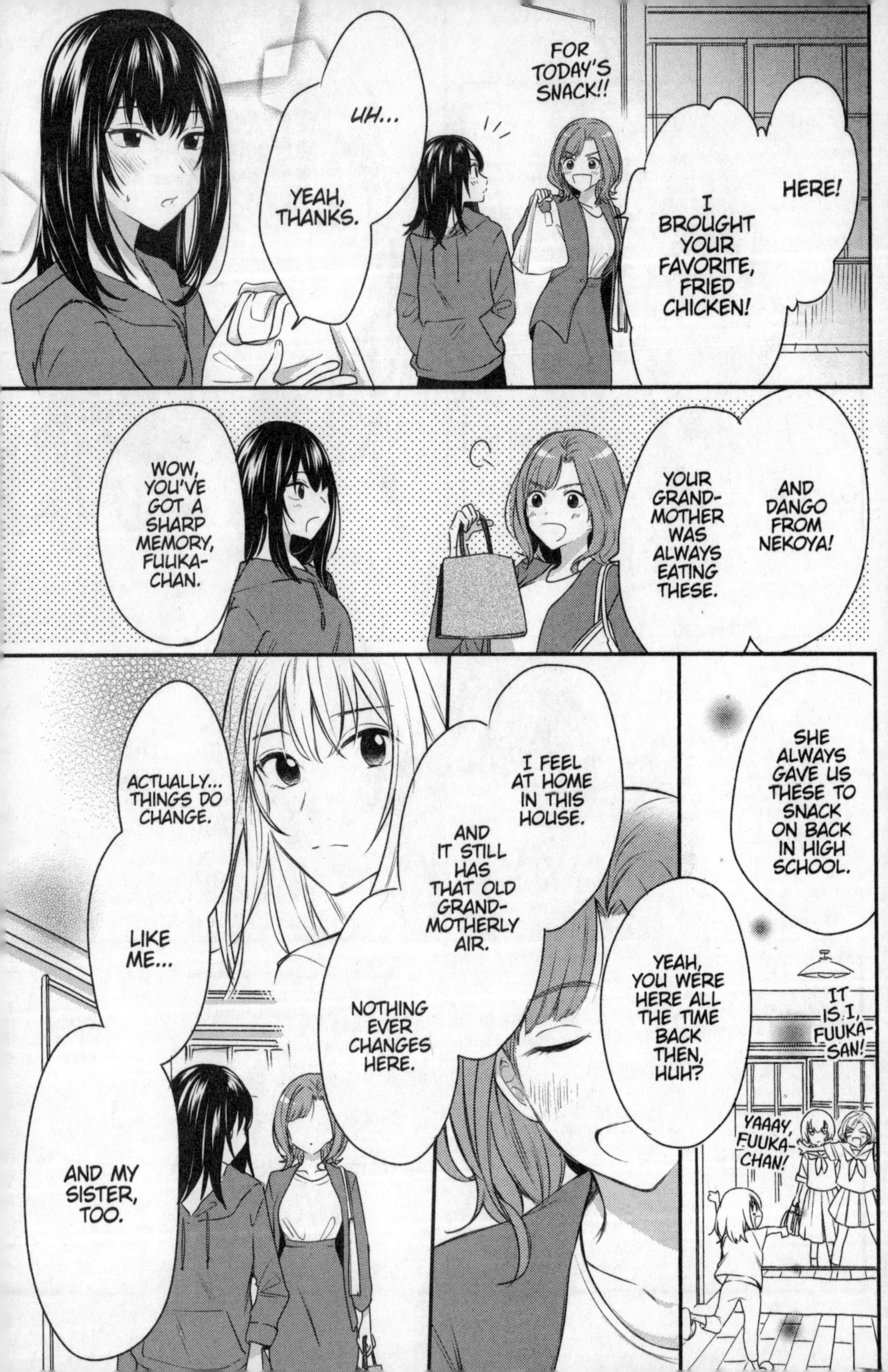
HERE!
I BROUGHT YOUR FAVORITE, FRIED CHICKEN!
FOR TODAY'S SNACK!!
UH...
YEAH, THANKS.
AND DANGO FROM NEKOYA!
YOUR GRAND-MOTHER WAS ALWAYS EATING THESE.
WOW, YOU'VE GOT A SHARP MEMORY, FUUKA-CHAN.
SHE ALWAYS GAVE US THESE TO SNACK ON BACK IN HIGH SCHOOL.
IT IS I, FUUKA-SAN!
YAAAY, FUUKA-CHAN!
YEAH, YOU WERE HERE ALL THE TIME BACK THEN, HUH?
I FEEL AT HOME IN THIS HOUSE.
AND IT STILL HAS THAT OLD GRAND-MOTHERLY AIR.
NOTHING EVER CHANGES HERE.
ACTUALLY... THINGS DO CHANGE.
LIKE ME...
AND MY SISTER, TOO.

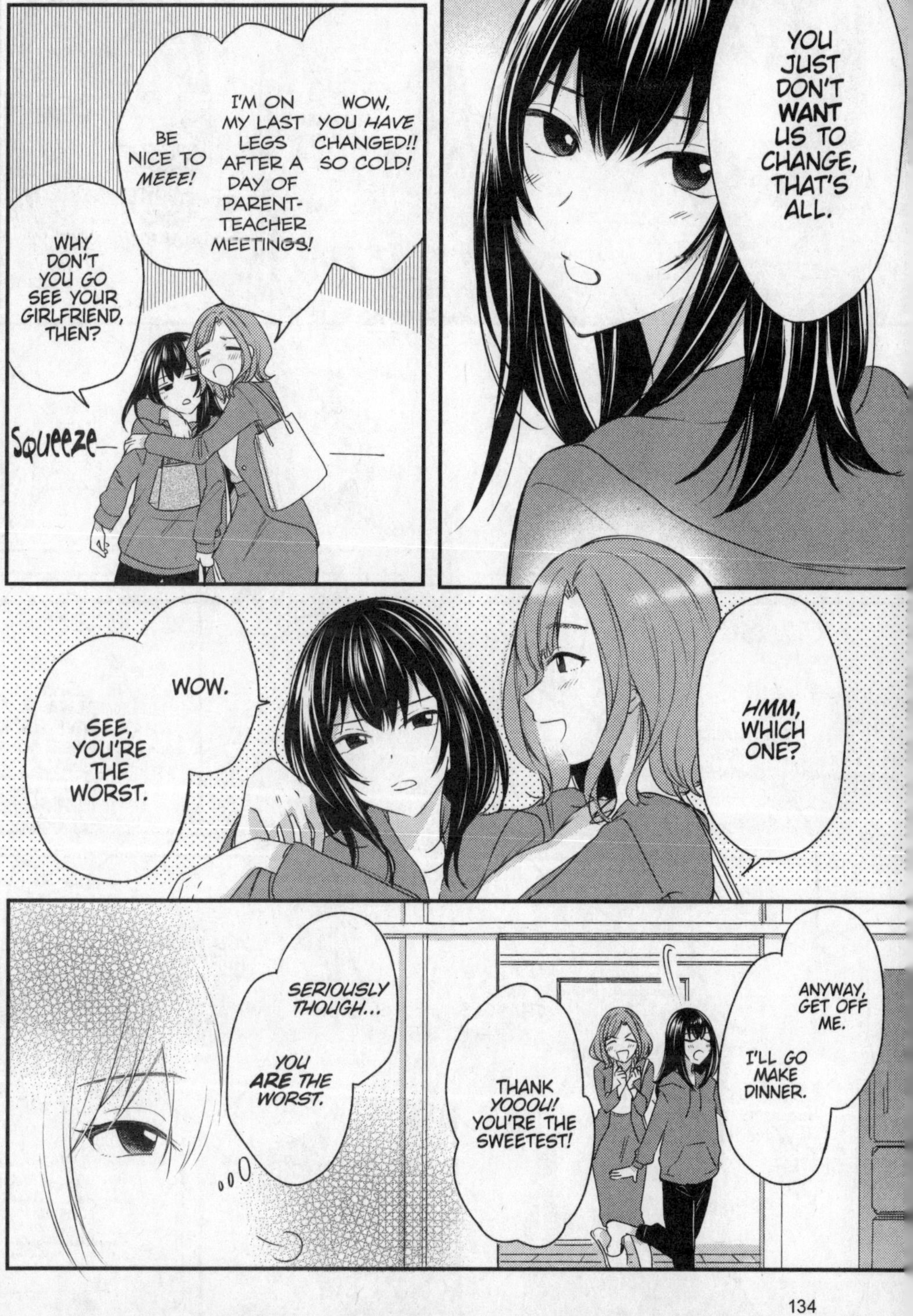
YOU JUST DON'T WANT US TO CHANGE, THAT'S ALL.
WOW, YOU *HAVE* CHANGED!! SO COLD!
I'M ON MY LAST LEGS AFTER A DAY OF PARENT-TEACHER MEETINGS!
BE NICE TO *MEEE!*
WHY DON'T YOU GO SEE YOUR GIRLFRIEND, THEN?
Squeeze
HMM, WHICH ONE?
WOW.
SEE, YOU'RE THE WORST.
ANYWAY, GET OFF ME.
I'LL GO MAKE DINNER.
THANK *YOOOU!* YOU'RE THE SWEETEST!
SERIOUSLY THOUGH...
YOU **ARE** THE WORST.

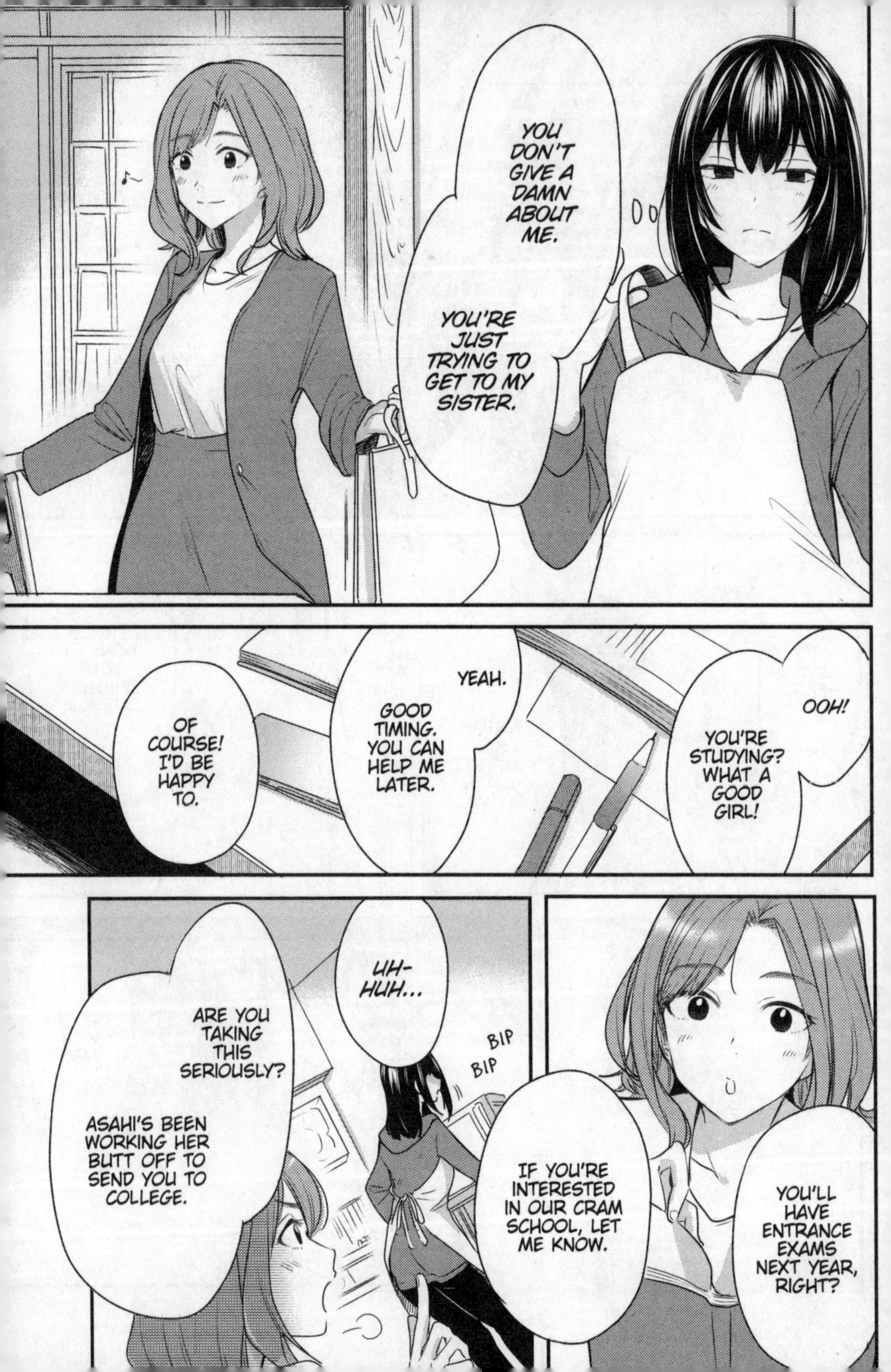
YOU DON'T GIVE A DAMN ABOUT ME.
YOU'RE JUST TRYING TO GET TO MY SISTER.
OOH!
YOU'RE STUDYING? WHAT A GOOD GIRL!
YEAH.
GOOD TIMING. YOU CAN HELP ME LATER.
OF COURSE! I'D BE HAPPY TO.
YOU'LL HAVE ENTRANCE EXAMS NEXT YEAR, RIGHT?
IF YOU'RE INTERESTED IN OUR CRAM SCHOOL, LET ME KNOW.
UH-HUH...
BIP
BIP
ARE YOU TAKING THIS SERIOUSLY?
ASAHI'S BEEN WORKING HER BUTT OFF TO SEND YOU TO COLLEGE.

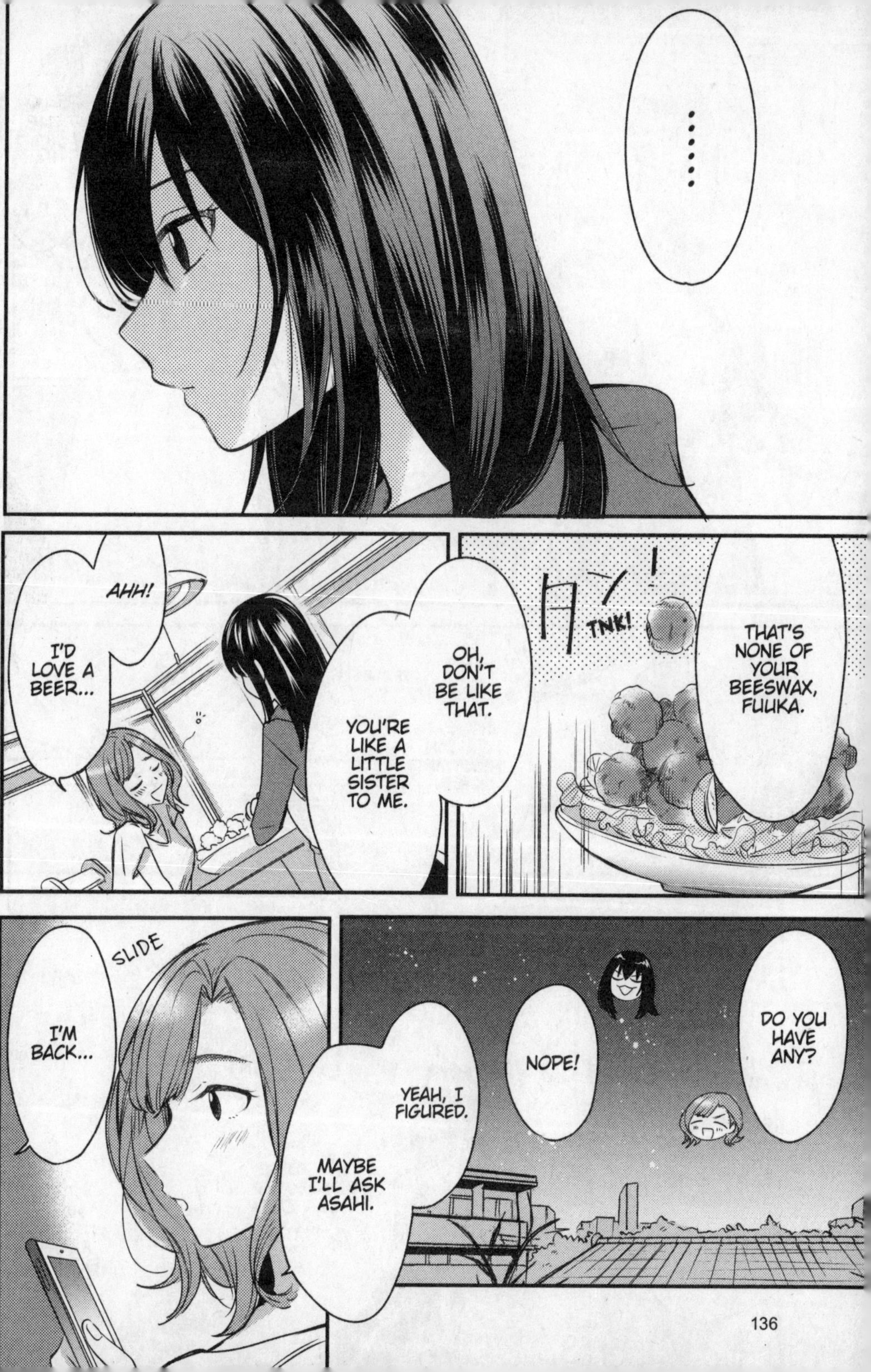
……
THAT'S NONE OF YOUR BEESWAX, FUUKA.
TNK!
OH, DON'T BE LIKE THAT.
YOU'RE LIKE A LITTLE SISTER TO ME.
AHH!
I'D LOVE A BEER...
DO YOU HAVE ANY?
NOPE!
YEAH, I FIGURED.
MAYBE I'LL ASK ASAHI.
SLIDE
I'M BACK...

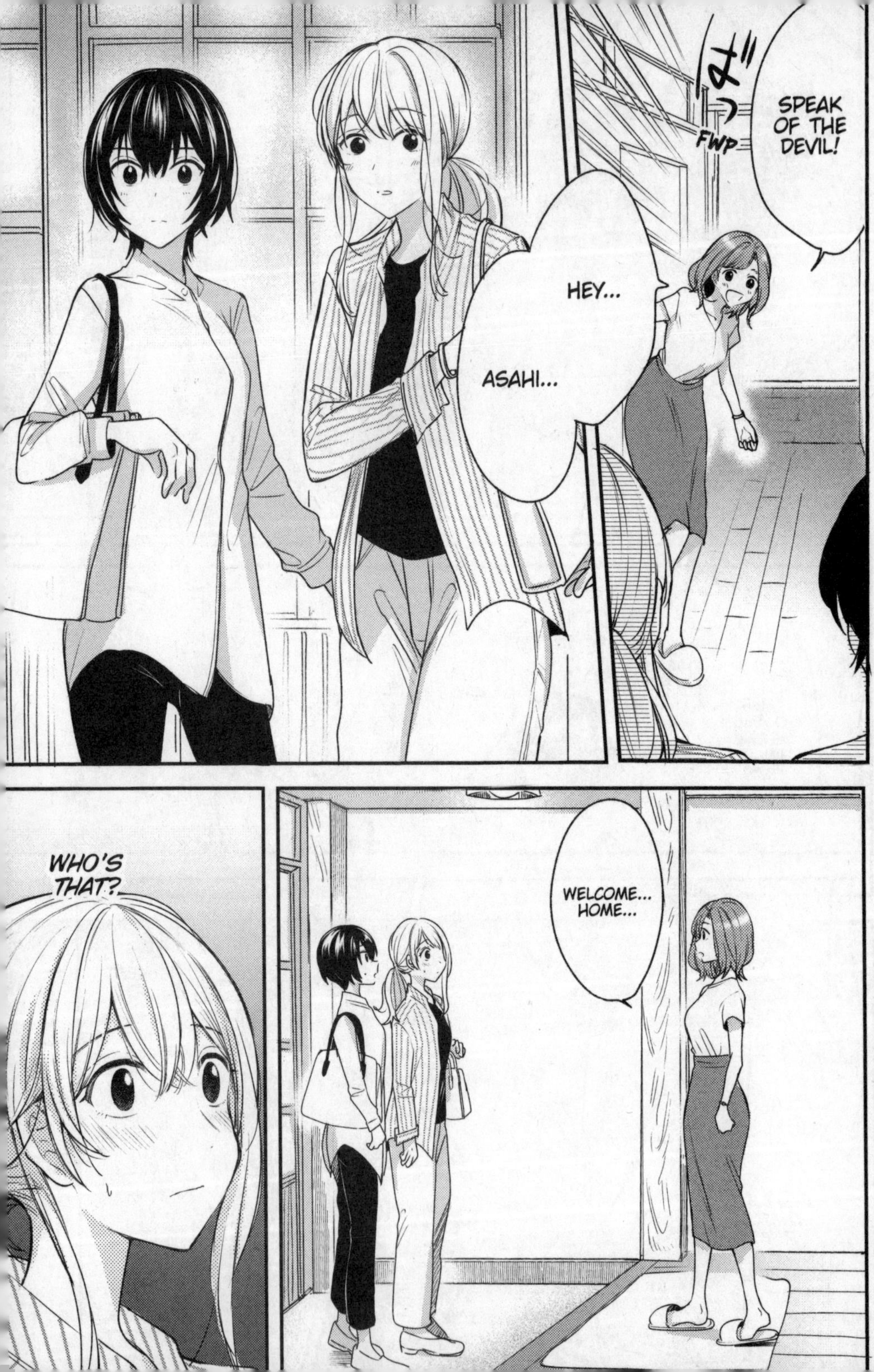
SPEAK OF THE DEVIL!
ばっ
FWP
HEY...
ASAHI...
WELCOME... HOME...
WHO'S THAT?

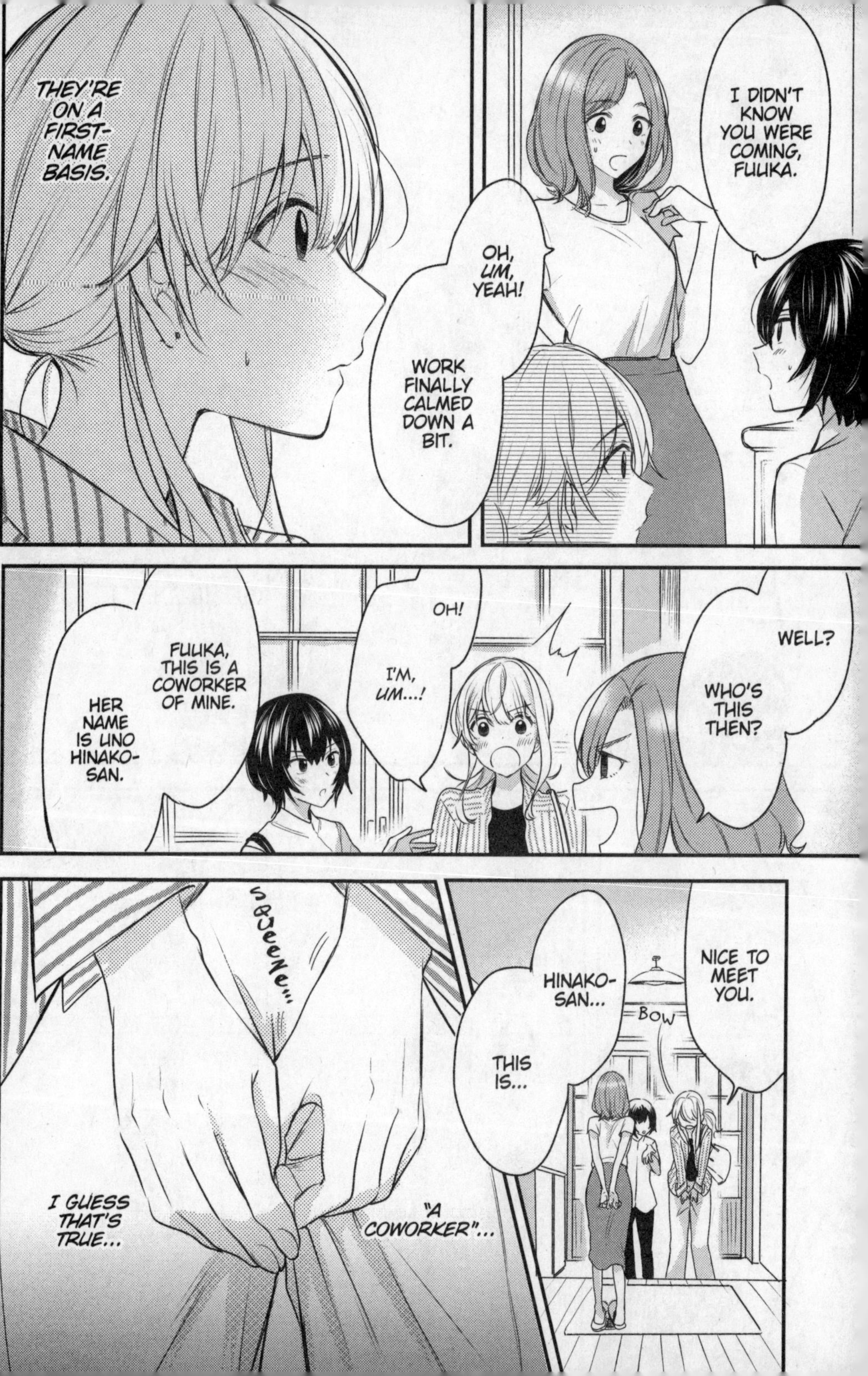
I DIDN'T KNOW YOU WERE COMING, FUUKA.
OH, UM, YEAH!
WORK FINALLY CALMED DOWN A BIT.
THEY'RE ON A FIRST-NAME BASIS.
WELL?
WHO'S THIS THEN?
OH!
I'M, UM...!
FUUKA, THIS IS A COWORKER OF MINE.
HER NAME IS UNO HINAKO-SAN.
NICE TO MEET YOU.
BOW
HINAKO-SAN...
THIS IS...
SQUEEZE...
"A COWORKER"...
I GUESS THAT'S TRUE...

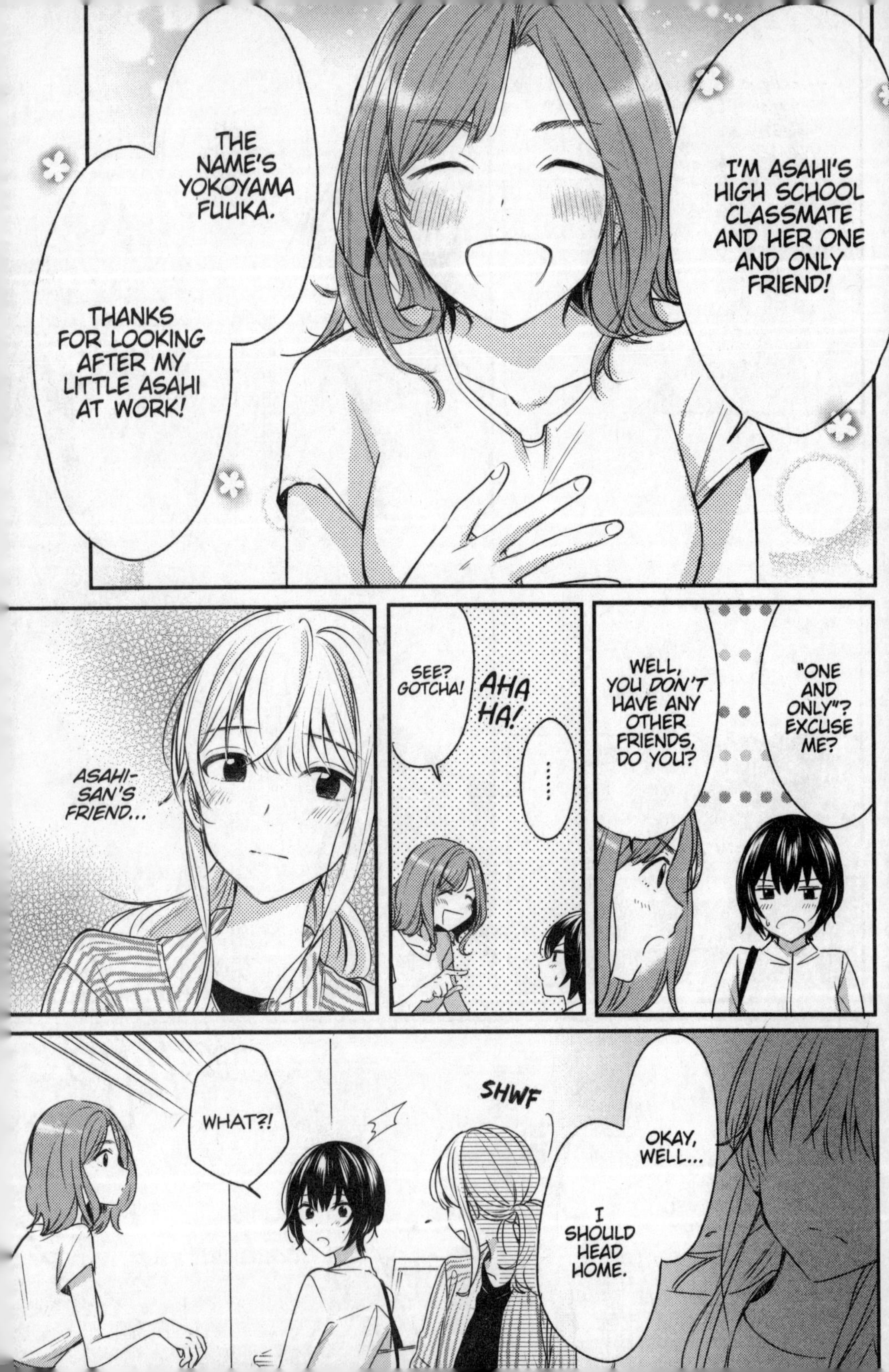
I'M ASAHI'S HIGH SCHOOL CLASSMATE AND HER ONE AND ONLY FRIEND!
THE NAME'S YOKOYAMA FUUKA.
THANKS FOR LOOKING AFTER MY LITTLE ASAHI AT WORK!
"ONE AND ONLY"? EXCUSE ME?
WELL, YOU *DON'T* HAVE ANY OTHER FRIENDS, DO YOU?
AHA HA!
SEE? GOTCHA!
......
ASAHI-SAN'S FRIEND...
OKAY, WELL...
I SHOULD HEAD HOME.
SHWF
WHAT?!

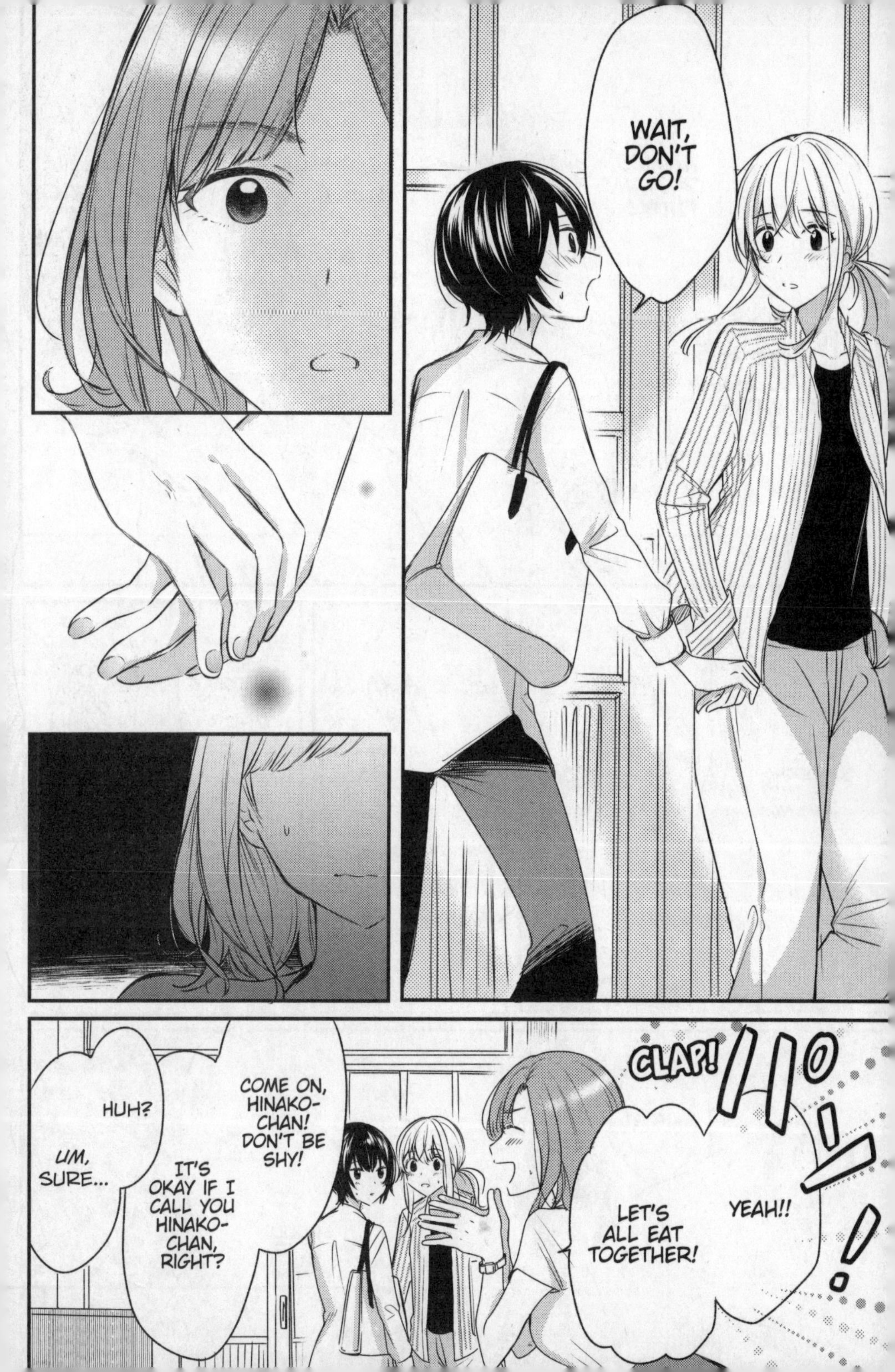
WAIT, DON'T GO!
CLAP!
LET'S ALL EAT TOGETHER!
YEAH!!
COME ON, HINAKO-CHAN! DON'T BE SHY!
IT'S OKAY IF I CALL YOU HINAKO-CHAN, RIGHT?
HUH?
UM, SURE...

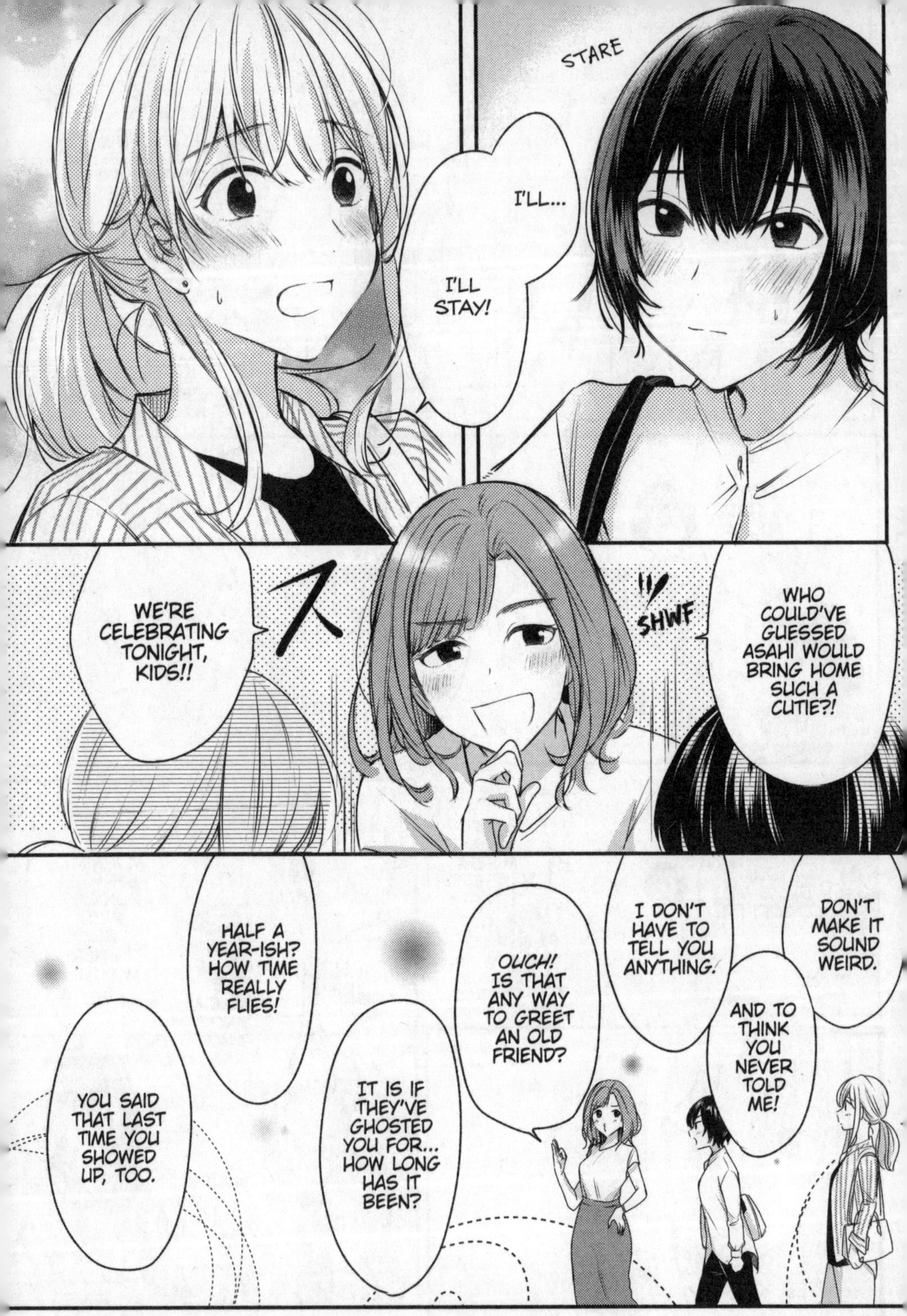
STARE
I'LL...
I'LL STAY!
WHO COULD'VE GUESSED ASAHI WOULD BRING HOME SUCH A CUTIE?!
SHWF
WE'RE CELEBRATING TONIGHT, KIDS!!
DON'T MAKE IT SOUND WEIRD.
AND TO THINK YOU NEVER TOLD ME!
I DON'T HAVE TO TELL YOU ANYTHING.
OUCH! IS THAT ANY WAY TO GREET AN OLD FRIEND?
IT IS IF THEY'VE GHOSTED YOU FOR... HOW LONG HAS IT BEEN?
HALF A YEAR-ISH? HOW TIME REALLY FLIES!
YOU SAID THAT LAST TIME YOU SHOWED UP, TOO.

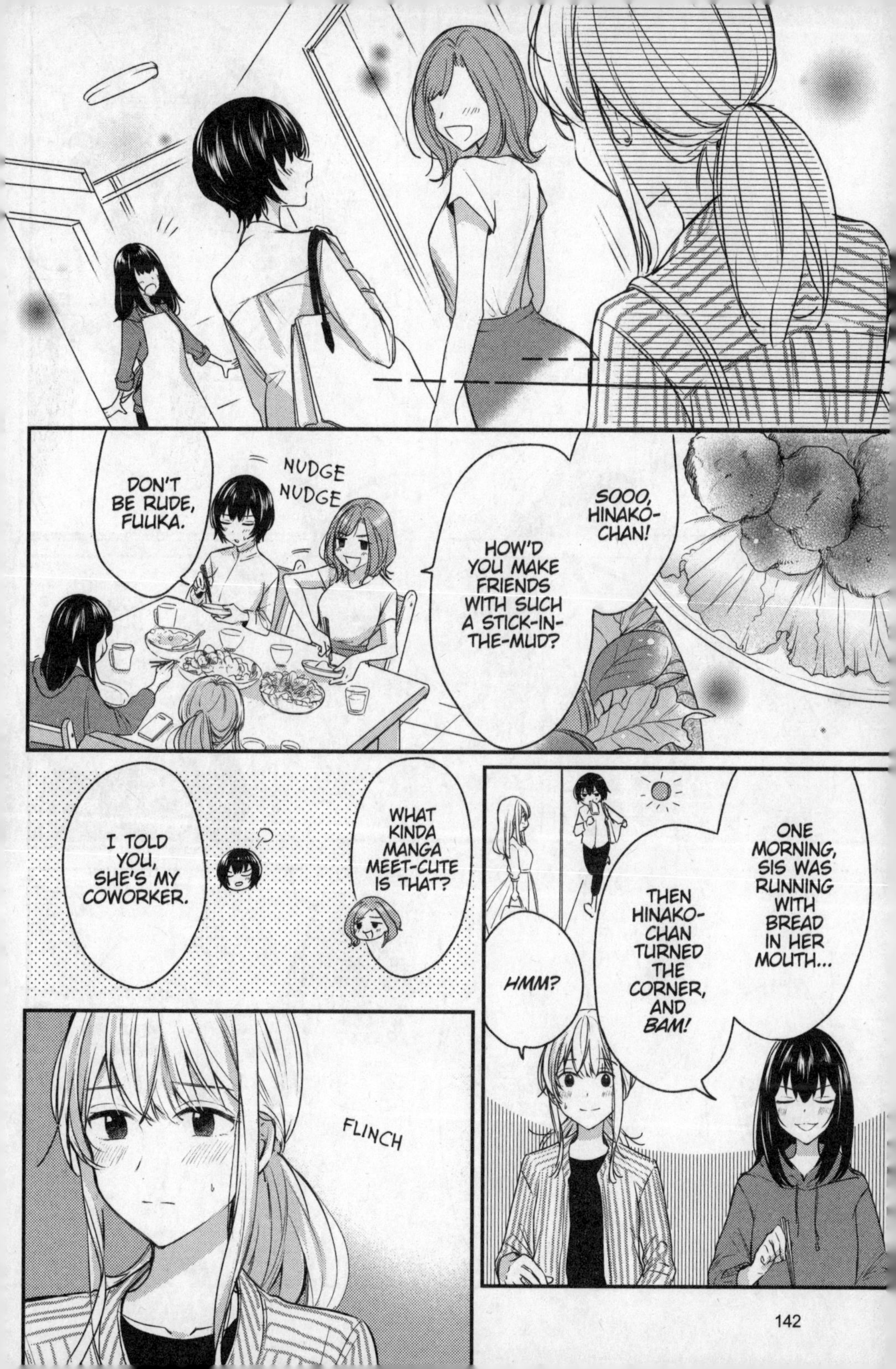
SOOO, HINAKO-CHAN!
HOW'D YOU MAKE FRIENDS WITH SUCH A STICK-IN-THE-MUD?
NUDGE NUDGE
DON'T BE RUDE, FUUKA.
ONE MORNING, SIS WAS RUNNING WITH BREAD IN HER MOUTH...
THEN HINAKO-CHAN TURNED THE CORNER, AND BAM!
HMM?
WHAT KINDA MANGA MEET-CUTE IS THAT?
I TOLD YOU, SHE'S MY COWORKER.
FLINCH

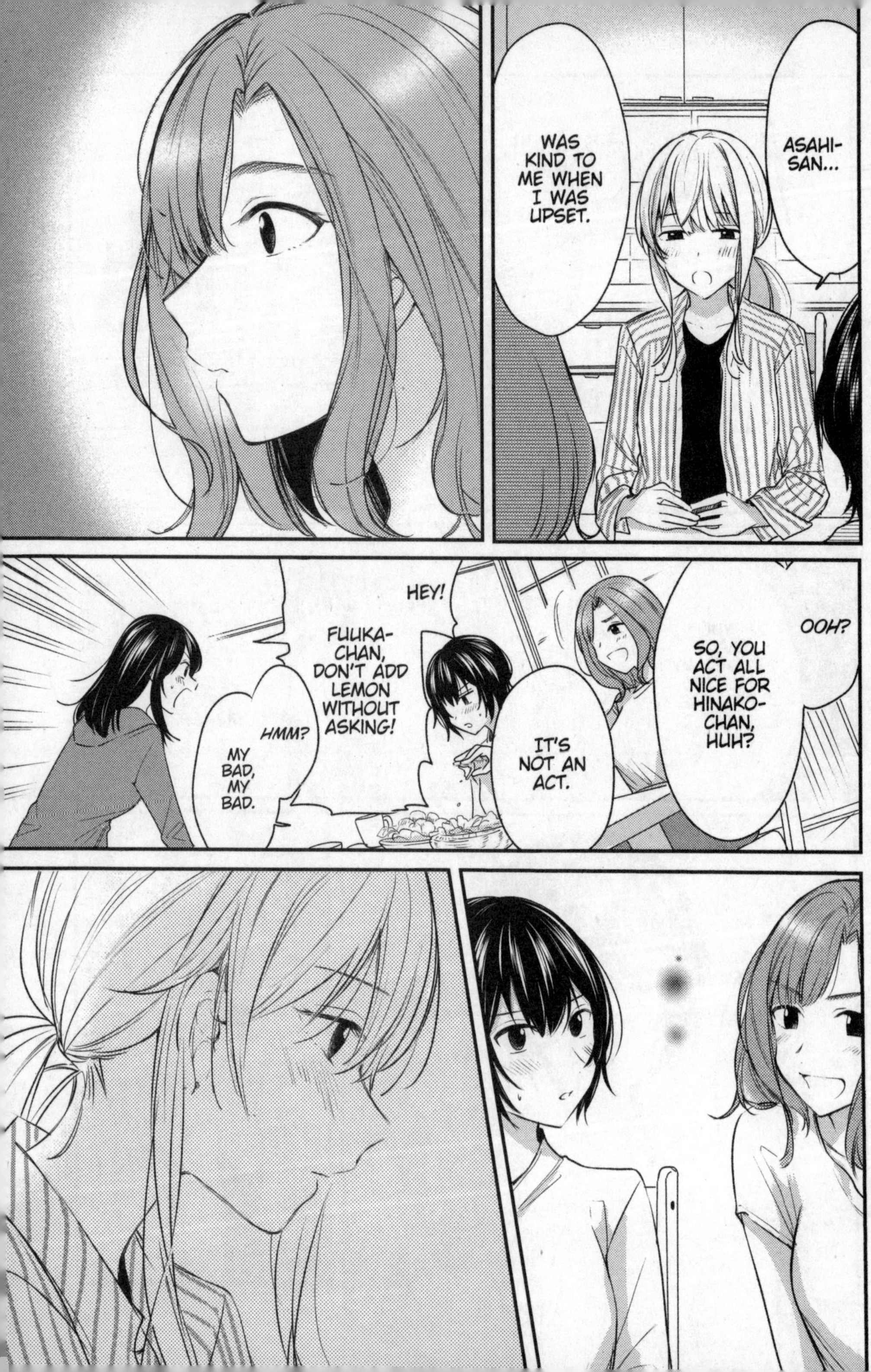
ASAHI-SAN...
WAS KIND TO ME WHEN I WAS UPSET.
OOH?
SO, YOU ACT ALL NICE FOR HINAKO-CHAN, HUH?
IT'S NOT AN ACT.
HEY!
FUUKA-CHAN, DON'T ADD LEMON WITHOUT ASKING!
HMM?
MY BAD, MY BAD.

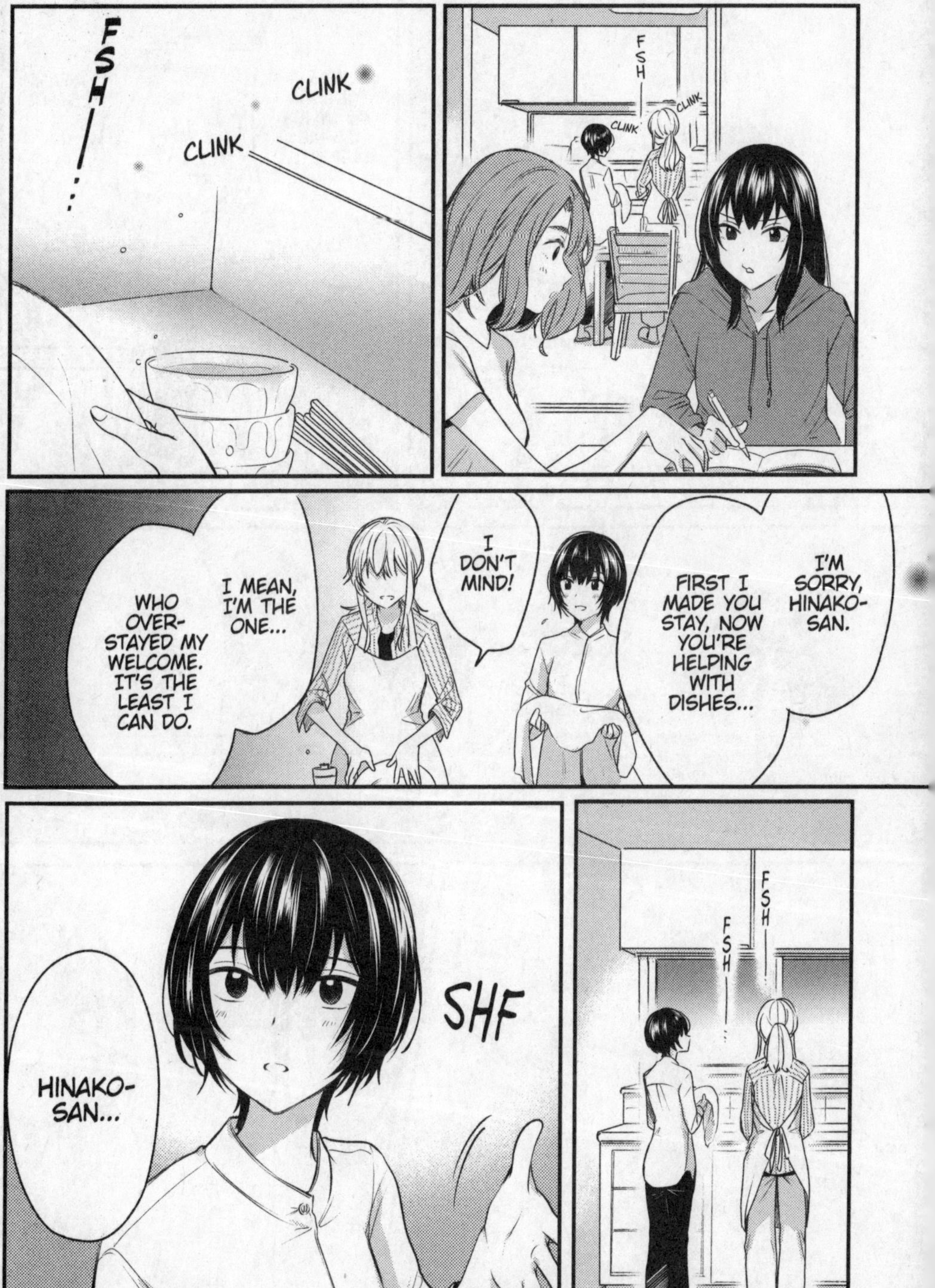
FSH
CLINK
CLINK
FSH
CLINK
CLINK
I'M SORRY, HINAKO-SAN.
FIRST I MADE YOU STAY, NOW YOU'RE HELPING WITH DISHES...
I DON'T MIND!
I MEAN, I'M THE ONE...
WHO OVER-STAYED MY WELCOME. IT'S THE LEAST I CAN DO.
FSH
FSH
SHF
HINAKO-SAN...

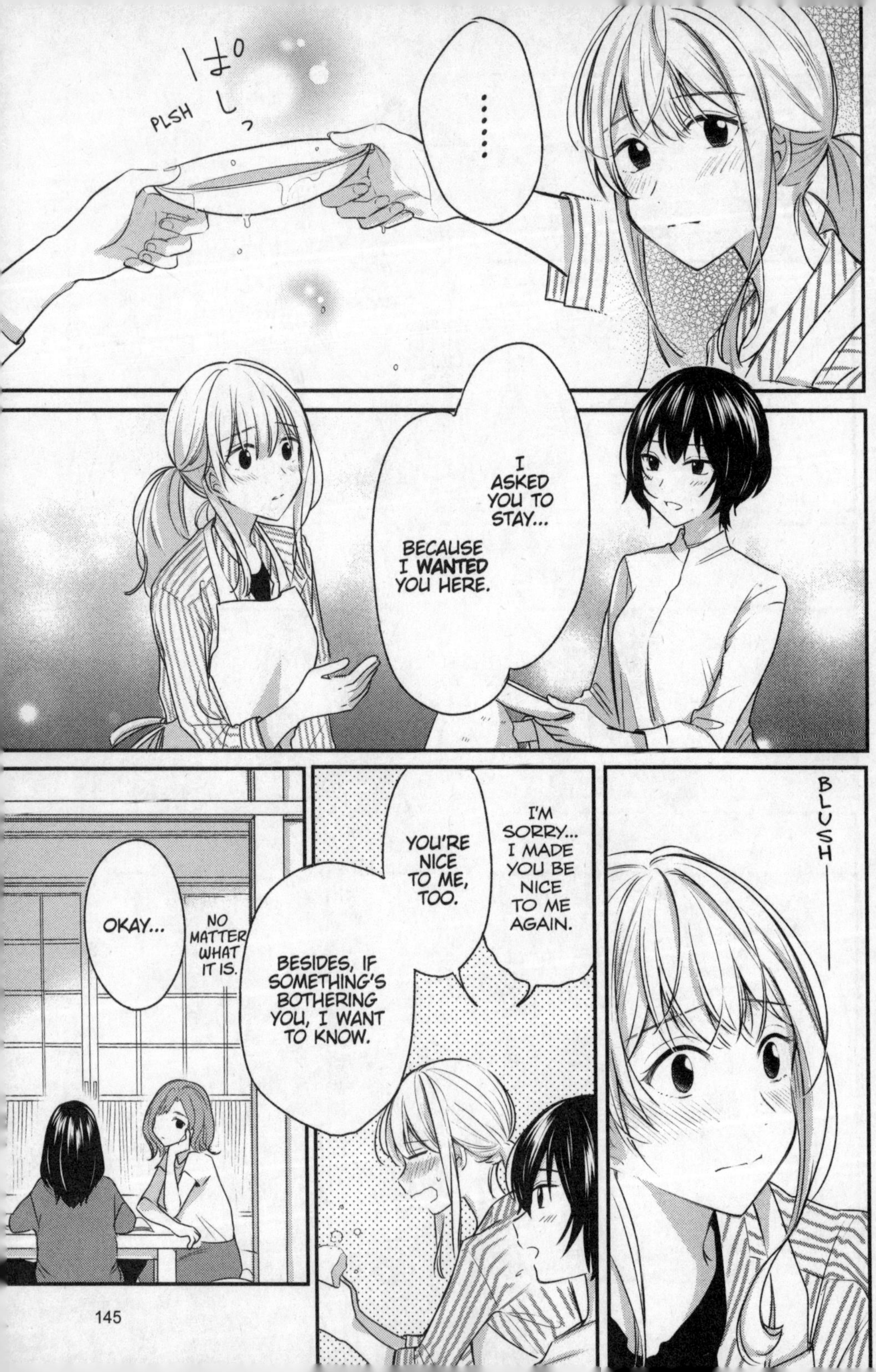
ぱしっ
PLSH
……
I ASKED YOU TO STAY...
BECAUSE I WANTED YOU HERE.
BLUSH——
I'M SORRY... I MADE YOU BE NICE TO ME AGAIN.
YOU'RE NICE TO ME, TOO.
BESIDES, IF SOMETHING'S BOTHERING YOU, I WANT TO KNOW.
NO MATTER WHAT IT IS.
OKAY...

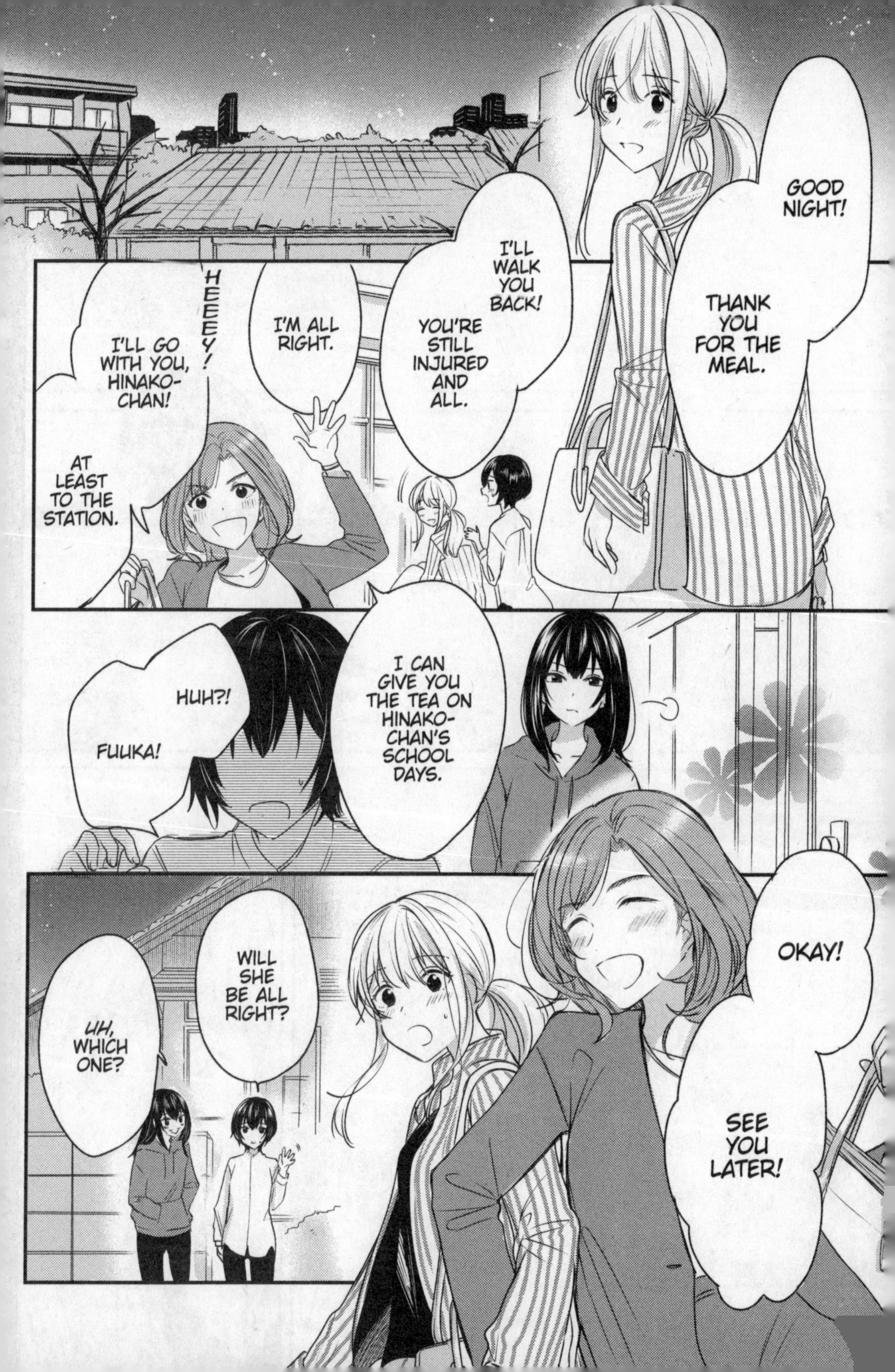
GOOD NIGHT!
THANK YOU FOR THE MEAL.
I'LL WALK YOU BACK!
YOU'RE STILL INJURED AND ALL.
I'M ALL RIGHT.
HEEEY!
I'LL GO WITH YOU, HINAKO-CHAN!
AT LEAST TO THE STATION.
I CAN GIVE YOU THE TEA ON HINAKO-CHAN'S SCHOOL DAYS.
HUH?!
FUUKA!
OKAY!
SEE YOU LATER!
WILL SHE BE ALL RIGHT?
UH, WHICH ONE?

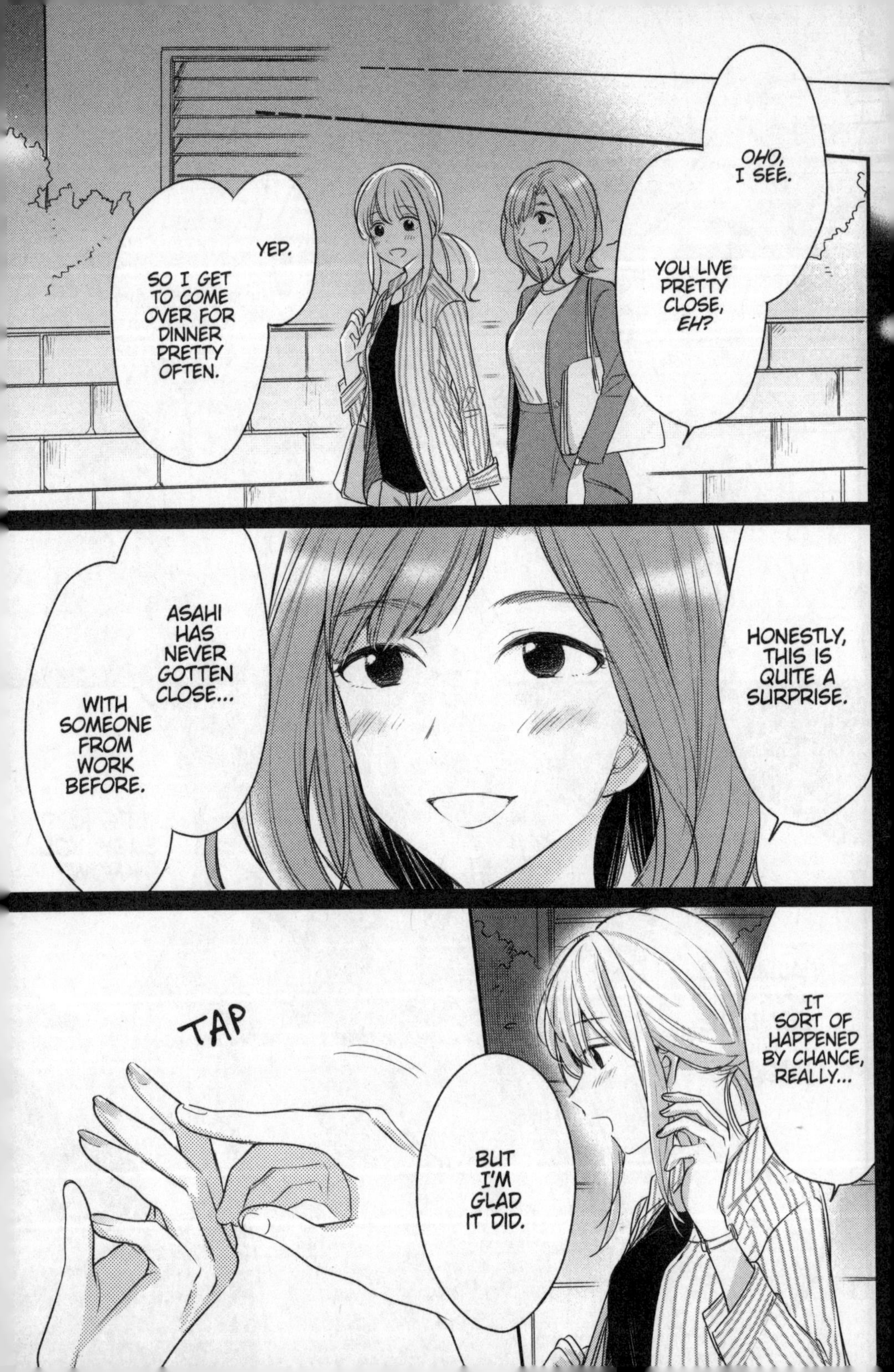
OHO, I SEE.
YOU LIVE PRETTY CLOSE, EH?
YEP.
SO I GET TO COME OVER FOR DINNER PRETTY OFTEN.
HONESTLY, THIS IS QUITE A SURPRISE.
ASAHI HAS NEVER GOTTEN CLOSE...
WITH SOMEONE FROM WORK BEFORE.
IT SORT OF HAPPENED BY CHANCE, REALLY...
BUT I'M GLAD IT DID.
TAP

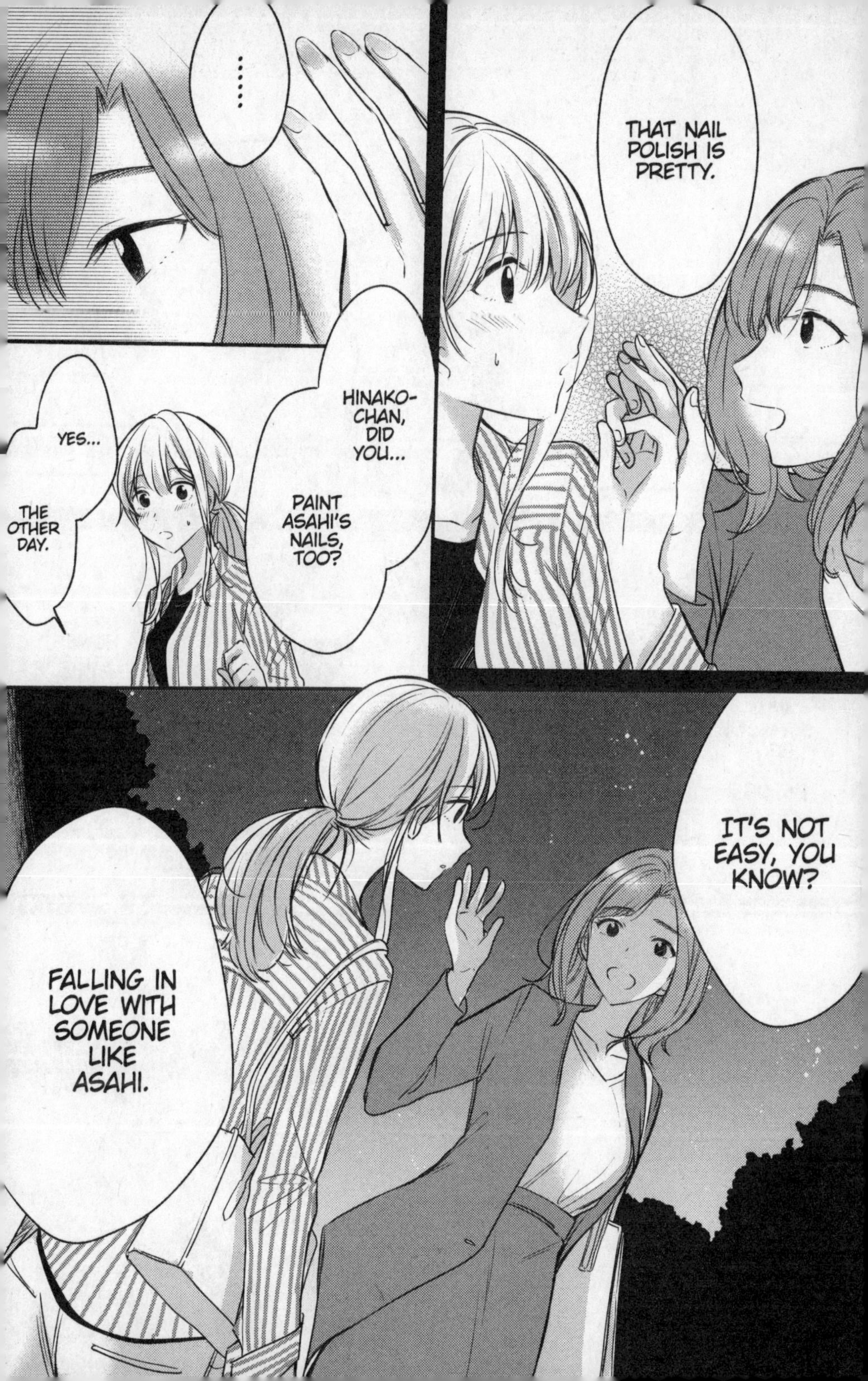
THAT NAIL POLISH IS PRETTY.
……
HINAKO-CHAN, DID YOU...
PAINT ASAHI'S NAILS, TOO?
YES...
THE OTHER DAY.
IT'S NOT EASY, YOU KNOW?
FALLING IN LOVE WITH SOMEONE LIKE ASAHI.

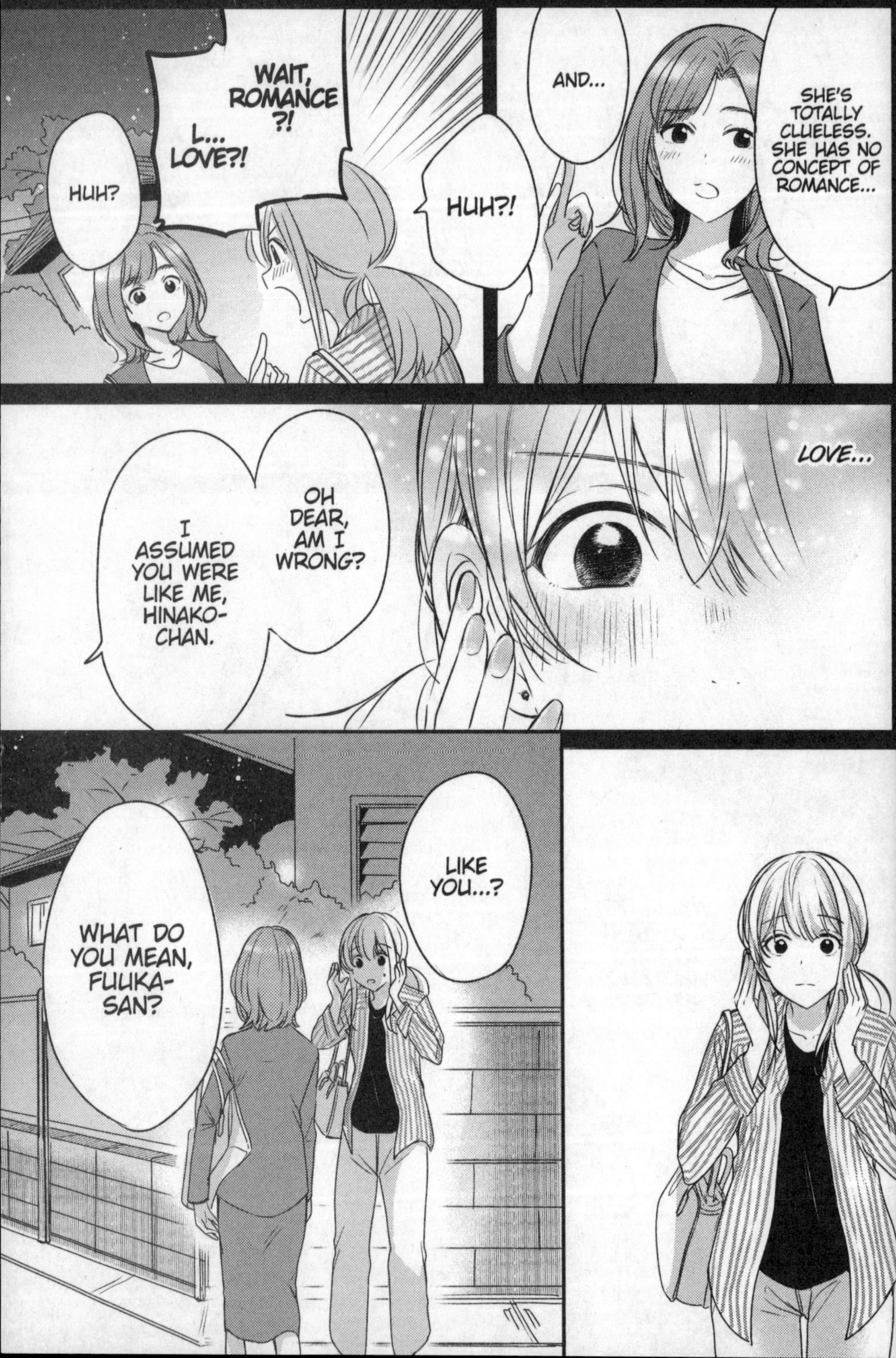
SHE'S TOTALLY CLUELESS. SHE HAS NO CONCEPT OF ROMANCE...
AND...
WAIT, ROMANCE?!
L... LOVE?!
HUH?!
HUH?
LOVE...
OH DEAR, AM I WRONG?
I ASSUMED YOU WERE LIKE ME, HINAKO-CHAN.
LIKE YOU...?
WHAT DO YOU MEAN, FUUKA-SAN?

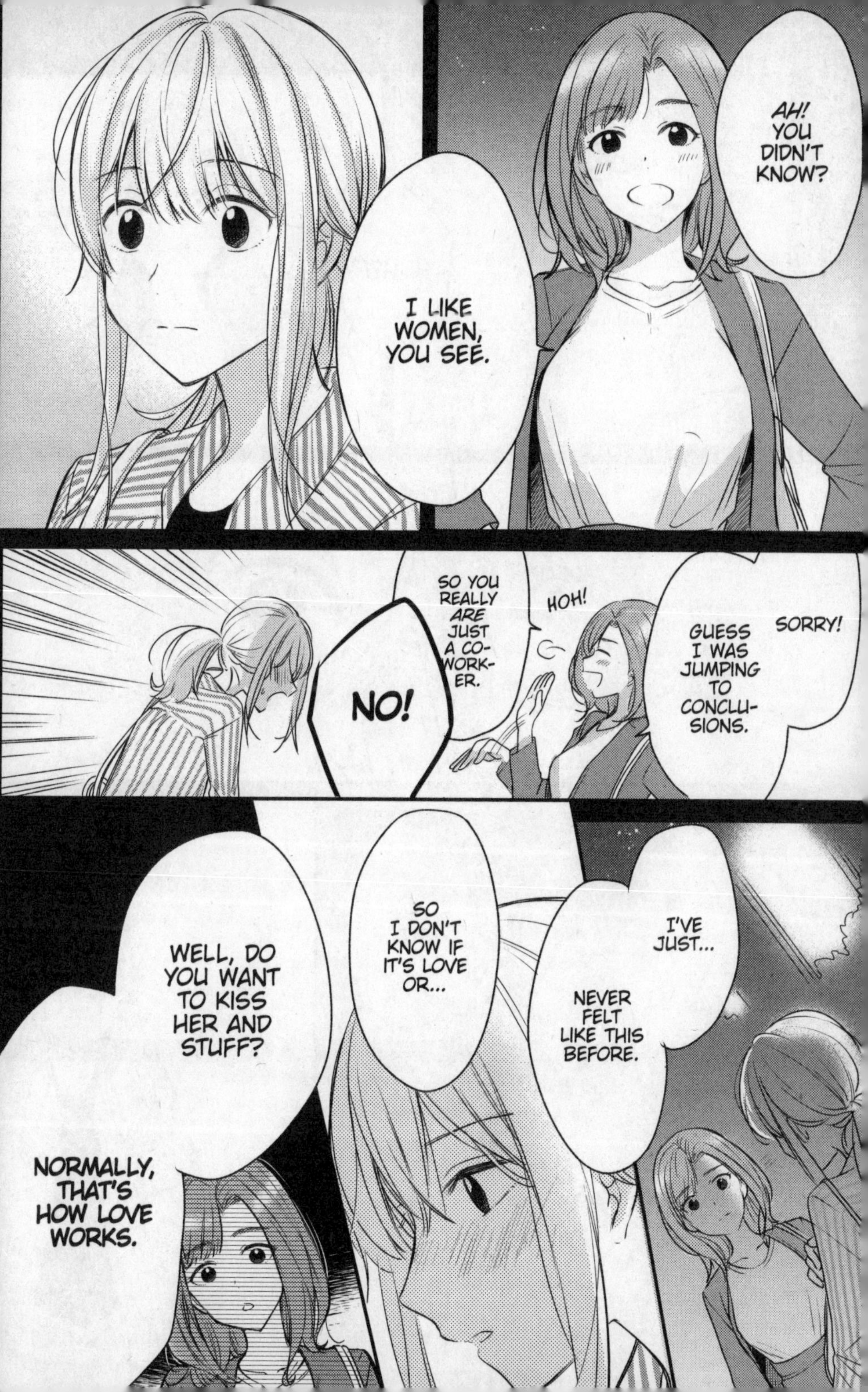
AH! YOU DIDN'T KNOW?
I LIKE WOMEN, YOU SEE.
SORRY!
GUESS I WAS JUMPING TO CONCLUSIONS.
HOH!
SO YOU REALLY *ARE* JUST A CO-WORKER.
NO!
I'VE JUST...
NEVER FELT LIKE THIS BEFORE.
SO I DON'T KNOW IF IT'S LOVE OR...
WELL, DO YOU WANT TO KISS HER AND STUFF?
NORMALLY, THAT'S HOW LOVE WORKS.

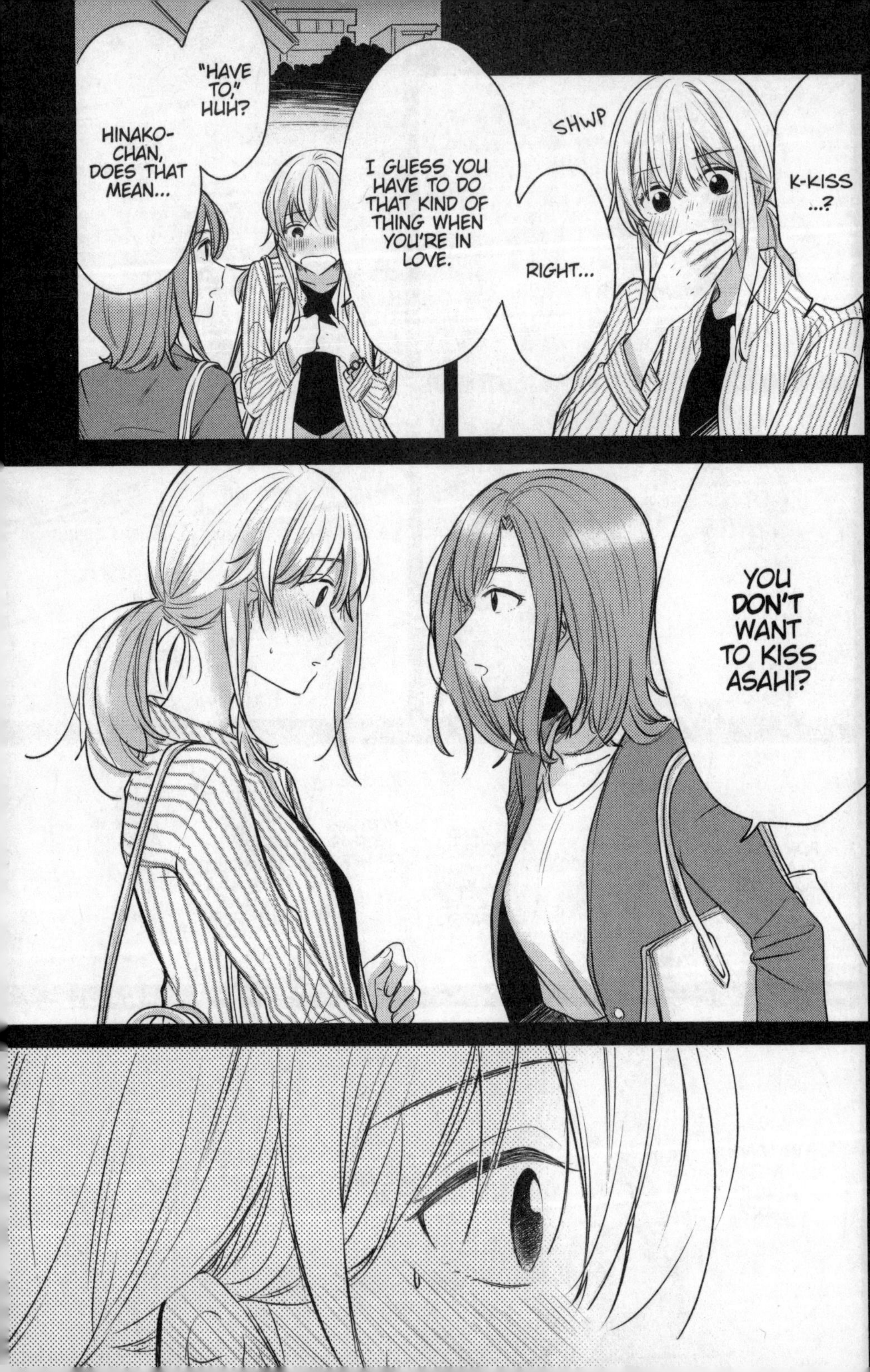
K-KISS ...?
SHWP
RIGHT...
I GUESS YOU HAVE TO DO THAT KIND OF THING WHEN YOU'RE IN LOVE.
"HAVE TO," HUH?
HINAKO-CHAN, DOES THAT MEAN...
YOU DON'T WANT TO KISS ASAHI?

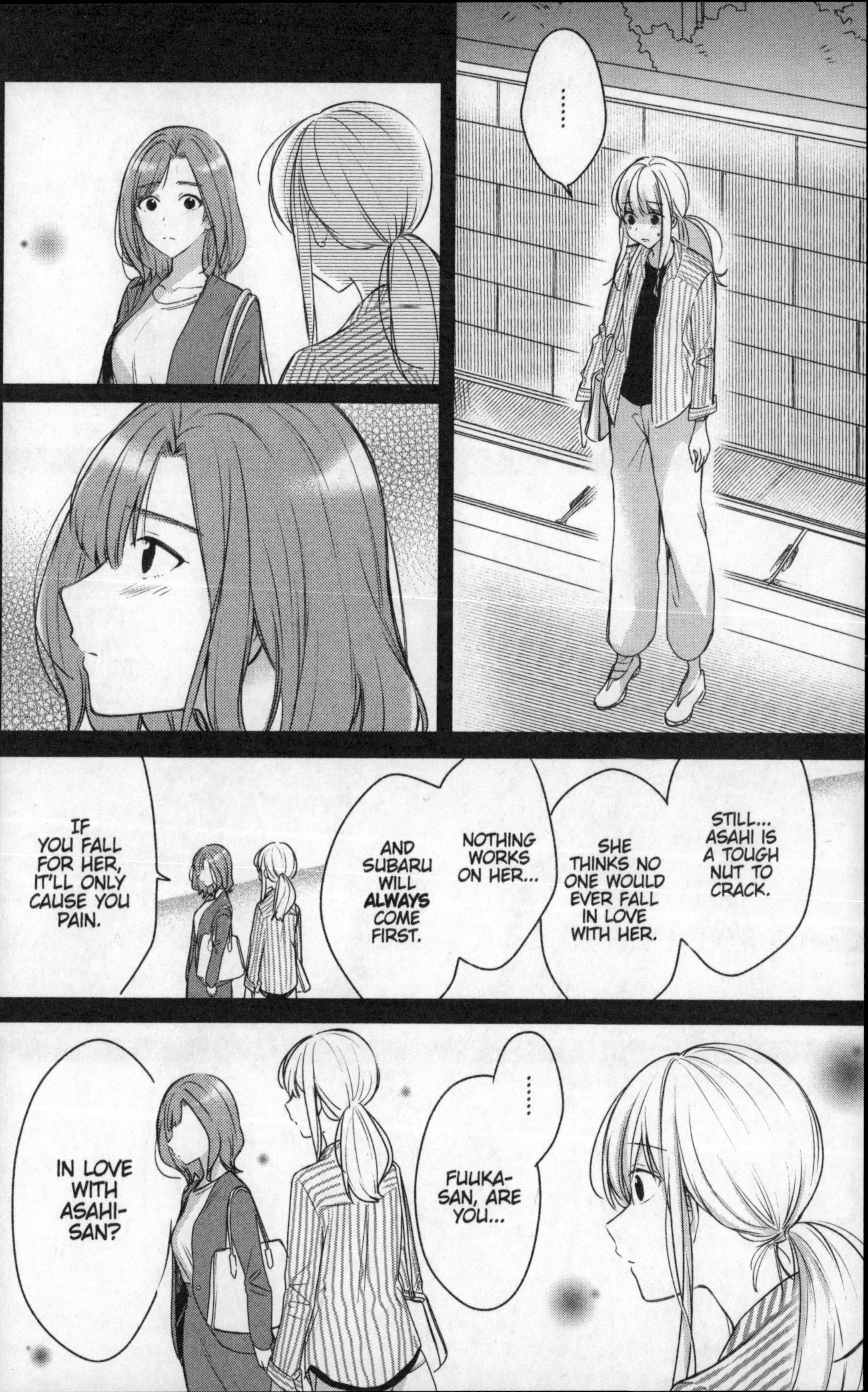
......
STILL... ASAHI IS A TOUGH NUT TO CRACK.
SHE THINKS NO ONE WOULD EVER FALL IN LOVE WITH HER.
NOTHING WORKS ON HER...
AND SUBARU WILL **ALWAYS** COME FIRST.
IF YOU FALL FOR HER, IT'LL ONLY CAUSE YOU PAIN.
......
FUUKA-SAN, ARE YOU...
IN LOVE WITH ASAHI-SAN?

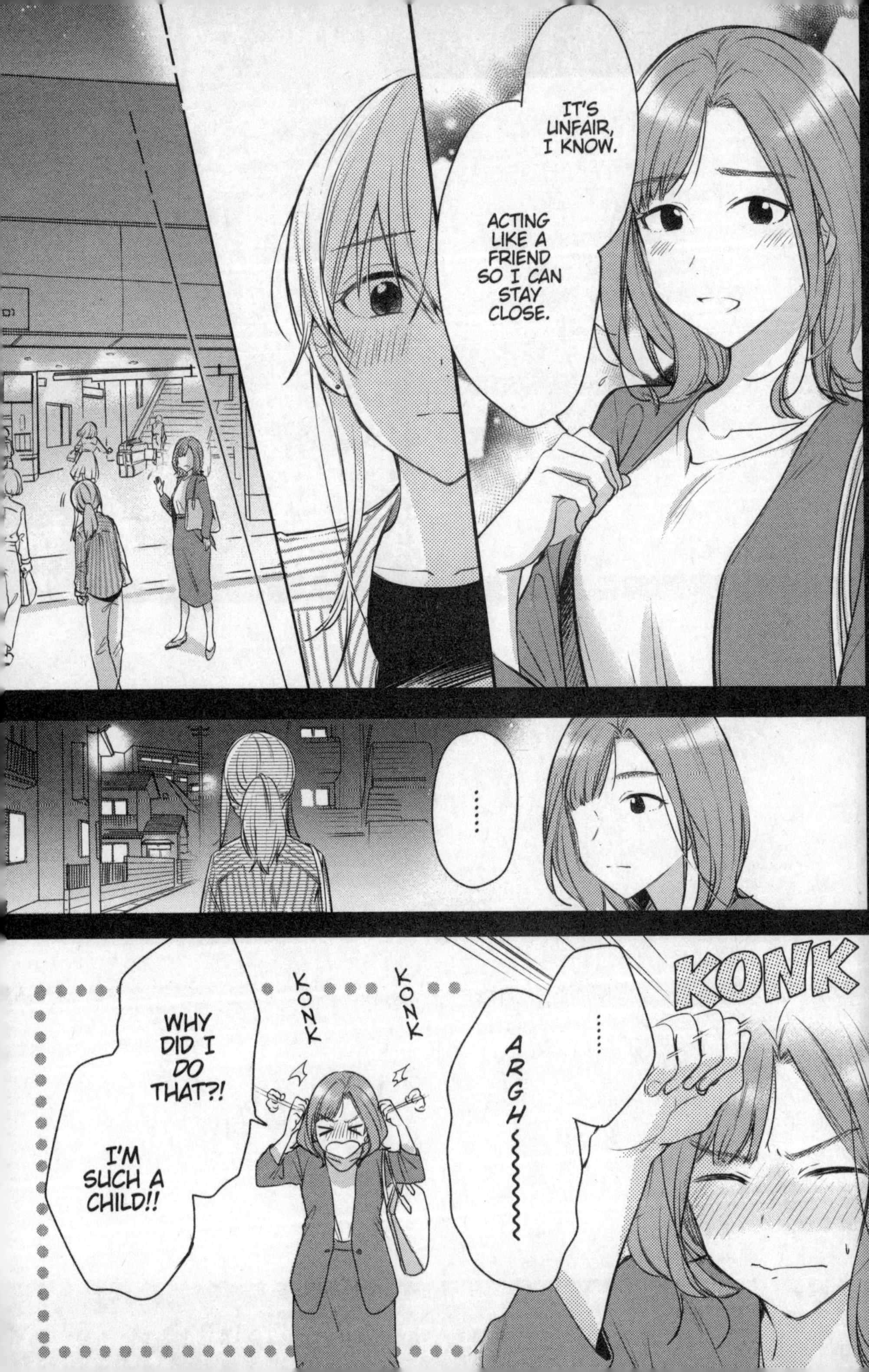
IT'S UNFAIR, I KNOW.
ACTING LIKE A FRIEND SO I CAN STAY CLOSE.
......
KONK
......
ARGH~~~
KONK
KONK
WHY DID I DO THAT?!
I'M SUCH A CHILD!!

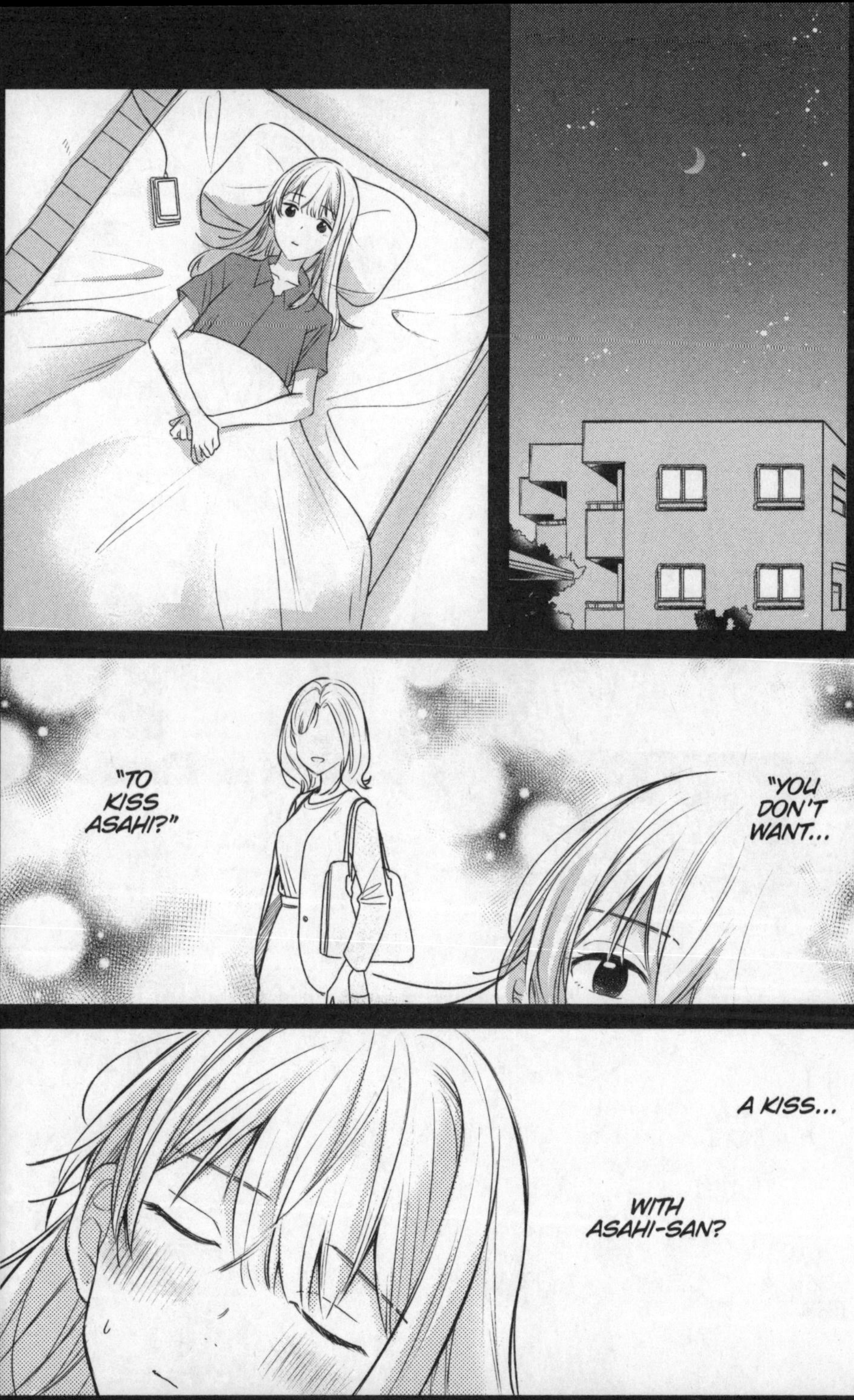
"YOU DON'T WANT...
"TO KISS ASAHI?"
A KISS...
WITH ASAHI-SAN?

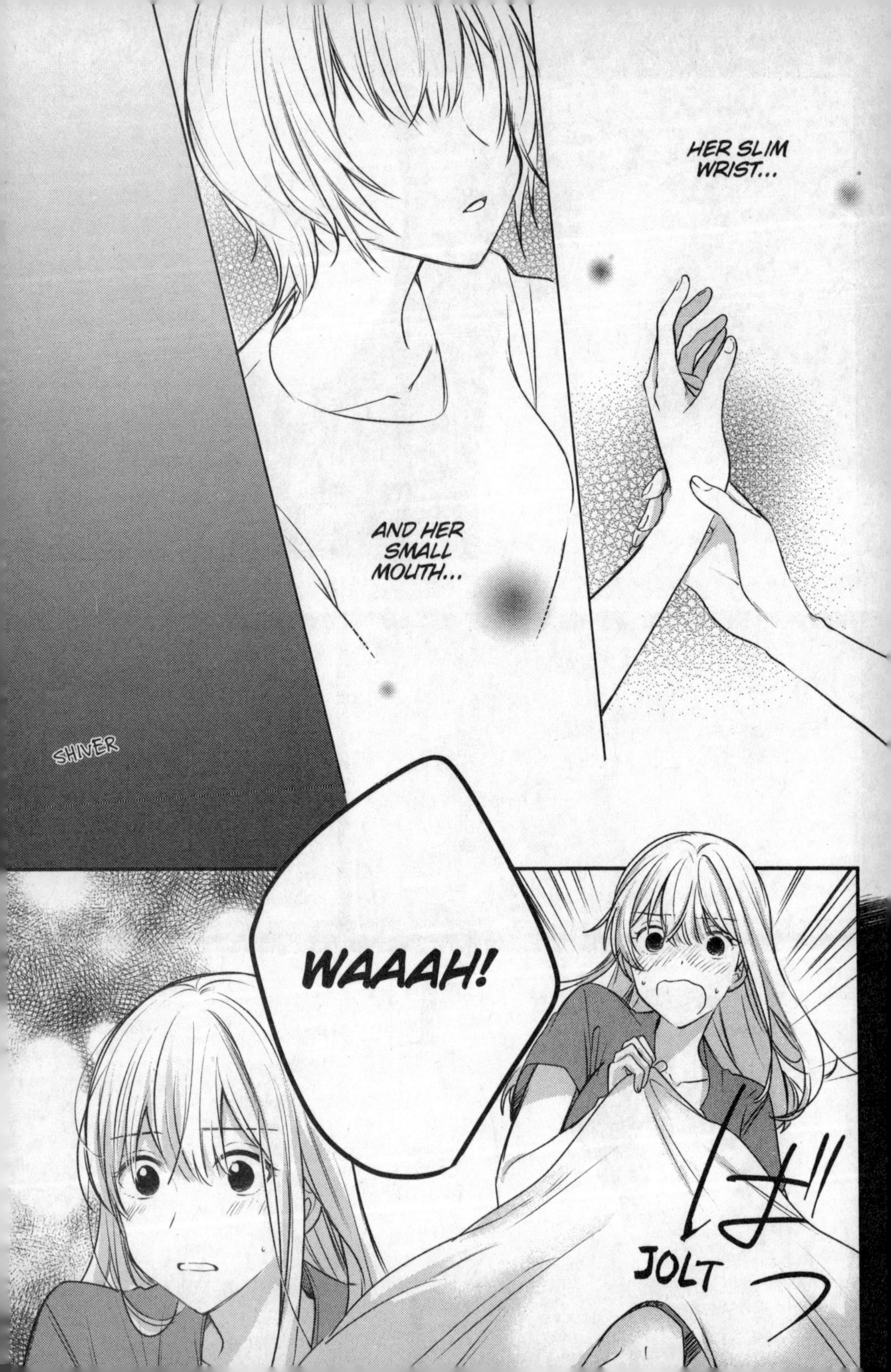
HER SLIM WRIST...
AND HER SMALL MOUTH...
SHIVER
WAAAH!
はっ
JOLT

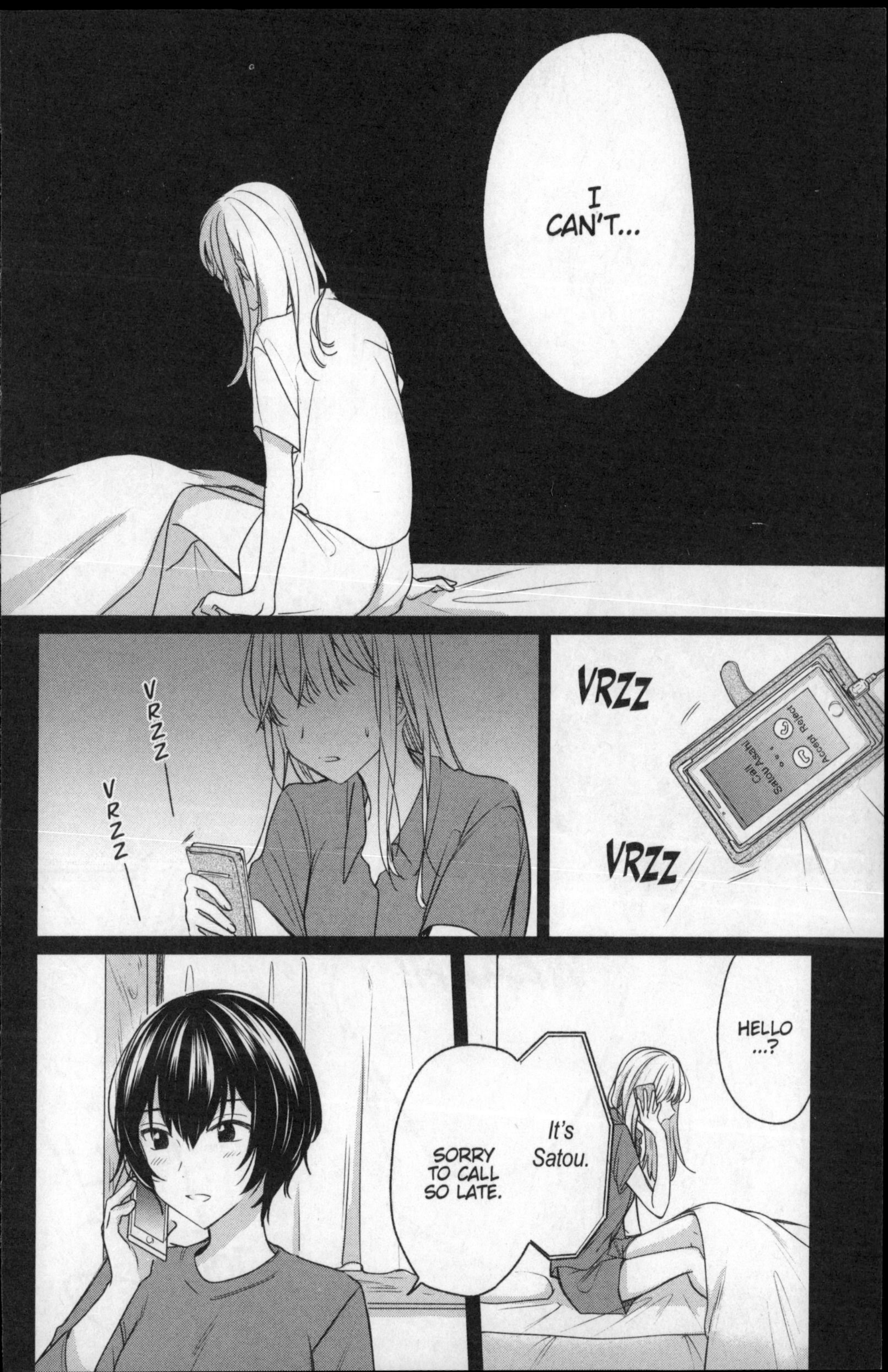
I CAN'T...
VRZZ
Satou Asahi
Call
Accept Reject
VRZZ
VRZZ
VRZZ
HELLO ...?
It's Satou.
SORRY TO CALL SO LATE.

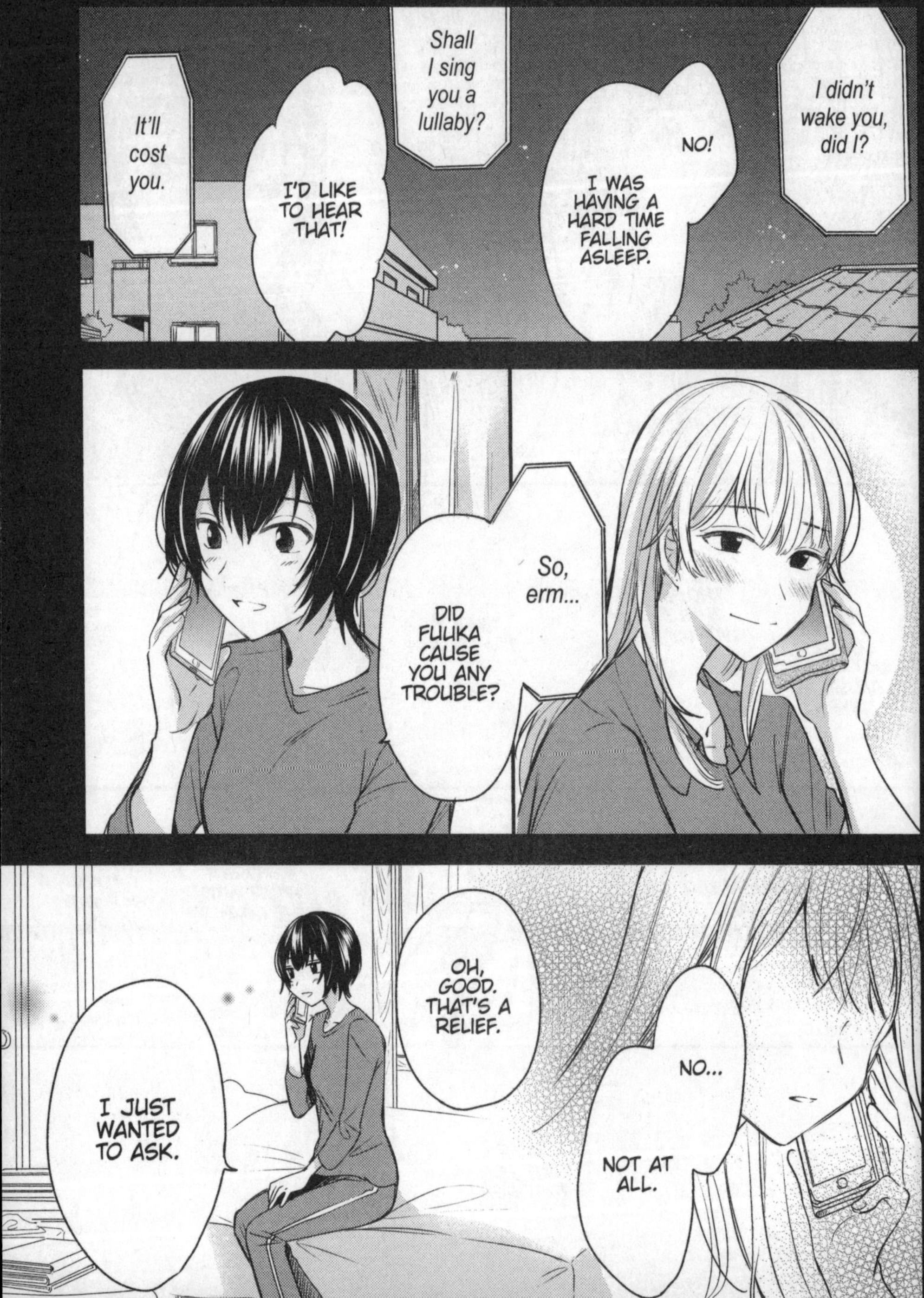
I didn't wake you, did I?
NO!
I WAS HAVING A HARD TIME FALLING ASLEEP.
Shall I sing you a lullaby?
I'D LIKE TO HEAR THAT!
It'll cost you.
So, erm...
DID FUUKA CAUSE YOU ANY TROUBLE?
NO...
NOT AT ALL.
OH, GOOD. THAT'S A RELIEF.
I JUST WANTED TO ASK.

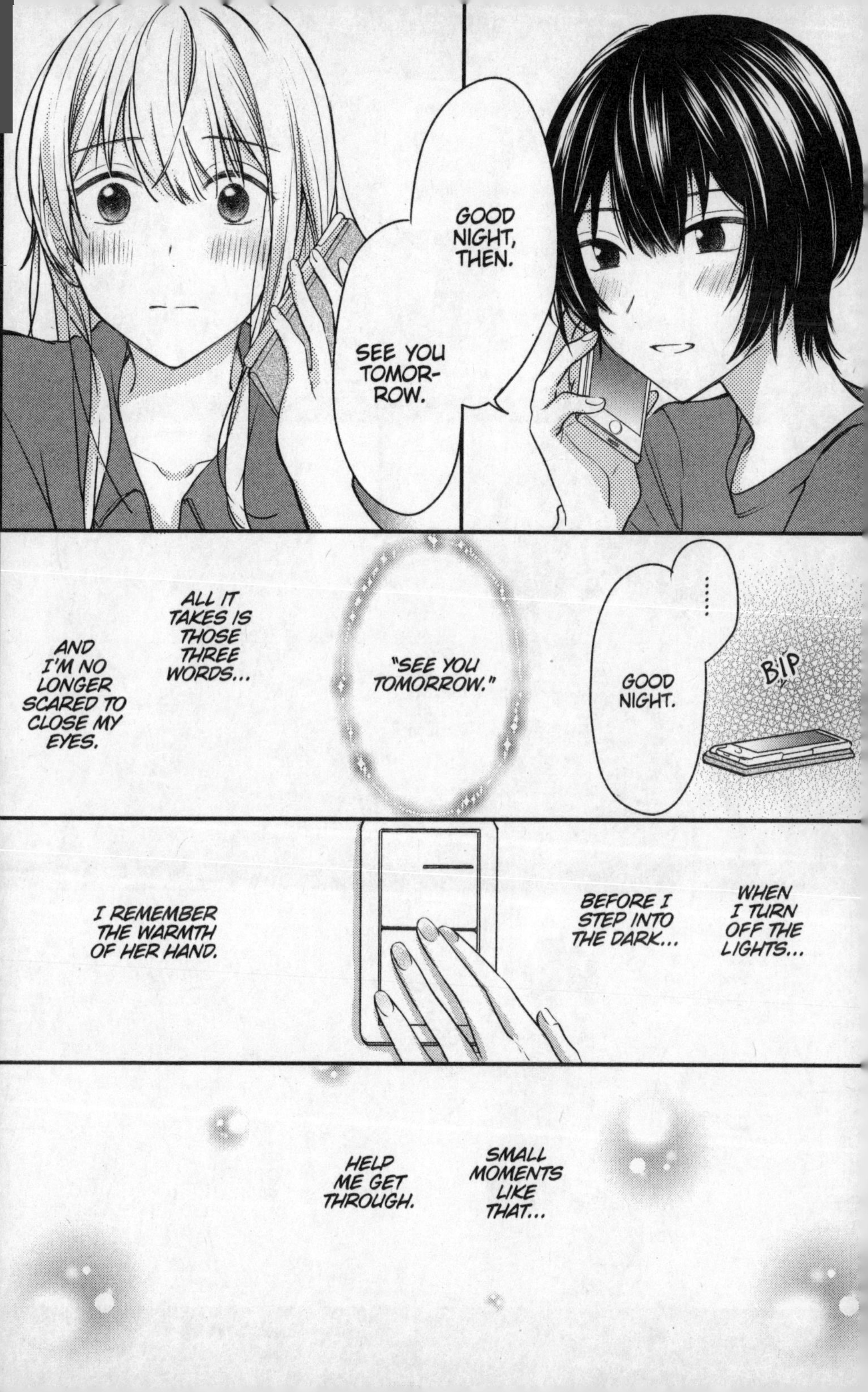
GOOD NIGHT, THEN.
SEE YOU TOMORROW.
......
GOOD NIGHT.
BIP
"SEE YOU TOMORROW."
ALL IT TAKES IS THOSE THREE WORDS...
AND I'M NO LONGER SCARED TO CLOSE MY EYES.
WHEN I TURN OFF THE LIGHTS...
BEFORE I STEP INTO THE DARK...
I REMEMBER THE WARMTH OF HER HAND.
SMALL MOMENTS LIKE THAT...
HELP ME GET THROUGH.

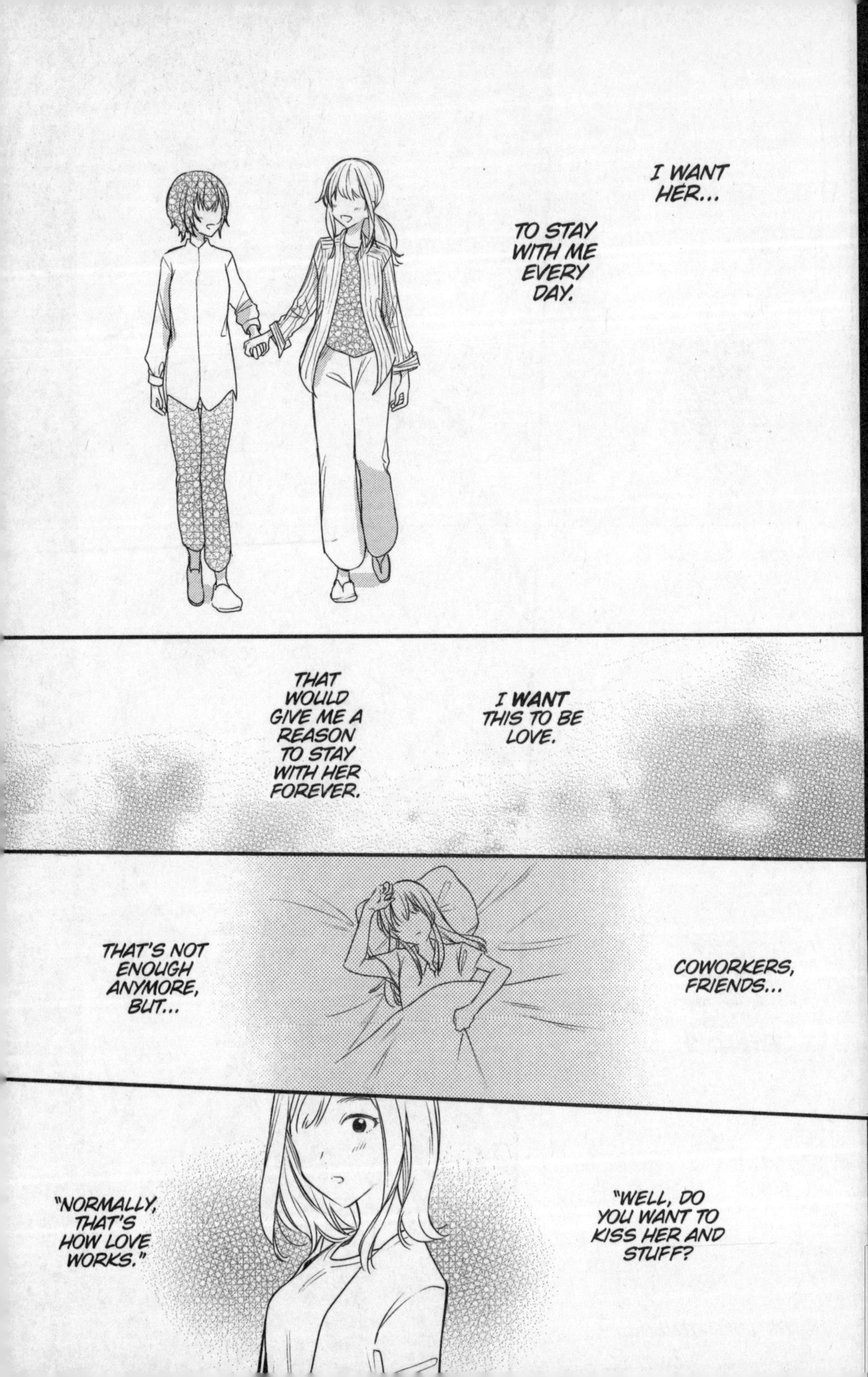
I WANT HER...
TO STAY WITH ME EVERY DAY.
I WANT THIS TO BE LOVE.
THAT WOULD GIVE ME A REASON TO STAY WITH HER FOREVER.
COWORKERS, FRIENDS...
THAT'S NOT ENOUGH ANYMORE, BUT...
"WELL, DO YOU WANT TO KISS HER AND STUFF?
"NORMALLY, THAT'S HOW LOVE WORKS."

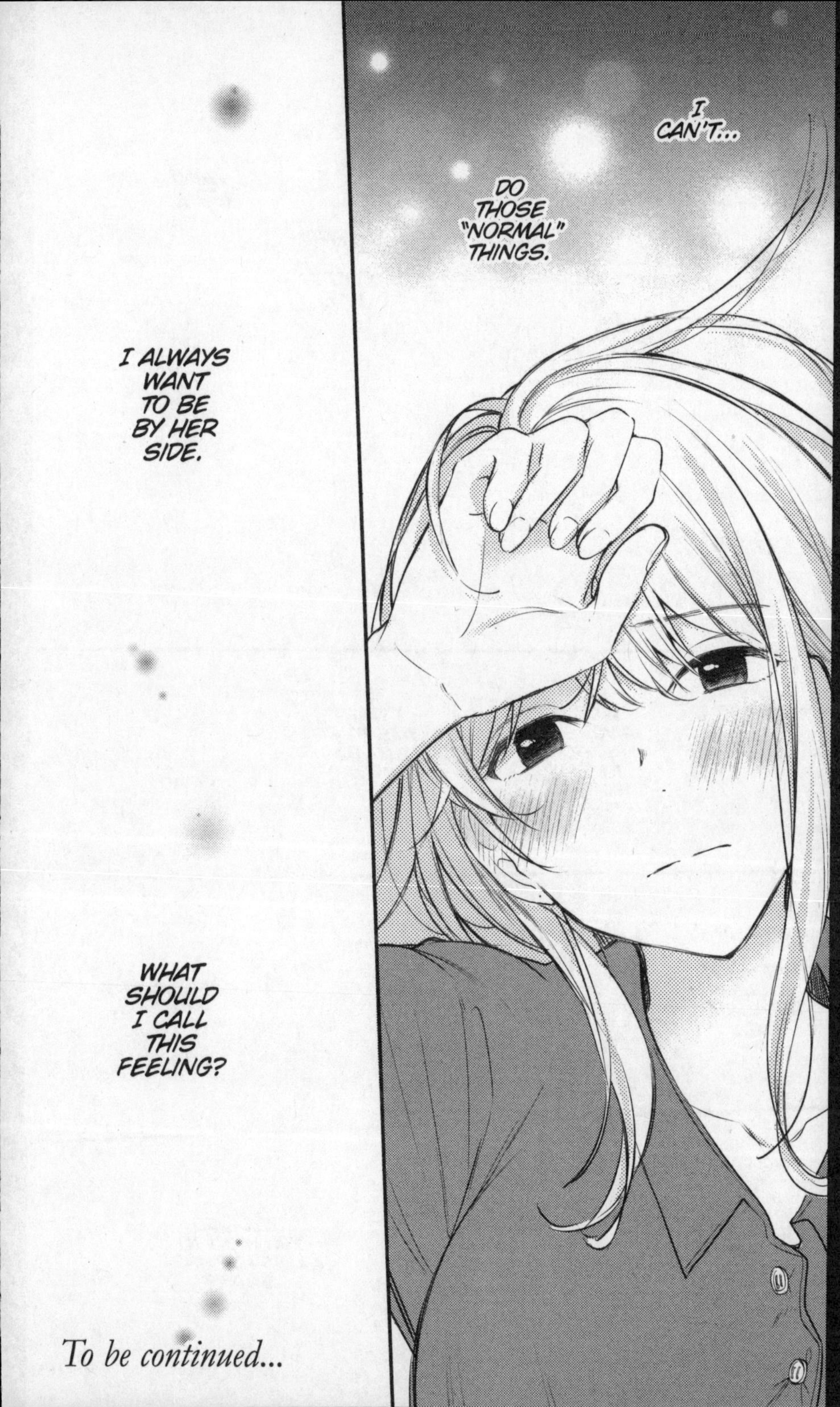
I CAN'T...
DO THOSE "NORMAL" THINGS.
I ALWAYS WANT TO BE BY HER SIDE.
WHAT SHOULD I CALL THIS FEELING?
To be continued...

Doughnuts
Under a Crescent Moon

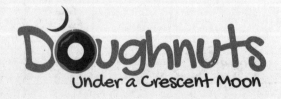

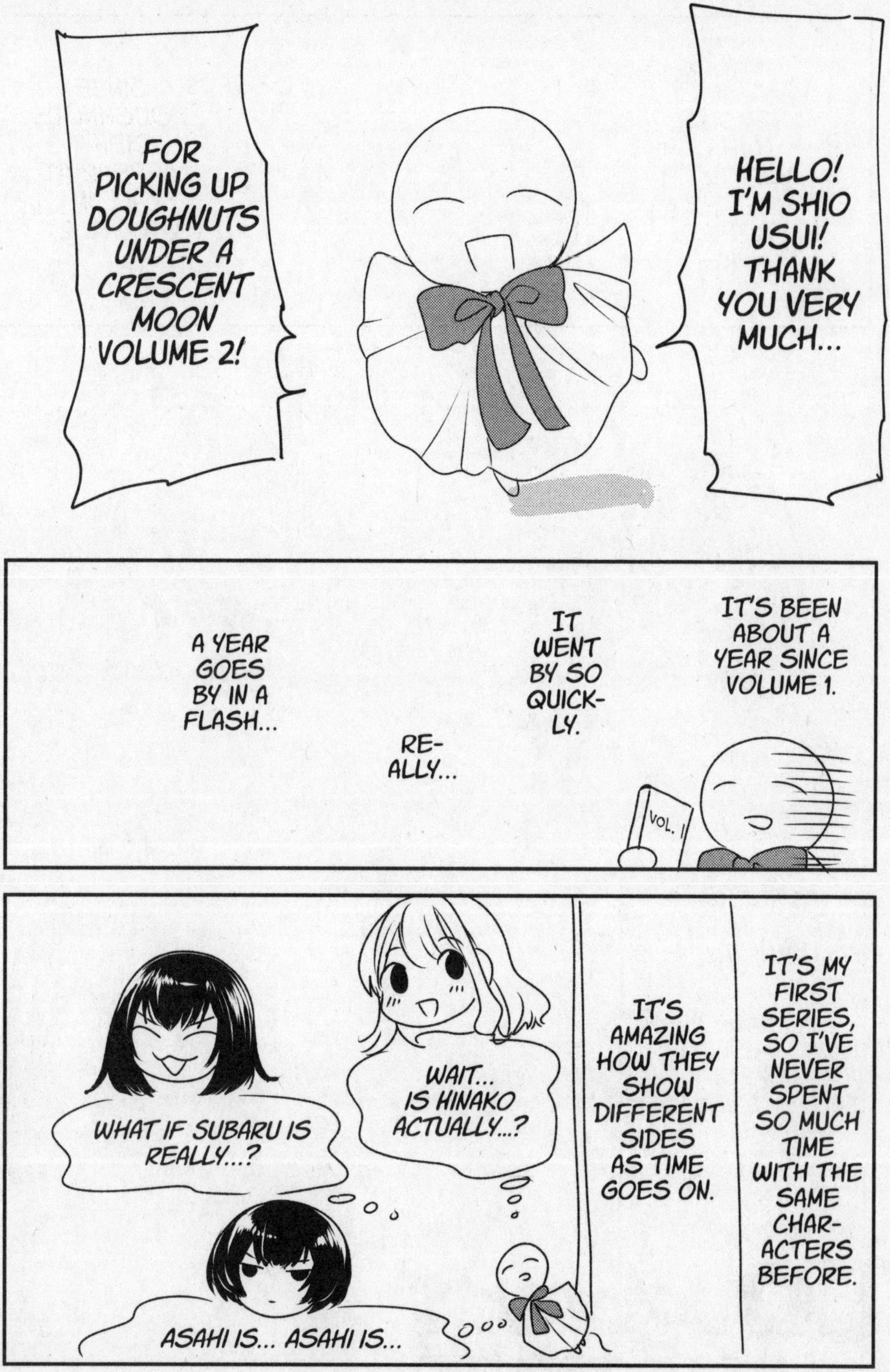
HELLO! I'M SHIO USUI! THANK YOU VERY MUCH...
FOR PICKING UP DOUGHNUTS UNDER A CRESCENT MOON VOLUME 2!
IT'S BEEN ABOUT A YEAR SINCE VOLUME 1.
VOL. 1
IT WENT BY SO QUICKLY.
REALLY...
A YEAR GOES BY IN A FLASH...
IT'S MY FIRST SERIES, SO I'VE NEVER SPENT SO MUCH TIME WITH THE SAME CHARACTERS BEFORE.
IT'S AMAZING HOW THEY SHOW DIFFERENT SIDES AS TIME GOES ON.
WAIT... IS HINAKO ACTUALLY...?
WHAT IF SUBARU IS REALLY...?
ASAHI IS... ASAHI IS...

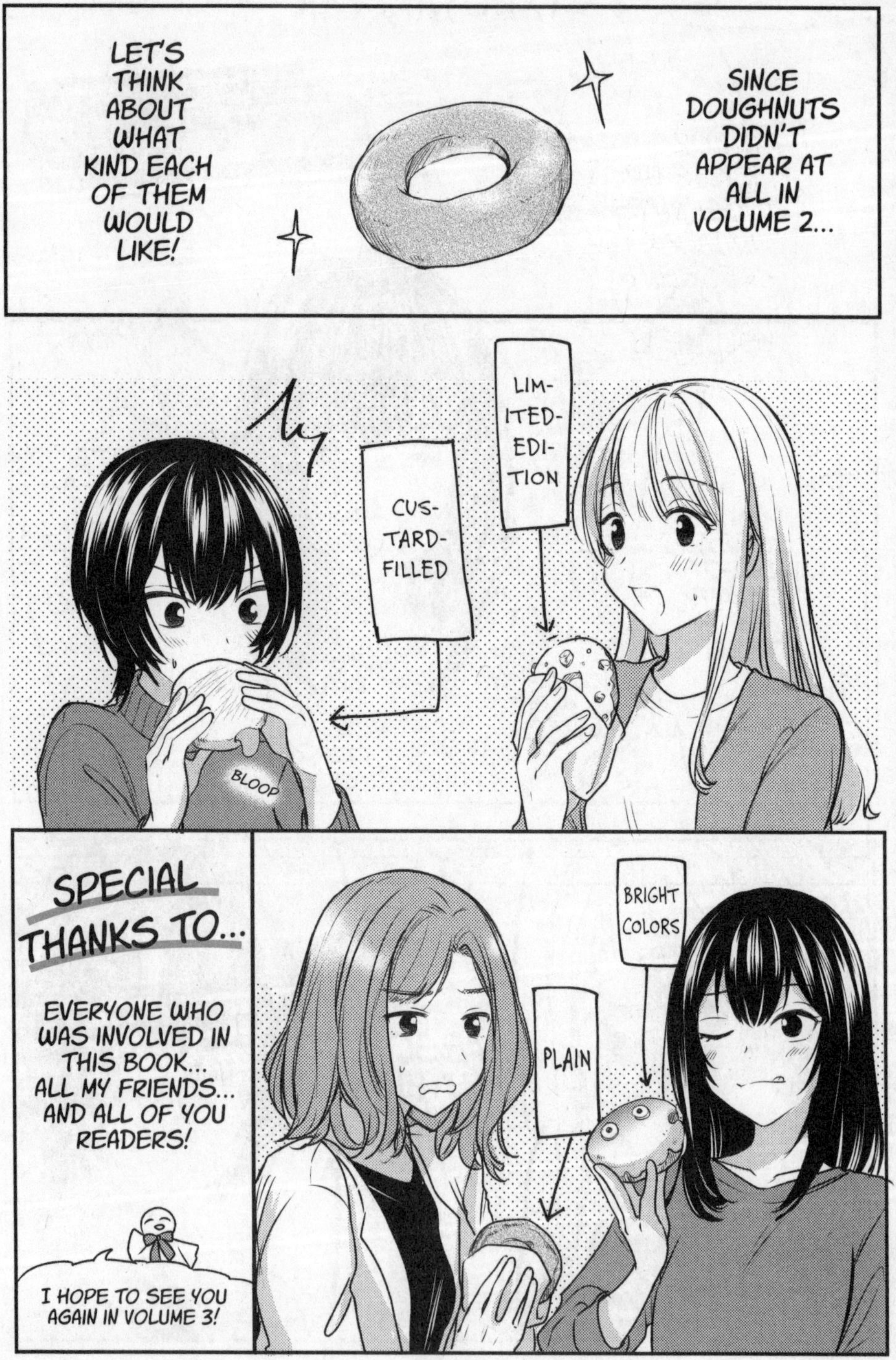
SINCE DOUGHNUTS DIDN'T APPEAR AT ALL IN VOLUME 2...
LET'S THINK ABOUT WHAT KIND EACH OF THEM WOULD LIKE!
LIM-ITED-EDI-TION
CUS-TARD-FILLED
BLOOP
BRIGHT COLORS
PLAIN
SPECIAL THANKS TO...
EVERYONE WHO WAS INVOLVED IN THIS BOOK... ALL MY FRIENDS... AND ALL OF YOU READERS!
I HOPE TO SEE YOU AGAIN IN VOLUME 3!

TAKOYAKI PARTY

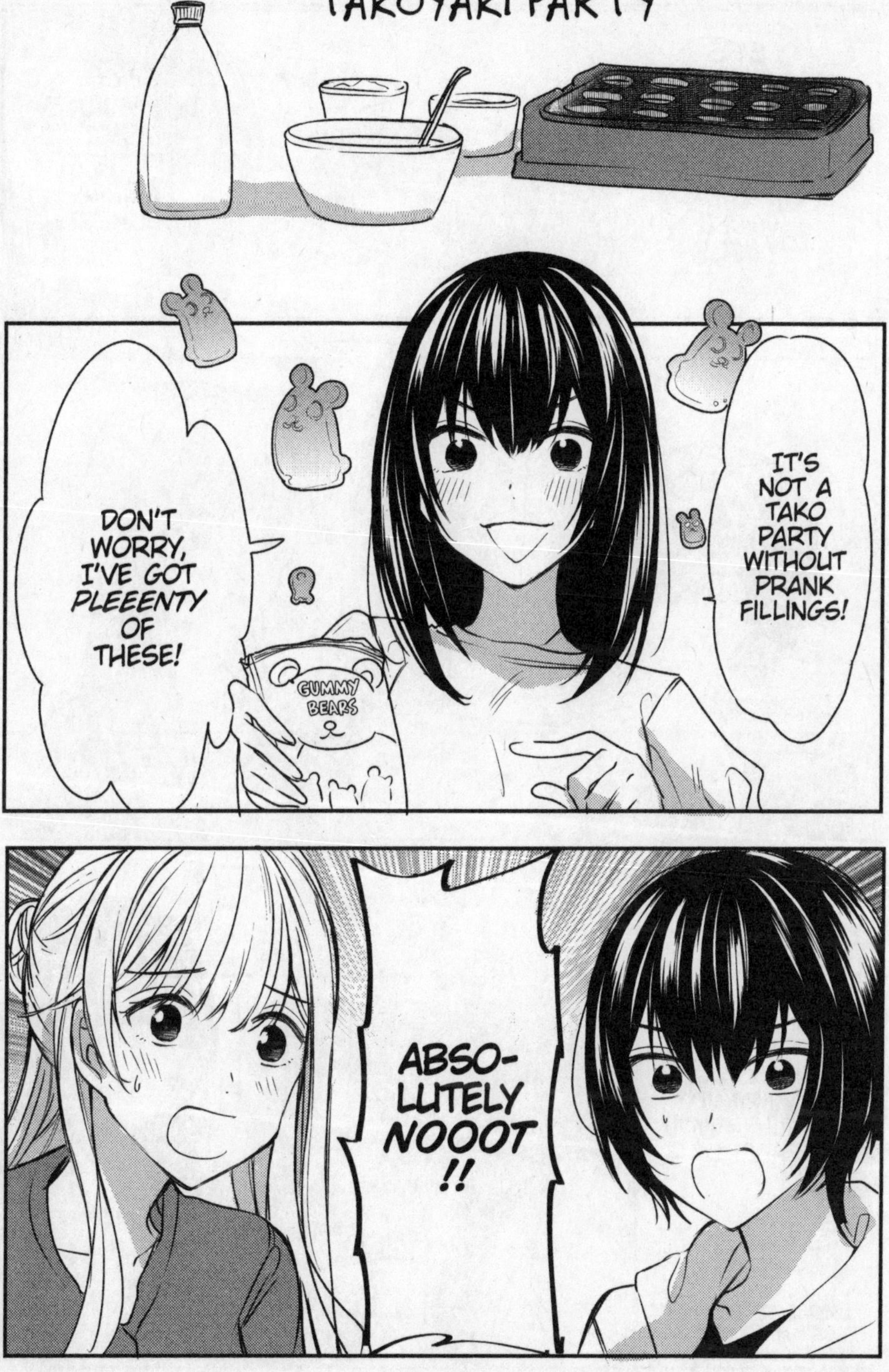
IT'S NOT A TAKO PARTY WITHOUT PRANK FILLINGS!
DON'T WORRY, I'VE GOT PLEEENTY OF THESE!
GUMMY BEARS
ABSO-LUTELY NOOOT!!

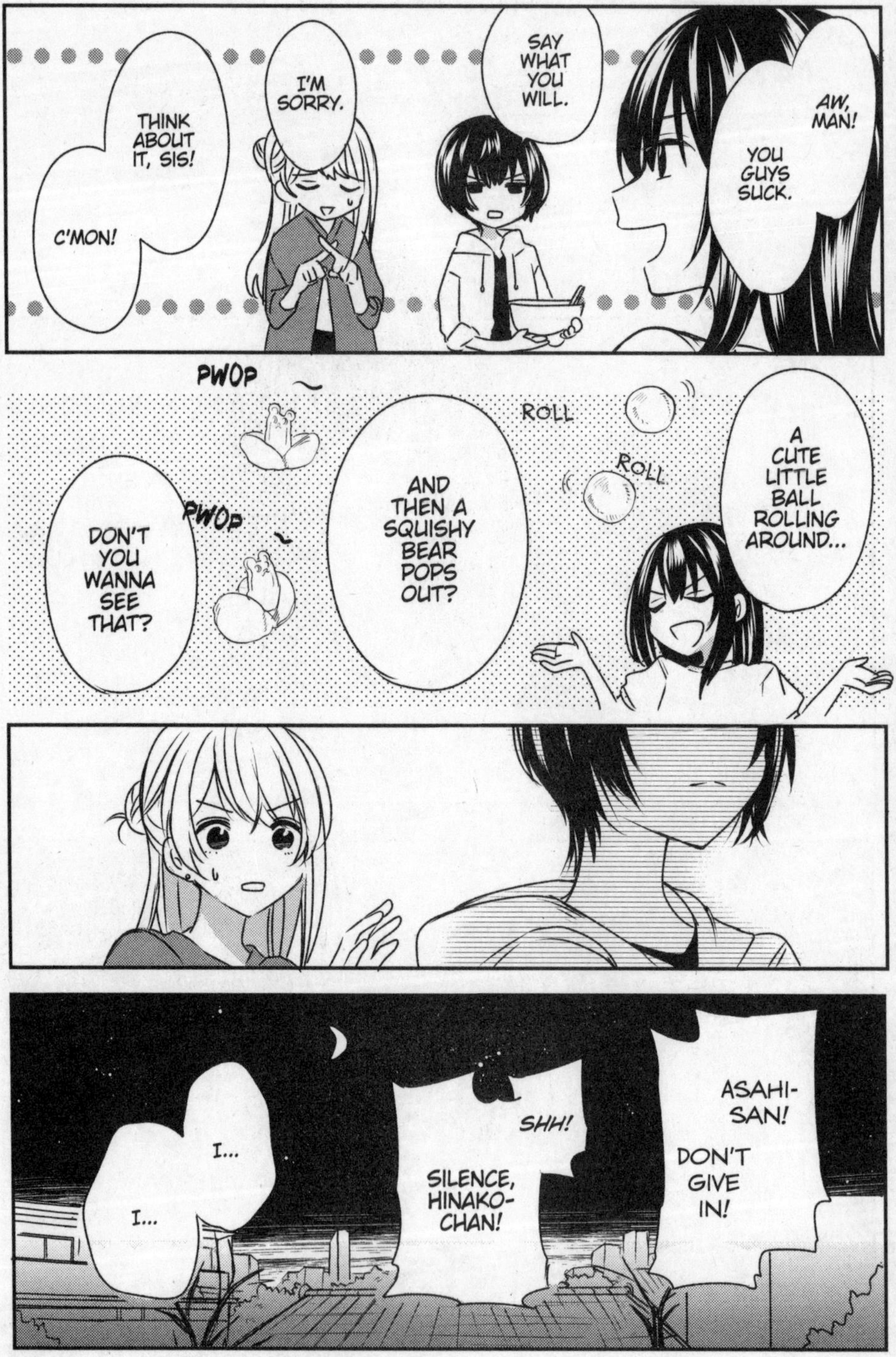
AW, MAN!
YOU GUYS SUCK.
SAY WHAT YOU WILL.
I'M SORRY.
THINK ABOUT IT, SIS!
C'MON!
A CUTE LITTLE BALL ROLLING AROUND...
ROLL
ROLL
PWOP
PWOP
AND THEN A SQUISHY BEAR POPS OUT?
DON'T YOU WANNA SEE THAT?
ASAHI-SAN!
DON'T GIVE IN!
SHH!
SILENCE, HINAKO-CHAN!
I...
I...

Doughnuts
Under a Crescent Moon

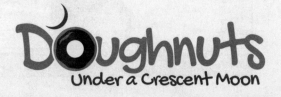

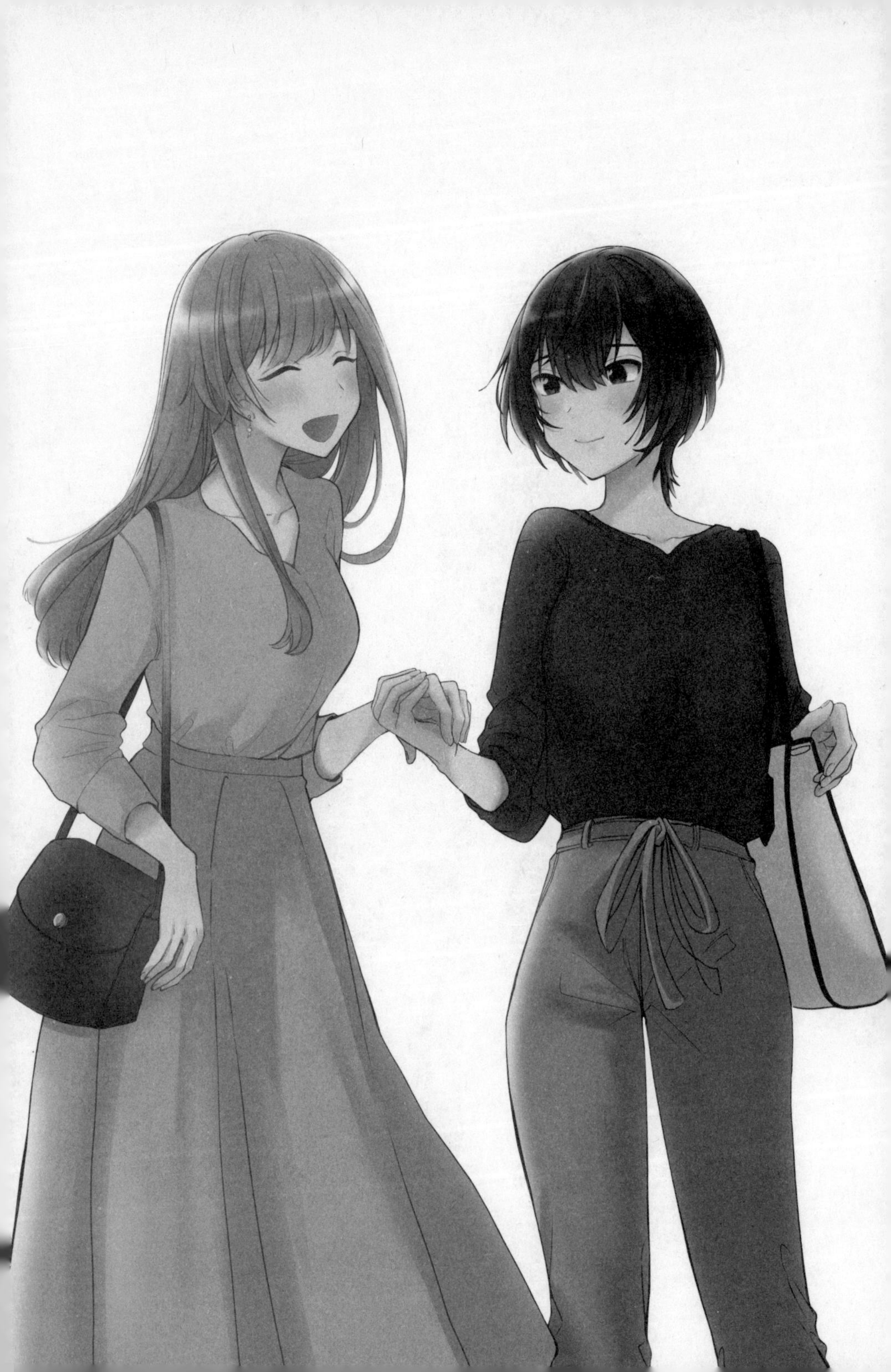

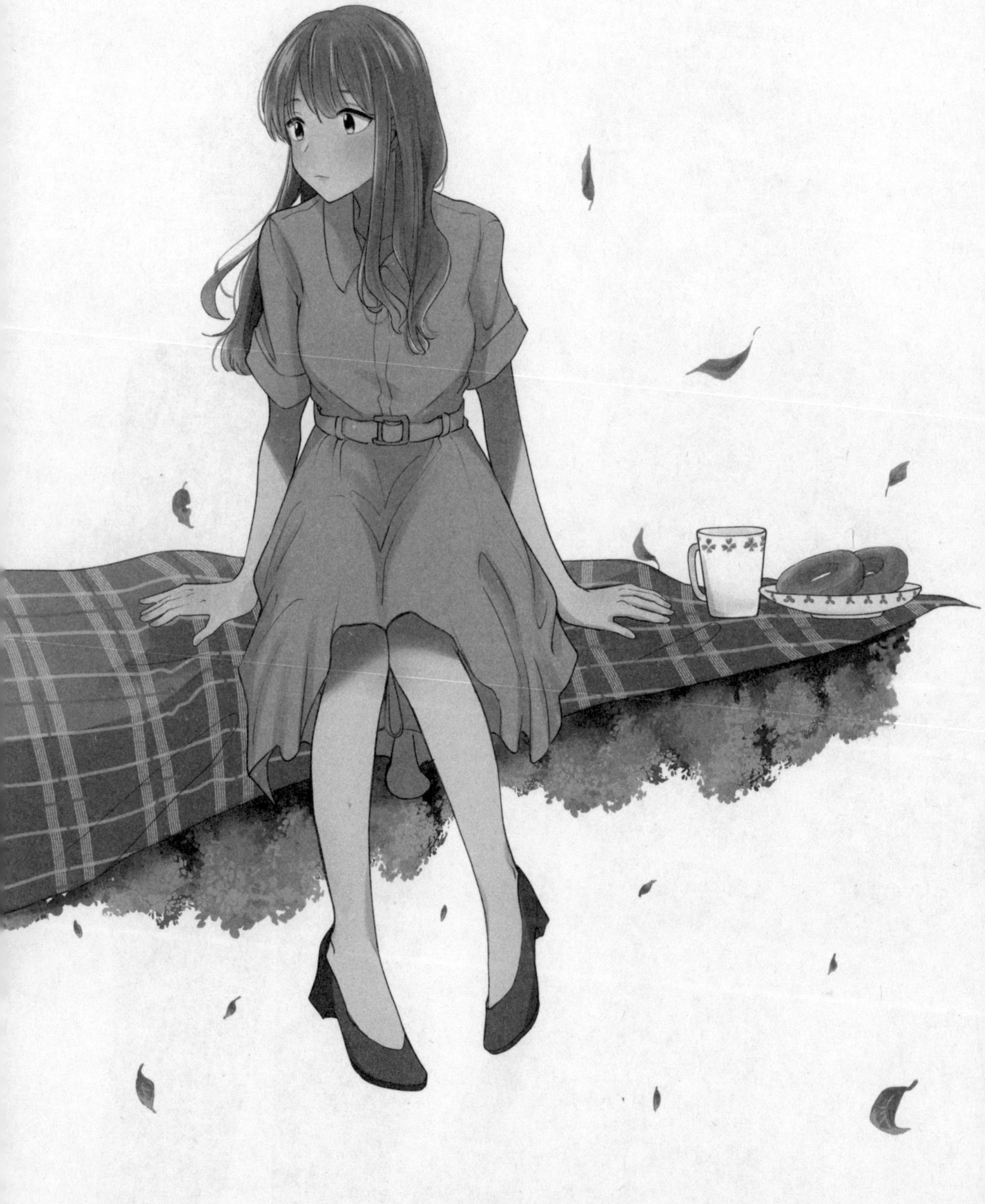

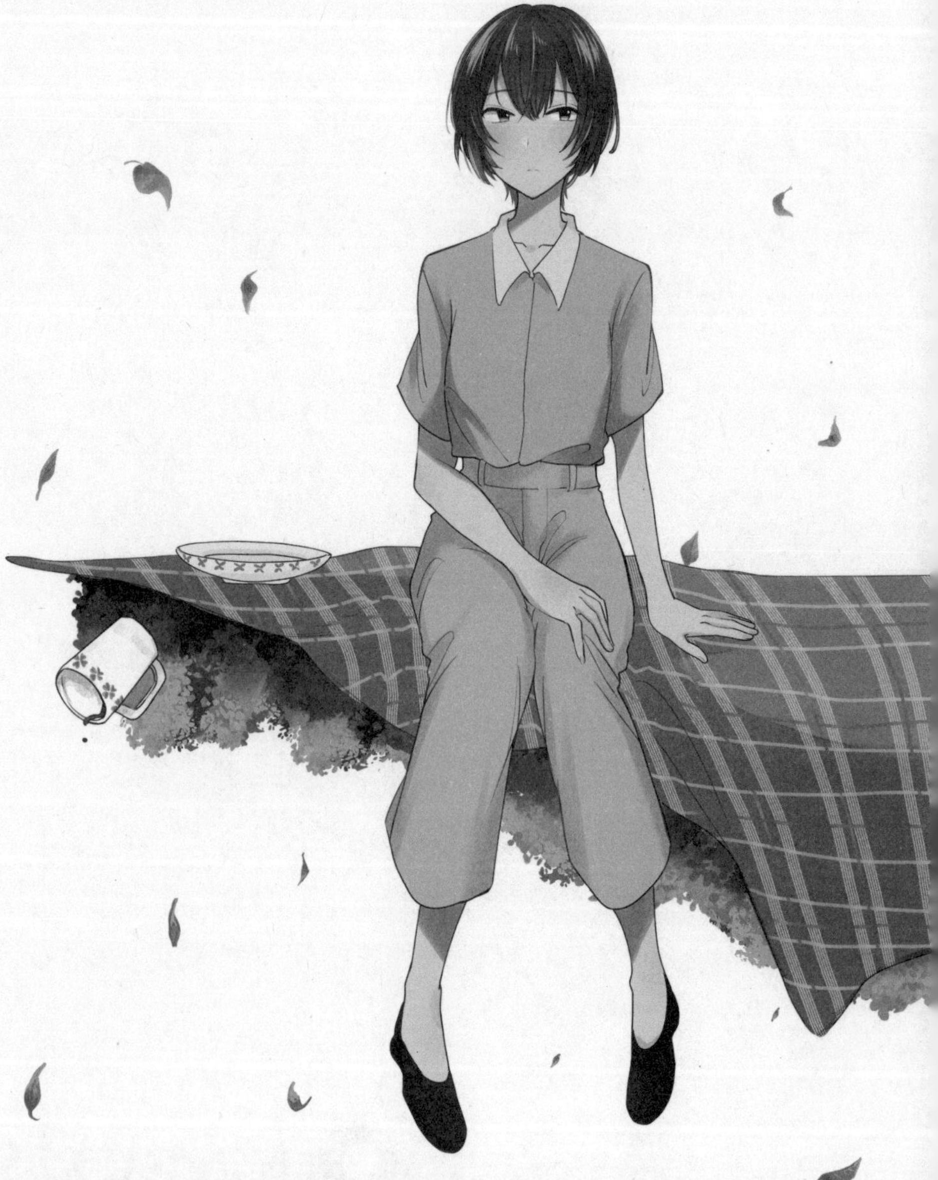

Doughnuts

Under a Crescent Moon

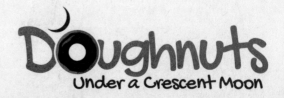

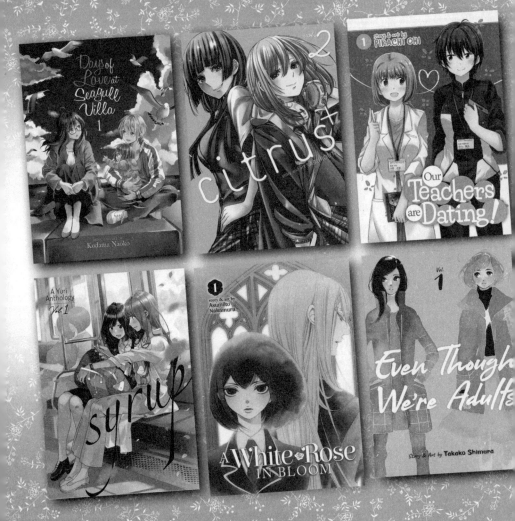

SEVEN SEAS ENTE

Dou
Under a Crescent Moon

story and art by SHIO USUI

VOLUME 2

TRANSLATION
Jenny McKeon

ADAPTATION
C.A. Hawksmoor

LETTERING AND RETOUCH
Rina Mapa

COVER DESIGN
Hanase Qi
(LOGO) George Panella

PROOFREADER
Kurestin Armada
Dawn Davis

EDITOR
Jenn Grunigen

PREPRESS TECHNICIAN
Rhiannon Rasmussen-Silverstein

PRODUCTION MANAGER
Lissa Pattillo

MANAGING EDITOR
Julie Davis

ASSOCIATE PUBLISHER
Adam Arnold

PUBLISHER
Jason DeAngelis

Kaketatsuki to Donuts Vol. 2

First published in Japan in 2020 by Ichijinsha Inc., Tokyo.
Publication rights for this English edition arranged through Kodansha Ltd., Tokyo.

Seven Seas press and purchase enquiries can be sent to Marketing Manager Lianne Sentar at press@gomanga.com. Information regarding the distribution and purchase of digital editions is available from Digital Manager CK Russell at digital@gomanga.com.

ISBN: 978-1-64827-246-2

Printed in Canada

First Printing: August 2021

10 9 8 7 6 5 4 3 2 1

FOLLOW US ONLINE: ***www.sevenseasentertainment.com***

READING DIRECTIONS

This book reads from ***right to left***, Japanese style. If this is your first time reading manga, you start reading from the top right panel on each page and take it from there. If you get lost, just follow the numbered diagram here. It may seem backwards at first, but you'll get the hang of it! Have fun!!

1
2
3
4
5
6
7
8
9

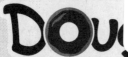

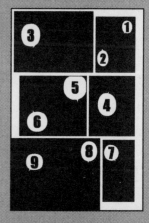